interrupting my train of thought

and your mother, and your dad

patricia dellio (1932 – 2009)

peter dellio (1934 – 2003)

contents

foreword i
introduction iii
the publications v

show no traces 1
the last phase of yours and yours and mine 31
whole new kinds of weather 49
some place back there 73
rain gray town 105
long journeys wear me out 123
fragments falling everywhere 159
if anything should happen 201
always window shopping 269
constantly aware of all the changes that occur 291
people always live and die in 4/4 time 331
in and around the lake 361
a friend i've never seen 415

appendix 435
acknowledgements 437

foreword

The first thing I noticed about Phil Dellio was that he sure liked Neil Diamond. The second thing I noticed was that I liked Neil Diamond a lot better after reading what Phil had to say. I was reading a copy of Phil's fanzine *Radio On* for the first time, riding a Charlottesville city bus in early 1991, wondering if my mind was playing tricks on me. This guy had provocative comments on recent hits by C&C Music Factory and the KLF; he also wrote about musty 1960s ballads by Herb Alpert or the Vogues. He had this mind-blowing ability to hear massive amounts of emotion or drama in pop hits that seemed ordinary to other ears, including mine. Everything sounded different after reading what Phil had to say. And he had a lot to say.

I knew Phil Dellio's voice would become a permanent part of my brain chemistry, and it did. He's one of my favorite writers on music, on film, on memories, on pretty much anything. *Radio On* was the best fanzine that ever existed—a kinda-yearly Xerox-and-staples symposium on the biggest radio hits of the moment, if "symposium" is the right word for a bunch of pop aesthetes arguing over Blind Melon or Salt-n-Pepa. It remains an inspiration to me—in my head, I'm always writing for *Radio On*, even if it's been 15 years or so since the last issue. (Not such a big hiatus in fanzine time, right?)

This collection—*Interrupting My Train of Thought*—is but a greatest-hits anthology from Phil's catalog. As a writer, he has little use for conventional wisdom—he keeps living up to the question posed in an early issue of *Radio On*: "Forget what you know: What do you hear?" He's obsessed with so many of the things I'm also obsessed with—Cheap Trick, *The Godfather*, Richard Nixon. Yet so many of my obsessions are ones I picked up from him, like Neil Young or Bill James or Pauline Kael. Neither one of us seems to be obsessed with Robin Zander's solo career, but there's still time. He's also one of the few writers I've ever encountered in any genre who does justice to that most elusive of topics, the Seventies. (A decade he already glossed in his classic exegesis with Scott Woods, *I Wanna Be Sedated*.)

In the two-decades-and-gravy I've been reading him, Phil has counted down three lists of his 100 favorite songs, with a different Number One each time—Gene Pitney's "It Hurts To Be In Love," Rod Stewart's "You Wear It Well," and Neil Young's "Only Love Can Break Your Heart." Each time, he's made that Number One sound fresh and new to me, no matter how many scuzillions of times I've heard it. And each time, he turns me on to buried treasures I've never even heard of. (If not for Phil, I would never have found Hot Tuna's "Sea Child," and I don't even like to imagine such a fate.)

One of the happiest memories of my life, for reasons tough to explain, is sitting with Phil and my wife Renée Crist in Toronto's Skydome in the summer of 1996, watching the Blue Jays play the Red Sox. Phil and I got giddily distracted by a middle infielder named "Wilfredo," setting us both off on several innings' worth of free-associating *Godfather* references. The same visit also involved a screening of *Raging Bull*, a lesson in the 1970s Canadian band Goddo (who sounded so ridiculous I was sure Phil was making it all up), and that great moment in the car when the Stones' "Under My Thumb" came on. Phil reached to turn it up, then hesitated, realizing there was a lady present; Renée reached over and turned it up for him, whereupon they both sang along and rocked out.

In one of his *Radio On* essays, Phil wrote about a short-lived Top 40 station in Toronto with a gloriously freewheeling playlist—he once heard the DJ segue from Public Enemy's "Can't Truss It" right into Madonna's "True Blue." In a way, Phil's book is like that radio station—a place where an essay on Neil Young, a highschool journal entry, or a Greil Marcus interview can seem right at home next to a riff on the Spice Girls or the Guess Who. His voice makes all these topics seem connected somehow. It's a radio station I've spent a couple of decades listening to and learning from. And it's one I never tire of turning up.

Rob Sheffield

introduction

It's the second half of the cruise—last third, probably. Time to gather up this stuff, put it between covers, then move on and forget about it.

I'd never really thought about a collection until a couple of years ago. (I'm not sure if collection is the right word, but I don't want to call it a best-of, and greatest-hits would be wildly off the mark; I'd like to think this is more in the spirit of K-Tel, a scattershot mixture of this, that, and the other.) The thing that got me going in the first place was the simple realization that it could be done—that I was in a financial position where I could publish it myself (i.e., continue to live in the luxurious lifestyle I'm accustomed to even if I didn't sell a single copy), and that I had a good idea of what would be in there and how I'd want the book to look and feel. It would be a book for me and for those who knew me, with a couple of hundred extra copies for the world out there. I could even include a few things that would, absent their original context, not always entirely make sense. And I wouldn't have to worry about that, either, because most of the people who'd read it would be able to put back the context on their own.

In a sense I've been self-publishing almost since I first started writing about music in 1985 (or '82, if school newspapers count). Maybe a third of what follows was written for publication in the conventional sense, but mostly I wrote for fanzines in the 1990s, and when that world started to fade away (for me, anyway—I bet there are still lots of fanzines defiantly and anachronistically plugging away, which is a heartening thought), I moved online. The conventional sense has never really worked for me, at least not since my involvement with *Nerve* at the very beginning, where I had the kind of editors every young music writer should be lucky enough to have. *Nerve* spoiled me; I didn't realize it wouldn't always be so easy. "Pitching," "shopping around," "spec," and all those other freelance terms—after *Nerve*, and with the occasional exception, what you'll find in here was my way of not ever having to say, think, or act upon those words again. Having a non-writing full-time job obviously had to be part of the equation, too. That's me; many others thrive in that world. In any event, from putting out your own fanzine to putting out your own book was but one short step temperamentally, even if it did take me 15 years to actually do it.

I knew it had to be a book book, though—I never for a second contemplated going the e-book route, which could have been done at considerably less cost, and would have made more sense about a dozen other different ways, too. I'll probably have to get an e-reader myself sometime in the next few years; my eyesight has never been great, but the last few years especially it's been a problem. So sending more dead paper out into the world is, to put it charitably, a little irrational. But I'm slow to change. I'm addicted to things—books, records, DVDs, baseball cards, drawers and shelves and boxes filled with junk of all sorts. I was that way 30 years ago, and I still am, even if that world is in the process of dying. (Whenever I used to go to a movie downtown, I'd always clear time beforehand to make the rounds of nearby book or record or video stores. No need to anymore; they're almost all gone.) Eventually, I do come around—for all the time-capsule hand-wringing over the advent of CDs found in "Vinyl Zombies" inside, I of course went on to acquire lots of them. But I'm not there yet when it comes to books. Psychologically, tactilely, and from sheer force of habit, I'm still a dead-paper person.

Explanations—I do too much of that, and there are more on the way, including one to lead off each chapter. I know that most of them have to do with things that don't really matter, a very good way of sidestepping the things that do. Because whenever I veer off in that direction, I usually end up in the same place as the Freedy Johnston song: trying to tell you I don't know.

the publications

Nerve: There's a look back at my time with Nerve in the autobiographical section, so I don't have to say a great deal here. You won't find much actual *Nerve* writing, though—there's not a lot I wrote then that I can read now without wincing. (More for the writing than what I chose to write about, although that figures in a bit.) There are a couple of full articles and interviews I still like fine, a few excerpts, and an early heads-up on Yo La Tengo. None of which changes how hugely important *Nerve* was to me; it's first on the list chronologically, and first in many other ways too.

Graffiti: A monthly glossy that existed alongside *Nerve*, gradually bringing in a lot of *Nerve* writers as contributors. I had a hand in some funny pieces that just wouldn't work in this book; also record and video reviews, some lists and sidebar items (*Graffiti* was like a 2014 internet site in some ways), and the occasional interview. Thanks to *Graffiti*, I got to meet Matt Bianco. He was very polite.

Innings: Baseball monthly edited by Martin Levin, lasted about a year—gone before Clayton Kershaw was born.

Radio On: A yearly fanzine read by about 30 or 40 people. Even more than *Nerve*, it remains the single most important project I was ever involved in. There's a partly true and partly fiction look back at its origins inside; it's the one publication that gets its own section.

Why Music Sucks: Frank Kogan's fanzine, started in the late '80s and lasting about a decade. I started contributing in 1994. *WMS*, together with *KITSCHener*, is where much of the autobiographical writing in here originated, including a piece on high school I can't imagine writing today.

Tapeworm: To an extent, the next three fanzines came out of the group of contributors found in *Radio On* and *Why Music Sucks*. *Tapeworm* was Jeff Pike's, and the core of each issue was based on a great 1990s idea: make a mix-tape, write about it, mail the tape and your comments to Jeff. The industry couldn't compete with all those tapes flying back and forth, so a collective decision was made to phase out cassette technology.

Martina & Kay's Big Secrets: Martina Eddy and Kay Wisniewski's fanzine. It only lasted two issues, but very original and a lot of fun. I got to write about libraries, where I spent a good deal of time in the mid-'90s.

KITSCHener: Sarah Riegel (daughter of *Creem* contributor Richard) started this when she was about 17, I think. Sarah asked a bunch of questions (*Why Music Sucks* was clearly a big influence) and you answered them. Of all the writing I looked at for this book, I was probably more surprised by how suitable my *KITSCHener* contributions were to this project than anything—I got to tell a lot of stories I never would have written about otherwise.

Homepage: My homepage, called "Phil Dellio's Homepage." (I was one of the first people to make use of focus groups when trying to decide on a name for it in 1997.) I remember I had little animated graphics along the bottom of the page for the first few years—a couple of dancing baseball bats, rotating film reels, that kind of thing. For a while, I was posting stuff on there semi-regularly, but now I mostly use it for my year-end ballot, the (very) occasional link, and maybe a couple of fifty-word think-pieces a year.

Popped/rockcritics.com: ...and at least a half-dozen other offshoot projects of Scott Woods' (one of which led to the record inventory that is so central to this book). Now approaching its 20th year. I think Scott's still figuring out what he wants to do with it.

Village Voice: A few reviews—a brief window opened when Chuck Eddy took over as editor—and a number of Pazz & Jop comments. I'm the guy who only votes for singles every year.

Cinemascope: A monthly film publication out of Canada. I wrote three pieces for them soon after the magazine was launched in 1999, all included here. It became more and more Cannes- and festival-oriented after that, leaving me like the guy in the Harvey Danger song who doesn't even own a TV.

Stylus: An online publication that was around from 2002-07. I contributed a long piece cataloguing every Neil Young cover version I could find (excerpted inside), and also a few song blurbs for their "Stypod" column. Wish I'd contacted them a lot earlier than I did—as I worked my way through the unwieldy Young piece, Todd Burns was my idea of an ideal editor.

ILX: These days, my thoughts and opinions pretty much end up one of two places: my classroom, where for the past 15 years I've been subjecting 12- and 13-year-olds to lots of stuff I suspect they could live without ("It was actually the third Moby Grape album that has my favorite song by them..."), and the I Love Everything/I Love Music/I Love Baseball message board, where ditto, except everyone's older. I was initially going to include more message-board postings than I ended up using (especially film-related: I'll often post some very quick first impressions right after seeing a movie). In the end, they were just too quick and too informal, even by my own lax standards. (Sometimes an ILX post was written as a direct response to someone else; I changed any names to a generic "you.")

Facebook Top 100/Facebook Top 50: The two times when Facebook was actually useful to me. The first was a months-long project where Scott Woods and I each counted down our 100 favorite songs. We'd both post a song every day—usually a YouTube clip, sometimes a Grooveshark link—accompanied by write-ups that were brief at first and got longer and longer as the countdown progressed. It was such a completely enjoyable experience that, as soon as we finished, I got in touch with Jeff Pike and Steven Rubio and we did it all over again with films. This time only 50, and only one of us would post each day.

Both countdowns involved Facebook groups, so there was lots of commentary from friends (in both the Facebook and real-life sense of the word) after every write-up. I wish I had room to include all of that—the discussion in the comments was central to what made both countdowns so rewarding. In the song and film write-ups included herein, I've left things in that have lost their context—references to group members, to previous posts, to YouTube clips, etc. If these seem puzzling, don't worry, the annoyance will pass in a matter of seconds.

Election Blog/Managing the Decay: The first wasn't actually a blog—I posted something on my homepage about Hillary Clinton early in 2008, started writing more and more frequently about Obama and the Democratic nomination, and before long was posting something almost every day, through the two conventions and right up to the election. Amazing, amazing few months. In 2012, Scott Woods and I set up an actual blog, named after one of the many entertaining barbs from the most entertaining presence in that election. 2008 was historic; 2012, taking its cue from Palin four years earlier, was pure freak-show.

Real Groove: Andrew Palmer's, out of New Zealand—a record-store giveaway, I think. I also contributed some to Andrew's *Brassed*, a softcore *Maxim*-type publication, where in lieu of payment I was promised models and weekend getaways on the ski slopes of Auckland.

Eye Weekly: Contributed two or three times, voted in their annual year-end poll from 1991 until it ceased in 2009. Those early ballots...there's no writing of mine that I'm happier to see boxed up in my basement.

Bill James Online: Every few months, I send a "Hey Bill"—an ongoing Q&A with the inventor of sabermetrics—to Bill James. He doesn't publish all the questions he receives, but mostly I've had good luck in getting mine onto his site and answered (28 so far—not like I'm counting or anything). One of them, a query about Andruw Jones' Hall of Fame chances, became the springboard for a lengthy analysis by James of Andruw's career. (His verdict: no.) I even tried to suggest he was wrong about something once—who's had more cover versions, Bob Dylan or the Beatles?—but very cautiously.

show no traces

Once I decided to go forward with a book, I felt that it should somehow begin in 1972 and end with Neil Young. And so this one does—except it starts not with Todd Rundgren and the Stylistics and the Carpenters, or with any of the other music that had such a profound impact on me that year, but instead with a re-elected president and an unprecedentedly popular movie.

Richard Nixon and the first two *Godfather* films have been regularly finding their way into my writing right from the start. Early on, I wrote a long piece for *Nerve* on early-'70s soul (not included here) that had Nixon all over the place; indeed, the Undisputed Truth's "Smiling Faces Sometimes" should have been played at Nixon's second inauguration. Somewhere along the way—you can see this most clearly in the John Cazale piece halfway through this chapter—the man and the film started to become one, turning up in my thoughts and in the flow of daily events in ways both expected (Nixon has become the Freddie Kruger of every presidential election-cycle, rising up from the grave again and again—a lingering backlog of audio tape will do that) and entirely intuitive ("Do you know who I am? I'm *Mo Vaughn...*"). A few months ago, when Jeb Magruder (Nixon's re-election manager) died, I reflexively thought of Johnny Ola's line from *Godfather II*, "One by one, our old friends are gone." When Gordon Willis (cinematographer for the *Godfather* films) died soon after, I thought of men huddled in darkened rooms, whispering—I thought of Nixon. The parallels and connections between them are unavoidable, and they continue to shadow both me and each other.

"Knockin' on Heaven's Door," Bob Dylan (1973)

Ma, take this badge off of me. I can't use it anymore. The greatness comes when you are really tested, when you take some knocks, some disappointments, when sadness comes. I remember my old man. I think that they would have called him sort of a little man, common man. He didn't consider himself that way. It's gettin' dark, too dark to see. I feel I'm knockin' on heaven's door. And so it is with you. It is only a beginning, always. The young must know it; the old must know it. Ma, put my guns in the ground. I can't shoot them anymore. The greatness comes not when things go always good for you, the greatness comes when sadness comes. That long black cloud is comin' down. I feel I'm knockin' on heaven's door. Always give your best, never get discouraged, never be petty. Always remember: others may hate you, but those who hate you don't win unless you hate them, and then you destroy yourself. Knock, knock, knockin' on heaven's door. We leave with high hopes, in good spirits and with deep humility, and with very much gratefulness in our hearts. Knock, knock, knockin' on heaven's door. We don't have a good word for it in English. The best is *au revoir*. Knock, knock, knockin' on heaven's door.

(#12, Facebook Top 100, 2010-11)

When Sadness Comes

Nine books on Richard Nixon that I'd ordered from AbeBooks arrived in the mail yesterday. I set a new standard for stupidity by accidentally ordering something (Richard Reeves' *President Nixon: Alone in the White House*) I owned not once but twice already—a copy on the shelf, and another one boxed away with some other duplicate books and movies. Weirder still, of the nine books, the Reeves turned out to be the only one that was damaged; as soon as I removed it from the box, pages started falling out. This may end up being lucky—if I can get a full refund, I'm off the hook. But if, as my initial contact with the seller would indicate, they're expecting me to spend five dollars shipping the book back in order to get a refund of six, obviously I won't follow through, in which case I'll have taken that standard of stupidity to a new level still.

I'm not exactly sure when I started collecting books about, by, or related to Nixon. When he died in '94, I think I'd already started; I vaguely recall it occurring to me that I'd missed my chance to get a book signed. (And I still believe that Nixon was so in need of validation that a friendly letter and some return postage would have been enough to make that happen, at least in the days before eBay.) In any event, it was somewhere around that time that I consciously decided that, as long as it was reasonably priced (under $10, let's say), I'd buy any and every Nixon book I came across.

Whenever Nixon's name comes up in conversation with someone, and I mention the books, and relate my fascination with the man, I always feel the need to immediately explain myself. I'm always sensitive to the fact that the assumption will be that I'm someone who views Nixon as a heroic figure, as somebody who was done in by the media, the counterculture, intellectuals, the Kennedys, liberals, etc., etc. (basically, that my view of Nixon is no different than what Nixon's view of Nixon was). No—my fascination,

I go on to clarify, can instead be attributed to two things.

First, there's the simple fact that Nixon was in office when I first paid any attention at all to politics—I sat in front of the TV as a 12-year-old and taped his resignation speech on a cassette recorder—and, even more than that, that he was absolutely central to a moment in time, the early and mid-'70s, that continues to this day to be of such paramount importance to my own imagination. So much of the music and so many of the films that I love from that time were either explicitly about Nixon, or implicitly about him. He was there in Michael Corleone, in Travis Bickle, in "Ambulance Blues," in "Smiling Faces Sometimes," in *Nashville*, in *Welfare*—he was lurking everywhere. And when the art wasn't so good, and a world was conjured up where he and the realities of the day were seemingly absent—*The Brady Bunch*, *Love Story*, K-Tel—that meant something too.

More personally, I've long recognized that I share in some of Nixon's worst character flaws. I won't dwell on that too much here, other than to scan a little chart I once drew up for *Martina and Kay's Big Secrets #2*, a fanzine put out by Martina Eddy in the mid-'90s, in which I contrasted myself with Nixon and LBJ:

Richard, Lyndon, and Me:	Nixon	Johnson	Me
VINDICTIVE	✓	✗	✓
SELF-PITYING/MARTYR COMPLEX	✓	✓	✓
MANIPULATIVE	✓	✓	✓
PARANOID/PERSECUTION COMPLEX	✓	½ ✓ *	✓
CONSPIRATORIAL	✓	✗	✗
POWER-CRAZED	✓	✓	✗
HOLDS GRUDGES	✓	✗	✓
OBSESSED WITH HOW OTHERS VIEW HIM	✓	✗	✓
LOYALTY OBSESSED	✓	✓	✓

*not really, though he did plant bugs and felt embattled from all sides over Viet Nam

Character Flaw Rating: Nixon- 100%, Johnson- 50%, Me-78%
References: Lyndon, Miller; Nixon (1962-1972), Ambrose
                                                          Phil

I was too hard on myself—I definitely don't view myself as a manipulative person today, and I'm not really sure why I thought I was at the time. As for the rest, well, much less so now than 15 years ago, but I can't say that it's not all some part of who I am.

Taken together—Nixon as part of my personal timeline, and also as a mirror into a corner of my own less-than-admirable self—I do maintain an unusual bond with him. It helps that I'm about five years too young to share in the visceral hatred of Nixon that demarcates the half-generation ahead of me—if I'd been 17 in '74 instead of 12, I doubt that bond would exist. And it helps even more that I've got some emotional and geographical distance as a Canadian. If I'd lost a family member or a friend in Vietnam, I'm pretty sure the visceral hatred would be there. (As I mentioned somewhere over in the Obama blogging, Palin has helped me to understand—to experience in the here and now—some of that Nixon-hatred.)

Every January 9, on Nixon's birthday, I show my students that amazing slow zoom that concludes the first David Frost interview—the shot that culminates with Nixon finally, after five agonizing minutes of stumbling and rambling and self-serving legalisms, coming as close to an apology as he likely ever came. (I first provide as much context as I reasonably can in a brief introduction, else I'm not sure the clip would mean anything.) Greil Marcus once compared the intensity of *The Godfather*'s slow zoom into Michael as he formulates the murder of McCluskey and Sollazzo to a similar shot in *Persona* where Bibi Andersson recalls her sexual encounter on the beach. I'd add the closing shot in *Long Day's Journey into Night* ("That was in the winter of senior year...") as being close to their equal, and I'd say the Nixon zoom is even more mesmerizing than all three. My students almost always remain quiet and focused for the duration of the shot; maybe they're connecting with something close to what I connected with at their age.

(homepage, 2009)

You Remember Merle, Don't You?

I don't know which I'd choose between *The Godfather* and *The Godfather Part II*. I used to think of them as a piece, then I started to develop a preference for the original, and now, after seeing *Part II* this summer and being overwhelmed by it as if for the first time, I'm not so sure anymore. I do know that I like seeing them back-to-back more than I do the chronologically reshuffled version (which loses some evocative transitions between generations), and that the qualitative gap between the first two films and *Part III* is greater than the gap between *Part III* and *Meet the Stupids*. Some notes on *Part II*:

Best single piece of acting: It's hard to know where to begin—from top to bottom, *The Godfather Part II* must have more great performances than any film ever made (if it doesn't, then only because *The Godfather* has more). My vote goes to John Cazale's breakdown scene when Michael interrogates and then disowns him. When Cazale blurts out "It's not the way I wanted it!" he does this thing with his arms that borders on an epileptic seizure. My favorite acting through the years has almost always come from people who underplay, a perfect example being Pacino here or Hackman in *The Conversation*. Cazale's cathartic unburdening of Fredo's resentment towards Michael crosses a line into some place where most actors look silly.

Best tantrum from Michael: He has four, and they're all riveting. 1) When he orders his underlings inside the Corleone compound to keep his would-be assassins alive ("Did you hear me, Rocco?—*alive*"); 2) When he visits Pentangeli soon after ("In my *bedroom*, where my *wife sleeps*..."); 3) When Tom breaks the news about Kay's miscarriage ("Can't you give me a straight answer anymore?—I said, was it a boy?"); 4) When Michael gets the truth from Kay ("You won't take my children...*You won't take my children*").

Best tantrum from someone other than Michael: Either Pentangeli in his first meeting with Michael ("and there's not gonna be *any trouble from me*") or Roth's reaction to Michael asking who gave the order on Pentangeli ("because this...is the business...we've chosen").

Michael's scariest moment: It's not one of his tantrums; they make you sit bolt upright, but he's at his absolute most sinister when, as he embraces Fredo at their mother's funeral, he looks up slowly and makes eye contact with Rocco.

Senator Geary's best moment: G.D. Spradlin is just brilliant in *Godfather II* (he's almost as good in *North Dallas Forty* as Nick Nolte's coolly heartless coach). There's his comic mispronunciation of "Corleone" at the communion, his contemptuously correct pronunciation of the same later that day, the catatonic shock on his face when he wakes up beside the butchered showgirl, his phony magnanimity at the Senate hearings, pretty much every last line of his. I love it in the Cuba sequence when he whispers to Fredo about getting him one of those "redheaded little Yolandas."

Tom Hagen's best moment: Along with *Godfather III*'s 900 other problems, the hole left by Robert Duvall's absence is incalculable. I think his greatest moment in *The Godfather* is the way he looks away from Tessio when he says, "Can't do it, Sally." In *II* I'd go with his affectionate farewell handshake with Pentangeli: "So long, Frankie Five Angels."

Pentangeli's best moment: To watch *Godfather II* is to fall in love with Pentangeli—he out-Clemenzas Clemenza, and with Michael and Tom reduced to empty shells through most of the film, he's the truest link to the spirit of the original. Easy choice: "Your father did *business* with Hyman Roth, your father *respected* Hyman Roth, but your father never *trusted* Hyman Roth—or his Sicilian messenger-boy, Johnny Ola."

Most shattering moment: Bookends: Michael's "You broke my heart, Fredo" kiss of death, brought full circle by his forgiving embrace of Fredo at Mama Corleone's funeral (see above).

Most powerful segue: The slow fade from the nine-year-old Vito sitting in his quarantined cell singing ("Vito Corleone, Ellis Island, 1901") to Anthony Corleone walking up the aisle at his communion 57 years later.

Pauses that last a lifetime: 1) Michael to Connie: "If you don't listen to me, Connie, and marry this man...you'll disappoint me." 2) Michael to Al Neri: "I don't want anything to happen to him [Fredo]...while my mother's still alive."

Best piece of violence: The violence in *Part II* is much less flashy (though no less effective) than the original's. The most startling moment for me is when young Vito puts the gun inside the already-dead Fanucci's mouth and takes one final shot.

Best historical allusion: There are at least two that stand out: 1) When Michael's being chauffeured through the streets of pre-revolution Cuba, besieged on all sides by kids banging on his car windows, there's a strong echo of Nixon's disastrous trip to Caracas in 1958; 2) The staging of Roth's assassination as he's escorted through the airport is clearly modelled on Ruby's assassination of Oswald.

Funniest line: Again, where to begin? Two that always get me: Michael's "He's been dying of the same heart attack for 30 years" line on Roth, and Connie's schlub boyfriend Merle—stupid, silly Merle—asking "Can I get a drink?" in Michael's office.

Three people to watch for: The easiest to pick out is Roger Corman as one of the senators on the investigatory panel—Corman was fairly well known when the film was made, so that counts as a cameo. More eye-opening are Harry Dean Stanton as one of Pentangeli's FBI bodyguards—he sits behind Pentangeli at the Senate hearings—and Danny Aiello as the Rosato brother who makes the attempt on Pentangeli inside the bar ("Michael Corleone says hello"). I'd seen the film probably 15 times before I picked out Aiello this year, more because of his voice than the shadowed view you get of him.

Who does Michael most resemble at the end of the film?: In Peter Biskind's excellent *The Godfather Companion*—from which I stole the format for this piece—there's an anecdote about how *II*'s final scene was referred to on the set as "the Hitler scene," and how Coppola specifically thought of Michael in terms of Hitler. The film came out in 1974; to me, it's impossible not to see Michael as a kind of *Final Days* Nixon as he retreats further and further into himself (a parallel drawn by many). "I don't feel as if I have to 'destroy' everyone, Tom. Just my enemies."

What else came out in 1974?: Among films that I love, there was *The Conversation, Chinatown, The Sugarland Express*, and *California Split*; *Badlands, Alice Doesn't Live Here Anymore, Thieves Like Us, Lenny, Harry and Tonto*, and *The Parallax View* were also 1974, and *Mean Streets, The Long Goodbye*, and *Serpico* were late-'73 releases that were either still in theatres or didn't really even get an opening until '74. Checking movie listings in those days must have been a lot like turning on the radio in 1965.

(homepage, 2001)

Hillary/Nixon

Very, very early in the campaign—before Iowa—I mentioned my support of Obama to an American friend, and he said he was surprised I wasn't instead rooting for the most Nixon-like candidate in the race: Giuliani. He was half-kidding—we both share a fascination with Nixon that's part generational, part temperamental, an odd mix of empathy and revulsion, and we continue to monitor the unexpected ways his shadow reverberates through American life. I know next to nothing about Giuliani beyond his post-9/11 ubiquity, but it didn't matter anyway, I told my friend, there was clearly a much better Nixon out there if I wanted to go that route: Hillary. I haven't seen any evidence yet that I was wrong.

She got off a line in her post-Bosnia-flap press conference yesterday that was Nixon through and through: "So I made a mistake. That happens. It proves I'm human—which, you know, for some people is a revelation." Unless Obama masks his neuroses exceptionally well, he seems to be more or less without them; she seems nothing but. She's always a beat or three off when addressing crowds, she's no less awkward trying to make convivial small-talk with reporters (something that came easy to her very un-Nixon-like husband), and I bet she comes out of this, whatever the result, with a finely-tuned enemies list. Prediction: the #1 slot will be held down by a portly man with a beard. I don't want to give the impression that her neurotic scheming makes her a typical woman. It doesn't—it makes her a typical Nixon. In the week after she lost Iowa, when she seemed headed for certain defeat in New Hampshire and a humiliatingly early exit, I said to the same friend that her "You won't have Hillary Clinton to kick around anymore" speech was close at hand. In the end, she never needed to give it. She may yet still.

(election blog, 2008)

The Conversation (Francis Ford Coppola, 1974)

I used the word "joyous" three times in my last post. Not much joy here—Alan Garfield's William P. Moran is even funnier (and scuzzier) than his ad-man in *The Candidate*, but that's about it for laughs. I won't try digging up the quote, but somebody I once came across called *Vertigo*, Richard Lester's *Petulia*, and *The Conversation* San Francisco's great trilogy of alienation, or ennui, or existentialist despair, or one of those really grim philosophical dispositions that people write papers about in grad school. *The Conversation* may also have been the film I was trying to remember earlier in this countdown when I said there was something else that had been blessed with serendipitous timing the equal of *The China Syndrome*. IMDB has its American release date as April 7, 1974, placing it somewhere in the middle of Alexander Butterfield's testimony before the Watergate committee (July 16, 1973, in which he revealed Nixon's in-house taping system) and Nixon's resignation on August 9, 1974. You could certainly say that that was savvy marketing on Coppola's behalf, but seeing as he had completed the script for *The Conversation* as far back as the late '60s, I'd say that whatever delays held up its completion as a film until 1974 transformed prescience into serendipity.

I have often felt that *The Conversation* is an even better film than the first two *Godfather*s. It's a meaningless comparison ultimately: one is small and moody and cerebral, the other is large and effusive and emotional, and it's almost difficult to reconcile them as being the work of one director. (I'm simplifying, of course—there's lots of moodiness in the *Godfathers*, and if cerebral just means smart, then they're cerebral, too.) I believe Coppola has gone on record as saying he felt closer to *The Conversation*, but that doesn't count for much as far as my own response goes (besides which, artists are not always their most insightful critics). What is less open to dispute, I'd say, is that it's either the definitive Nixon film, or at the very least one of two or three on which you might hang that title. And, as you may have guessed by now, that's worth a whole when it comes to ranking my favorite films.

The Conversation is a Nixon film not just because of the obvious, that Gene Hackman's grubby surveillance expert is like a composite of Hunt, Liddy, Segretti, and all of Nixon's other low-level operatives, the plumbers and dirty-tricks experts who themselves functioned as a subversive extension of Nixon's paranoia. You don't need all the middlemen; in many ways, Hackman's Harry Caul is Nixon himself. He's socially inept, ultra-secretive, conspiratorial, shadowy and anonymous, and he's able to dissociate himself completely from the morality of his actions if called to account. Pestered by Moran about a job of his that once led to someone's gruesome murder, Harry just brushes it aside: "It had nothing to do with me—I just turned in the tapes." As Caul skulks around San Francisco in his grey, rumpled raincoat, trying to remain as invisible as humanly possible as he implicates himself deeper and deeper in some shady corporate power-play he only dimly understands, he's like a phantasmagoric embodiment of the last miserable months of Nixon's presidency. He's Nixon and he's Nixon's henchmen rolled into one, trying to navigate his way through a maze as murky and unknowable as Watergate.

I overdo the Nixon stuff, I know. *The Conversation* is just as spooky if viewed as a Big Brother parable, or as a foreshadowing of the YouTube/Facebook/Google world we live in today, where notions of privacy are (voluntarily and otherwise) slipping away. There's a recurring moment in *The Conversation* where Harry is suddenly horrified to find his universe flipped on its head and himself the one being surveilled—happens at least four times. If the film had been made today, he'd be a computer hacker who gets hit with identity theft.

Hackman's performance is one of the greatest ever, I think, while character acting never got any better in the '70s than Garfield and John Cazale. One last thing: much like *Marathon Man*, you'll always remember *The Conversation* by a single line of dialogue. You hear that line two different ways by the time the film's over, and—ingeniously on the part of Coppola—the puzzle at the center of everything hinges on the difference.

(#14, Facebook Top 50, 2011)

The Godfather Re-imagined (I)

Rob Sheffield and I have been engaged in a back-and-forth e-mail game over the past year, the premise of which is that anything that happens in life can be meaningfully re-enacted through scenes from the first two *Godfather* films. Northrop Frye might have called such a game "The Great Code," but "The Six Degrees of Fat Clemenza" works too. In that spirit, and continuing with something that Rob started in the last *Radio On* and expanded in *Rolling Stone*, here's a short teleplay that begins inside the Oval Office in November of 1996:

BILL CLINTON: "I'm sorry about the other night, Monica...You gotta blow me, so turn around—on your knees, facing me. [Monica begins.] I guess I'm getting too old for my job. Too grouchy—can't stand the aggravation. You know how it is."

[A voice is heard from the other side of the door.]

GEORGE STEPHANOPOLOUS: "Mr. President? Mr. President, you in there?"

BILL CLINTON: "What?"

show no traces

GEORGE S.: "The First Lady wants to see you."

BILL CLINTON [long pause]: "Yeah, one minute."

[Cut to George S. as he smiles and walks away. Monica Lewinsky's voice can be heard from inside the Oval Office.]

MONICA: "Mr. President!"

[Scene #2: A reception room elsewhere in the White House, five minutes later. The First Lady is listening intently to Yasser Arafat.]

ARAFAT: "I don't know what to do. My army's weak. It's weak. If I had this territory on the West Bank, it puts me right back on top again. But this man out there, he won't give it to me; the head of Israel."

HILLARY CLINTON: "What's his name?"

ARAFAT: "Netanyahu. He won't give it to me—he says there's no chance. No chance. Oh, Mrs. President, I don't know what to do. I don't know what to do."

HILLARY CLINTON: "You can act like a man! [Slaps Arafat in the face.] What's the matter with you? Is this how you turned out? A respected international terrorist who cries like a woman? '*What can I do?! What can I do?!*' What is that nonsense? Ridiculous. [The President quietly enters the room; the First Lady casts a quick glance in his direction.] You spend time with your family?"

ARAFAT: "Sure I do."

HILLARY CLINTON: "Good. Because a man who doesn't spend time with his family can never be a real man. Come here, Yasser...You look terrible. I want you to eat. I want you to rest a while. And a month from now, this Tel Aviv big shot's gonna give you what you want."

[Dissolve to a montage of newspaper headlines covering the next 15 months, culminating in the public revelation of the Lewinsky scandal in January of 1998. Shots of the President jogging, the President

11

golfing, and the President eating are interspersed, and the sound of old piano rolls fills the soundtrack. Fade in to scene #3: A group of Clinton's closest advisers—James Carville, Paul Begala, Ann Lewis, Rahm Emanuel, Lanny Davis—are huddled in a darkened room, plotting a counterattack to the new Lewinsky allegations. Mickey Kantor enters and hands a small package to Carville; he opens it to find a blue dress with a visible stain.]

CARVILLE: "What the hell is this?"

BEGALA [grimly]: "It's an Arkansan message. It means the President sleeps with the interns."

[Scene #4: A PBS studio, later that night.]

JIM LEHRER: "Mr. President, is it true?"

BILL CLINTON: "Don't ask me about my personal life, Jim..."

JIM LEHRER: "Is it true?"

BILL CLINTON: "Don't ask me about my personal life..."

JIM LEHRER: "No."

BILL CLINTON: "Enough! [Slams his fist down.] All right. This one time—this one time—I'll let you ask me about my personal life."

JIM LEHRER: "Is it true? Is it?"

BILL CLINTON [long pause; he looks directly into the television camera—imploringly, earnestly, tenderly—and his voice becomes very quiet]: "No."

[As the studio camera starts to pull back slowly, the President's advisers emerge from the wings and surround him. James Carville kneels down and kisses the President's hand.]

CARVILLE: "Mr. President."

[The camera continues to pull back, and the familiar and haunting refrain of Fleetwood Mac's "Don't Stop" is heard on the soundtrack. When the camera has moved beyond the threshold of the room's entrance, Paul Begala walks over and slowly closes the door. Fade to black.]

(*Radio On*, 1998)

Frost/Nixon

I avoided *Frost/Nixon* when it was in theatres, bought a cheap DVD last year, continued to leave it on the shelf, finally watched it the other night. The guy who plays Frost is good—same guy who was in the play, I think. It's mimicry rather than acting, and he overuses a couple of facial expressions, but boy, he had the voice down pat (and an interesting conception of the character to go along with it: nice guy giving it his best in the midst of official-journalist condescension). Didn't get what Langella was doing at all. Anthony Hopkins didn't really look or sound like Nixon, yet it was an idiosyncratic interpretation that made sense to me—the Andy Hardy aspect was a great touch. Langella speaks slowly and deeply, and barely even hints at Nixon's insecurities and neuroses. To me at least, he didn't even remotely suggest Nixon.

(ILX, 2012)

Locked in the Attic Again

Perfect set-up for something I wanted to call attention to, Scott: it's Nixon's birthday. He'd be 99 today.

If there's one thing I'd count on this election cycle, it's that Nixon will pop up at some point. He always does—as many people have pointed out, he simply cannot be killed. The last couple, I think it was via old tapes where he was holding court on McCain and Kerry; there was definitely stuff that came out in '96 in connection to Dole, and in '92 having to do with the first Bush. (Can't remember if there was anything in 2000 or not.) Assuming Romney's the nominee, there must be lots out there between Nixon and Romney's father. In 1966, there was a point where George Romney was the leading candidate for the Republican nomination…there's a tracking chart on his Wikipedia page that has him eight points ahead of Nixon in November. He was soon overtaken, had a meltdown prior to the convention when he announced he'd been brainwashed in Vietnam, and ended up serving as HUD secretary during Nixon's first term.

I'm guessing more tapes'll turn up. Something along the lines of this: "Let's give that crazy Mormon son of a bitch HUD. Goddammit, let's bury him—keep him buried where he can't hurt us. No one gives a fuck about HUD. I mean, Jesus Christ, Bob, does anybody here even know what that stands for?"

(Managing the Decay, 2012)

"South Side," Moby

Moby: "You know any good spots on the South Side?" Gwen: "Yeah, I'll think about it." Moby: "Well, think about it while you're drivin', will you? I wanna hit New York sometime this month." (4.0)

(rockcritics.com, 2001)

Lynyrd Skynyrd

I was talking to someone at work just last week about "Sweet Home Alabama," refuting the notion that it was intended as a show of support for George Wallace. I've come across such an interpretation of the song on at least a couple of occasions. Depends on what you make of the first two lines in the third verse: "In Birmingham they love the governor/Now we all did what we could do"

To me that seems clear: we didn't vote for the guy but the rest of the state did, so get over it. Coming back with the rejoinder about Nixon and Watergate is brilliant (as is the use of rhetoric in the Muscle Shoals verse), so much so that I always took the bit about "Does your conscience bother you?" at face value, an accusation that it was the rest of the country that was to blame for Nixon's re-election. Checking the appendices of *The Making of the President 1972*, though, I see what should have been obvious all along: Alabama voted overwhelmingly for Nixon, with a 73% level of support that ranked behind only Georgia and Mississippi. So now I'm not really sure what that line means. In any event, I continue to hear "Sweet Home Alabama" as a perfect combination of wisdom, anger, joy, humour, and audacity. That Neil Young had added it to his set-list within a year or two of its appearance isn't surprising; when you're cut down to size that convincingly, all you can really do if you're smart enough, and have a good enough sense of humour yourself, is wave the white flag.

(record inventory, 2005-06)

show no traces

Nixon (Oliver Stone, 1995)

I was considering *Wall Street*, an overheated junk bond I've seen more times than I care to admit (powered in part by a drug called Charlie Sheen), but it occurred to me just two nights ago that *Nixon*'s the one—I absolutely have to have *Nixon* on my list.

I'll start where Steven left off with *Sid and Nancy*: I wouldn't go into this preoccupied with what you know about Nixon. Getting your head around Anthony Hopkins' off-putting interpretation is the first and biggest leap you have to make. He's not trying for precise mimicry at all—Dan Ackroyd, Rich Little, etc.—nor is he seizing on one aspect of Nixon's personality and running wild with it, the way Philip Baker Hall takes Nixon's paranoia and elevates it to the nth degree of delirium in *Secret Honor* (a more acclaimed Nixon film I don't like nearly as much). It's more like Hopkins spends the whole film tentatively trying to feel his way into the character, always a half-beat off, never quite sure which Nixon he's supposed to be at any given moment. Which is, of course, perfect; Nixon himself spent the entirety of his public career groping around for some semblance of an authentic self, and he seemed no less awkward or embarrassed inside his own skin than Hopkins does. It's a weird, heavy (literally; Hopkins is always lurching around with his shoulders slumped), but ultimately affecting performance.

Factually—well, it's Oliver Stone. As with *JFK*, he conflates, reshuffles, and creates "counter-myths" (a favorite Stone word) whenever it suits his purposes to do so. There are probably a thousand little fibs scattered throughout *Nixon*, and, to me, it wouldn't be very interesting to start cataloguing them. Here's one big one: the idea that RFK's assassination was the trigger that led Nixon to seek the presidency in '68. If you're at all familiar with the actual timeline, that's laughable; Nixon had decided as early as the impending Goldwater debacle in '64 that he'd be the guy to pick up the pieces, and I wouldn't even doubt that he started thinking about running within five minutes of finishing his infamous concession speech in '62. That's a more serious transgression, because it misrepresents something fundamental about Nixon's character.

Even that doesn't matter, though. Stone gets the story right in broad outline, and he also gets at something much harder to pin down. Here's how Greil Marcus describes the experience of watching the film in an essay on J.T. Walsh included in *O.K. You Mugs* (Walsh plays Ehrlichman): "One night, though, flipping channels after the late news had closed down, I happened onto *Nixon* running on HBO, and I didn't turn it off. I was pulled in, played like a fish through all the fictions and flashbacks, dreaming the movie's dream: waiting for Watergate." "Dreaming the movie's dream"—I love that line. There's something very sad and very majestic about *Nixon* (a nod to John Williams' score on that front), and even if you despise Nixon as much as most people who'll take the time to seek out the film almost certainly do, I think you end up feeling the weight of the man and the full scope of his centrality to post-war America; like Neil Young's "Campaigner," it takes you to a place where you can say, "Okay—there was a life there." Everything ends, as it should, with footage of Clinton's eulogy in 1994. It's a movie I expect I'll be revisiting once every year or two for the rest of my life.

(#48, Facebook Top 50, 2011)

Natural Born Plumbers: John Cazale and the Character Actors of the 1970s

American cinema in the 1970s will always be remembered first and foremost as a legendary decade for directors (the familiar litany of Coppola, Scorsese, Altman, and company), and secondly as a time when a new generation of lead actors superseded the Waynes, Newmans, and McQueens of the '60s (Nicholson, De Niro, and Pacino preeminent among them). It's not a decade famous for its character actors, those familiar-but-elusive faces that turn up in film after film to commandeer the proceedings with some memorable bit of business that stays in your mind long after everything else is forgotten—certainly not in the way that the 1940s, the height of the studio system, is widely regarded as the high-water mark of character acting. In *O.K. You Mugs*, an anthology of writings on the art of character acting, editors Luc Sante and Melissa Holbrook Pierson define the specialized appeal of the character actor this way: "As they reappear in one film and then another, it is as if they are returning in our very dreams; these characters take on character."

Defined as such, the '70s was actually a time of unforgettable role players. Their names haven't as yet been accorded the same mythological status as Walter Brennan, Ward Bond, Harry Carey, Sidney Greenstreet, or Elisha Cook Jr., but men like Allen Garfield, Ned Beatty, Peter Boyle, Bert Remsen, Harry Dean Stanton, Michael Murphy, Burt Young, Billy Green Bush, and G.D. Spradlin left behind a body of work that was absolutely integral to the key American films of the era. If, like me, much of your movie-going sensibility was shaped by that time and place, De Niro's "You talkin' to me?" monologue in *Taxi Driver* is like scripture; but you probably cherish Peter Boyle's densely layered a-man-is-what-he-does lecture in the same film (culminating in his "It's not Bertrand Russell, but what do you want, I'm a cabbie" apologia, a masterpiece of redundancy) just as much.

And most of all, you cherish John Cazale. Dead at 41 by cancer, Cazale's filmography is endlessly fascinating in its haiku perfection. His career consisted of five films over a seven-year period: the first two *Godfather*s (1972/4), *The Conversation* (1974), *Dog Day Afternoon* (1975), and *The Deer Hunter* (1978). All five received Academy Award nominations for Best Picture (inexplicably, Cazale himself never earned a supporting nomination); three of them won, *The Conversation* lost to one of the other five, and only *Dog Day Afternoon* was beaten by a film that didn't feature Cazale. Leaving aside the validity of the Academy Awards as a barometer of artistic worth (other than to observe that the awards given out during the '70s tended to be more adventurous than at any other time in history), that's a combination of brilliance and brevity unmatched by even James Dean. I've gotten into the habit of referring to Cazale as the Velvet Underground of actors, insofar as everything he ever did has its own secure niche in film history, without a single misstep along the way.

In trying to place Cazale according to Luc Sante's classification of character actors ("Some character actors are foxes and some are hedgehogs: the fox knows many things, while the hedgehog knows one big thing"), I'd say he was a hedgehog with a little bit of fox in him. His specialty, on full display in all his films but one, was everything that fell on the vulnerability end of the emotional spectrum: weakness, ineffectuality, fragility, resignation, invisibility. When Talia Shire pleads with Pacino in *Godfather II* to forgive Cazale's Fredo, she pins down his overriding persona perfectly: "He's so sweet and helpless." To think of Cazale is to recall first his sad, imploring eyes, the mixture of inadequacy and shame he conveyed—he was one instance where the overused adjective "haunted" is justified. Cazale's performances elicit feelings of protectiveness, a sense of having to look out for a younger sibling. Coppola expertly plays upon this instinct in the *Godfather*s by turning the Fredo-Michael relationship on its head: it's the older brother who grudgingly submits to being watched over by the younger brother, in time coming to resent the arrangement so deeply that humiliation gives way to betrayal.

In *Godfather II*'s scene inside the Corleone compound where Michael questions and then disowns Fredo, this resentment and humiliation reach their breaking point. Cazale has had relatively little screen time up until then—two significant scenes in *The Godfather* (most memorably, toadying up to Moe Greene to the withering dismay of Michael) and a lot of jumping through hoops in *II* (his debauched wife, Johnny Ola)—which makes his confrontation with Michael all the more remarkable. In a brother scene that stands alone with Brando and Steiger in *On the Waterfront* for its purity and intensity, Cazale seizes his big moment by venturing to a place where almost any actor would look foolish. He completely melts down—when Fredo snaps at Michael that "It's not the way I wanted it," Cazale does a thing with his arms that borders on epileptic seizure. It's a startling transformation.

Cazale's hedgehog-like ability to do one thing exceedingly well—to recede into the background and meekly defer to his superiors— also shapes his portrayals of Stan, Gene Hackman's assistant in *The Conversation*, and Al Pacino's accomplice Sal in *Dog Day Afternoon*. Stan is the least neurotic of Cazale's characters, but he's also such a cipher that he's reduced to the role of chattering lapdog to Gene Hackman's Harry Caul, maybe the most socially inept of '70's movie-loners. Harry manifests a painfully evident inferiority complex with just about everyone he encounters, but in his working relationship with Stan, it's Cazale who's shut out and made to feel like an intrusive amateur: "It wouldn't hurt if you filled me in a little bit once in a while, Harry—did you ever think about that?" So he quits to go work for Harry's number-one competitor, the despised William P. Moran (Allen Garfield), as a means of both revenge and retaining some self-respect. It takes all of a few nice words and a vague promise from Harry to bring Stan back into the fold—with a shrug betraying apathy as much as it does loyalty, Cazale reasserts himself as the ultimate pushover.

By the time of *Dog Day Afternoon*, Cazale's an empty shell. Sidney Lumet's casting deftly echoes the Fredo/Michael relationship by again placing Cazale in a position of feckless subservience to Pacino. Cazale's Sal is afraid of everything: of Pacino's wired unpredictability, of guns, of cancer, of planes, of being reported as a homosexual on local news broadcasts. Cazale comes up with a vibrantly tacky look for Sal—with his long hair, cheap suit, and extra-loud '70s tie, he's like a rough sketch of Benicio Del Toro's character in *The Usual Suspects*—but the eyes are more lifeless than ever. A lot of Cazale's screen time in *Dog Day Afternoon* consists of little more than a blank, uncomprehending stare at the unfolding circus around him. Pacino gyrates and schemes and exhorts; Cazale just stands by and waits for the bottom to fall out, which of course it eventually must.

Cazale was enough of a name after *Dog Day Afternoon* to get second-billing to De Niro in *The Deer Hunter*. Perhaps feeling boxed in by an emerging pattern of variations on Fredo, Cazale used his newfound visibility for a masterly about-face. This time, all the fumbling silences and little-man significance go to De Niro, Christopher Walken, and John Savage (too much so—at times their lines seem to have been written by Barton Fink), while Cazale reinvents himself as a womanizing, vainglorious blowhard, again named Stan, who stays home and cultivates a moustache while his friends go off to war. Stan is crude, self-aggrandizing, reckless, and 99% bluff—it's like Fredo has been inhabited by Moe Greene. When Cazale starts spewing invective at De Niro's grandiloquent "this-is-this" rationale for not lending him some hunting boots—a scene of comical miscommunication that anticipates *Raging Bull*'s "Did you fuck my wife?" interrogation—he's a profane motormouth far removed from anything Cazale had previously attempted. Stan was a beautifully crafted adumbration of where Cazale might have gone if he hadn't died—proof, really, that he could have gone anywhere.

If Cazale was the most purely gifted of '70s character actors, Allen Garfield may have captured the tenor of the times better than anyone else. There's no more emblematic '70s image to my mind than Garfield stalking around in *Nashville*, waving off Ned Beatty and Michael Murphy with his mantra of "I got no time, Delbert—*I got no time!*" In *O.K. You Mugs*, Greil Marcus envisions the late J.T. Walsh as a reflection of Bill Clinton: a charming lout drifting from one tawdry role to another inside an ambiguous "haze of sincerity." That's the kind of irresistible analogy one can easily overdo, and to prove it, I'm going to overdo a different one: I've always viewed Garfield and many of the '70s' other key character actors as extensions of Richard Nixon, the inescapable white whale of another time.

Cazale was Nixon the brooding, self-pitying outsider—the eternal wallflower who felt inferior to East Coast intellectuals, the part of Nixon that wanted to crawl out of his own skin. You can easily envision *Godfather II*'s compound scene played out between Nixon-as-Fredo and JFK-as-Michael: "I was in the White House before you, Jack, and I was stepped over!" Ned Beatty was Nixon the mechanical bumbler, the one who couldn't work a tape recorder properly; Burt Young and Peter Boyle were Nixon the uncouth slob (all those expletive-deleteds); and G.D. Spradlin (Senator Geary in *Godfather II*, Nick Nolte's imperious coach in *North Dallas Forty*) was Nixon the coolly manipulative despot. Garfield had some Nixon in him too, but most of all he was the ultimate Nixon flunky: the compulsive wheeler-dealer, sweating under his collar as he works the crowd, backroom rot with a smile. Garfield's political ad-man in *The Candidate* (a prototype lifted intact from *The Selling of the President 1968*, Joe McGinniss's account of how the "New Nixon" came to be) and his squalid wiretapper in *The Conversation* were two of the most gleefully amoral small-time operators of the era, natural born plumbers on the order of Hunt and Liddy. (Even as Ronee Blakley's avowedly apolitical husband/manager in *Nashville*, Garfield still managed to come across as a weasel-for-hire.) When Garfield offered his assessment of some welfare mothers gumming up one of his ads in *The Candidate*, his words were as sure a marker as "Ohio," *Joe* (Peter Boyle as the phantasmagoric embodiment of Nixon and Agnew's "silent majority"), or *All in the Family* that the Nixon decade was well underway: "Grim scene, baby, grim scene...You look uptight and uncool. Nobody's listening and nobody's digging you." To which Garfield, Robert Redford, and everyone within earshot burst out laughing.

The peculiarly feral quality of Garfield can be found in Steve Buscemi's best work during the '90s, just as Cazale and his contemporaries have their own modern-day equivalents in Philip Seymour Hoffman, Michael Imperioli, and Luis Guzman. In time, stray moments from this current generation of character specialists will seem much more vital than most of the huffing and puffing that now pushes them into the background (or a lot sooner than then—a few seconds of Guzman and Don Cheadle clowning around in *Traffic* is worth the whole Michael Douglas subplot). John Cazale packed more of those moments into five films than anyone I can think of. In Coppola's hollow *Godfather III*, Fredo is only present as an absence, as empty space on a rowboat; Michael is consumed by the memory of standing at the window, looking out on the one murder that in time will come to weigh heaviest of all on his conscience. That flashback to the empty rowboat is *The Godfather III*'s most resonant image—tribute to the enduring power of the first two *Godfather*s, but perhaps even more so to the deep impression left behind by Cazale.

(*Cinemascope*/rockcritics.com, 2001)

Fight for the White House

I found something called *Fight for the White House* in a Wal-Mart junk bin for $7. Measured in pop-music terms, it's legitimacy looked to lie somewhere in the neighborhood of a *La grande storia del ROCK* LP, if that means anything to you—I was anticipating three discs of ancient footage out of a Méliès film. It's actually pretty excellent. I've watched about two hours' worth so far, with another six to go.

Mostly it consists of TV commercials for every election going back to 1952, four or five for each side, with the balance given over to things like

Nixon's Checkers speech, debates (almost an hour of Carter and Reagan in '80), and campaign material. I looked at all of the commercials from '64 to '92 the other night. Anything involving Nixon, of course, is a highlight for me. There's a bizarre ad from '72 meant to showcase his "human" side: dancing at his daughter's wedding, conducting business on the phone, taking the piano for a rendition of "Happy Birthday" in honour of Duke Ellington. (If you want a can't-lose bet, ask someone to name the presidential TV ad in which Duke Ellington appeared.) There's one moment you'd never see today: Nixon sitting with Ehrlichman inside the Oval Office, dismissively referring to some state politician who's giving Nixon grief on property taxes as a "clown." Also fascinating is an E.G. Marshall spot for Humphrey from '68, where one-by-one he stands next to oversized photos of the three candidates and offers his appraisal of each. So how appalled by/terrified of Wallace were mainstream Democrats? The commercial leads with him. (There isn't, unfortunately, any third-party ads included in the package. I can live without John Anderson—I'm sure his spots were as electrifying as the man himself—but Wallace, Perot, and Nader all tipped elections, and it'd be nice if they were here.) Amazingly enough, the whole thing finishes with Obama, Clinton, and McCain ads from this year. I think the Wal-Mart truck must have been parked out back as DVDs rolled off the assembly line.

(election blog, 2008)

Godfather sightings

I'm almost positive that Corrado Gaipa (Don Tommasino, Michael's wheelchair-bound mentor back in Italy) plays the old uncle in *Big Night*[1]; there's no mistaking Alex Rocco in *That Thing You Do!*, especially since he's still doing Moe Greene 25 years later. I thought for sure Rocco was going to accuse one of the Wonders of banging secretaries two at a time.

(#5 video, year-end ballot, 1996)

"Dues," Ronee Blakely (1975)

I recently did a two-part Nixon show on CKLN, hooked in with the anniversary of his resignation—iconic Nixon songs, songs that were on the Top 100 the week he resigned, sound clips, a variety of cultural flotsam and jetsam circa 1974 (e.g., a news report on Patty Hearst, movie trailers for *The*

---

1   Not true; Gaipa had been dead for seven years when *Big Night* came out.

Godfather II and *The Parallax View*), etc. One thing I thought about a lot was the perfect song on which to finish, and I must say I was quite proud of myself for settling on this. It takes care of the easy part—conveying some sense of where the country was at in 1974—but there are any number of songs that would have worked just as well on that level. "Dues" does something else: it's a possible map as to where Nixon's head might have been at as he climbed onto that plane and headed back to San Clemente. (Another song that's got it covered both ways: "Knockin' on Heaven's Door.") Okay—I'll now do what anybody writing about anything should do as often as possible, which is to hand it over to Pauline Kael:

"When (Blakley) stands on the stage of the Opry Belle and sings 'Dues,' with the words 'It hurts so bad, it gets me down,' her fragility is so touching and her swaying movements are so seductively musical that, perhaps for the first time on the screen, one gets the sense of an artist's being consumed by her gift...At one point, she sings with the mike in one hand, the other hand tracing the movements of the music in the air, and it's an absolutely ecstatic moment."

(#92, Facebook Top 100, 2010-11)

Forrest Gump

Simply as a matter of style, there are a couple of more basic problems: the computerized lip-synching is inept, and there are enough heavy-handed portents to make you feel like you're four years old. The worst offender is the Nixon segment: 1) Upon learning that Forrest has nowhere to stay, Nixon says that "I know a hotel for you" (good; cut the scene there and the point has been made subtly); 2) Move to Forrest inside the Watergate, phoning the police because he spots burglars across the way (enough already); 3) Just in case you're still finding your bearings, the camera pans to a close-up of some hotel stationery—"Watergate Hotel." At this point, I thought that maybe a big title card would come up explaining, "AND THAT'S WHEN HE HAD TO RESIGN." This is just one example of the kind of overkill that recurs throughout. Now, I know that this isn't going to bother anyone under the age of, say, 20, but clearly that's not who this film was made for. Bill James once wrote that he started *The Baseball Abstract* because he wanted to be able to mention Babe Ruth without having to stop every time and explain who he was. Robert Zemeckis wastes a lot time in *Forrest Gump* trying to explain who Babe Ruth was. (Strangely enough, when I saw *The Babe* with John Goodman, I remember being depressed because the filmmakers didn't want to spend any time trying to explain who Babe Ruth was—mostly they just wanted to recreate scenes from *Animal House*.) (5.5)

(*Radio On*, 1994)

Rob Base

I wonder how many actual copies of the Lester Bangs album exist. 1,000? 5,000? However many there are, take the square root and subtract seven, and that's how many people bought *The Incredible Base*, Rob Base's follow-up to *It Takes Two*. D.J. E-Z Rock gets a prominent thank-you in the credits, but judging from his complete non-participation on the album proper, that was obviously meant to smooth over some grim, Corleone-style parting-of-the-ways beforehand: "That's it, E-Z Rock—you're out."

(record inventory, 2005-06)

Evil

One point on which we part company is the idea that Nixon was evil. Sorry, don't believe that, no more than I believe George W. was/is evil. You could spend a month cataloguing Nixon's faults, and yes, he had much blood on his hands. As to the former—the small-mindedness, the paranoia, the manipulation, etc.—I recognize them as human failings, some of which I share. He had an inordinate number of them, an almost perfect storm, but I recognize the person there. In terms of the latter—the thousands upon thousands of deaths in Vietnam that he could have foreshortened—to me that's a complicated mixture of Nixon's personality, the institution of the presidency, the American character, the male character, etc., etc. If I'm not mistaken, you describe almost every post-war president as evil. If you believe that, fine. I don't. Sorry to be obvious (naive, I'm sure you'd say, my Kay Corleone to your Michael), but to me evil is Hitler and Manson and the like.

(ILX, 2011)

Our Nixon

Surprise, surprise, I liked *Our Nixon*. It basically follows the standard timeline, from inauguration through to the resignation of Haldeman and Ehrlichman, but it moves along casually, and it never feels like events are being ticked off a checklist. Nixon doesn't fulminate much—there are phone calls with Haldeman where he sounds bemused by events, and even one, after a Vietnam television address, where he sounds stoical. (And another, right after Haldeman's resignation, where he's almost certainly been drinking.) The one time he really gets going, on *All in the Family* and Greek philosophers, is something. There's a bit with the Ray Conniff Singers that moves from a funny introduction by Nixon—no lie—to a fairly stunning moment that I don't recall ever reading about. The highlight for me was a brilliant choice for the opening-credit music. It's not just a great song (not period music), it lays out the entire film in a way that makes perfect sense.

(ILX, 2013)

The Godfather Re-imagined (II)

NEWT: We can't wait. I don't care what David Gergen says about inevitability, Romney's weak, that's it. That's the key for us. Gotta get Romney.

CALLISTA: Lemme ask you something, Professor. I mean—what about Paul and Santorum, huh? What do we do with these...nuisances?

NEWT: They wanna have a debate with me, right? It will be me, Santorum, Paul, and Romney. Let's set the debate. Get our Twitter people to find out where it's gonna be held. Now, we insist it's a public place—an auditorium, a town hall, some place where there's people so I feel safe. They're gonna shake hands with me when I first meet them, right, so I can't be frothing at the mouth then. But if Bill Kristol can figure a way to have opposition research planted there for me—then I'll kill 'em all.

(ILX, 2012)

All the President's Men (Alan J. Pakula, 1976)

This is the last film on my list I've actually been looking forward to writing about. My next two have been listed already, and my #1 and #2 I've written about before. Other than stray comments on the message board, though, I'm pretty sure I've never written a word about *All the President's Men*, which has slowly but inexorably made its way into my Top 10 over a number of years—going all the way back to its original release, really. I say I'm looking forward to writing about it because, more so than the music countdown, where my comments sometimes only addressed songs at a 45° angle at best, here I've been trying to zero in on what exactly it is I love about the films I've been listing. So now I get to find out what it is I love about *All the President's Men*.

A good place to start is Richard Nixon, 37th president of the United States. Have I mentioned that I have a long-standing fascination with Nixon? Every other film, you say?—okay. He only actually appears once in *All the President's Men*, and his placement is just perfect: right at the end, on a TV monitor nobody's watching inside the offices of *The Washington Post*. He's just back from China and making a triumphant appearance before Congress, and his return coincides perfectly (Hollywood does like to massage timelines) with Woodward and Bernstein having just achieved a major breakthrough in their Watergate investigation. He looks distracted, but I may just be projecting.

There've been two films the past few years where I saw a number of reviews that compared them to *All the President's Men*: *Zodiac* and *The Social Network*. *Zodiac* because it was similarly a meticulously detailed procedural enacted on a large canvas, and there was also the newspaper angle linking them together; with *The Social Network*, it was the challenge of documenting living history that more or less happened yesterday. I would endorse the comparisons on both counts. No matter how many times I watch *All the President's Men*, I become completely immersed in the minutia of Woodward and Bernstein's detective work as if for the first time; like the three principals in *Zodiac*, they make their way through a labyrinth of setbacks, small gains, and sudden moments of clarity. As to the second point, I applaud the risk Pakula took in diving right back into Watergate at a time when I imagine most of the American public was Nixoned out to the point of exhaustion—even though it was probably commerce and star availability that dictated that decision.

I've read that journalism schools filled up to capacity after *The Post* led the way in bringing down Nixon. That romantic notion of the investigative journalist as hero is on full display in *All the President's Men*, the culmination of Murrow and Cronkite beforehand, a moment worlds away from the contempt in which the media is held today. (Rather loud descendents like Glenn Greenwald and Matt Taibbi keep the moment alive, I suppose.) Hoffman and Redford carry it off with just the right balance of movie-star dash, gonzo scrambling, and odd-couple tension. ("Is there anywhere you *don't* smoke?") Kael had problems with what she perceived as the film's fixation on Bernstein's Jewishness, and I can see that, but Hoffman's pretty great nonetheless.

Character actors—three of my remaining films are pinnacles of character acting, beginning with this one. Jason Robards won the Academy Award as Ben Bradlee, everybody remembers Jane Alexander (just nominated, but she did get a job in the Clinton administration), Jack Warden and Martin Balsam and Ned Beatty are inner-circle Hall of Fame character actors, and Robert Walden as Donald Segretti is oddly affecting. Best of all, Hal Holbrook. When Steven posted *The Third Man* the other day, I started thinking how it was a perfect segue into *All the President's Men* and the character of Deep Throat, who has the same elusiveness as (and is shot very much like) Harry Lime. I've also got to mention the woman at 1:22 of the trailer; she's as mythical to me as the Erik Satie woman in *Goin' Down the Road*.

So here's a clip of Holbrook, followed by the trailer. If I could link to anything, my first choice would probably by the famous overhead shot inside the Library of Congress (referenced in *The Simpsons*—makes me laugh just thinking about it). If you had to distill the idea of a vast, unknowable conspiracy into a single image, that would be the shot.

(#5, Facebook Top 50, 2011)

The Objective Reality of the Campaign

I'd been tuned out enough the last couple of days to not even realize that Nevada was yesterday until I flipped the TV on in the morning, and whenever I had CNN on for the rest of the day, it was just background drone, up to and including the results. (Even Sullivan didn't post once about Nevada yesterday.) But I made it a point to watch Gingrich's late-night press conference. Newt + big loss + press conference promised to be a strange kind of fun. And it was.

Victor David Hanson has something up on *The Corner* making the obvious comparison to Nixon's '62 press conference. True enough, with a couple of differences: Gingrich was there to announce he's ready to be kicked around for a few more months, and whereas Nixon genuinely despised the press, Gingrich only pretend-despises them—he was courting the assembled reporters mightily, and having a great time doing it. Speaking of which, the weirdest moment of all for me came after he finished, when CNN's David Gergen, with heavy heart, observed that he can't remember a presidential candidate who was more "driven by hatred" than Gingrich. Huh? A quick check of his own résumé may help Gergen jog his memory.

So Gingrich still has lots of venom left to spew. How much notice anyone takes from here on in, I don't know, but he's still the most compelling reason by far to keep watching. Alex Castellanos, who was responsible for that creepy Jesse Helms ad twenty years ago ("Hands") but is probably the funniest guy on all the panels right now, had a great line on *Meet the Press* this morning: "Romney won every demographic last night except for divorce lawyers and narcissists." True up to a point—Canadian election bloggers don't vote, but we're for Newt too.

(Managing the Decay, 2012)

The Godfather I & II (Francis Ford Coppola, 1972/1974)

Another jersey (or jerseys) that I've been trying to retire from my travels as a film-goer. I saw *I* in the new Lightbox theatre a few months ago, part of their own 100-greatest rollout to celebrate their launch, so I feel like I'm finished with that one. They didn't play *II* for some reason; if that should turn up one day at the new place—and that day may never come—I'll give that another go too. And that's it—no more meetings, no more discussions, no more Sollozzo tricks. As I once wrote somewhere else, the best approximation I can give for how many times I've seen the first two *Godfathers* is some percentage of my life. TV doesn't help—I stumble over them somewhere once or twice a month. I want out, I really do.

I was very interested in *Sight & Sound*'s decision to combine votes for the two films in their 2002 poll. I assume they'll do the same next year, but going by some of the pushback I've encountered in my own discussions on the matter, maybe they'll back off. As I mentioned in my Apu comment—and please, chime in on this—I think they made the right decision. The main argument against combining them, as I understand it, is that you may have people voting for *I* who don't think nearly as highly of *II*, or vice versa. And in almost any other analogous case, I'd agree with that; even with the Apu films, there's a meaningful gap in how much I like the first compared with the other two. (I cheated by listing them together—there are parts of the second and third I just wouldn't want to lose.) You'd have to survey all the people who cast individual votes for *I* or *II* in the *Sight & Sound* poll to know for sure, but I strongly suspect that almost everybody who voted only for *I* loves *II* almost as much, and that those who voted the other way, *II* but not *I*, are in the same boat. (For a dissenting view, go back to Jeff's *Godfather* comment and follow the link to his page.) So I doubt that actual *Godfather* voters were bothered by the decision, but I can see where someone who would have preferred to see something else in the top 10 would be.

I know—I'm shadow-boxing around the films themselves, because 1) I'm invariably going to repeat stuff I've written and said elsewhere, and 2) I assume that everyone else knows them inside-out too. They're just such a fact of life by now. I remember last spring being in the store down the street where I go to buy lunch sometimes, and I made some obscure reference to *The Godfather* in a conversation with John and Andrea, the store's owners. It was an incomplete allusion, almost a test, and I looked immediately at John (Italian) to see if he could complete it. Of course he did.

If you watch movies for big themes, the first two *Godfathers* have them. Like *Citizen Kane*, and like one of my two remaining choices, it aspires to say big things about America. It's not just my being Canadian that makes we want to sidestep that stuff—as you may have noticed, I'm just not in general a theme guy when it comes to movies. (Now and again I'll figure something out about some film that I think other people have missed, and I'll feel really pleased with myself.) I've always been fascinated by the way Michael's end in *II*—hunkered down inside his compound, surrounded by his henchmen, obsessed with destroying not everyone (or so he says) but "just my enemies"—eerily mirrors the final days of, sorry, the Nixon presidency, which came about just a few months earlier. But I also realize that both films mostly draw their material from Puzo's novel, and also that films take a while to get made—the made-to-order parallel to Nixon was probably accidental. You could just as easily see Hitler's last days instead.

So the themes are there for me, even though I don't dwell on them, and so is Gordon Willis's extraordinary cinematography (especially in *I*), a million little details in the art direction (you can spot a poster for a Jake LaMotta fight at one point), towering lead performances, and of course the audacity of Coppola's direction. Meticulous, deliberate audacity—the audacity of someone who has total control of every second.

With of all of that, I once again find that the supporting performances in the first two *Godfathers* are what have made the most lasting impression on me over the years. If you could map out a film's characters in a hierarchy according to screen time—something like the way the Corleone family is rendered on that chart during the Senate hearing—*I* and *II* would have more unforgettable performances at the sixth, seventh, and eight levels than any film ever made. The senator who says "No, I'll allow it" with regards to Michael's prepared statement—he's somewhere down around the seventh level, and I wait for that line every time. The way Johnny Ola says "Anisette," Enzo the baker's touching loyalty ("For your father—*for your father*"), the Cuban diplomat who introduces everyone down in Miami...there are just so many of these bit parts scattered everywhere.

I've gone even longer than my usual longwinded entry. Single most memorable screening of my life: seeing *I* and *II* back-to-back in the early '80s at the Nostalgic, a ridiculously tiny upstairs rep theatre (long gone) that seated maybe 60 people. That was the night that did it for me, and it's another reason why, 30 years later, I want to list the two films together.

(#3, Facebook Top 50, 2011)

Washington Behind Closed Doors

I'm a couple of hours into *Washington Behind Closed Doors*. Not what I thought, which is that it would be exclusively about Watergate. It starts in '67 or '68, even before "Dick Monckton" wins the presidency. It's fun matching character to person—most are obvious, some less so (probably some composites in there). Jason Robards (wisely) makes no attempt to sound like Nixon, instead giving glimpses here and there; he snarls some vintage Nixon to end the first episode, which I won't quote here (telling you something about what was still acceptable on network TV in 1977). Has a lot of CIA-connected stuff that I didn't realize was such public knowledge so close to Nixon's presidency...It's based on one of Ehrlichman's books (not a whitewash; he was clearly in revenge mode), so maybe this had a hand in getting that out, or maybe the big Senate hearing on the CIA had already happened—not sure of the timeline. Cliff Robertson fairly wooden, Andy Griffith a decent (though not really remotely similar) LBJ, Stefanie Powers quite gorgeous.

Finished this tonight. It's close to artless—there was one nice shot of Andy Griffith/LBJ and Cliff Robertson/Richard Helms outdoors as the camera drew back at a critical moment—and it lurches along from storyline to storyline, with occasionally pointless detours (the entire marital situation of Robertson). But then there'd be a really strong scene and it'd pick up for a while. Robards is as valid as any other Nixon I've seen. He emphasizes some things (Nixon's persecution complex), minimizes or bypasses others (the social clumsiness), adds little flourishes the whole way through (his bizarre clowning around on Air Force One seemed especially Nixon-like). Robert Vaughn's Haldeman is so robotically sycophantic and callous, he's funny—his ongoing exasperation with Nicholas Pryor (most annoying character in the whole thing, not sure who exactly he was supposed to be) is great. Two people I knew from *Save the Tiger*: Thayer David as Hoover, also Lara Parker. Matches up well with *All the President's Men*, ending at exactly the moment where the earlier film begins. Meg Foster's eyes are weird beyond compare. She looks like a glassy-eyed Stepford wife.

(ILX, 2014)

August 9

Who was Richard Nixon? He was supposed to be Quaker. Some say his father was a lemon rancher. Nobody believed he was real. Nobody ever saw him or knew anybody that ever worked directly for him, but to hear Woodward tell it, anybody could have worked for Nixon. You never knew. That was his power. The greatest trick the Devil ever pulled was convincing the world he didn't exist. And like that, 39 years ago today, poof. He was gone.

(ILX, 2013)

the last phase of yours and yours and mine

Most of this section is drawn from something I've come to call "the record inventory." For a little over a year in 2005 and 2006, I catalogued my record collection online: an alphabetical list of the approximately 3,500 albums I own, with comments and stories about whichever of them I felt like writing about, plus accompanying lists of the songs I'd want to save if had to choose. I swiped the idea from Scott Woods; he eventually bailed, I carried on.

At least 37% of the inventory was more or less about the music on those albums—a lot of that can be found over in the pantheon section. But it was the detours I enjoyed most: linking certain albums to whatever critics and books were solely responsible for my owning them, discovering that I had a few records tragically mis-alphabetized on my shelves, regretting a few dozen high-school favorites I once sold to a co-worker at Sunrise Records. A lot of the time, I tried to reconstruct the details of when and where I bought a particular album, and would also write about the stores where they were bought. And thus, to a large degree, the inventory became the story of my life as a record collector.

I've continued to buy a few dozen vinyl albums a year in the decade since, almost all of them at a twice-a-year record show I attend in Toronto. (Completely avoiding the insanely overpriced 180-gram reissues that are making a—temporary, I'm positive—comeback in stores.) A co-worker at my school also gave me a few hundred from her father-in-law's collection that I'm still wading through to see what can be salvaged. Meanwhile, my cheap metal shelving is ominously wobblier than ever, while the inventory remains online, but not updated. No plans to ever do so—the albums I accumulate now are without stories.

Vinyl Zombies

I spend a lot of time complaining to people about CDs, and I know they come away thinking I'm elitist or reactionary or stubborn or obsolete or just plain stupid. There's a measure of truth in each point, but I'm helpless at this stage to change my way of thinking. If CDs were to eliminate records once and for all, then for me, and many people like me, acquiring recorded music would lose a lot of its meaning. Since the music itself is supposed to be the be-all and end-all, this requires some explaining.

From the time my interest in Top 40 radio moved from casual to obsessive in the winter of '72—the mumps followed closely by the German measles opened up a whole new world—to the time I stopped paying close attention in 1975, I owned few albums. Probably about 10 or 20, every one in awful condition, an odd assortment of Ray Stevens (first aural hero) and the Partridge Family and *The Who Sell Out* (funny voices and a great cover) and the Beach Boys, who did "Little Honda," which would set my dad to doing this really silly dance if the spirit so moved him. Most of the records were appropriated from the pile my parents kept in the basement—they didn't know the Who from the Cowsills, but my dad once owned a variety store that carried albums, which he often brought home when they didn't sell. I did buy singles during this period, but basically the radio was everything.

In 1975, a couple of things happened: a portable stereo (w/8-track!) was passed on to me by my parents, and I fell under the influence of some senior basketball players who used to sing Neil Young songs while riding the team bus. The music they enthused about interested me because it fell outside my radio experience (Spirit's *Dr. Sardonicus*, one of my first favorite albums, and Genesis' *Lamb Lies Down* were their other big records), so, stereo now in tow, I decided to jump into the fray and start an album collection. I began, I'm not sure why, with the simultaneous purchase of *The Worst of Jefferson Airplane* and (oops) *Weird Scenes Inside the Goldmine*. Both were bought at G&S Stereo, a landmark of Georgetown's cultural heritage ("Even the bus stops at G&S's door"). With an eye towards the future, I made it a point to treat whatever albums I bought with great care. Somewhere along the way I bought Logan and Woffinden's *Encyclopedia of Rock*, and soon after stopped listening to the radio altogether; my assimilation of pop music became completely bound up in filling gaps in my collection. Albums, both mysterious and sacred artifacts in their own right and as building blocks in the drive to own everything worth owning, occupied the forefront of my imagination. They became psychologically, pathologically, linked to currency—whenever I had money, I bought an album. My mom was baffled. And not very happy.

This went on at the rate of an LP-per-week for four years, some real good'uns mixed in with your Gentle Giants and Moxys, leaving me with 200 or so albums as I started university in 1979. Now, 200 albums is of course nothing, but I'd sit back and look at them and feel overwhelmed with satisfaction: independent, wealthy, discriminating, alive. Like God, more or less.

the last phase of yours and yours and mine

Collecting records is tantamount to feeling like God.

Living in Toronto quadrupled my record-buying universe. No more sneaking records past mom, I was now free to buy and buy and buy without fear of repercussion. Record stores were refuge from the numbing vapidity of classroom ritual—they seemed to form a safety net around the U of T campus, and I was forever lighting off to one between classes, my enactment of Holden Caulfield's farewell to Pencey, "Sleep tight, ya morons!" I can vouch that half my post-secondary education was spent combing any one of the following: the huge expanses of Sam's and A&A's, the amazing clutter of the original Cheapies, the old locales of the Peddler and Wheels (imports adding new complexities to the decision-making process), and, the biggest godsend of all, the Vortex/Driftwood/Around Again axis, where even with a little money you could get your fix and come away with a record.

There was just too much latitude. My first two years at school, I didn't have much money to last the year once accommodations were taken care of—enough, though, if I would have rationed it sensibly. But I just ploughed ahead and bought records, emptying my account by Christmas each year. I would then spend the second term borrowing each week to pay back the next. I'd borrow from friends, from people in my residence, from my grandmother, and sink the money into records; I'd go home to Georgetown on the weekend, borrow from my mom with a promise to pay her back in the spring, then return to Toronto and pay my debts on Monday. By Wednesday I'd need to buy a record, so I'd start all over again. Once work started in the spring, I'd have my mom paid back over the course of two cheques—after which I was in the clear for the rest of the summer, and could start making Saturday treks into Toronto to buy three-four-five albums a week. My expanding collection was turning into a labyrinth of possibilities but also frustration: the more I bought, the more I needed. The publication of *The Rolling Stone Record Guide* and Christgau's '70s book accelerated my completist's mania.

By third year, I had moved in with my grandparents. Rent-free. It was at this point that records really began to consume me. It was like being handed fifteen hundred dollars in disposable income and told to make sure to spend it, because you were living an unreal life anyway in which a well-paid job cutting grass in a cemetery was waiting for you each summer, six summers in a row with nobody but Portuguese Virgil to non-communicate with, and all that was expected of you in return was occasionally to affect expressions that made you look emotionally run-down or intellectually inquisitive or haunted by the future or some other code whereby the university student is granted an extended hall pass to duck out of the human race until a degree flutters down from the sky and your mission is complete.

My last three years at school were basically one big record-buying binge; I felt like a real comic-book hero swooping into class each day with an album or two tucked under my arm and a who-gives-a-fuck retreat to the corner desk. Records were my link to the outside world, my declaration that I may be sitting here but don't get the idea I'm happy about it. When I graduated in 1984, I had made it up to about a thousand albums.

Since then, my addiction has taken on self-destructive proportions. Low rent and a non-existent lifestyle leave me with money to burn. My last two jobs have been within scurrying distance of all my favorite record haunts. Working in a record store has given me access to discounts, plus I get free records through work and writing. Whereas I was mostly guided through school by the desire to have a well-rounded collection—even when buying extravagantly I bought with purpose—I now buy a record quite frequently just for the hell of it, so I can cart it home and look at the cover two weeks later and try to guess what I was thinking when I bought it. It's a little game I play. I've got this floating, to-be-played pile of 50-75 albums on the floor, many of which have been sitting there for weeks and months. I've flipped past these records a hundred times and they completely mystify me: Jerry Murad's "Fabulous" Harmonicats, a Peaches and Herb album from after they stopped having hits, Wavis O'Shave, *This Is Hawaiian Music*, A Flux of Pink Indians, *Welcome to the LBJ Ranch!*, the First Class album with "Beach Baby," the Elektrics, *Beat Street Vol. 2*, *The World of Susan Jacks and the Poppy Family*, *The Cult Live at the Lyceum*—there's really no excuse to bring that stuff into your home if you're 26 years old.

But I'm just getting started. I'm still fascinated by the existential act of buying a record, more and more able to take pleasure from the way a decade-plus of my life zig-zags through the boxes of albums that spread from a corner of my apartment. There's a story, or a few words, to go along with every record. It's beautiful how they take up so much space, because why would anyone want ten years of living tucked away in a little storage unit? Who could ever have a story to tell about a particular CD they bought? "I had twenty dollars, so I bought this CD...compact, isn't it?" I'm telling you, those things are vile. They're spiritually void.

That's my version of the mania. For corroboration and comparison, I spoke to a couple of people with collections that dwarf mine (now approaching a second thousand): Gerry Michaels, 34, who has around 15,000 albums,

the last phase of yours and yours and mine

including one of the country's best rare-Canadian collections; and *Nerve*'s own Tim Powis, age unspecified, who numbers among his 3,000-plus pile an actual ESP release by the legendary Godz and the Bruce Springsteen album *Born to Lose*.

I asked Gerry how it happens that someone wakes up one day to find 15,000 records sitting in his living room, and whether or not he should immediately call the police.

"I think you hit a point where all of a sudden you say I want to start re-collecting the records I had as a kid. Before you realize it, you've gone too far—you start picking up records and saying I want that, I want that and I want that, but within two or three years you look back and realize you've got all this other stuff you didn't really go out looking for. It was just there and you picked it up. Ten years down the road you look again and say geez, this has really gotten out of hand. You've gotten to a point where you want to collect one copy of every record ever made.

"It is like a drug. No matter where I go, I run into records. When I go up to Sault Ste. Marie, like last Christmas, I go downtown to some to the second-hand shops—there's a second-hand music store that has a large selection of records in the back, and I'll always pick up four or five from him. I'll still get my fix. If I go down to visit my folks in Port Colborne, I'll always check out the area, and there are five or six flea markets every Sunday.

"This past Christmas day I just resigned myself to the fact that everything's closed so I'm not gonna find any records. So I just put it out of my mind for the day."

As Gerry and I spoke, two cats wandered about the room. I wondered if Gerry might trade one of them for the Reign Ghost album he's currently mad for?

"The cats aren't mine."

Oh.

Tim Powis is the kind of person where, if you run into him on the street, your first words after "Hello" are automatically "What, record d'ya buy?"—he's always got a new acquisition on hand. Tim traces his irrational need to own the entire Touch & Go catalogue to the magical summer of love.

"I've always bought a lot of records. I started around the time of *Sergeant Pepper*. That's what turned me around—I became a total psychedelic hepcat. My parents gave me *Sergeant Pepper* for my birthday, and then I went out and bought *After Bathing at Baxter's* and that Rolling Stones one with the 3D cover. From about 1970 onwards, I became a really obsessive record buyer. And I bought real sludge, too. Like Flash, a Yes spin-off band with Tony Kay, the original organist. I'll never live that one down.

"Things really got going when I lived on Baldwin Street across from Around Again Records. That's when I started buying jazz, because around that time I decided it was time to get interested in something other than this kid's stuff. It got so every day when I got home from work I would go into Around Again and come out with three or four jazz records.

"I can't walk by a record store without going into it, and I can't come out of a record store empty-handed. Sometimes it bothers me and I think I buy too many records. I can't stand it, it's almost like an addiction. I just feel...usually I set out for a record store with something specific I want to buy in mind. Very seldom do I head for a record store because I need a vinyl fix. But there's so many records I want, it goes without saying that I can't imagine any circumstances in which I would not go into a record store. On the other hand, I've got so many records it's absurd. How long would it take me to listen to all those records again? Probably until I die."

Although the increasing unavailability of certain jazz records has Tim considering a CD player, he remains a devout vinyl sympathizer.

"An album is the right size—it's 12 inches, it's substantial. I hate cassettes and I hate CDs. I think they're ugly little things, and I don't think they sound that great, and I don't give a fuck about surface noise. What the hell, who wants pure music? It's nice to have some little reminder that what you're listening to isn't just wafting in on the breeze. It's nice to know I have this little sound system that's producing this music, and I can hear the little earmarks that this is my sound system, all these imperfections. You go into a CD department of a record store and it's depressing looking at those stupid little six-inch wide things."

A way of life is insidiously being phased out before our very eyes. But there's still time. There are a billion records circulating out there, and they're not about to evaporate into thin air. You have a bunch yourself. Watch out. We're coming. VINYL ZOMBIES!!!

(*Nerve*, 1988)

How is your recorded music collection organized? Why do you use this method?

Ninety percent of my records are arranged the simplest way of all: alphabetically by artist, chronologically within a given artist. Sorting by genre, as some people do, would be confusing and ultimately impossible; it can also be a little creepy, like this one person I know who arranges his records by genre so you can be impressed by the regal breadth of his jazz collection. I do keep separate whatever classical records I have, for the practical reason that I just don't know a lot of the composers' names well enough to go searching for a particular one if I want to hear some classical. They're filed before the alphabetical part starts, along with 12-inch singles (same rationale, as many are by obscure people I'd never remember if I had to go looking for one; if I subsequently buy an album by someone where I already have a 12-inch, both go into the alphabetical section) and multi-artist compilations. These latter I arrange by genre—doo-wop, punk, country, etc., highlighted by my four-album worldbeat collection (*Rainy Night in Tokyo*, *This Is Hawaiian Music*, *Beautiful Hawaiian Steel Guitar*, and *The Three Smiles*) and one-album comedy section (*Welcome to the LBJ Ranch*). I should really move *LBJ* into the alphabetical section, seeing as it's not a compilation, but I think it's important that everyone have a comedy section. An alternate plan would be to move my Oi! compilations into comedy. The strange thing about my records is that from day one I've been filing them backwards. If you can picture four of those tall industrial shelving-units side-by-side, the compilations start in the bottom right-hand corner of the unit at the far right, zig-zagging right-to-left up through the 12-inches, classical, more compilations, and the A's and most of the B's; then down to the bottom shelf of the next unit for the rest of the B's, continuing the same right-to-left/up-then-down pattern through to the Michael Zager Band, the Zantees, Zapp, the Zarkons, Warren Zevon, and the Zombies in the top left-hand corner of the unit at the far left. In terms of the way we read, everything is 100% backwards and upside-down. I never set out to do this, it just happened, and by the time I realized (or someone pointed out to me) how unnatural this was, there was no way I was going to take everything down and start over. I had my best chance to do so when I moved a couple of years ago, but it still would have been a tedious process. I also flip through magazines in a back-to-front direction. Movies, books, and baseball games, I start at the beginning.

(KITSCHener, 1997)

Be-Bop Deluxe

The Beck double and Be-Bop Deluxe date back to high school, meaning they're among the first hundred or so albums I ever bought. I bet I haven't put on *Modern Music* in 25 years. What do I remember of it? "Modern music, on the *raaayyydiiiooo*," and that's about it. I'm not sure how it survived the time I sold a couple dozen mullethead albums to Randy, a guy I used to work with at Sunrise Records in Toronto; *Modern Music* has Randy written all over it. I've written before about how I now regret this transaction. There was a moderately hard-to-find Canadian album included in the deal, *Moxy*, but much more important than that, I handed over a small, really personal corner of my record-collecting autobiography. I'm having a hard time remembering what else I parted company with, but a few titles come to mind (I'm checking each one as I type to make sure it's indeed M.I.A.): the CSNY best-of *So Far*, Gordon Lightfoot's *Sundown*, Don McLean's *American Pie*, a Renaissance double-live (!)—a mix of '70s singer-songwriters, metal, and art-rock, all of it bought when I was in grades 10-13. Most of what I've just listed is ho-hum ordinary, but the Renaissance LP gives a better idea of some of the horror-show dreck that was in there—basically, I was just embarrassed at the time to own some of these records. (This as I was avidly buying Die Kreuzen and Scratch Acid and all the other Renaissances of their day.) So dumb. I probably got about 40 dollars for the lot. I'm amazed it never occurred to me that somewhere along the way I might be really glad that that small corner of the story was still there on the shelf, good for a laugh if nothing else, maybe even important in some hard-to-describe way.

(record inventory, 2005-06)

Polly Bergen

There are maybe a dozen records in my collection that fall into the Polly Bergen category: old original-issue LPs that I bought solely because they were cheap and virtually brand new. The Bergen record is from 1957, on the maroon Columbia label, a mono issue that the *Goldmine Record Album Price Guide* lists for $30.00 in near-mint condition. Such alleged value is meaningless to me. As I've indicated already, I haven't sold a single album since the great Randy Debacle of 1986; price-guide listings (like baseball-card listings) are theoretical anyway, since in reality you'd be lucky to get $2.50 from one of Polly Bergen's grandchildren for the album. Such records are not investments—what I love about them is how good they look when you take them out of the sleeve and inspect them under the light. My attraction has all the considered sophistication of Homer Simpson: "*Mmmmmmmmnnnnnnn...shiny.*"

(record inventory, 2005-06)

the last phase of yours and yours and mine

Clifton Chenier

There are a few subsets running through my collection of things I bought because of specific books. They almost all trace back to the late '70s and early '80s, when the now out-of-control desire to canonize—I'm as guilty as anyone; I would appear to be doing exactly that right here—first started to take hold. Some of the more esoteric examples: there's the *Stranded* subset (Jesse Winchester), the Logan and Woffinden *Rock Encyclopedia* subset (Family's *Bandstand*—the Logan book was the one with color reproductions of album sleeves, so that was an extra hook), the *Christgau's Record Guide: Rock Albums of the '70s* subset (James Talley's *Got No Bread, No Milk, No Money, But We Sure Got a Lot of Love*), the *Rock Critics' Choice* subset (which explains the goofy Can album), and, most influential of all, the *Rolling Stone Record Guide* subset, the book that had a lot of future rock-critic weasels such as myself discovering their great mission in life: to collect every single five-star album as designated by the all-knowing, all-seeing *Guide*. Hence the Clifton Chenier album, my one and only zydeco record.

(record inventory, 2005-06)

Buck Clayton

The Buck Clayton albums were part of a large purchase I made from the father of somebody I worked with at the record store—British guy, can't remember his name. The father was making the transition to CDs and selling off almost his entire collection at $5 a record, a little more for doubles. I bought a lot: 40 or 50 albums, at least $250 worth. Thinking back on it, there's no way I would have been in any kind of financial position to spend that much all at once, but I did, and quite likely without much hesitation. I always used to tell myself that if the price was good enough, go ahead and buy; 20 years down the road the albums will still be with me, and whatever I paid for them, and whether or not I could have afforded to pay that much, won't make any difference at all. From my vantage point today, I'd have to say I was right.

(record inventory, 2005-06)

interrupting my train of thought

Eddie Cochran

I keep coming across LPs that belong to big, memorable bulk purchases. Three of the Eddie Cochran albums were among a bunch of French imports that turned up for $5 each at some store in the Eaton's Centre (weird, because I don't remember the Eaton's Centre as ever housing a worthwhile record store, yet I'm positive that's where it was). I also came away with a handful of reissued Fats Domino originals, and maybe a dozen Blue Note titles, including *Herbie Nichols Trio*, one of the guys A.B. Spellman profiled in *Black Music* and something I coveted at the time. Record stores, both retail and used, tended to react one of two ways to the great vinyl funeral of 1988-1991: a few treated records as a suddenly extra-precious commodity and raised prices accordingly, while most of them threw in the towel at some point and more or less started giving stuff away.

(record inventory, 2005-06)

Dells

The Dells album belongs to probably the most infamous budget-line series of reissues ever: the *La grande storia del ROCK* series out of Italy. There was a Pussy Galore album that meticulously parodied the generic cover art ("cover art") shared by *La grande storia* albums, although I'd have to check, they may have altered the tagline to read *La grande storia del ARTY PIGFUCK THAT PEOPLE ARE INEXPLICABLY GETTING ALL WORKED UP OVER*. The albums themselves were hit or miss. Some were very obviously of highly suspicious origins—field recordings of Gary Puckett & the Union Gap, demo tapes unearthed from before Freddy & the Dreamers really got it together—but some, like *The Dells*, were perfectly legitimate reshufflings of original material dating back to the '50s; theirs has stuff lifted from 1959's *Oh, What a Nite* on Vee-Jay (pictured inside—gatefold cover + Italian liner notes), filled out with other songs of similar vintage. Half the *La grande storia* albums were single-artist, half threw together as many as five or six artists, and the groupings could be surreal: the Everly Brothers share #12 in the series with Disco Tex & the Sex-O-Lettes, Lloyd Price and John Travolta are both found on #29, and Sam Cooke, the Crewcuts, and Iron Butterfly vie for space on #42. They were generally priced somewhere between a pack of gum and book of matches. The changeover to CDs actually increased the market for such semi-legal entrepreneurship tenfold, I guess because CDs are cheaper to mass-produce—any Wal-Mart dump bin

the last phase of yours and yours and mine

is filled with every kind of budget configuration and reconfiguration imaginable, most of them with obviously no connection whatsoever to the original recordings they pretend to compile. The phenomenon lives on, but the *La grande storia del ROCK* series had a lunacy and an aesthetic all its own.

(record inventory, 2005-06)

Fleetwoods

Almost every album I own is in excellent shape. That was a decision I made right from the outset, when I started collecting records in the mid-'70s: that I'd be really particular about how I handled them, and then, when I started buying used LPs a few years later, that I wouldn't buy anything unless it was in very good condition. Maybe this was a by-product of having seen so many junky, scratched-up records among the four of five piles kept in the basement by my parents, I don't know, but I'm glad it was something I continued to be mindful of over the next 20 years. (The biggest test came during the half-dozen years in and around university, where album-playing often went hand-in-hand with beer and pot and acid and ether and all those other things Ian MacKaye warned us about; I'm surprised my copy of the Replacements' *Let It Be* isn't octagonal, but it seems fine.) Anyway, *The Fleetwoods' Greatest Hits* is possibly the only album I have that is in fairly poor condition. To look at it, it seems like it might play OK—a lot of light surface scratches—but I remember it sounds bad enough that I don't even want to check right now. I'm not sure why I felt at the time that I couldn't wait for a better copy—it's not as if used Fleetwoods albums are immediately scooped up the moment they're put out. I've always thought of the album as only being provisionally part of my collection, and that I'd replace it sometime. Its provisional status is now entering its third decade.

(record inventory, 2005-06)

Hagood Hardy

The Hagood Hardy album (yes, I'm a little defensive about that one and feel the need to explain its presence) was part of the last huge record buy I ever made, 75-100 classical albums I found at a garage sale after moving back to Toronto in the mid-'90s. The seller was essentially giving them away—I think I paid $10 for the lot. Most looked to be unplayed, and there were a lot of doubles. It was such a great deal, I actually started to spin some ridiculous scenario in my mind whereby the albums were being sold unbeknownst to the real owner, who I figured must have been away on vacation at the time. When I suggested this to the wife of a friend, she gently brought me back to reality: "Um, it's 1995—no one wants albums anymore." Good point. It took me over a year to make it through half of them, and eventually I just gave up; some are filed away still unplayed, the only part of my collection that hasn't been listened to at least once. Getting back to Hagood—who isn't classical (I'm not sure what he is) but was part of the deal—*Maybe Tomorrow* leads off with "(Love Theme from) Missouri Breaks." I've never seen *The Missouri Breaks*, which is generally viewed as one of those auteurist debacles that gradually transformed the American film industry in the mid-to-late '70s. I always thought it was Nicholson and Brando and a bunch of horses. I didn't know it needed a love theme.

(record inventory, 2005-06)

International Submarine Band

I mentioned the International Submarine Band's *Safe at Home* a couple of days ago, something I had coveted since reading the Gram Parsons entry in Woffinden/Logan's encyclopedia: "an album which is assumed to represent the beginning of country-rock and copies of which now change hands for a king's ransom." I'm not sure at what point I bought the Woffinden book—sometime around the end of high school or beginning of university—but that was likely the first time I became aware that such a thing as really valuable records existed. "'King's ransom'—wow, that sounds impressive, I think I'd like to have one of those." When I found a sealed copy of *Safe at Home* at Toronto's Around Again a few years later, I remember getting all worked up that I'd stumbled over this once-in-a-lifetime discovery, even though every conceivable sign—the price (a very paltry ransom of seven or eight dollars), the "DJ Copy - Not for Sale" stamp on the record, the fact it was still sealed, the oddly unreal look of the cover art (which was in actuality the only legitimate thing about it), the sheer fortuitousness of it all—suggested it was a fake. I wanted to believe: "Who'd ever bootleg something that no one except me even knows about?" The most ridiculous part of the story was when I had the album with me back at class that day, and I eagerly shared all the details of my good fortune with Viveca Gretton, my great fantasy-land crush through most of university. I want to say something like "I'm not sure what kind of reaction I was hoping for" at this point, but I think I do know, and that's the really sad part: "The International

Submarine Band's *Safe at Home*? The one that changes hands for a king's ransom? That's so amazing! I need to re-evaluate you—let's get married."

(record inventory, 2005-06)

MC5

I actually had an 8-track of *Back in the U.S.A.* at one point. Some other 8-tracks I remember owning: *The Best of the Guess Who*, *Exile on Main Street*, *Let It Be*, *Harvest*, the Stampeders' *Against the Grain*, the Tee Set's *Ma Belle Amie*, Three Dog Night's *Harmony*, a Polydor compilation with Derek & the Dominos' "Bell Bottom Blues," a K-Tel '50s compilation with a jukebox on the cover that was heavily advertised at the time because of *American Graffiti*, and, after that, I'm drawing a blank. We had at least 30 or 40 of them around the house—most of all, I remember us listening to 8-tracks on a green fold-out portable as we drove down to Florida sometime in the mid-'70s. Whatever you may have heard about how bad 8-tracks were, they were twice as hideous as that: bad sound, clunky packaging, zero durability, ridiculous formatting. The Ramones would have had their first couple of LPs come out on 8-track; never seen one, but I bet there was an "I Don't Wanna Walk Around with You" (Pt. 1) and "I Don't Wanna Walk Around with You" (Pt. 2) on the first. I'm trying to think of one good thing to say about them, and I can't. So how was it that for a couple of years everyone got so excited about 8-tracks? It's not normally like the music-buying public to get all worked up over every bit of new technology that comes along.

(record inventory, 2005-06)

Otis Redding

Otis Blue may have been the first import I ever bought—either that or the weird German copy I have of *Loaded*, part of the "Original Rock Classics" series. I didn't even know what an import was when I found *Otis Blue* at the old Queen Street Record Peddler in Toronto—I distinctly remember being very excited that I'd stumbled over an original copy of an album I coveted because of the write-up and the picture in Woffinden and Logan's *Rock Encyclopedia*. This would have been 1979; discovering the Record Peddler and Records on Wheels, and finding out that long-unavailable LPs were still being printed elsewhere in the world, accelerated my record-buying habit significantly, and simultaneously learning of Toronto's growing network of used stores—Vortex, the Vinyl Museum, Around Again, Driftwood—sent it through the roof.

(record inventory, 2005-06)

Swingin' Medallions

Taking everything into consideration—age, rarity, supposed value, musical interest—my greatest find over two decades of flipping through delete bins was the Swingin' Medallions' *Double Shot (Of My Baby's Love).* It's an album I probably would have been pretty lucky to find near the beginning of my time buying records—by 1976, it would have been 10 years old (having no idea at the time who they were, I of course would have flipped right past it)—but the really amazing thing is that I instead found it right near the end, sometime in the late '80s, and also that it turned up in my hometown of Georgetown, at the very same store where I bought most of my earliest albums 15 years prior, G&S Television. They were only a year or two away from relocating and changing their name—it had originally been owned by the Laing family, daughter Christine being high-school crush #117, but new owners had taken over sometime earlier—and their album section had dwindled away to almost nothing by that point. They still racked a couple of dozen deletes, though, and *Double Shot* was one of them. I'm still astounded that this one record could have bounced from warehouse to warehouse for 25 years and somehow remained unclaimed. My copy's stereo, which is too bad: according to a note on the back, "the sound quality of any Smash Monaural recording is actually enhanced on a Stereo phonograph." It would have been nice to experience the Swingin' Medallions, an audiophile's dream, with that extra bit of enhanced sound quality.

(record inventory, 2005-06)

James Taylor

I tried for many years to get a vinyl copy of James Taylor's Apple debut. I think the closest I ever got was a badly worn and overpriced copy at the store Jonathan Lipson used to operate on Yonge St., the Incredible Record and Book Store. (I think that was his name, and I think that was the name of his shop—I'm trying a number of searches on Google and not having any luck.) It was a dreadful place that managed to get local media coverage and maintain a customer base because Lipson had a colourful biography—according to the one page reference I did find (where he's unnamed), he used to be the Grateful Dead's gardener. (Petunias, tulips, daffodils, that kind of thing.) Meanwhile, the pricing system went something like this: abused records went for seven or eight dollars, anything in good shape that no one would ever conceivably want started at 10 or 12, and if it was something in good shape that was also desirable, forget it—$20, $25 and upwards. Among all the used stores in the city I ever walked into during the '80s heyday, it may have been the only one where I'm pretty sure I never bought a single record. Really, more than his biography, I think it was location that kept him in business—Yonge St. was still kind of touristy in those days, and I bet he sold a lot of criminally overpriced records to a lot of people who'd never been in a huge space filled with used vinyl. In any case, after waiting another 10 or 15 years, I finally found Taylor's Apple debut on CD. I'd be listing "Circle in the Sun" and "Something in the Way She Moves" from it, and I'm tempted to list the version of the latter found on *Greatest Hits*. Close enough for horseshoes, but it's still a slightly inferior version of the original, especially in the absence of the harpsichord intro. I'm not sure who had control of the Apple catalogue by 1976—the Beatles? Allen Klein? Billy Preston?—but it's surprising something couldn't have been worked out. Have I mentioned that James Taylor's in the Rock and Roll Hall of Fame? Strange—he doesn't play rock and roll.

(record inventory, 2005-06)

Cherry Vanilla

When I was writing about how bad the Incredible Record & Book Store was a few entries back, I said it was the worst Toronto record store I ever walked into. I added the part about "ever walked into" only after realizing that there were so many record stores around the city at the time, the dozen or so I frequented on a regular basis represented only a part of what was out there—all the key ones, I'm pretty sure, but I didn't have a car at the time, and there were lots of out-of-the-way stores scattered around the city that I didn't have the initiative to bike out to. Occasionally an album will turn up that I associate with a store I was in no more than once or twice, and that probably wasn't in business much longer than a year or two, in some cases not even that long. I got the Cherry Vanilla LP at some place out in the east end, just above the Danforth, somewhere around Pape or Greenwood; I vaguely recall it being a very cluttered and small space, more likely a general junk shop that happened to carry records than an actual record store. For a time I (reluctantly) kept a scratched-up copy of

Freak Out! in my collection that I bought from a shop at the lower end of Parliament St., somewhere below Gerrard; again, I retain a dim memory of the general look of the place—much more spacious than the store above, with a large window display—but don't remember being in there more than the one time. I'll be listing a copy of *Jackie Wilson's Greatest Hits* shortly that was bought at the north end of Church, just below Bloor; that definitely wasn't a record store, with more of an elegant, wooded look common to antique shops. So maybe there weren't that many record stores proper after all, but there was no end to the book and knick-knack and thrift shops that had records for sale, and I'm sure I only ever made it into a small percentage of them. The stores where I bought all these records were almost as much a part of this story as the records themselves, and thus far I've mainly mentioned them in passing; towards the end, I may try to write a more detailed rundown. I know for sure that two of the used stores are still in business, as is one of the retailers; another one of the retailers may be, but I'm not sure. The rest are long gone.

(record inventory, 2005-06)

Youth Youth Youth

Youth Youth Youth was a Toronto hardcore band led by a guy named Brian Taylor, a first-ballot hall-of-famer in the annals of Snotty Record Store Clerks (Canadian Chapter). Anyone who has ever spent any amount of time in record stores has his own personal list; they've even been commemorated in a Hollywood movie, *High Fidelity*. I was one myself for a couple of years, although my own snobbishness tended to be directed towards co-workers whose musical tastes varied from my own rather than customers. There was a guy at Records on Wheels who was pretty bad—I just barely remember him—and also Shadowy Men on a Shadowy Planet's Don Pyle, who worked at Driftwood. Brian's perch on Mount Olympus was based on his expertise and insider-status within the Satanic Corpsefucker Thrash-Metal world; I once tried to engage him in some conversation about Hüsker Dü's impending first visit to Toronto, and, maybe because I looked more like a budding ornithologist than a Manson-family castoff, not much more than a hateful grunt issued forth. (I really have no idea what a typical ornithologist looks like, but I think you get the point.) I'm not sure where he is now, but I bet it's like Lou Reed in that one Bangs interview and he's moved on to fusion-era Herbie Hancock.

(record inventory, 2005-06)

the last phase of yours and yours and mine

Melodiya label

I bought the four albums leading off this group from the Vinyl Museum during its final year or two, when they all of a sudden had boxes and boxes of brand-new stuff on the Russian Melodiya label. I think it was all a dollar a record when they first put it out, and by the end everything was a quarter. Most of what they had was in the 10" format; I just took a look, and along with *Black Market Clash* and Billy "the Kid" Emerson's *Crazy 'Bout Automobiles* and the handful of other pop-related 10" records I own, there are 40 Melodiya titles, only about a quarter of which I got through before boxing them. This would have been the mid-late '90s, timing that doesn't make it difficult to figure out how it all ended up in a used record store in Canada. From an online article entitled "Rebirth of a Record Company":

"'The most valuable recordings had long since made their way to the West and were being handed from one firm to another,' said Andrei Troshin, chief editor at Melodiya. 'It is almost impossible for us to take them to court for this. Many recordings were stolen and all of the catalogues at Melodiya were destroyed in 1991—people were working to cover their tracks. Fortunately, the thieves were too lazy to steal everything and there were copies of most of the recordings.'"

To anyone who remembers the Vinyl Museum, it's amusing to think of it as a firm. Anyway, it was a one-of-a-kind haul (as much as I did buy, I should have picked up a copy of everything out there), and, in view of the circumstances by which it was made possible, I felt a little like Jon Lovitz in *The Wedding Singer*: "The Soviet Empire is falling apart, and I'm reaping the benefits!"

(record inventory, 2005-06)

whole new kinds of weather

The don't-blame-them section—my influences, which have been either admirably or sadly fixed in place for three-plus decades now. You're supposed to grow all the time, connect with new voices, challenge your assumptions, think about things anew. I try to do those last two as much as possible, but as far as new voices go, it all starts with the people I write about here. No offense to Anthony Lane at *The New Yorker*—I have friends who think he's great—but even in 2014, I don't come out of a movie wondering what Anthony Lane thinks about it. I'm much more interested in what the reaction of a woman who's been dead for almost 25 years would have been.

The influence of Pauline Kael, Greil Marcus, Bill James, Stanley Kauffmann, Jim Bouton, and Robert Christgau on my own writing is sometimes easy to spot, and at other times could only be detected by me. Sometimes it's stylistic, sometimes it's a shared enthusiasm, more often it's a way of looking at something. In the interview with Marcus I did for *Nerve* in 1987—the only interview I've reprinted in this book (Joey Ramone, Johnny Thunders, Richard Berry, Martin Degville—I passed over some giants)—there are ideas I've always tried to keep in mind when fumbling around for an explanation of why I love some song. Above all else, that the important thing is not what the artist intended, but rather what does it feel like to listen to this piece of music?—what does it remind me of, what puzzles me about it, what meaningless event in my own life does it speak to? "What I'm interested in is what happens when you listen"—it's an approach that can send me off on a tangent, one that may begin with autobiography and end with a dumb joke, but, to me at least, that's a more entertaining, surprising, and (I hope) insightful path than filing a general report on the emotional well-being of Bruce Springsteen or Kanye West.

To get into the influences section, you have to be someone I don't know. That precluded some other important influences, all of whom can be found over in the acknowledgments.

Do you ever read one of Christgau's reviews and go, "What the hell is he talking about?"

Marcus has had more of an influence on me than Christgau, but I'll give this a go. The one thing that links all the critics that loosely make up my frame of reference—Kael and Kauffmann and Sarris in film, Marcus and Christgau and a few others in music, Bill James in baseball (he hates having his work reduced to this, but part of what he did in the *Abstracts* was rate players)—is that with all them, I crossed a point somewhere along the way where their personalities drew me in, and I wanted to know what their opinion was about anybody and everybody. I can't describe how or why that happens, but it does. How often I agree with them matters a little but not a lot. I haven't been interested in what Marcus is interested in for years, yet I'll still read him whenever I get the chance; Christgau's enthusiasms often lose me (especially when he veers off into world music, about which I know next to nothing), but I still have this compulsion to look in on the Consumer Guide wherever it happens to reside and see what he thinks about things. There are many other high-profile film and music critics who write well and knowledgeably, yet they don't mean a thing to me. I can't even really defend that statement—it's just something that happens or it doesn't.

Marcus's discography at the end of *Stranded* is pretty much my favorite piece of rock-critic writing ever. A friend and I have developed a whole shorthand around it, cryptic references that the other person picks up on immediately. "The Rolling Stones would have killed to make this album" (especially when wildly misapplied), pulling your car over to the side of the road when you hear something for the first time (especially when wildly misapplied), etc. Plus it's where I first encountered so many records I'd never heard of before—Hackamore Brick, Savage Rose, Colonel Jubilation, Jesse Winchester, many others. Not that all of them turned out to be quite as advertised.

(ILX, 2012)

Brian Kellow Interview

Something I've said more than once over the years is that the three biggest influences on me among writers are Pauline Kael, Bill James, and Greil Marcus. I consider myself lucky to have had some contact with two of them. I interviewed Marcus back when I first started writing, and he later contributed a few comments to my old fanzine; the past couple of years I've submitted the occasional question to the "Hey Bill" section of James's website, and he's responded to most of them. Something I often regret, though, is that I never sent any of my writing to Pauline Kael. I've primarily written about music the past 25 years, but I wish I'd sent her a piece I wrote about the best uses of pop music in Scorsese's films—an idea that I bet has been done to death now, but which I think was fairly novel when I wrote it up for Scott's *Popped* website in the late '90s—or a couple of pieces I did for *Cinemascope* around the same time, which would have been a couple of years before Kael's death. I have no idea whether I would have had any success in getting anything to her, whether she would have liked any of it if I had, or even whether she would have bothered reading it in the first place. I'm guessing she was bombarded with stuff on a constant basis and from all directions—from the now infamous Wes Anderson solicitation to see *Rushmore*, to fan letters and invitations and everything in between.

Letter from Kael arrives in the mail: "Thank you for the Scorsese article, Phil. I don't know what you've got here, young man…"

Wasn't meant to be. Some consolation arrived this past year by way of *A Life in the Dark*, Brian Kellow's biography of Pauline Kael. If you check in regularly with rockcritics.com, you'll know that Scott recently posted a number of links to reviews of Kellow's book (sometimes reviewed in tandem with *The Age of Movies: Selected Writings of Pauline Kael*, the third career overview of Kael's reviews). I'm tempted to say that it's amazing the amount of interest—often rawly contentious—that Kellow's book has generated, but I suspect that anyone who has ever strongly felt the pull of Kael's writing would not be surprised. People have been arguing about Kael since the mid-'60s; the arguments didn't stop with her retirement in 1991, and they didn't stop with her death in 2001. There are a couple of ILX threads devoted to Kael where I've been posting the last couple of years, and while (to the best of my knowledge) no one on there ever personally knew Kael, some of the back and forth can get very barbed on occasion. That's Kael. That readers can still feel so strongly about her in 2011—and I can't think of another writer I've ever argued about so much; a couple of music writers are close—is, to me, the truest barometer you'll find of just how strong that pull was. (Or, if you aren't a fan, of how strong your aversion is. Kael's detractors have always been fierce. But as I say in the accompanying interview, "the circle of people I travel in"—Jesus, where do I come up with this stuff?—is almost exclusively made up of fans.)

Between the message board, Kellow's book, reviews of the book, and James Wolcott's *Lucking Out* (in which Kael figures prominently) on top of all that, I'm a little Kaeled out at the moment, but before I hand it over to Brian, let me say that I think *A Life in the Dark* is excellent. Its portrayal of Kael did not in any way conflict with my sense of her as a reader (I feel like

I have to stress that; some reviews written by friends of Kael's—some, not by any means all—disagree), and my recognition of her influence on me has deepened. A lot of Kael's own words make their way into *A Life in the Dark* via review excerpts, and I liked that: the excerpts—and the almost month-by-month timeline of the films that caught Kael's attention—construct a parallel story, the story of American film from the late '60s through to the late '80s (but American films in the '70s especially, which has always been my own frame of reference), that is inseparable from Kael's. Does Kellow always agree with Kael's verdict on specific films? No—he'll sometimes say so. Did I? No. Do I always agree with Kellow's occasional disagreements with Kael? No. Does any of that detract from the book for me? No. The main thing was that it always felt like I was reading someone who'd been as permanently shaped by the likes of *Reeling* and *Deeper Into Movies* as I've been, ever since first discovering Kael at some point near the end of high school. There's an oft-quoted line of Kael's (a friend has it on the masthead of his blog) from her introduction to *For Keeps*, one of those earlier career overviews: "I'm frequently asked why I don't write my memoirs. I think I have." True—I wouldn't try to argue that Kael's body of work did not leave behind a complete world. But I'm still very glad that *A Life in the Dark* exists.

(rockcritics.com, 2012)

"Buzzin' Fly," Tim Buckley (1969)

I suppose this is the point where folk music stops being folk music and turns into art song; I also considered the very arty Vashti Bunyan's "Love Song," but I figured it would have been somewhat redundant so close to Angela Strange and Jennifer Lewis. Consider "Buzzin' Fly" my little tribute to Lillian Roxon, whose *Rock Encyclopedia* was where I first read about Tim Buckley back in…I don't know; I have it in my mind that there was a copy back in my grade school, but I may be jumping the gun by a couple of years—it may have been in middle school. I rarely have cause to look at the book anymore (before the very un-Roxonian Wikipedia came along, I'd often check it for discographical information), but on the rare occasions that I do, I'm always surprised by how engaging Roxon's tone is, and how much better it holds up than other early rock criticism. Which may be because, as others have pointed out, she's not at all writing rock criticism—it's a somewhat gossipy, in-love-with-the-scene fan's book, with enough mock portentousness to make the inane sound Really Important, and enough humour to make the Really Important sound fun. You're lucky I'm not listing Earth Opera or somebody like that here—her book influenced me that much.

I won't make the trip downstairs to look up Roxon's entry on Tim Buckley, but: 1) I slightly prefer a demo version of "Buzzin' Fly" I have on *The Dream Belongs to Me: Rarities & Unreleased 1968-1973*, where I first encountered it a few years ago, but the original studio version's close enough; 2) *Coming Home*'s soundtrack is highlighted by two songs of Buckley's from *Goodbye and Hello*; and 3) I remember once reading an interview with John Lydon where he was asked what he was listening to, and he said something like, "The usual stuff—(reggae album), (some Can-type album), and Tim Buckley."

(#33, Facebook Top 100, 2010-11)

Bill James

My favorite iconoclast is baseball writer Bill James, who 15 years ago completely turned around the way I look at baseball. James is also theory-driven—his *Baseball Abstracts* from the '70s and '80s are full of them, things like the Johnson Effect, the Brock6 System, Similarity Scores, the Reservoir Estimation Technique, the Shotton Syndrome—and I can see parallels between James and Chuck Eddy, a comparison jokingly made by Chuck himself in a recent *Philadelphia Inquirer* interview/article on *Accidental Evolution*. There's one major difference for me: James's attacks on conventional baseball wisdom in those *Abstracts* weren't merely startling, they were also amazingly, irrefutably, wonderfully true. Once you'd read James, it was no longer possible to take seriously the idea that Steve Garvey might be as good a baseball player as Mike Schmidt, that entire offenses could be constructed around the stolen base, or that the mark of a good baseball team was that it won the close games. All of these views were taken as self-evident at one time (some still are, unfortunately); with clear and devastating logic, James came along and demonstrated how there was no truth whatsoever to them, or to many other accepted truisms about the game. But the guiding principle with James was always to uncover what was true; he didn't waste any time trying to convince you that Bill Plummer was a better baseball player than Steve Garvey (much less that Bill Plummer was a better baseball player than Mike Schmidt). It's pretty much impossible to "fake 'em out every time" in a baseball argument—empty theories are very easy to disprove.

(*Popped*, 1998)

Rolling Sabermetrics and Statistics Thread

There's a blogger in California I read, Steve Rubio (a *Prospectus* writer when it was still fairly new, I think), and the other day he linked to the following from Jennifer Doyle, who seems to mostly write about soccer. I love what she says, and she captures some of my own feelings when I get into old-vs.-new-stat discussions on this board:

"Beware of sports writers who pretend to mastery of the facts. I come across a different version of these people in academia—they can recite a bunch of dates, or quote Hegel, and for this reason they seem to think that they've figured it all out. The ones who listen, however, who have a good sense of humor and know how to hold contradiction in their head without trying to resolve it—those are the ones who are most likely to say something interesting, something insightful, something new...Reader, beware of the sense of mastery which comes at the cost of a sense of wonder."

I have no problem at all with VORP and WAR and the like, as long as you view them as just more pieces of the puzzle. But I sometimes get the feeling that when someone throws VORP at me, it's like when someone yells "Challops!" on ILM, or "Muslim!" in Palin World—it's meant to end the discussion, not add to it. Obviously, we're a million miles ahead of the days when people used to think Steve Garvey was the best hitter in baseball because he'd go bat 700 times and knock in 100 runs. (Pointing out, however, that even Bill James revised his thinking on Garvey when he reissued the *Historical Abstract*—one of many reasons I like James so much more than his disciples.) I wouldn't want baseball arguments to return to that level of thinking. But to echo Doyle's last sentence above, if your belief in the infallibility of VORP and WAR lead you to shrug your shoulders at the prospect of Pujols or Votto winning the Triple Crown, that's a place I don't want to end up.

I'll have more to say on this in my upcoming book, *VORP: The God That Failed*.

(ILX, 2010)

Chuck Eddy & the Holy Greil

My interview with Greil Marcus and Chuck Eddy is right near the top of my favorite *Nerve* pieces. If I didn't mention as much in my contribution to Scott's *Nerve* retrospective, that's only because it was an interview rather than something I really wrote.

I have a vivid memory of how different it was to talk to each of them. I wrote to Greil beforehand, to get his phone number and to see if he was receptive to an interview. I sent along a piece on junky '70s music that Scott and I had written (a precursor to the book we later wrote on the same subject) for *Graffiti*. Greil wrote back to say he enjoyed the piece and to give him a call. When I did call soon after—this is the part I remember so clearly—there was a long pause, followed by an intimidatingly impatient "Just a minute." I think he later explained that I'd caught him at a bad moment, but at the time, I wanted to crawl under a rock. ("I was just being polite, doofus—I didn't mean for you to *actually call*.") I remember also that when we finished, I asked Greil if he'd put together some kind of index or bibliography of his writings that we could publish alongside the interview. More withering exasperation: "I can't do that..." It was, indeed, a pretty strange request. You always remember the bad stuff first, and I'm laughing at these two specific lowlights now. Greil was in fact great once the interview got going, and after publication he sent a nice follow-up postcard that is visible on the bulletin board pictured in the *Nerve* piece.

I'm guessing Marcus had been interviewed many times by 1986; I don't know if this was Chuck's first interview (I seem to remember him mentioning another one he'd recently done), but it was close enough that he couldn't have been more accommodating or enthusiastic. That it was someone from Canada must have made the experience even more novel and unexpected, comparable, I suppose, to me getting an interview request from Iceland tomorrow. It was actually Chuck's wife, Martina, who fielded my first call (I must have gotten the number through directory assistance), so as soon as he got on the line when I called back, he was ready to go. And, as I wrote in my preface to the interview, that's exactly what Chuck did—probably not as breathlessly as I indicated at the time, but even today I remember the conversation as a blur. A friendship developed from there, one that's had its ups and downs over the years. The downs are adumbrated in a line from the intro: "even though I rarely agree with him about anything," a gap that I have personalized at times. Hüsker Dü = Big Country—all we needed was Bette Davis in the wings telling us to fasten our seatbelts, it's going to be a bumpy ride.

interrupting my train of thought

Whenever I take a look at an old *Nerve*, I especially love anything that's hopelessly dated. I think my favorite part in the whole Greil/Chuck interview is either the burning question of whether or not the Cro-Mags deserved space in *Spin*—the Cro-Mags??—or the part where, given the chance to ask Marcus his opinion of anybody, I stepped back, took a good hard look at history and posterity and all of that, and got a few words from him on... Anita Baker! It's invaluable that I was able to get that clarified for future pop-music scholars.

Phil Dellio: In the last [1985] Pazz & Jop poll, Tim Somner suggested the time has come for the '70s critics to bow out. How do you feel about the long-term domination of yourself, Bob Christgau, and Dave Marsh?

Greil Marcus: I don't see myself in any sort of dominant position in any way—I just write a column and say what I think. Until I started the *Voice* column a year or so ago, I did it in a small-circulation art magazine, and before that in a magazine that wasn't circulated outside of California. All I'm doing is writing about stuff that continues to interest me in a very intense way. I'm still struggling to make sense of it and feeling vitalized by writing about it. But I don't consider myself a player in a game of taste-making, or any sort of a critical powerbroker or anything like that. When Tim says the '70s critics should bow out, my response is, "I guess I don't have to worry—I'm a '60s critic." I don't know who he's talking about when he said that—I really don't. There's another thing, too, to get obnoxious about it for a moment. People will stop reading me and Bob and Dave and people of that ilk—if that is an ilk—when other people come along with better ideas, a more intriguing writing style, more stamina, and more commitment to the subject matter. There's nothing surprising about that.

Dellio: A few months back you commended Steve Albini's highly personal diary in *Forced Exposure*. Do you think the people at *Forced Exposure* are writing out of genuine conviction, or just looking for a forum to make a name for themselves?

Marcus: I don't know the people on *Forced Exposure*, so I don't know what their motives are. As someone who reads the magazine, I often get the feeling they're just writing for fun. And that could mean dozens of things. To try to piss people off—easier said than done. I *don't* know why Byron Coley keeps dropping the g's off his words. It's *so* affected. I talked to him on the phone recently—I've never met the guy—and told him he's just gotta stop that. It's like a quadruple irony, and I got lost somewhere on the double irony.

One of the reasons I like Steve Albini's writing is because he isn't working within someone else's form. He's working within his own. I was very moved by that diary. I really thought the guy was talking about real things. Making a fool of himself, shooting himself in the foot, and not giving a damn—he was gonna say it and leave himself completely naked. I don't think he was trying to be provocative, and I don't think he was copping a pose; I think he was really trying to figure out what the fuck he wanted to say, and to say it to its limit. And I think he did a real good job.

Dellio: What do you think about Chuck Eddy's writing?

Marcus: I liked Chuck's writing a whole lot when I was first seeing it in the *Voice*, but I guess I've gotten the impression over the past year or so that he's trying to convince himself that what he's saying on the page is true. Like, "I'm supposed to like this album, so I like it, and I'm gonna write about how great it is." You see the letters H-E-L-P tearing through the lines. So I'm not convinced by what he's been writing lately. Maybe I'm wrong, maybe he believes it with all his heart and soul. But if he doesn't, I don't have any idea what's going on with him.

Dellio: Since interviewing Peter Townshend and Elvis Costello earlier this decade, you seem to have completely given up on interviews.

Marcus: I've never done interviews. I did the Townshend because the person who was supposed to had cancelled at the last minute, and my editor called me up desperate. I did the Costello simply because I'd always wanted to meet the guy. I'm real glad I did because we've become friends, and we talk, and he's really quite a guy.

But I'm not an interviewer—I'm not good with it and I'm not comfortable. What's wrong with me is I want the other person to like me. And that's fatal for an interviewer. The best interviews come when you ask stupid questions. You say, "Is it true your mother's really a dolphin?" And the guy says, "No! Where did you hear that? She's not a dolphin, she's a *burrow*. And let me tell you how she got to become a burrow..." And he'll tell you everything.

Obviously, if you want the guy to like you, you're not going to ask if his mother's a dolphin. So I'm not cut out to be an interviewer.

interrupting my train of thought

Dellio: Would you agree, as Chuck Eddy wrote earlier this year, that radio is in its worst shape ever?

Marcus: Look—except for a few years, and they were mostly in the mid-'50s and mid-'60s for AM, and in the late '70s for college FM, the state of radio has *always* been the worst in history. There was a time in around 1959 when I stopped listening to the radio because it almost made me physically ill every time I turned it on. All I'd hear was Debbie Reynolds singing "Tammy." There was another time like that in the late '60s, the early '70s were beyond belief, and the early '80s were astonishing. Top 40 or hip FM—whatever the standardized form of pop music might be—has an infinite capacity for dullness and stupidity. We'll never know when we hit bottom. So sure, I completely agree with what Chuck wrote—except it's not the worst in history if you want to take a longer view than six months.

Dellio: How about the mid-'70s, the radio that Chuck Eddy and a lot of other newer writers grew up with?

Marcus: Well, I thought "The Night Chicago Died" was really funny, and "Beach Baby" was a truly wonderful record. But it was one of those fallow periods. And since it wasn't *my* period, in the sense that it wasn't when I was first starting to write or argue with my friends about music, it was just a time I had to get through. One of the great things about major changes in pop music, like Elvis or the Beatles or the Sex Pistols, is that unless you're a lot smarter than I am, it's a shock. Moving along in the mid-'70s it was, "Jesus, seems like it's gonna be like this forever." The ultimate nadir was reached with that song "How Long" by Ace. Remember when that record came out? There's a mid-'70s record for you. Well, rock critics all over the country said, "Hey, this is good! This is kinda interesting! Maybe this is gonna be a good new band!" I mean, *that* bland piece of shit? It couldn't get any worse than that, Chuck Eddy to the contrary.

Dellio: I take it that it still means something for you to hear a song over your car radio, as opposed to sitting at home.

Marcus: Yeah, because it's a surprise, it's more tactile, you're closer to the speaker, your hand's on the dial. I find it a lot of fun to be moving along and have something come on that will take me out of the day, take me back 20 years, confuse me in terms of a context, or just hear some song that I'm thinking, "What the *fuck* is that?"—something I've never heard before that just sounds great or weird. I think that's a lot of what living a good life is all about, to be able to be surprised like that.

Dellio: The collection of Lester Bangs's writing that you're editing was undertaken soon after his death five years ago. Has there been a delay in getting it out?

Marcus: It took a good while to collect everything we could collect. That meant gathering all the material from his apartment, which was thousands and thousands of pages, some of it in order and some of it not, then shipping it out to me; it meant gathering hundreds and hundreds of published articles from obscure sources, as well as from the *Voice*, *Creem*, etc., and getting all the stuff in one place and me going through it, dividing it into piles of 'yes,' 'no,' and 'maybe,' and then starting to read it and think about it.

But I finished the book last June, and it will be coming out in September. I think it was worth the wait. I hope it will have a big effect on how not just rock'n'roll, but culture or politics or anything is written about. I think people are going to see new possibilities for talking straight and for talking twisted when they see this book.

Dellio: Do you think people who write about rock'n'roll still tend to write in the shadow of Lester Bangs, or with Lester Bangs in the back of their mind?

Marcus: Well, I don't know. He's certainly on my mind, and I know he's on Dave's mind in the sense that he's a literary conscience. Often you'll write something and you'll say, "God, that's pretentious—Lester would kill me." Of course, people felt that when he was alive, too. That's not just a function of his being dead.

Dellio: Between your columns in *Artforum* and the *Voice*, you usually manage to say a few words about most performers. I wanted to get your thoughts on a few I've yet to see you comment on. The Jesus and Mary Chain?

Marcus: I thought [*Psychocandy*] was a good record, but in a real cold way. I always tried to get my British friends to explain to me why they're so big and important and controversial over there. I've got some smart British friends, but they never could explain it to me.

interrupting my train of thought

Dellio: Anita Baker?

Marcus: I think Anita Baker is ridiculous. Any time you hear somebody bringing back this kind of genteel, effete black music—the same number the Pointer Sisters pulled in the early '70s when they gave concerts with "Black Tie Recommended" printed on the tickets—it's an incident in class politics that has nothing to do with music.

Dellio: Robert Cray?

Marcus: I don't like Robert Cray, and I particularly dislike his new album [*Strong Persuader*]. What really puts me off about him is that you just can't do blues in the self-conscious way you can do a lot of other things. You can't get up and say, "Ladies and Gentlemen, now I'm gonna do a blues song," without immediately sounding ridiculous. There's something very demagogic about that. The Bonzo Dog Band could do it, but they were supposed to be ridiculous.

Dellio: R.E.M.?

Marcus: The most boring of the boring—forget it.

Dellio: Both "Real Life Top 10" in the *Voice* and "Speaker to Speaker" in *Artforum* are fairly free-form in what they draw upon for subject matter. How does each take shape?

Marcus: For "Real Life," I keep a running file. Whenever anything crosses my path that might conceivably go into the column—something I hear on the radio, a book I see in a store, a strange news story I see in the paper, something I might see at an art exhibit—I write it down. You need a balance: I don't think it would be much fun to read a column about ten records, or ten books, or ten movies.

I suppose the subject of "Speaker to Speaker" is, "What does it mean to be a listener?" What are we doing when we listen? What happens? What doesn't happen? What could happen? I really am a critic in the sense that I don't give a shit what the artist intended, or what he meant. I couldn't care less. What I'm interested in is what happens when you listen. If the artist made a record intending to convince all right-thinking people to send money to the I.R.A., but the record is in Swedish and nobody can know that, it's sort of pointless to discuss the guy's intentions. What you really have to discuss is what is it like to hear a record in Swedish, and does it have a good beat?

Dellio: The last couple of years you've written a disproportionate amount about Elvis Costello and the Mekons. What do you see in them?

Marcus: They provoke me more, they give me more to think about, they give me more visceral pleasure, they upset me more, than any other people. But I don't like the new Mekons album [*Honky Tonkin'*]; I didn't like *Blood and Chocolate*. I don't like everything those people do. But for the last few years, it's true, they've been the people who have gotten under my skin.

It just so happens with the Mekons that when I started to write about them, they weren't much being written about. So I had both a cause to trumpet and a subject to explore. And with Elvis Costello, to be perfectly frank, I don't think anybody else writes anything halfway intelligent about him. And I don't know why; don't ask me why no one else wrote a whole column on "Pills and Soap," because it sure as hell deserved it. You could write a whole column on his version of "Withered and Died," an old Richard Thompson song.

(*Nerve*/rockcritics.com, 1987/2003)

Ball Four

Buried somewhere near the beginning of this site's existence, there's a piece on the film *Rushmore* wherein I went back and reread *The Catcher in the Rye* for the first time in a decade-plus. The movie reminded me of the book; more specifically, Max Fischer reminded me of Holden Caulfield. I don't know—thinking about that now, the connection seems a little tenuous beyond the prep-school angle.

I've just finished rereading Jim Bouton's *Ball Four* for something I've been working on, a rereading that in this case spans at least 25 years. I remember getting Dave MacIntosh to read it during the *Nerve* days, and also Scott Woods, although Scott tells me now that he'd already read it at that point. I probably read it again myself around that time. That would have been the mid-'80s, so let's say 25 years. Jim Bouton turned 75 this year. He's older now than Casey Stengel was when he managed the Mets.

Unlike my revisitation of *A Catcher in the Rye* 15 years ago, *Ball Four* held up just fine this time around. Much better than that, actually—I've never felt surer about naming it as one of the key influences on my writing, on me as a baseball fan, and on my general outlook on life. Yes, I have a general outlook on life. I'm not sure if mine is any more philosophical than the one espoused by Joe Schultz in *Ball Four*—"Well, boys, it's a round ball and a round bat and you got to hit the ball square"—but I bow down to Joe in the philosophy department, so no shame there.

When I first read *Ball Four* in high school, the thing I most gravitated towards was its jaundiced view of the player-coach dynamic. Bouton's two managers in the book—Schultz in Seattle, and then Harry Walker after he's traded to Houston—mostly got a pass, but the inane proclamations and less-than-forthright maneuvering of some of the other coaches, particularly Sal Maglie, had special resonance for me at a time when I lived out my own version of *Ball Four* as the mop-guy on my high-school basketball team. I loved the humour, loved Schultz (a character beyond the powers of literary invention), and pretty much loved anything having to do with baseball in those days, but it was the book's confirmation of my growing sense that the people running the show were clueless that meant the most to me then.

That part is still there, of course, and it still makes me laugh. Eddie O'Brien ("Mr. Small Stuff") checking up on every last pointless detail, Maglie second-guessing so often that Bouton has to invent the concept of the first-guess second-guess, Sibby Sisti puttering around on his little cart for no discernible reason beyond qualifying for a pension—*Ball Four* remains my *Catch-22*, *Dr. Strangelove*, and *Mad* magazine all rolled into one, the book that more than anything else hyper-sensitized me to the clear and present absurdity all around. (Sisti does get off what is possibly my favorite line in the book, after the Pilots' first and last annual father-kid game: "Forty runs, for crissakes, and nobody gets knocked down.") But it was a couple of other things that jumped out at me even more this time. The fact that I'm a coach myself now, and a teacher who nags my students about every last pointless detail, I'm sure none of that has any connection to my evolving viewpoint.

The first was how incredibly good Bouton is on the major issues of the day, primarily race and the war. *Ball Four* was written squarely in the middle of a famously chaotic moment, the events of which should be familiar, and far from dodging what was playing out in the rest of the country, Bouton tries to make sense of things. He closely observes the interactions between white and black players on both the Pilots and the Astros, noticing key differences between the two clubs. He ridicules the idea that Houston would be asking for trouble if they traded for Dick ("Richie," as he was called against his wishes then) Allen down the stretch: "*Humph*. I wonder what the Astros would give to have him come to bat just fifteen times for us this season." And he's open about his own fallibility, admitting that his views on integrated marriage—remember, this is a notoriously conservative sport almost 50 years ago—have been upended. With regards to Viet Nam, he's completely on the side of those protesting the war. So much so that he (along with kindred spirits Steve Hovley and Mike Marshall) senses reluctance among the other players to engage him on the subject. Which is not always a bad thing—in the case of hard-line farm guy Gene Brabender, Bouton describes him as someone who looks like he'd "crush your spleen" if you got under his skin.

Coming full circle from the high-school me, the other thing that really came through this time was how much of an unabashed fan Bouton is. I think I always picked up on that sentiment, but never so clearly. There's a love and a reverence for the game all through *Ball Four*, often for those very same absurdities that otherwise exasperate Bouton. You see this especially in his back-and-forth with Brabender and Fred Talbot, or Wade Blasingame over on the Astros, guys he has zero in common with beyond the game itself. But they're all able to make him laugh—they're all bonded by the somewhat surreal nature of what they do for a living, bonded by their derision for the coaches and owners, and bonded by the same insecurities that were a given with guys who existed at the margins in the years before free agency. (The emergence of Marvin Miller and the player's growing labor awareness is one of the book's most vital subplots, as is Bouton's ongoing struggle to master a schizophrenic pitch, the knuckleball.)

There's a heavily-trafficked website called Baseball-Reference where you can sponsor a player's stat page. You pay them a set amount, you get your name on the page as the sponsor, and you get to write a line or two about the player. If you want to sponsor Willie Mays or Ted Williams, forget it, unless you're willing to pay a few hundred dollars a year. (Mays and Koufax are both available at the moment, somewhat surprisingly; Mays goes for $455, Koufax for $305.) But you can also sponsor pages for as little as $10 a year, and yes, the Seattle Pilots were just waiting there for me, alone and unloved and unsponsored. Right now, I've got three Pilots: Merritt Ranew, Talbot, and—quite possibly my proudest possession in the world—Joe Schultz. I plan to sponsor a few more, I've just been lazy about following through. Bouton himself, unfortunately, looks to be out of reach—the "Law Offices of Jeffrey Lichtman" have had the page for a number of years now (probably out of my price range anyway).

The sponsorships are just one of many indications of how strongly *Ball Four* has stayed with me through the years. More than a great baseball writer, Bouton—like Bill James, like Joe Posnanski—is simply a great writer. I can't think of a better illustration of that than the book's famous closing sentence:

"You see, you spend a good piece of your life gripping a baseball, and in the end it turns out that it was the other way around all the time."

Honestly, that's as good as *The Great Gatsby*'s closing sentence.

(homepage, 2014)

Casualties of War (Brian De Palma, 1989)

One war film only. I considered *Paths of Glory*, but one Kubrick is enough. *The Deer Hunter* and *Apocalypse Now* (and, to a lesser extent, *Coming Home*) had a huge impact on me as a teenager, but, not surprisingly, that has waned over time. I still think *The Deer Hunter* has remarkable passages, and also some juvenile sentiment that dates badly; *Coming Home* has problems too, balanced by some very moving scenes. (I recently called it the opposite of Joe Rudi: Rudi was an overrated underrated baseball player, *Coming Home*'s an underrated overrated film.) *Apocalypse Now*...is famous.

So: *Casualties of War*. The last few years of Kael's tenure, I don't think I was on the same page as her. She seemed to gravitate to stuff like *Scrooge, Club Paradise, Dirty Rotten Scoundrels*, films I wasn't even remotely interested in, while *Stranger Than Paradise, sex, lies & videotape, Miller's Crossing*, and others were either bypassed or, at best, accorded qualified, disinterested praise. It felt at times as if the more a film aspired to, the more seriously it took itself, the less chance it had with her. That's a simplification, of course, and it's also a tendency that had been part of her writing forever. I just felt like it became magnified towards the end. But with *Casualties of War*, she nailed it. I don't know if it was her last epic review in the style of her reviews for *Last Tango* and *Nashville*—*Enemies: A Love Story* was in there too, and I'm too lazy to check which came first right now—but it's the one that I prefer to think of as her equivalent of Ted Williams' final home run. *Casualties* got lost in the late-'80s spate of Vietnam films—*Platoon, Full Metal Jacket, Born on the Fourth of July, Good Morning Vietnam*, two or three others—and in 1989, it probably didn't get 10% of the attention that *Do the Right Thing* did (which I like fine). Kael is the only critic I remember who was alert to how masterful it was, and she took that and ran with it like it was 1975.

The few war films I like tend to have relatively few combat sequences—not sequences in the field, but actual combat—and that's true of *Ca-*

sualties. The scene I've linked to is representative of much of the movie: one prolonged game of mental chicken between Sean Penn's Sgt. Meserve and Michael J. Fox's Private Eriksson, triggered by the abduction and then gang-rape of a Vietnamese peasant girl. A story I've told before: there was a local critic who dismissed *Casualties* at the time by saying it was another De Palma "kill the bitch" film. Twenty years later, I still count that as the single stupidest line of film criticism I've ever read. (Sorry—I considered "most irresponsible," but "stupidest" is a better fit.) De Palma's treatment of the girl is humane and shattering beyond words.

There are a couple of missteps, especially a scene where Fox needlessly and clumsily starts musing aloud about stuff we can figure out for ourselves (his "maybe it matters more" monologue). And Penn gives a highly stylized performance that you may recoil from—the clip will be a good test of that. Otherwise, pretty close to perfection I'd say. Last word to Kael:

"(Some movies) have more imagination, more poetry, more intensity than the usual fare; they have large themes, and a vision. They can leave us feeling simultaneously elated and wiped out...*Casualties of War* has this kind of purity."

(#38, Facebook Top 50, 2011)

"An Impression," No Age/"North Sea Girls," Wussy

This is the fourth year in a row I've voted for Wussy, so I'm running out of things to say about them. Wussy, you're not going to be famous. Looking forward to *Attica*—great meet-me-where-I-come-from title. I'm late to No Age. At first I was going to list "C'mon, Stimmung," which is about as melodic as skronk ever gets, but here and there the vocal bugs me. No such problem with "An Impression"; quite beautiful, especially when it morphs into *Another Green World*. I want to go back and hear all their previous records.

My exposure to both bands came via Christgau. A few months ago, the Consumer Guide bowed out for the second or third (fourth?) time. (It hasn't always been called the Consumer Guide, but as long as there were capsule reviews with letter grades, it still felt like the Consumer Guide.) My guess is it won't be back this time, and that saddens me more than I would have expected. After devouring his '70s book in my 20s, and then really caring about Pazz & Jop results all through the '80s, I basically shut out Christgau through the '90s. I'd been writing for a few years by then, and was putting out a fanzine with a number of Pazz & Jop voters as contributors. I was mad that I wasn't getting a ballot myself (why I thought Christgau would know about my fanzine without someone actually giving him a copy, I'm not sure). Somewhere in there a friend and I put out a book on pop music in the '70s, and I made sure that we omitted Christgau in the acknowledgements, where we listed a few key music books covering the decade— against mild objections from my friend, as I remember it, but he didn't make an issue of it. One review made mention of Christgau's '70s book, hinting that it was an odd omission. Anyway, for as long as it lasted, it was an excellent grudge. Like many of my grudges it was secret, so the world went ahead as before.

These days I defend Christgau when message-board posters pick over some CG entry from 40 years ago. ("How did he not know that Black Sabbath would have critical cachet in 2013? What the hell was he thinking?" I'm exaggerating, somewhat.) Not that there's a great deal of that right now—after he left the *Voice*, the number and intensity of arguments about him seemed to diminish. People who were edited by him almost always single him out as the best line-editor they ever had. I wish I'd had that chance, but I don't know how enjoyable that would have been—whatever stylistic influence he had on me disappeared soon after I started writing, and I like to leave in all the "well"s and "I don't know"s he obviously had no patience for, so maybe it would have been a demoralizing experience. But as someone who got into my bloodstream early on—I continued to check the Consumer Guide reflexively, through all its incarnations and right to the very end (if it is...)—he belongs up there with Kael, Marcus, Bill James, and Stanley Kauffmann as a compass. Kauffmann died this year, and I paid tribute to him elsewhere. Call the Wussy and No Age songs partly my belated tribute to Christgau.

(#8/9, year-end ballot, 2013)

Hey Bill

(Asked by: Phil Dellio, 12/30/2011) Bill: This isn't the most precise question, but I'll give it a go anyway...Do you believe—or do you know of any studies that indicate—there's a correlation between teams who play better late in the season (as opposed to April and May) and winning divisions/pennants? This springs from some recent back-and-forth I had over the relative merits of Verlander and Bautista for MVP. Obviously, all wins count equally in the standings—a win in September is a win in June is a win on Opening Day, etc. But in making the case against Bautista, I remarked that it bothered me that he was so much more formidable in April and May than

he was the rest of the way, while Verlander was close to unbeatable the last two months. But I don't know if I'm placing importance on something—the notion that players have added value if they perform well down the stretch—that has no basis in fact.

(Bill James) Well...in general championship teams play better late in the season...The league "pulls apart" late in the year; the .400 teams play .350 baseball, the .600 teams .650 baseball...actually .640 or something, but the gap widens. It isn't what you were asking, but there IS a correlation between playing better later in the season and winning the pennant.

It has been shown that playing well late in the season has SOME carryover value to the next season. If you take two 90-72 teams, but one was 50-31 the first half, 40-41 the second half, while the other was the opposite, the team which played better late in the season has some advantage in the next season. But I am not aware of any study that shows that teams that play well late in the year have a meaningful advantage in post-season play.

On a related issue...I remember we used to have people in the field who would fume about late-inning homers being counted as more important than early-game homers, etc. We just hadn't worked out a coherent way to think about the problem. Eventually we all came around to the concept of "leveraged" situations, a concept with which people are comfortable, so people stopped bitching about game-time performance being given additional weight. It's not unreasonable to think that late-season performance in a pennant race is ALSO leveraged performance, and should be given weight.

One of the greatest rock'n'roll songs of all time, by the way. "The Weight."

(Asked by: Phil Dellio, 6/19/2013) Bill: The other day, Bob Costas got a little sarcastic about the Mets going crazy over their extra-inning win over the Cubs ("another sign of the decline of Western Civilization"). On a message board where I post, a couple of people took umbrage at Costas's derision. While I agree that he maybe shouldn't have targeted the Mets (a little celebration in the midst of a rotten season seems understandable), I also find the recent ritual of treating every walk-off win like the 7th game of the World Series a little excessive and puzzling. Any idea when this took hold? I don't remember teams doing this in the '70s or even the '80s for mid-season games of no special consequence.

(Bill James) It's the last ten years. But you SHOULD get excited when you win a game in dramatic fashion. If you don't, you're not participating in the emotional experience of the game.

Used to be, I think, that players didn't celebrate on the field out of the fear of "showing up" the opposition. The practice of lining up on the field to congratulate everybody on the win started in the late 1970s, and the jumping around celebrating kind of grew out of that. Since you're on the field anyway, it seems natural to express your passion for the game. There's nothing wrong with it.

(Asked by: Phil Dellio, 7/4/2013) Bill: In light of Chris Davis, Jay Jaffe compiled a chart the other day of all the players who've had 30 HR by the All-Star break; the chart also included how many they hit after the break and their total for the year. The fewest after the break (excepting strike years and injuries) were 10, by Mays in '54 and Reggie in '69. A reader comment offered an explanation for Mays—that Durocher asked him to concentrate on spraying the ball around the second half (no idea whether that's true or not). Any recollection of what happened with Reggie? His walk rate went up—once every 6.5 PA first half, once every 5.5 second half—and the All-Star Game wasn't until July 23 that year, but they wouldn't seem to wholly explain such a drastic 37/10 split. I also notice that he had 24 doubles and two triples before the break—63 extra-base hits! His slugging average dropped 260 points the second half.

(Bill James) The strikeout was invented in mid-season.

(Bill James Online, 2011-13)

Calmly Disagreeing: Stanley Kauffmann (1916-2013)

When film critic Stanley Kauffmann died a few weeks ago, Scott was in the midst of a series of posts devoted to rock critics who, at some point in their careers, expressed a declining interest in writing about music. Did Kauffmann ever experience something similar, I wondered? He began at *The New Republic* in 1957, and he was still at it when he reviewed *Our Nixon* just prior to his death at the age of 97. That's 50-plus years of writing film reviews for the same publication—it wouldn't appear that he ever got bored of seeing and writing about movies, and I don't recall him ever saying so in any of the interviews I've read with him (many of which are collected in *Conversations with Stanley Kauffmann*). But who knows? He did slow down considerably the past few years, sometimes only appearing in the magazine every couple of months. Maybe there was a moment in there, back when he was still only 93 or 94, where he stopped and thought, "This film reviewing thing, I'm not really sure if it's for me."

Kauffmann, as I've written many times before, influenced me almost as much as Pauline Kael. Or maybe his influence was every bit as great—it's just easier to detect Kael when I look at stuff I've written. I can pick out little stylistic flourishes here and there, and in terms of her favorite films and directors, there's overlap with my own favorites all over the place. If Kauffmann had a signature style when he wrote, something as instantly recognizable as Kael's whirlwind advocacy (I know that's a simplification, but I think it's a fair description of the reviews she's most famous for— *Nashville*, *Last Tango*, etc.), I'm not sure how you'd describe it. Whenever I'd mention him on the ILX message board, the general perception seemed to be that he was bookish and a little stodgy. Not John Simon, maybe, but another guy who came from some place that had an inherently supercilious attitude towards film—in Kauffmann's case, from a background that included theatre criticism, book publishing, and even a few novels. And while there were a few directors he venerated for a time—Antonioni and Bergman in the '60s, and Oliver Stone at the beginning of his career, are the first three that come to mind—I don't associate him with specific directors (Altman, De Palma, Peckinpah) or moments (American film during the '70s) the way I do Kael. I almost want to say that he especially kept the latter at arm's length— as Kael rhapsodized over *The Godfather* and *Jaws* and *Carrie*, Kauffmann would instead devote his reviews to noticing small virtues in the likes of *The Hired Hand* and *Desperate Characters*, all the while writing much more skeptically about the era's defining films—but again, a simplification. Sometimes, as with *Close Encounters*, Kauffmann rhapsodized, while Kael wrote admiringly of many smaller films.

Two paragraphs in, and I'm lost in explanations and clarifications. For whatever reason, I read and reread Kauffmann's collections incessantly for a time—he was one of those critics where I reached a point of needing to know what he thought about every film of interest to me. His key work is found in *Figures of Light* (covering the late '60s), *Living Images* (early '70s), *Before My Eyes* (mid-late '70s), and *Field of View* (early '80s); there's also *A World on Film*, his first collection, where he discovers Bergman and

Antonioni, and wades through the dying years of the Hollywood studio system, and *Distinguishing Features*, devoted to the late '80s and early '90s. I just realized now that I don't own a copy of his final collection, *Regarding Film: Criticism and Comment*, which came out in 2005. Or maybe I should say latest, rather than final—I expect there'll be another one collecting his last few years of reviews sometime soon. Anyway, I just put *Regarding Film* on order.

I never found Kauffmann's writing bookish or stodgy; there was humour, curiosity, detours into personal anecdote, a thorough knowledge of film history (a history that unfolded right alongside his own life—someone pointed out that he was born the year after *Birth of a Nation*), an ability to connect film to the other arts that was never pedantic (Kael had that too), an ongoing willingness to re-see and re-evaluate (very different than Kael there), and a way with words that was lucid and spare and, to me as a reader—and I know this sounds odd—comfortable. I had a degree of comfort with Kauffmann's reviews that I don't think I've ever reached with another critic.

He was both a participant in the great film-critic free-for-alls of the 1960s—I always thought of him, Kael, Andrew Sarris, and John Simon as the epicentre of those battles, probably because of their ubiquity, with Manny Farber and Dwight Macdonald and everyone else kind of buzzing around at the edges—and also slightly removed. He didn't snipe away with great glee like Simon (who has now outlived the other three, presumably good karma for a lifetime of gentle collegiality), but there are allusions to Kael and Sarris in his reviews—when he refers to "all the advance fuss" over *Last Tango in Paris*, he's surely looking in one direction—and discussions of auteurism here and there. (Kauffmann wrote a review of Kael's *I Lost It at the Movies* for *Harper's* in 1965, but I've never read it, and it isn't collected in any of his books.) He was hardly oblivious to the surrounding din, nor were the other three oblivious to him. Kael talks about Kauffmann a few different places; she seemed to be a little perplexed by him, and he and Macdonald and Simon represented one kind of film criticism she took on in the early '60s. ("I always thought that the reason Stanley Kauffmann and I so rarely agreed on things was clear if you looked at his measured walk versus my incautious quick steps"—which is probably just a nice way to say stodgy. Sometimes I like quick and incautious, more often I gravitate towards measured.) Somewhere, I can't remember where, I recall reading Kauffmann taking a second look at auteurism—he was always taking a second look at things—and giving it credit for bringing to the fore certain films and directors that might otherwise have been forgotten; he's also on record as saying that he missed the boat with the '60s great critical lightning rod, Godard. As acrimonious as the '60s and '70s could get among film critics, Kauffmann kept that acrimony out of his own reviews, and he didn't seem to come out of that period with calcified views.

I only occasionally read Kauffmann's reviews these past few years—he almost exclusively wrote about small foreign films I knew I'd never see, by choice or otherwise. (The reviews were sometimes behind a paywall, too.) When he did write about something I was interested in, I can't say I always found the results as rewarding as his work 30 years ago—the *Our Nixon* review consisted of little more than description. But I'm not really sure if you should expect a critic to be topping himself at 97, and there's no real precedent for seeing how the work of other 97-year-old critics holds up. (George Bernard Shaw? I don't know.) There's a line in his *Raging Bull* review—"this film, like some (though not most) good art works, is finally 'about' the fact that it incontrovertibly exists and, by existing, moves us"— that to me serves as rationale enough for those later reviews.

(rockcritics.com, 2013)

Pauline Kael

There's one very dead lady six feet underground somewhere enjoying this argument immensely. (Unless she's not: "One guy says auteurist, the other guy says not an auteurist, and I'm lying here thinking, 'Why I am listening to these two dumb fucks argue about whether or not I'm an auteurist?'")

(ILX, 2010)

some place back there

This was the easiest section of all to put together. Wall-to-wall song comments (ratings notwithstanding, they're not exactly reviews, even though I characterize them as such just below; I'm not sure what you'd call them), all chronologically drawn from a single source, ten stapled fanzines sitting in a box in my basement. Or nine stapled—one of them has hi-tech ring binding.

If I were to make a list of my favorite decades for music (miraculously, I don't think I ever have), the '70s and the '60s would unsurprisingly be at the top. Irrational nostalgia would have them in that order, too—I'd be happy to make the case that the '70s was a phenomenal decade by any objective criteria, but I wouldn't try to convince anyone that it was a better decade than the '60s. Doing so would require complicated formulae involving vectors and leveraged situations and the Marshall Tucker Band, and I'd also have to lie a little.

So far, so good, but third place is where I'd lose most people: the '90s. I hope this section, and also a good part of the Top Ten section, will get across what I got out of the music—which, for at least the middle part of the decade, amounted to Nirvana and Nirvana's shadow on one side of a split-screen narrative, with hip-hop's ever-ascendant stranglehold on popular culture on the other. (I do realize all simplifications are dangerously simple. There was also Right Said Fred and Sister Hazel and lots else.) Apart from the music itself, though, something else lay behind my affection for the '90s, something that I've come to believe is often the unacknowledged guiding factor for most anyone who writes about music in terms of your level of engagement with the subject at hand. When you're writing regularly, when you feel you're part of things—part of "the conversation," if you will—music sounds better. It's not just that you hear more, you're more alive to what you hear. Even if, as in my case, it's one tiny corner of the conversation, and what you say never leaves the room.

Radio On made all of that happen for me through the '90s, becoming the backdrop to a most entertaining decade: scandals everywhere, a pretty good approximation of LBJ in the White House, and Top 40 hits that seemed important enough at the time for extra-close attention from the revolving assemblage of 15 or so enthusiasts who helped me fill the pages of each issue.

----

interrupting my train of thought

The Story of Radio On

Scott Woods and I put together the first *Radio On* over the summer of 1991. It was 16 pages long, Little Peggy March was on the cover, and we photocopied and mailed out about 40 copies to friends and some people suggested by Chuck Eddy, plus another few hundred to military personnel stationed in Kuwait. Most of the issue consisted of Scott and I reviewing and rating 40 singles then being played on the radio; there was also a very funny debate on Madonna (the fate of the world depended upon Madonna at the time), a debate on the John Waite Rule, some scribbled commentary from Chuck, and an old-fashioned chart ranking of all 40 songs based on our ratings. The guiding purpose of *Radio On* was to call attention to a lot of important music that wasn't being written about elsewhere, music that would, over time, come to define an era: Huey Lewis's "Couple Days Off," Another Bad Creation's "Playground," the Rebel Pebbles "Dream Lover." Included among the Top 10 for that first issue were Men Without Hats' "Sideways" and Maestro Fresh-Wes's "Conductin' Thangs." People are still talking about these records.

The second installment (later that same year) was twice as long, the third (spring 1992) longer still. Chuck had gotten other people interested—Chris Cook, Rob Sheffield, Michael Freedberg, Amy Linden, Frank Kogan, Jack Thompson—and they in turn brought others along: Renée Crist, Patty Stirling, Gavin Edwards, many others. Number 4 (1993) came in at 86 pages and had reviews from 19 contributors; 104 pages and 24 contributors for #6 (1994); a peak of 128 and 23 for #7 (1995), the last issue I typed before switching over to a computer (after a long and acrimonious court battle, I had wrested control of *Radio On* away from Scott and was putting it together myself by this time); 100+ pages for #8 (1996) and #9 (1997); finishing off with a smaller, online-only #10 engineered by Jeff Pike (plus a handful of print versions that Kate Lewis took the trouble to assemble) in 1998. The commitment to important, overlooked music never wavered: Porno for Pyros's "Tahitian Moon" in #8, Paul McCartney's "The World Tonight" in #9, the last big hit by the Paul Main Project in #10.

Each issue also featured three or four Top 100 lists from both regular and one-time-only contributors, photocopies-of-photocopies-of-prints of photos by Chris Buck, and an end-section where people wrote about pretty much whatever they wanted (as opposed to the reviews section, where people wrote about pretty much whatever they wanted). Getting each year's issue out took up the whole of my summers from 1992 to '97, a valuable means of not having to think about my continued apathy in remaining a supply teacher.

You can still find the last two issues of *Radio On* online (for how long, I don't know), but all extant copies of numbers one through eight are in the sole possession of about 50-100 people scattered across the continent—getting hold of them may necessitate forged identity, sexual favours, or multi-thousand-dollar bids on eBay. The Rebel Pebbles and Men Without Hats, meanwhile, are no longer with us. Huey Lewis is presently a much-in-demand movie star. I still spend my winters telling kids to pay attention and stay in their seats, except now that I'm full-time, I get to say it to the same 27 kids every day.

(rockcritics.com, 2002)

"I Can't Make You Love Me," Bonnie Raitt

When I used to get especially morbid towards the end of my radio show, there were a few folk and folk-country songs I would invariably mix in with whatever doo-wop and other self-pitying ballads I was playing. Most were sung by females, most were piano-based: Richard & Linda Thompson's "A Heart Needs a Home," Tom Rush's "No Regrets," Fairport Convention's "Who Knows Where the Time Goes" (or Judy Collins'—I know some people find her prettified version intolerable, but I like it almost as much), some Mary McCaslin or Nanci Griffith, and a Roches song that I believe is called "I'd Really Love to See You" (it's from the *Nurds* LP). To hear such songs at 5:00 in the morning, especially sitting alone on the third floor of an empty building, certain that nobody's listening to you not just now but maybe not ever, is, as hokey as this sounds, shattering—I played them, listened closely, thought about things, rarely went on air. This record belongs in that company. For as long as it's been out, I'm always thinking about hearing it if I'm driving home from the city late at night, hoping some DJ will play it. When it happens, it washes over me. I feel empty, alone, afraid, and that's about the truest listening experience I look for these days. (9.0)

(*Radio On*, 1991)

interrupting my train of thought

"I'm Too Sexy," Right Said Fred

An historic record—after 10,000 rock stars who look like total dicks, a couple who look like actual penises. Sad to say, but I'm too prudish for this song. I'll happily motherfuck-this and motherfuck-that along with the most obscene juvenilia, but this makes me blush. I check the front mirror and I'm blushing. I still draw the line at the t-word when I sing along—I always trail off to a mumble when they get to the t-word. But I've long since been won over, rendered giddy enough to abandon whatever feeble attempts I was making at figuring it out, trying to decide if it was the most preposterous thing I'd ever heard or if some very clever people just wanted me to think that. I rarely get anywhere with such pursuits, I should know by now that the distinction's hardly worth making, and anyway it gives you the answer right in the song, the verse that goes "I'm too sexy for my hat/ This is the most preposterous thing you've ever heard." (You have to listen closely, that second line sounds a little bit like "What you think about that?") There's the most puzzling moment in the video when the guitar player—the guy who totes around the guitar—sits on a stoop and appears to be seasick. This seems to be triggered by a woman who passes by. Obviously this song was meant for Tom Jones and somehow got mixed up with Van Morrison in the mail. "What's New Pussycat?" 1965—7.0; "Faster Pussycat, Kill! Kill!" the Bosstweeds, 1965—8.0; "Can Your Pussy Do the Dog?" the Cramps, 1986—5.5. (7.5)

(*Radio On*, 1991)

"Let's Talk About Sex," Salt-n-Pepa

I think this must have started out on paper as the most obvious thing in the world, an anti-censorship tract, but something happened. The result, even more than "Summertime," is my idea of joy and wisdom, novelty and durability, playfulness and grace, without a trace of self-importance or contrivance, glitches I can happily abide by when I'm swept away by something for other reasons ("Here We Go"'s a good example, "Shiny Happy People" too), but which I'd just as soon not have cluttering up my enjoyment. Instantaneously this had me singing along with what I could, trying to learn what I couldn't keep up with (parts of it still trip me up—I can match Shirley Ellis line-for-line on "The Name Game," but I'll never be a rapper), and, as it

some place back there

dogged "O.P.P." up the charts, rooting for it to come out on top. It didn't, but as grand as "O.P.P." was in its own right, I think this will stand taller down the road—there's a lift in the "all the good things, all the bad things, that may be" refrain that's warm and lyrical beyond expectation no matter how many times you've heard it. It's that lift which explains, I believe, why this was able to hang around so inordinately long on CFTR's Top-6-at-6:00, the kind of fickle, time-sensitive thing that usually chews up novelties (I don't use the word pejoratively, as you might guess) quickly. Three months after release, even after it had begun its descent on the countdown proper, it was still there, like a bunch of people that day had suddenly had the "all the good things" part run through their mind and felt compelled to call up in appreciation. (On the other hand, it was also usually #6, making you wonder if it wasn't the DJs themselves who put it there for that great beginning—as soon as you heard "Spinderella-cut-it-up-one-time," you knew it was 6:00.) The first verse houses the most amazing tease: it gives you a whole bunch of ways you might choose not to hear this song, a dare rendered so assuredly and so intricately it seems like there's nowhere for the record to go, and then at the last second it pulls you in for good—"Will that stop us, Pat?/I doubt it/All right then, come on Spin" opens things up like Petula Clark singing "Well, if you like, I'll tell you more" in "I Know a Place." The second verse tells a touching story; no judgement is handed down, and it even spares a few kind words for me. (And I've never been completely sure whether it's the prez or the press who's next on her list—the ambiguity's perfect.) It keeps bouncing forward, first into that wonderful "take it easy now," then the last bit where they joke around about the radio not playing this, which they knew would be impossible, which is why their joking around seems so right, so in place. That's about 10% of what's here, 80% I couldn't even begin to describe, and the other 10% I'll mention only reluctantly, because Chuck thought my Bo Diddley/Clarence Thomas analogy last issue was a little strained (I agreed, a little). This record appeared, and began its ascent, during the Thomas/Hill hearings; peaked around the time of Magic Johnson's announcement; and started to fall alongside the Kennedy-Smith trial. I don't mean to trivialize those events (like this could trivialize anything—it's too good), and I'm definitely not looking to bestow false significance on a record that doesn't need anything it doesn't already have. But that was the backdrop—it was there, I was aware of it, and it resonated. In the end, maybe all that needs to be said is this: half or more of what makes it to the radio is an empty invitation to have sex; this is an invitation to talk, and it's sexier by miles. (10.0)

(*Radio On*, 1991)

"Jump Around," House of Pain

I'm amazed at how bracing these two-three note rap songs can be—"Jump Around," "The Choice Is Yours," "Warm It Up," one of the two versions of "La Schmoove" I hear, the one with the guitar (same split as "The Choice Is Yours," one's great and the other's lame—really, they're like two different songs). There's nothing to "Jump Around," but once the squawking starts it never lets up. If you go by the video those are bagpipes causing all the commotion, but it sounds more like a rabid horse whinnying. (Can a horse be rabid? I'll have to check my Osmonds records.) I still find the idea of thick-accented Irish rap sort of goofy, but only when I think about it after the song's over. Seeing as we're in the grip of this non-stop jumpathon, has anyone ever heard Voice of the Beehive's "Jump This Way"? I got it cheap on a BBC series recently, so I don't know if it's on any of their regular albums. It's a little like L7's "Pretend You're Dead," and a lot like the Primitives' "Crash." It's easily my favorite 25¢ record from over the summer, way ahead of the Kix album that set me back 52¢, and probably my favorite song heard since last issue. (8.0)

(Radio On, 1992)

"Deeply Dippy," Right Said Fred

If this drove you up the wall, it probably came on like "Winchester Cathedral" or Tiny Tim. Believe me, I sympathize, but the sad truth is I loved it all summer. It's those "Sweet Caroline" horns: the Foundations, the Spiral Starecase, Alive & Kicking, lots of stuff that freezes 1969. There's also the way the guy sings "Oooh, my love/let's set sail for seas of passion"; it seems to owe a lot to David Bowie and Bryan Ferry, so maybe I should give them another listen. And if you felt stupid for not liking the summer's two biggest stupid-novelty-songs, "Deeply Dippy" was possible proof that you hadn't lost your sense of humor/sense of stupidity. Unless you just thought it sounded passionate. That's the line score: 1969, David Bowie, stupid, passionate. (7.5)

(Radio On, 1992)

some place back there

"Rhythm Is a Dancer," Snap

More semantic adventures inside the seduced-by-seduction/tempted-by-temptation house of mirrors; maybe Genesis can answer back with "Rhythm He Don't Know Me." I like it much better than "The Power," which had the same fascistic sound I shrink back from in KLF singles (the urban ones, that is). There's some beauty here, and, thanks to the title, some mystery too. (7.0)

(*Radio On*, 1992)

"Friday I'm in Love," Cure

I said I found Rick Dees funny last issue, which must stretch credulity if his TV show or landmark deep-house record is all you know about him. I don't know how well he'll transfer to the page, he does a lot of creative stuff with radio, but here's something from a few weeks ago: "It was 1982, ten years ago today, that Robert Smith of the Cure was on the verge of suicide. Fortunately for Robert he flew home to England, got off the plane, and suddenly realized he was just ugly—but alive. Ten years later, he's livin' the high life!" Judging from the inspired self-deprecation that begins "Friday"'s video, I bet Robert Smith would appreciate Rick's capsule history: out of bed, down the stairs, flop around some, muss your hair, and turn into the Cure just in time for the song to begin. (6.5)

(*Radio On*, 1992)

"November Rain," Guns N' Roses

"Everybody needs some time all alone"—I can't argue with that, it's a beautiful thought, and it's probably behind dozens of my favorite songs. I don't especially believe it from Axl Rose, he wants to be alone like Madonna wants to be alone, but it's affecting anyway. (Yet if Madonna sang it, I'd believe her—it's good that I'm fair that way.) This is really corny, though, and if a ballad strikes me, the guy who gave "(Everything I Do) I Do It for You" an 8.0, as corny, chances are it's ten times cornier than that. I'm overwhelmed by one future scenario for this record: that on November 2, the eve of the election, it's going to be used by one or more of the networks to score a gooey, slow-motion collage re-tracing the campaign from day one—the *Chariots of Fire* thing, with shots of Bush and Clinton and the insane man with the Whitey Herzog haircut looking beaten, weathered, ennobled, stepping off airplanes with the wind whipping around them, bravely looking off at some point just beyond the camera's range, statesmanlike and magnanimous and all alone in that cold November rain. I see it all so clearly, especially if the aging incumbent's still trailing. Images like these make it even harder for me to accept this for what it's supposed to be, but I guess I still count it as an empty improvement over the previous *Use Your Illusion* singles And how about that video?!? They managed to get every last extra signed up, all that's missing is the climactic chariot race. (5.5)

(*Radio On*, 1992)

"People Everyday," Arrested Development

"Speech" is an unusual name: if he ever gets thrown in prison like James Brown, it'll be the birth of the Free Speech Movement all over again. I think he has the friendliest voice on the radio right now, which because he's so surly in videos might seem like a strange statement. I find the bounce in his voice so engaging, it doesn't even bother me that the words could be deemed preachy (maybe Preach would have been a good name). I'm not sure they are, though—skipping back one single, how come it's OK for Richard Marx to yearn for some imagined home but not him? "Tennessee" was a beautiful summer song, the best there was this year along with Janet/Luther, and even if you didn't want to bother with the story, you could use it like "Panama": I never had any idea what Van Halen were carrying on about, but whenever the chorus arrived you got to shout out "PANAMA!", just like the mere mention of Tennessee triggered Arrested Development's great chorus. "People Everyday" has the same dreamy languor to it, as suggestive of "Everybody Is a Star" as "Everyday People," with "Clean Up Woman" buzzing around in the background. I like it even more than "Tennessee." The reference to Ice Cube always makes me laugh—it's hard to tell whether it's a putdown or a plug (there's a prominent "who?" called out in response), but either way it's just funny to hear Ice Cube's name in the middle of drive-time. On a more inexplicable level, I love the sound of the words "Gruber brothers." Part of me knows that they've totally lost (or ignored) the focus of "Everyday People": if you're going to make a big issue of distinguishing yourself, an "African," from the "black man" you stomp, obviously you're going to have large numbers of listeners both black and white tuning ou completely. Part of me knows that, the rest doesn't care. Those "*wo-oh-wo-oh-iiiiii*"s near the end—they're so graceful, they can sing about anything they want and I'll be with them. (8.5)

(*Radio On*, 1992)

"Plush," Stone Temple Pilots

I started to read an interview with them at the newsstand, and a little ways into it I closed it up. All the putdowns of Pearl Jam and this group as commercializations of Nirvana seem silly to me, not too far away from what happened with Milli Vanilli, but as soon as I started reading, and they started trying to prove they were just as genuine as what they're supposed to be betraying, I realized it wouldn't take much for me to hate them too. Better just to hear them on the radio—this is good, almost as good as "Alive" or "Even Flow," both of which I've been hearing for a year now and like a lot. It is strange that the Stone Temple Pilots singer looks so much like the Pearl Jam singer, even imitating his every mannerism (especially the comic-book twitch in his eyes), but it can't be an oversight, I'm sure someone must have pointed this out to him. Musically, "Plush" is very complicated. One part triggers me to sing 'We've Only Just Begun": when he sings "Whe-ee-en the dogs have found her" (?), I segue into "Watchin' the signs along the wa-aa-ay." Meanwhile, same part, you can hear "25 or 6 to 4" underneath. You really have to pay attention, there's lots happening here. (When I interviewed Chuck for *Nerve*, June 1987, I singled out "Howls from the Heartland" as one of his better pieces and described it as "a tour through Midwestern grunge." I have no idea whether I got the words from Chuck's article or not. If I didn't, then I too am an important co-founder of this popular musical genre.) (7.0)

(*Radio On*, 1993)

interrupting my train of thought

"Creep," Radiohead

The subject is unusual for a Top 40 hit, but there's one place where it's common: you're-so-perfect-I'm-a-creep is behind countless horror films. Besides obvious examples like *The Phantom of the Opera*, *The Wolf Man*, *Psycho*, and *The Fly*, films where the realization's anguished, there's also the ones where it turns sadistic and sometimes gleeful—*Freaks*, *Peeping Tom*, *Blue Velvet*, and especially *The Texas Chainsaw Massa*cre, where Leatherface's creep-brother taunts the captive girl at the dinner table. I like all those films, a little or a lot. (The Who, "I Can't Reach You," 1967: "You fly your plane right over my head/You're so alive and I'm nearly dead." "I Can't Reach You" is "Creep" written and sung by a shy teenager who could put words together poetically.) If I were rating "Creep" for its idea, or for how often I share the same feelings, I'd give it a high mark. It's a song, though, and all it takes to kill the whole thing for me is the way he sings "you're so very special." Really, I don't like the way he sings anything. (4.0)

(*Radio On*, 1993)

"Insane in the Brain," Cypress Hill

House of Pain's horse is here—it bolted the stable, ran around the block three times, and now Cypress Hill has it. You'd think "Insane in the Brain" would be strictly a love-it-or-hate-it proposition, but I find it not quite commanding but in no way annoying. I always turn it up, I imitate the voices, I think they're a hilarious novelty to take number-one on the album chart, and needless to say I'm looking forward to spending the next few months in various classrooms with 12-year-old kids who've been listening to this in their spare time—that'll be a lot of fun. Who's sampled for the great ending? I keep thinking Roger Miller for some reason, but I don't think so. When the shorter and rounder guy is not singing with Cypress Hill, he bats cleanup for the Detroit Tigers—big RBI man, about 500 for the past four years. (7.0)

(*Radio On*, 1993)

"No Rain," Blind Melon

I wish I could hear this as a 12-year-old might, which was how old I was when I saw *Go Ask Alice*. "Dear Mr. Fantasy" and "It Ain't Easy" sounded extremely mysterious on the soundtrack; I thought of them as "drug music," and a couple years later I heard "Cowgirl in the Sand" and *Twelve Dreams of Dr. Sardonicus* for the first time, and they were drug music too. "No Rain"'s countryish ebullience notwithstanding, there's something in it that evokes those same feelings in me ("Insane in the Brain" doesn't), a kind of early-'70s what-the-older-kids-listen-to wonderment. (The singer looking like a young Ozzy Osbourne plays a part.) I love it, so much so that I really do envy 12-year-olds who must be fumbling around for words to describe it to their friends. I came across a straightforward explanation of the video that I would have been just as happy not knowing—where the storyline's from, I mean—but it's still among my favorites of the year. The little bee-girl's eyes lighting up upon spotting her new misfit friends, the three quick fade-to-blacks and how it's timed to the song's break, is just perfect—warm, funny, inspirational, one of the best video moments ever (right up there with Cyndi hugging her mom). (8.0)

(*Radio On*, 1993)

"Pets," Porno for Pyros

I used to play "Jane Says" a lot on the radio, and I used to joke about it because I didn't want to let on how much I liked it. You can't blame me, can you? It was a hokey song, but its hokiness was part of why I liked it—so pretty that the way its words strained to be the Velvet Underground was affecting. "Pets" seems quite sublime to me, not hokey at all. "We'll make great pets" is probably the one lyric I will take away from 1993. I don't go in much for doomy science-fiction, and I wouldn't claim any insight for "Pets," but the line stays with you like the last shot of *Planet of the Apes*. The guitar parts—the lyrical wash and the quiet interludes—couldn't be better. Looking at the video, Perry Farrell is right at home on this list: him, Lenny Kravitz, Prince Be, the Stone Temple Pilots singer, these people must be a joy to be around on a full-time basis. I would never have guessed I could like a Porno for Pyros song this much. (8.5)

(*Radio On*, 1993)

"Hip Hop Hooray," Naughty by Nature

I hadn't planned to, but I've got to say some words in defense of what may end up being my number-one song at year's end. The thing that's never stopped amazing me about "Hip Hop Hooray" is how pretty it is. Its words are as intricate as "O.P.P."'s, and just as difficult for me to follow, but it doesn't go by in a blur like "O.P.P."—it has the same easiness and contentment that I loved so much in "Summertime." I'm talking about how it feels: again, I can't always pick up on what Naughty by Nature's singing about here—they clip a lot of words—which is frustrating, because I like to sing along with the radio. (A few weeks ago I signed a book out of the library that had the lyrics to "O.P.P.," thinking that I might try to learn them. I never bothered to once I got the book home, so maybe it's not that important to me after all.) The phrases I do hear clearly are masterful: "Because I'm naughty by nature/And not 'cause I hate ya" is subtle, and "Let's start a family today" couldn't be more unexpected. There's the chorus too, and there's also the video. The gunplay at the end with the water pistols, a slight pause at one point and these pretty notes playing in the background, gets at something much deeper, more humane, and more elusive than the boring diatribe of "Everything's Gonna Be Alright." (9.0)

(*Radio On*, 1993)

"Backwater," Meat Puppets

Casey Kasem prefaced "Backwater" with a brief Meat Puppets biography that had them "laboring away in obscurity" until now. At first I flinched, because my own impression of the Meat Puppets is that they're more or less famous—not as famous as Madonna, more famous than Roxette or Jodeci. But that says more about me and what I was paying attention to in 1984 than it does about them—Casey Kasem's right, they are pretty obscure. I wrote an article on the Meat Puppets when they were at the height of their obscure fame, just after *Out My Way* came out. In the middle of a pretentious plea for why Top 40 radio should have been playing them at the time, even though I didn't know the first thing about what Top 40 was playing instead, I had a coherent sentence: "I think 'The Other Side' would sound terrific blasting from a car radio." Taking the record out now to see if I was right, I've discovered two things: 1) I must have had a very forgiving infatuation with the Meat Puppets, because it would sound not-bad at best, and it would also sound out of place; 2) Song titles were not considered important in 1986, and writers were encouraged to make up their own—what I meant to say was "Not Swimming Ground," where the words "the other side" are used a lot. Anyway, even though "Backwater" seems decent enough, with a little of what I used to like about the Meat Puppets (the harmonies) and a little of what I didn't much like even then (the choppy rhythm, the parts that drift into borderline heavy metal), I initially thought they'd gotten much worse as measured against what I remembered of *Out My Way*. Now I think they've probably only gotten a little worse. I would have been just as content misremembering. (I do like "We Don't Exist.") (5.5)

(*Radio On*, 1994)

"Stay (I Missed You)," Lisa Loeb

I find it hard to believe that the way she is in her video is the way that she really looks; no one looks like that anymore, it's as if she wandered out of *The Sterile Cuckoo*. Too good to be true from my vantage point, so invention or not I think she's extremely fetching. After she finished playing "Stay" on Letterman, she whispered into Dave's ear that "I have something for you." It made my own ear a little heartsick. (6.0)

(*Radio On*, 1994)

"Bizarre Love Triangle," Frente!

I want to use Frente! as a flimsy excuse to write about O.J. Simpson—you want to read some more about O.J., I can tell, especially something extra-lengthy and fuzzy-minded. There was talk in the beginning that a love triangle was behind it all, but that quickly became obscured by everything else. That's not what I want to write about, nor is it the everything else—abuse, race, the legal process, the media, all the major issues that have been sustaining the intense coverage throughout. Going back to the first few days after the freeway chase, there was another peripheral matter that attracted a lot of commentary before fading away: the question of whether or not O.J. the football player had ever been a "real" hero. It faded away,

I think, for two reasons: as the story developed, and the 911 calls and the other gruesome details came forth, it would have been redundant to waste time arguing about whether O.J. had ever been a hero, and anybody trying to make the case that he had been would have found himself subjected to certain ridicule; also, the argument had been settled in those first few days anyway—from what I saw, every single person who volunteered an opinion on the matter agreed that no, O.J. Simpson had never been a hero. I heard this from William J. Bennett, which didn't surprise me; I heard it from four out of four panelists on *The Capital Gang*, one of whom, Al Hunt, I generally like because he takes a commonsense, gray-area approach to things instead of simplifying them (a rarity on panel shows); I even heard it from Bob Costas, which kind of shocked me—Costas has always broadcast sports as an unabashed fan, frequently talking about what it was like to grow up in awe of Mickey Mantle. (Mantle's recent problems—and Strawberry's, and every other sports scandal of recent years—became part of the O.J. Simpson discussion.) But they all agreed: O.J. was famous, he was a celebrity, he was a gifted athlete, he was a '70s phenomenon, he was a hundred other glamorous but insubstantial things that made the story such a national obsession, but in no way was he ever a hero.

Being a lifetime sports fan—baseball primarily, but a sports fan more generally—it drove me up the wall to keep hearing this. William J. Bennett was the worst, dismissing whatever reverence O.J. had received during his football career with a condescending shudder, as if thousands upon thousands of football fans had been deluded in a way that William J. Bennett hadn't been. Knocking arch-conservatives is easy, especially one who has appointed himself a public arbiter of virtue, but that's not my purpose in singling out Bennett. I see him on TV all the time, and normally I don't mind him; he's pompous, but at least he's not hysterical. His stand on O.J. was offensive, though, because first and foremost Bennett's a politician, one who's positioning himself for a run at the presidency in 1996, and no one in that situation should be passing judgement on someone else's heroic attributes. Obviously—so obviously that I feel redundant in mentioning it—Bennett's job for the next two years is about as unheroic as can be: he has to go out each day and shape every single word he says to the specific goal of being elected president. He'll be saying some things that are true, some things that he thinks are true but aren't, and lots of things that he already knows aren't true but has to say anyway. So even if Bennett can't figure out why anybody would have ever considered O.J. a hero, he can at least contrast what an athlete does with what he himself will be doing for the next two years, and maybe he can understand why people are more inclined to revere athletes than politicians—athletes are a lot more spontaneous in how they express themselves than William J. Bennett's ever allowed to be, and there's something about spontaneity that engenders trust and admiration.

But Bennett never came out and identified himself as a hero, even though that's what he in fact meant; he instead said what all the others said, that the real heroes in society are doctors, teachers, police officers, Gulf War veterans, and parents. (That was the standard list; one person I heard included lawyers, which was funny.) They all said it with a noticeable measure of self-satisfaction, like they were engaging in heroics themselves merely by saying this. It's a list that's meant to intimidate—who isn't going to feel stupid saying a football player is heroic if "heroic" also means raising a family or dying for your country? The other way they had of discrediting O.J. was to measure him against a strict dictionary definition of hero, meaning "one who shows great courage." No one would argue that skill in carrying a football is the same thing as courage.

The dictionary argument is easy to knock down—that's one definition of hero, but Webster's also lists five others, including the idea of being "admired for achievements and qualities." I don't see how anyone could make the case that choosing sports heroes doesn't involve admiration based on achievements and qualities (you can test that further by looking up "qualities"). Even if a literal definition did run contrary to widespread perception—which it doesn't—I still think it would be a cheap argument. As for aggrandizing doctors and teachers in the abstract, that's harder to counter, but I'm not sure that it has much to do with actual doctors and actual teachers. Sometimes I'll get fed up with a kid at school, and I'll make myself feel better by thinking how nice it would be to break a baseball bat over the kid's head (a metaphorical bat, of course, one produced by the world-famous Metaphor & Bradsby Co. of Louisville, Kentucky). I'll immediately feel guilty for even thinking that, and I'll feel even worse when I tell myself that full-time teachers never have thoughts like that. Later, when gingerly describing my troubles with the student to a teacher on staff, I'll get something like this: "Oh yeah, him—don't you just want to take a baseball bat to his head?" I've seen lots of teachers who are great at what they do, but the conversation in the staff room is as mundane and unheroic as anything else—lots of complaining, lots of counting down to 3:00 (or to Friday, or to summer vacation), crude sex jokes, the same stuff I've heard at every other job I've ever had. And then I think about myself, the probability that I'll be teaching full-time within the next few years, and the abstraction becomes even sillier. I'll still be the same ridiculous person I am now, with all the same hang-ups, all the same accumulated pettiness, and all the same prurient thoughts. Will I just be a bad example of a heroic profession, or will the whole profession suddenly become less heroic with me on board? And what if on every staff of 25, there are 10 or 12 people just like me?

"Hero" can mean whatever you want it to mean, but there should be some room for having it mean what people actually think it means, the way they use it in everyday conversation. When O.J. Simpson broke 2,000 yards in 1973, he was right up there with Muhammad Ali and Bobby Orr in larger-than-lifeness, one of those occasional athletes who captures the public's imagination in a profound way—like Willie Mays did, like Michael Jordan did, like Ken Griffey is doing today. I don't think it would have been necessary to survey 1,000 kids in 1973 to get an affirmative answer to the question of whether or not O.J. possessed heroic qualities; I'm pretty sure you could have surveyed 1,000 doctors, teachers, and parents and gotten exactly the same answer. It was this youthful, spontaneous, larger-than-life version of O.J., one I hadn't consciously thought of in years, that made his indictment and the subsequent chase so jolting and unsettling. It wasn't because he was merely famous, and it wasn't because he was a celebrity; I can think of lots of celebrities more famous than O.J. where the story wouldn't have reached me, and a lot of people like me, in quite the same way. If Jack Nicholson were to become implicated in an identical story tomorrow, it would be just as remarkable, but I don't think it would have nearly the same resonance. OK, that's a bad example, Nicholson seems like someone who'd be mixed up in double-murder—let's say Barbara Walters then. There'd be just as much shock and puzzlement, but I can't see the words "An American Tragedy" appearing on the cover of *Time* beside Barbara Walters' picture. She's ultra-famous all right, but no one believes that she's done great things; Jack Nicholson has done great things, but I doubt that even his most ardent fans have deep feelings about him as a person. I certainly don't, and his performance in *Five Easy Pieces* means more to me than football ever has.

The view forwarded by Bennett and the others was that this is where people make a mistake when it comes to athletes—they fail to differentiate between on-field accomplishments and the off-field person. That's true as far as it goes, but it doesn't explain what John Updike meant when he wrote of the "immense open anguish" experienced by Red Sox fans when Ted Williams retired, which also seemed like a common reaction to the Simpson story (especially in Buffalo) before it was reduced to a freak show. Updike was aware of Williams' sour off-field demeanor when he wrote those words, but it didn't change how Williams the baseball player had affected him. (Please don't think that I'm equating murder and wife-beating with refusing to tip your cap after a home run; again, I'm talking only about O.J. in the 1970s.) With something as purely of the moment as sports, there isn't any point in differentiating between on-field and off-field—if sports means anything to you, there are invariably athletes who are going to leave an impression that will last your whole life. Of course I consider my parents heroic, but I can honestly say that I never had a teacher, from kindergarten through university, who affected me to the degree that Johnny Bench did when I was younger. That's not a knock on my teachers, and maybe it's a significant absence in my life, but it never happened. I don't feel compelled, however, to minimize the effect that a teacher may have had on someone else; I know it happens all the time, and with the right teacher it could just as easily have happened to me. So why can't Bennett and the others accept the idea that something similar can happen with athletes, and that with O.J. Simpson something indeed did? If athletic achievement can stir something so deep and so long-lasting in people—what the moment felt like, the inexplicable significance of a number like 2,000 or 61, the elation when you witness something as perfect as Joe Carter's home run last year—then obviously the impact of sports goes well beyond celebrity and fame. If it's not a kind of heroism, and I'd again point to the idea of capturing people's imagination through extraordinary accomplishments that are beautiful in the context of ordinary life, then heroism doesn't make any sense. It's not the day-to-day kind, granted, which is really what the others are talking about, but that doesn't make it any less of a factual reality. Bob Costas knows that it's real, and it was disappointing that he didn't make the effort to say so. (5.5)

(*Radio On*, 1994)

"Closer," Nine Inch Nails

When I made a Fields of the Nephilim joke in issue #2, it was partly in reference to the radio show that used to precede mine on CIUT—"New Powers," a Nine Inch Nails-type show. I used to come into the station each Friday night around 11:00, and there would be Chris hunched over the turntable, drinking Black Label as his usual assortment of favorites played: Current 93, Controlled Bleeding, Boyd Rice, Diamanda Galas, Laibach, Zoviet France, Nurse with Wound, that whole crew. It was like walking into Buffalo

Bill's bachelor pad in *The Silence of the Lambs*—after Chris mumbled his customary underworld greeting, I'd make it a point to disappear into the record library until it was time for me to take over. I didn't think I'd get a chance to hear "Closer," but I was flipping around after midnight and caught the video on MuchMusic's *City Limits* show. It was just what I thought it'd be: "I want to desecrate you," the singer bound up and ready to be beaten, a bald woman in a mask, "I want to fuck you like an animal," a rotating pig's head, a side of beef and a little Lewis Carroll girl on a couch, "my whole existence is flawed" (I'd actually be content if my existence were merely flawed)...It doesn't seem as if this genre has expanded its horizons much in the last five years, so these points are based mostly on nostalgia for my old radio show. Nine Inch Nails, Kings of Nostalgia. (4.0)

(*Radio On*, 1994)

"Nappy Heads," Fugees

My favorite quote of the year comes from Kevin Mitchell of the Cincinnati Reds, hinting to a reporter that he'd like to return to San Francisco so he could play with Bonds, Strawberry, and Williams: "Three guys like that in a lineup...Might as well put a machine gun on 'em and send 'em to Ruwaiti"—as everyone who reprinted the quote pointed out, Kevin's unique amalgamation of Rwanda, Kuwait, and Haiti! "Nappy Heads"'s spaciness is reminiscent of "Scenario," and as such I think it's pretty neat, but what I'd really like to hear is some of that new-school Ruwaitian rap. (My second favorite quote of the year is from
Charlie Hough, 46 years old going on 90: "I'm not officially retired, but I do officially stink.") (6.5)

(*Radio On*, 1994)

"Regulate," Warren G

This gets a 6.0 easy, because it sounds good and it makes me laugh; whether I'm laughing at it or with it—at it, I think, but it may be more knowing about its silliness than I realize—doesn't matter, or at least only matters for half-a-point's worth of difference. I know it's about a world that's real, and even though that world is a million miles away from mine, it does come alive and I do respond—in "Fantastic Voyage" and *Menace II Society*, not here. In "Regulate" I hear a comedy routine, and that starts me to devising parodies based on the world I actually live in, where the most traumatic societal inconvenience is either sitting down to watch a video that the last person forgot to rewind ("I can't believe this is happening in my own town") or an extra-long red light at the corner of Delrex and Highway 7 ("Damn—what next?"). Here's a list of eight comedic elements which conspire to undermine "Regulate" for me: 1) The little-brother syndrome (I know about Warren G and Dr. Dre; is Nate the little brother of Snoop, or has he just adopted the "Dogg" surname by way of paying homage?); 2) "We're *damn* good" in the opening sample is even funnier than it should be if the song's meant to be taken seriously; 3) Nate Dogg's vocal—weird at all times, almost unearthly when he sings "Nate Dogg and the G-Child were in need of something el-el-else"; 4) Phrases like "the G-Child"; 5) Chuck pointed out the bit about Lawrence Welk to me when I first started hearing "Regulate," and I haven't been able to hear that line any other way since; 6) The thought that Tom Jones might cover this one day—"Think I better regulate now!"; 7) The fact that I haven't got a clue what it means to regulate; 8) It's the only song of the entire G- funk era to employ the Noel Cowardish adjective "tad." (6.0)

(*Radio On*, 1994)

"Sabotage," Beastie Boys

I only know this through the video, and it's the one video in a thousand that has made me like a song I think I probably would have hated otherwise—videos routinely affect me by degrees, but they don't often perform alchemical miracles. The "Sabotage" video, though, is an amazing recreation of a specific kind of grade-Z action movie I remember, the kind that has been rendered obsolete by the huge budgets that go into action films today. (I take it that the grade-Z ones still exist in the straight-to-video market.) It makes me think back to two in particular, *Firepower* (1979) and *The Man with the Icy Eyes* (c. 1970). I can't find a listing anywhere for *The Man with the Icy Eyes*, but it definitely exists—I saw it two or three times in the early '80s on Global TV in Toronto. I think Keenan Wynn's in it, and it's as good a bad movie as I've ever seen. *Firepower*, which was playing at the Georgetown theatre when I was an usher there, has the kind of cast that gives resonance to the words "tawdry international intriguer": James Coburn, Eli Wallach, Sophia Loren, Anthony "Tony" Franciosa, George Grizzard, Vincent Gardenia, and, making it probable that someone's renting it out this very moment, O.J. Simpson. According to Leonard Maltin's synopsis, "Inane, complicated story has Loren seeking revenge for murder of her chemist husband." As far as I can tell, that's the same plotline as the inane, complicated "Sabotage" video—Sir Walter Stewart is seeking revenge for the murder of his chemist husband, but Nathan Wind and Vic Colfari want to keep him neutralized until they can get word back to Alasandro Alegré ("The Chief") that Sir Walter's on the prowl. The highlight is a spectacular shot of someone (Fred Kelly, I think) getting thrown off a bridge, maybe because he knew a little too much and was trying to shake down Vic. The camera hardly stops moving the whole time, and when the three of them—don't ask me which three, but that's how many are left standing—walk down the street in the final shot, you really feel like justice has somehow prevailed. (7.0)

(*Radio On*, 1994)

"Freak Like Me," Adina Howard

I like lots of obscene records, but very few which I'd call crude. (To me there's a difference: N.W.A. and the Angry Samoans are obscene, "Wynonna's Big Brown Beaver" and Sir Mix-a-Lot are crude, and don't ask me to explain the difference because I can't.) Before "Freak Like Me," I don't know that I've ever found a record both crude and beautiful. Barking dogs as a verb—it kind of makes censors obsolete, and there's probably more poetic imagery to be found in an average AC/DC record. But the dogs are spellbinding, and so is everything else about "Freak Like Me." There's the wah-wah, the Dre-like synthesizer, the compulsiveness with which Adina Howard pursues her hobby, the sharp rap in the middle—I could make a decent-sized list of all the rap interludes I've liked in non-rap records—and most of all there's the contentment behind "It's all good for me," the first hip-hopspeak to mean anything to me in a while. It took me forever to pick up on the concept of Gs—four issues ago, when Amy Linden referred to John Mellencamp as a G in her review of "Again Tonight," I thought she'd made a typo so I changed it to J ("Let's break 'em off another one of them J-hits")—but I've been right on top of "it's all good" since I first noticed it in Biggie Smalls' "Juicy." It's a resonant phrase, a grace note, and when I hear it now it's as the inverse of Charles Crumb's "How perfectly goddamn delightful it all is, to be sure." There's an acceptance behind the words which seems very real to me, and it finds a perfect—and perversely anomalous—home in this record. (8.5)

(Radio On, 1995)

"Misery," Soul Asylum

The fascination of "Misery"'s words aside, it strikes me as a major improvement over "Runaway Train" on sound alone. There's the sparkle of good pop music here, something I just could not hear in "Runaway Train." There's a part near the end where the harmonies get to be a little too precious, perhaps, but everything else falls into place—it only takes one dumb part to kill a delicate pop song, and "Misery" doesn't have any. As for what it all means, on that I go back and forth. At first I thought the obvious, that this was a self-deprecating joke on their surprise stardom. I like hearing the song that way, and the image of CDs rolling off an assembly line is a good one—unlike Henry Rollins, who can turn self-deprecation into an act of monumental purgation more agonizing than root canal work, "Misery" is smart, modest, and funny. Before long, however, I caught on to the other interpretation, the one that I've since read is causing the group some trouble—the Kurt Cobain/Courtney Love interpretation. That's where I start to have mixed feelings. Conceding that there's still truth to the song if that indeed is what's going on, the smugness and self-serving meanness of such an attack should be obvious—if that's all you have to say, I'd rather hear a blank, ambiguous "hey man, nice shot" and have it left at that. Soul Asylum must also have a formidable blind spot if they can't see a connection between the timing of their own success and the success of Nirvana that preceded it by a matter of months. (Maybe because they've been around for so long, they feel entitled to pretend that the connection doesn't exist.) And yet, because these contradictions seem so brazen to me, I've started to take an odd sort of enjoyment from the Kurt Cobain interpretation: it must have taken a lot of chutzpah to put such a song out, and the fact that it keeps me guessing and saying to myself "Does he really mean what I think he means?" is not a bad thing. I do think they're most likely writing about themselves. (7.0)

(Radio On, 1995)

"Shimmy Shimmy Ya," Ol' Dirty Bastard

More line-dancing—every time I turn on the TV, people are line-dancing. "Shimmy Shimmy Ya"'s about the weirdest song on this list, I think. I tend to find weird rap music much less off-putting than weird rock music—I'll stick with it in a way that I won't with rock, and in the end it usually has some appeal for me. This is no doubt because my idea of what rock music should sound like is much more inflexible; a rap song as generic as "Sick of Myself" I'd tune out instantly (something else that turns me off about "One More Chance"), but with Matthew Sweet I'm able to take pleasure from the familiar. Conversely, "Shimmy Shimmy Ya" is gruff, shapeless, off-key, and as confusing to me as Captain Beefheart. Captain Beefheart I can hardly listen to, "Shimmy Shimmy Ya" holds my attention the whole way. (6.0)

(*Radio On*, 1995)

"Scream," Michael Jackson

Most of "Scream" is a trade-off: the ugliest voice in pop music (when it turns into that guttural, strangulated thing) in exchange for a few seconds of Janet whispering, the usual there's-no-song-here problem for that one dramatic guitar break (which sounds like the opening of "Mama Told Me [Not to Come]"), all the nonsense in the video for the fact that it does look good, etc. It's not the worst single Michael Jackson's ever made, and it's a long way from the best. How much benefit of the doubt you give it in the end probably depends on the simple fact of whether you believe he was wronged or not. I'm very conventional on that point: my gut feeling is that he did virtually everything he was accused of doing. Believing this as I do, whether I'm right or wrong, it stands to reason that virtually everything he's done since in the way of confronting the charges—the televised press statement, the settlement, the interviews, the marriage, the petulance of "Scream"—has been kind of appalling. Since he may very well have been falsely accused, my reaction to "Scream" may not have a thing to do with the truth of the record. But I'm on no shakier ground than someone who concludes he was falsely accused and from there accepts the record at face value. I sat in with my Dad for a few minutes of a Peter Gallagher made-for-TV movie last month, and there was a line that sums up my feelings about "Scream" perfectly: "Your self-righteous indignation has made you persona non grata in this town." (5.0)

(*Radio On*, 1995)

some place back there

"Woo-Hah!! Got You All in Check," Busta Rhymes

My favorite song over the spring. Impossible to sing along to, but I had fun trying (and I always knew when a woo-hah was coming up). I think this makes for an infinitely more fascinating if-I-ruled-the-world song than Nas's—the guy who's singing it actually does rule the world, albeit from somewhere inside a rubber room, and now that he's taken over he's going to crush all our heads, like the character from the Kids in the Hall sketch. It also reminds me of a more famous TV sketch, the one where Gilda Radner's little-girl character used to rule the world from inside her bedroom; I can easily imagine that little girl jumping around and singing "Woo-Hah!!!" as pillows and toys go flying through the air. There's an alternate version of this that I taped off Much, one with Ol' Dirty Bastard, and although I don't like it nearly as much (the music is noticeably different), the video's worth seeing for the way it makes the rubber-room idea explicit. When Busta Rhymes was all over other people's videos as Buster Brown, he used to drive me up the wall. He hasn't really changed any, so I'm kind of in check when it comes to explaining my fondness for "Woo-Hah!!!" That little piano part that runs all through the record has a lot to do with it, and when it comes to call-and-response, I guess I'm temperamentally much more of a woo-hah than a hey-macarena or choo-choo person. (8.0)

(Radio On, 1996)

"Bulls on Parade," Rage Against the Machine

With some help from Al Franken, I think I know where this group got their name. Franken, referring back to the Thomas-Hill hearings, likes to point out how Strom Thurmond is the only guy in Washington old enough to refer to a microphone as "the machine." If you watched the hearings, you might remember the many times where someone would be giving testimony, and Thurmond could be heard squawking in the background, "Towinnama-sheen! Towinnamasheen!!"—ornery-old-codgerspeak for "Talk into the machine!" Strom was raging against the machine, and a fledgling group of angry young hip-hop fans was inspired by his tenacity. (3.5)

(Radio On, 1996)

interrupting my train of thought

"Fastlove," George Michael

A new and more mature George Michael—that's not merely déjà vu all over again, it's more like The NeverEnding Déjà Vu. This has been going on since at least "A Different Corner" (from when I only dimly knew who he was, but looking back at that pretty good single today, I can see how it was a song very much in line with where his career went from there). He's the hardest-maturing man in pop music, and if he matures any more, he's going to start befriending people like Andy Rooney and Gerald Ford; he's going to accelerate the aging process to a point where he kills himself with excessive maturity. That aside, "Fastlove" does have one of the funniest lyrics I've heard this year: "Why don't we make a little room/In my BMW/Searchin' for some peace of mind." I think that was the subtitle of the Thomas Merton book I read a few years ago. (4.5)

(*Radio On*, 1996)

"Pepper," Butthole Surfers

Before I lost interest in the Butthole Surfers after *Rembrandt Pussyhorse*—nothing to do with them, I just turned my attention elsewhere—I liked their trippier psychedelic side the best, a sound they'd obviously grown up with and could approximate well. The scatology of "Lady Sniff" seemed dumb and obvious to me; I liked "Hey," "Gary Floyd," and almost all of *Rembrandt Pussyhorse*, especially "Waiting for Jimmy to Kick," "Mark Says Alright," and their cover of "American Woman." "Pepper" is a continuation of that—patched together from "Loser" and the Nails cult-hit though it might be, it's still strange and exciting and great to sing along with, infinitely better than anything I thought they'd be doing at this point in time. At first I thought it was a song about a group of people who were all in love with this one girl named Diane, sung with the second syllable accented; there was a girl in Texas, she had magical powers of attraction, and she was the cause of all these spectacular car crashes and horrible unnatural deaths (like in *Carrie*). Well, sometimes I mishear—as you know, it's *dyin'* that they're all in love with, and dyin' and death tend to go together. So it's really a song about thrill-seeking nihilists, none of whom is named Diane. (I'm also guessing that it's about actual people that they knew, which would make it like Jim Carroll's "People Who Died," though much more oblique and less pushy.) But not everyone in the song's a nihilist, there are also those who like to bask in the sun and drink life in, except at certain points it seems like the two groups of people are one and the same. I don't know what it is they're trying to say—as the chorus points out, it's hard to look through other people's eyes and hard to know what you look like through theirs. But it all sounds great, especially the gorgeous sun-grope guitar. (8.0)

(*Radio On*, 1996)

"Pretty Noose," Soundgarden

The most bracing heavy metal I've heard since at least "Sweet Child O' Mine" (with which it shares a piercing bit of echo off the top, "alright-alright-alright-alright" taking the place of "cry-iii-iii-iii") and, for all I know, all the way back to "Black Dog" or "Whole Lotta Love." The sound of it hits me as a dozen different contradictory things at once: dense, clean, chaotic, beautiful, concise, brutal, just one big wash of drone and clang and swirl. Most of all, it has what "Sick as a Dog" and Hüsker Dü's best songs had, the thing that Metallica's kind of heavy metal never has, and what I didn't think "Black Hole Sun" had, either—some chime to it, some Byrds. I play it in the car all the time, and it affects me the same way that this kind of music, at its best, has affected me ever since I was a teenager: I look out the window at everything that's going on—a man walking his dog, someone buying a paper, kids hanging around a store—and it all looks absurd and slightly surreal. The song becomes soundtrack music, slowing the world down and turning everything on its head. (8.0)

(*Radio On*, 1996)

"Jack-Ass," Beck

Kaleidoscopic wah-wah that could go on a Delfonics record, low-register cowboy-folk vocal that belongs to 1970 (Skip Spence, Kris Kristofferson, David Ackles, others I've never heard—it's none of them in particular and all of them at once), and all my favorite words: drifting along, loose ends, puzzles, strange, the cool of the evening. It's like the Warren Oates character in *Two-Lane Blacktop* has come back 25 years later and made a record; he never got grounded, he's now in orbit. (8.5)

(*Radio On*, 1996)

interrupting my train of thought

"You Keep Me Hangin' On," Reba McEntire

A couple of years ago, I came across a Pam Tillis concert on the country video station. She had some well-known guests with her—Marty Stuart or Alan Jackson, I think, plus another woman. Tillis and her guests took turns on a Beatles medley at one point, and I recall that they did a pretty good job of it. When Tillis introduced what they were going to do—"We're going to do a Beatles medley now," or however she said it—she turned defensive and apologetic, as if the reaction from the audience was much less than she'd hoped for. This is how she reassured them: "Did you know that the Beatles were really influenced by country music?" Yes, they were, and I guess I don't blame Tillis for using that to try to win the crowd over; she had to say something. But the whole idea of someone having to legitimize the Beatles...How many people have covered "You Keep Me Hangin' On" already? I can think of two other hit covers, and Whitburn lists four altogether, beginning with Vanilla Fudge in 1967. That's the impression I got as I sat there watching Pam Tillis that day: New Country, especially when it comes to piffle like Confederate Railroad, or Brooks & Dunn, or Reba McEntire doing a Supremes cover—the stuff that's supposed to pass for lively and fun—is music made by and for people who are 30 years slower than the famously swift Vanilla Fudge. (4.5)

(*Radio On*, 1996)

"Free to Decide," Cranberries

Along with the Cranberries song, one of the most heavily aired videos on MuchMusic right now is by the Wild Strawberries, a Canadian band. There's another Canadian band, the Gravelberries, whose claim to fame is that one of its members is Mike Myers' brother. Haven't heard them. I was never a major Raspberries fan, though I do like "Overnight Sensation"—if you have their greatest-hits album, you know that a couple of old Mike Saunders reviews are quoted on the inner sleeve. Halle Berry, now her I love—if I were starting up a band of my own, I'd definitely consider naming it the Halleberries. Two of the last three N.L. MVPs were Barrys, neither of whom was Halle's ex-husband (but one of whom shares his matinee good-looks). The Cranberries deserve a less frivolous review than this one. I was at a barbecue this summer where their previous album was playing on the portable CD for a good hour. "This band sure has lingered" I thought to

some place back there

myself, and sitting there on a hot summer day, lingering's not a bad way to go. This one doesn't quite linger, but at least it doesn't lumber. There's a title that Metallica can use some day: "Lumber." (5.0)

(Radio On, 1996)

"Where It's At," Beck

This is about the same mythic place commemorated by Dobie Gray in "The 'In' Crowd," Petula Clark in "I Know a Place," and Fred Flintstone in "The Twitch." As someone who only owns one turntable and a telephone, I've only been to that place three or four times in my life, and I felt very uncomfortable there. I haven't been back since at least 1988. I do like "Where It's At," though, even if it took a little while. For all its surface similarity to "Loser," I think there's a major difference: whereas "Loser" appeared to be aimless but was actually quite precise, "Where It's At" strikes me as screwing around plain and simple. But that's OK—it's still very different from everything else on the radio, still the work of a likeable and surprisingly accessible eccentric, so I look past its pretensions and end up finding it borderline hypnotic anyway, especially the beginning. I'll never see Beck in concert, but having read what he likes to do with his lyrics when playing live, I've been working on some possibilities for "Where It's At" that I hope to pass on to him someday: 1) I got four Black Labels and a kidney stone; 2) I got Aesop's Fables and a dial tone; 3) I got nine Clark Gables and a David Cone. (7.0)

(Radio On, 1996)

"Walking Contradiction," Green Day

I'm surprised—after concluding that I'd probably always like Green Day a little without ever liking them a lot, this is easily my favorite song of theirs so far. (I seem to appreciate Green Day through the wrong end of the telescope: until now, I never thought they got any better than "Longview," while "Basket Case" was the only thing I didn't care for.) "Walking Contradiction" bridges the convincing punk-rock of "Longview" to the sweetness of "When I Come Around"; it feels wistful to me, much like "Hip Hop Hooray" did three years ago, and the way the chorus goes up a notch on the word "walking" is one of those great pop moments that can only be felt, not described. The same mood is reflected in the fool's-paradise expressions worn by the group in the excellent video, which unfolds like "Sabotage" choreographed around the travels of three Forest Gumps. (I have another theory about the video, a more pretentious one: that they're three of Nick Carraway's "bad drivers," blissfully making their way through life without ever noticing all the damage they leave in their wake.) MuchMusic provides director credits during its Friday countdown, and I couldn't help noticing the name on this one: Roman Coppola, Francis's son. I got three Green Days and a Corleone. (8.0)

(*Radio On*, 1996)

"The Difference," the Wallflowers

MuchMusic plays "The Difference" incessantly—five times a day, it seemed like, when I was doing a lot of videotaping and trying to track down songs from the list. It's as ordinary as can be, I wouldn't know what to say about it, but I can't resist trying to place Jakob Dylan on the father-son baseball spectrum. I'll do this from his end of the equation, not worrying about finding the right match for his father. You'd have to start with someone like Nolan Ryan or Pete Rose to do that, and until a couple of weeks ago, neither of their sons had even made it to the majors.

So: Jakob Dylan is definitely not Barry Bonds, Ken Griffey Jr., or Roberto Alomar. He will not be a first-ballot inductee into Cleveland one day. (Do they have a five-year waiting period there? A Veteran's Committee? I saw an ad in *Billboard* where a group of famous musicians was campaigning to get Johnnie Johnson inducted, much as a group of famous baseball players has been campaigning for years to get Ken Keltner into Cooperstown. On a related note still, I came across the following in a wire story on the movement to grant Mother Teresa official sainthood: "However, only five years after death can the bishop begin collecting proof of the 'heroic virtue and reputation of holiness' of a person.'" The Vatican, like Cooperstown, has a five-year waiting period.) Nor is he Moises Alou or Jose Cruz Jr., not unless he has much more to offer than "The Difference" or "One Headlight." Alou's had a couple of star seasons so far, and he should be good for at least a couple more; it's still way too early to say much about Cruz, but my conservative guess is that he'll hit upwards of 250 home runs in his career—I'd say there's a better chance that he'll hit a lot more than 250 than a lot fewer. But Jakob Dylan has already had a more successful career than Eduardo Perez, Tony's son, who turns 28 this year and hasn't done much of anything after five years in the majors. That leaves the great middle ground, lineup fillers like Brian McRae, Ed Sprague, and Bret Boone. These guys have all had their moments—Boone was great the year of the strike, McRae scored 100 runs last year, Sprague knocked in 100—but they're not stars, not even minor stars. They're just there, hopefully not too much longer in Sprague's case. (5.0)

(*Radio On*, 1997)

"The Impression That I Get," the Mighty Mighty Bosstones

I like equivocation. If I had my own hit single out, it wouldn't be called "Anarchy in the U.K.," I'd go with something more along the lines of "The Impression That I Get." Let's see... "If You Say So." "That Would Depend." "Well, I'm Not So Sure That's a Good Idea." "I Guess I Can See What You Mean." "Whatever, Nevermind." I'm pretty sure it wouldn't have anything to do with ska, but having my name on this would be OK—it sounded especially good as between-innings music at the N.Y.-Penn League game I saw outside of Cooperstown this summer. People need to be made more aware of the strange things that are going on at minor league parks all across America. At this particular game, the Vermont Expos vs. the Oneonta Yankees, hometown Oneonta players received a free sub from a local supermarket-deli whenever they hit a double. That's fine, except the PA announcer would come on and award the prize immediately upon the play's completion; as the player stood there dusting himself off, news of his free sub was boomed out across the stadium. There were four or five doubles hit, and every time the same ritual unfolded. One guy hit a triple, and he got a sub and a free haircut. I guess they had to throw in an extra little something, otherwise what would be the point of continuing on to third? (7.0)

(*Radio On*, 1997)

"Listen," Collective Soul

One of my projects next summer is going to be to invent a special dance for all these Collective Soul singles. I don't know what it will look like, but the Axl Rose serpentine move will figure prominently. While I'm at it, I might write a *Seinfeld* script:

Jerry: "They're true riff monsters, you know. I do hope you realize that."

George: "Monsters of the riff. Love to riff monstrously."

[A buzzer sounds.]

Jerry: "Yeah?"

Voice on intercom: "It's Elaine."

Jerry: "Come on up." (5.5)

(*Radio On*, 1997)

"Quit Playing Games (With My Heart)," Backstreet Boys

Just like with "Macarena," "How Bizarre," and the Beatles, we're a full year ahead of you in Canada when it comes to the Backstreet Boys. What happens is, the record companies fly all 25 million of us to the Northwest Territories, where we stand around in a circle and give thumbs-up or thumbs-down to a number of bands being considered for international stardom. That's why you've never heard of Scrubbaloe Caine; they never made it through the screening process. (5.0)

(*Radio On*, 1997)

"Return of the Mack," Mark Morrison

I've written before how much trouble I sometimes have trying to get a song's title from the radio. I heard "Return of the Mack" at least 10 times before a DJ identified it—I liked the song, so it was becoming rather maddening. I went ahead and dubbed it "Yolanda" after a while—exactly like Sarah, I was hearing "You lied to me" as "Yolanda," though I never thought to fill in the "Mae" part. I liked a Yolanda in grade 4, Yolanda Sluik, who was Dutch and a half-foot taller than everybody else in my grade. She may have been the first supermodel, I'm not sure. Anyway, "Return of the

Mack"'s as good as "This Is How We Do It." After all this time, I'm still not sure what a Mack is. If you were to draw a picture of what goes through my mind when I hear the word, it would look a little fuzzy and abstract. "What's that thing in the middle?" "That would be the Mack—it went away and now it's back." (7.5)

(*Radio On*, 1997)

"Your Woman," White Town

The Pet Shop Boys are an obvious precedent, but what this really makes me think of is "Baker Street" or "Year of the Cat": minor-key atmospherics writ large. Especially "Year of the Cat"—I could never be your woman" is as suggestive and enigmatic as I remember the Peter Lorre line being 20 years ago. (Truthfully, it completely baffled me for the longest time, until I heard Rick Dees explain that it was a straight guy writing about his unrequited love for a lesbian. Not exactly complicated, so I don't know why I missed that. When you start turning to Rick Dees to explain the universe to you, you may have a serious problem on your hands.) The part where the singer targets her highbrow Marxist ways is so brazenly pretentious, so wildly anomalous on the radio, that I actually love it. Slandering someone for her highbrow Marxist ways—in the annals of Top-40 spitefulness, it's not exactly "96 Tears," is it? "Your Woman" and "Wannabe" are the two songs I'll most identify with my half-year as a full-time teacher; kids were gung-ho for the Spice Girls, I connected more with White Town. (7.5)

(*Radio On*, 1997)

"If You See Him/If You See Her," Reba/Brooks & Dunn

I'd rate this lower if I didn't think the idea of a duet between a singer and a duo were so inherently funny. When Reba McEntire looks deep into her singing partners' eyes like you're supposed to with this kind of song, what does she do? It's probably like one of those terrible job interviews where you're in front of a panel and you have to remind yourself to keep moving your eye contact from one interviewer to another. Hank Kingsley: "Sex is not wrong...sex is a loving act between two or more consenting adults." (5.0)

(*Radio On*, 1998)

"Zoot Suit Riot," Cherry Poppin' Daddies

On behalf of the Coasters, Sly & the Family Stone, and the Clash, I would ask that this group publicly admit to having an improper relationship with the word "riot." (1.0)

(*Radio On*, 1998)

rain gray town

I think of myself as having two hometowns. There's Toronto, where I was born, and where I've now resided more than half my life, but there's also my Thomas Wolfe/*Bus Riley* hometown, the one where I grew up, went to high school, and presumably can't go back to, the hometown of everyone's imagination. That would be Georgetown, a small town—really small when I was a kid, still relatively small today—about 45 minutes northwest of Toronto. When I finished university and moved out in 1984, I figured that, beyond the usual family get-togethers, I was clearing out for good. Not so—I found that I continued to return there in some of my writing, first in *Nerve* and then (especially) in some fanzine pieces. (I eventually physically moved back there for a few years at the age of 30, when I started teachers college. Unexpected, humbling, awkward.) Obviously I had left behind some things that I hadn't quite resolved, things I wasn't even aware of until I started writing about them. Most of what lingered concerned high school.

There was a documentary I saw earlier this year at Toronto's Hot Docs Festival called *Beyond Clueless*. Basically, it was a massive collection of clips from 200+ American films set in high schools—all of them from the '90s and '00s, which ensured, the director explained, that he didn't end up with a John Hughes tribute. (Thankfully, I'll add.) I liked the film, but I couldn't relate much of what was there to my own high school experience. Which is funny, because in the big high-school piece that starts this section, I make the same complaint about the then-new *Dazed & Confused*, a film that gets better and better every time I revisit it. When it comes to cinematic depictions of high school, I'm apparently like *Seinfeld*'s Kramer and the velvet scrunchie: very particular.

Anyway, the whole subject was very much on my mind 20 years ago. Something will still, on occasion, catch me by surprise and get me wandering down that road again, but mostly I've found newer things to brood about these days.

Draw a social map of your high school or some job or other place, and, like, you know, how people talked, and stuff, and categories like "hoods" and "preppies" and "dirtbags"; or write about your life, or something.

interrupting my train of thought

I attended Georgetown District High School from 1974 to 1979, a time frame that puts me halfway between the incoming freshmen and the graduating seniors in *Dazed and Confused* (set in the spring of 1976, when I would have been finishing grade 10—high schools in Ontario go to grade 13). *Dazed and Confused* seemed somewhat hollow to me, but the problem is mine, not Richard Linklater's. If you look back at high school as an adult, with affection (or at least wry amusement) for what's universally silly about it, Linklater had just about everything right—not just the easy iconography, the music and the clothes and the language, but also a little of what was mean and petty and wasteful, the stupid humiliations that no one feels any nostalgia for. (*Fast Times at Ridgemont High* did a better job of dredging up the unfunny stuff.) But after spending two days searching through microfilm at the local library, I realize (not for the first time; I renew this realization every few years, triggered by something like this assignment) that in some ways I'm not really over high school yet, that what I feel about that time is still too mixed up to afford much humor or understanding. I know for certain that I'm not the least bit closer to being an adult today than I was when I left GDHS. That's the first thought that comes to me in trying to remember myself 16 years ago.

For one thing, I was too young. I started high school when I was 12, the result of a fall birthday and a skipped grade (from 6 to 8, which has to be the worst possible moment to move someone ahead; I don't think it's done at that late a stage anymore). I was too young, and too shy and socially inept to begin with. If high school can be plotted as a series of Erik Erikson-type obstacles that you're supposed to navigate successfully on your way to leaving with a good sense of self and a healthy psychological makeup, then I failed them all. Everything since has been wrong—out of order, incomplete, inauthentic. I didn't catch up then, and I still haven't.

The social map of GDHS (1,500 students total, about 200 in my graduating class) was exactly like that of every other high school. I don't remember all the names then in use for the different groups, but they were pretty basic, and I'm sure that more than a few of them are still around. They're all kind of dismal and crude anyway, so I'll recast them here as "sports people," "academic people," "sex people," "drinking people," "drug people," "good-citizen people," "invisible people," "misfit pariah people," and all the subcategories, shadings, and overlap therein. (I don't recall any great philosophical divide between the drinking people and the drug people.) The very best thing to be was someone who was a good student, who played on a couple of school teams, who was friendly and well liked, who drank but didn't make a career of it (that's what university would be for; to drink yourself stupid in high school relegated you to some kind of dark reprobate colony, like Wayne Thompson or Gary Blaskovic), who went to parties and who had sex (or who at least went out with someone, if it was possible to do the one but not the other—in 1979, unlikely), who seemed to float effortlessly in a world of their own. They were the most admired people in the school: John Wright, Nancy Phillips, Jennifer Thompson, Gord Miller, Heather Clarke. There were another 30 or so with only slightly less presence, a group that included all of our class's most beautiful girls: Karen Gregson, Chris Pekala, Sandy Smith, Michele Giesen, Charlene Cox, Marilyn Thorne, the girls who went out with guys who were already in university. At the farthest edges of the map were the misfit pariahs: Fergus Lewis and June Morris are the two that come to mind right away, though I might be forgetting someone just as obvious. (I make this cruel statement in the belief that both have gone on to become better-balanced individuals than I.) No matter how unfulfilling my own memories of high school, I would not have wanted to be Fergus Lewis. His account of those years would be much more interesting and unusual than mine.

    The simplest way to place myself on the map is to say that I was an academic person who fought against it. The one constant in how I did this, central to my friendships and to how I wanted to be viewed by others—the desperate need for approval that's the most destructive thing I took away from high school (or rather never managed to shed while I was there; it took shape long before)—was basketball. Grades came easy, but didn't mean anything; being on the basketball team, no matter how demoralizing it was to hardly ever play, or how much I dreaded the final posting during fall tryouts, was how I measured my place in school. (The dread of final posting: in grade 11 I was certain I wasn't going to be on the list, so the night before I phoned the coach at home—Gene Howland, my nemesis throughout—in order to feel him out. When he realized what I was up to, it turned into one of my worst phone conversations ever.) That two of my three best friends were fixtures on the team made being there that much more important. Acceptance, approval, and a place on the basketball team were inseparable to me.

    Or at least that's how it was for the first three years. Up until grade 11, I wanted more than anything to be one of the admired people in my class; I remember being preoccupied with things like the number of girls I could count on to say hello to me in the halls. I was sure that it was only a matter of time until I moved into that special group of 40 I mentioned earlier. But grade 11 was terrible—summed up by my either quitting or getting kicked off the basketball team (a little bit of both, really), though there were other traumas too—and by year's end it was clear that I'd been left behind in what seemed like an unspoken closing of ranks. Everything that mattered was going on elsewhere, mysterious transactions hidden from view. The school had rearranged itself in the space of a few months, and I was now a permanent onlooker.

When I think about my change in outlook from that point forward, the feeling I get now is one of deep resentment, of sourness and revenge. I built walls around myself: the emotional support of my three closest friends (Steve and Norm from the basketball team, Dave who I worked with at the golf course), the intellectual arrogance of knowing that school was still supremely easy for me at a time when it was finally starting to defeat some of those same people who'd shut me out, and the accumulation of various outside influences that were starting to make a lasting impression on me. There was music, of course: an obsession with Neil Young in grades 12 and 13 (especially *Everybody Knows This Is Nowhere*, *Tonight's the Night*, and "Ambulance Blues"), all the *Dazed and Confused* glop before that. (Al Green and the Carpenters, "Anticipation" and "Hello It's Me"—music from a slightly earlier time that most overwhelms me now—had been all but forgotten by 1979.) I was seeing all the famous American films of the late '60s and early '70s on TV for the first time, *The Conversation*, *Midnight Cowboy*, and all the Altmans, and they went a long way toward shaping me; I was most susceptible to things like *The Graduate*, *The Heartbreak Kid*, and *The Paper Chase*, romantic daydreams that spoke directly to the desire and sense of better-things-ahead I associate with that time. And although I was never much of a reader in high school, *Ball Four* and (big surprise) *The Catcher in the Rye* came along at just the right moment and had a profound effect. With all of that to hide behind—and also the inevitable drinking and messing around with drugs that I did with Steve—I spent much of my last two years being as disagreeable and abrasive as I could.

I went back to the basketball team in wade 12, but mostly so I could entertain myself (and Norm and Steve) making a mockery of it. I was Jim Bouton now, wildly overdoing the inane chatter, making a great show of fake sorrow after losses, closely observing all the petty maneuvering of Coach Howland. (I actually got an award for "team spirit" my final year, something that amused the three of us tremendously; maybe Gene was trying to one-up me in irony.) I especially loved to antagonize Paul Krowchuk and Bill Rivers, two of the team's stars. Inside the classroom I was even worse. There had never been a time when I was less than sure I was the smartest person in the room, and to that I now added pretension and meanness. I remember laughing my way through a particularly ludicrous history presentation by (a perhaps drunk) Gary Blaskovic one afternoon; when Mrs. Linney got called away from the room moments later, Greg Thoms stood up and suggested that someone needed to bash my head in, and that maybe he'd like to do it right there. (I picked up Greg hitchhiking a few years later and got along with him fine.) The full weight of my gee-whiz facetiousness was reserved for the likes of Ross Jeffrey (valedictorian) and Bill Kent, people whose big crime was being blandly friendly and more popular than I. As long as I had an audience, I was especially obnoxious toward Ross. Grade 13 was when most people started to settle down, to emotionally grow up; I got more and more unbearable, and I can see now where I was just getting warmed up for the next 15 years. My last act of what I thought was self-assertion, but was in fact self-negation, was an abrupt change in plans that winter to study English and film at university, rather than pursue the math that came so easy to me and which I loved much more than I was willing to admit at the time. It was the single dumbest decision I've made in my life, the perfect finish to an incomprehensible five years.

That was my high school. I've simplified the story, garbled it no doubt, and left out what I want to—it's impossible not to. When I say I'm not over it, what I mean is that I've never rid myself of the idea that I left without ever getting the chance to explain myself, to talk to and to get to know people whose friendship I obviously wanted very badly. This feeling that a part of my life was left unfinished has caught me up a few times in the intervening years, most vividly in a couple of instances involving classmates who had disappeared from the picture by grade 13. (That was something new and strange about high school: how someone you'd gone to school with for as long as you could remember would one day simply not be there anymore. The only time people left in the elementary grades was when they moved away, and it was always preceded by a certain amount of ceremony.) Denise Curtis was someone I identify more with my junior high than with high school—what Jennifer Thompson was to GDHS, Denise was to Centennial Middle School—but for as long as she was around, which I guess was until grade 11 or thereabouts, she was always among the most beautiful girls in my grade. When I moved back to Georgetown in 1990, I'd occasionally see her at the Shoppers Drug Mart where I think she'd been working for a number of years. The last time was around Christmas two years ago; I did what I always do, I turned away quickly without saying hello. A few months later, I heard from Dave (still a close friend) an absolutely horrible story concerning

interrupting my train of thought

Denise, the worst story I'd ever heard about someone I went to school with: similar to what happened to George McGovern's daughter recently, only worse because Denise lived through it, if you can imagine what that might involve. I was sure that Dave must have heard wrong—he didn't even live in Georgetown anymore, and it was only last Christmas I'd seen her—but I went to the library and found out he was right. This reached me like hardly anything ever reaches me anymore, and I immediately got it in my mind that I was going to send Denise the most beautiful tape I could compile, along with a long anonymous letter that would explain all the time I'd wasted and all the regrets I'd had since I used to look at her in grade 8 and wonder what it would be like to be friends with someone like that. Of course I never did: someone assured me it would be an extremely thoughtless thing to do (someone who I hadn't met until after university, who was not a part of my past), and I didn't need much convincing anyway, as the idea to do it anonymously should make clear.

The abrupt departure of Yvonne Burke in grade 11 was the one that really puzzled me. I'd been going to school with Yvonne since grade 1: for many of those years she was in my class, we accelerated together in grade 6, I went to a dance with her that same year (I can't remember if it was 11 or 12 words I managed to get out that night), we both got our middle-school letters, we danced at graduation that evening, we had classes together in high school, she'd always been around. To repeat something I've said too many times already, she was always one of the most beautiful girls in my grade; she was also as quiet and awkward as I was, which together with our common past made it easier for me to talk to her. Sometime in the middle of Mr. Moore's grade 11 calculus class, Yvonne started becoming very erratic—behaviour, appearance, everything—and within weeks of first moving to the back of the room, she left school and never came back. Obviously whatever happened had something to do with drugs, but as a full explanation this just didn't go together with Yvonne; there must have been more to it, something more complicated that led to a breakdown of sorts. A few years later, during university, Dave (again) ran into Yvonne at some country club where he was curling. She was perfectly fine—the way he described her was exactly as I remembered her before those strange few weeks.

That was a happy ending, but for someone as self-absorbed as I it was the same ending, the same feeling of unresolved sadness as Dave related the story to me. Since moving back to town, I'll sometimes take my bike out after the dinner hour, right around the time that dusk starts to set in; I'll invariably make it a point to ride by the houses of grade-school friends who moved away long ago—the Karolidis house, the Hutchinson house, the Lenski house—and I'll also end up gravitating toward Yvonne's house on Pennington Crescent, which, according to the sign over the garage, is still occupied by her parents. I have this idea that one time she's going to be visiting, and she'll be walking out to her car just as I pass by. She's not with anybody, of course, so we go somewhere to talk, and as best I can I try to recount what I've been doing since last that I saw her, try to make myself known like I never did the first time around. I explain that however normal or satisfactory the general path of my life might seem, the fact is I'm unhappier and even less sure of myself than I was fifteen years ago. That's the kind of drama I play out in my mind, and that's what I mean about not getting over high school.

(*Why Music Sucks*, 1995)

Spirit

The "Prelude - Nothin' to Hide" pick is mostly a nostalgic nod to one of my two favorite high-school al-bums (the other whichever Neil Young LP I most liked at the moment—it alternated between *Tonight's the Night*, *Everybody Knows This Is Nowhere*, *After the Gold Rush*, and *Zuma*). I must have listened to *Twelve Dreams of Dr. Sardonicus*, oh, two or three hundred times in grades 10 through 12—between Spirit and Neil, I think I single-handedly logged 31% of all human hours spent listening to David Briggs productions in 1977. My friend Steve and I followed the lead of the senior basketball team—good guys Mike Stankovic and Paul Nichols, plus Doug Lamb, who, uh, wasn't such a good guy—for some of the albums that dominated my life during that time, and they tended to be linked by their pot-related utilitarianism. Listening to *Sardonicus* today, something I made a point of doing in its entirety, was odd. I could have done a lot worse—it's about as song-driven as high-concept psychedelic art-rock ever got; just about every melody came back to me instantaneously—but I'm positive I would have had more fun had Cypress Hill been here to share the experience. And please don't ask me to explain the concept. Something to do with someone named Dr. Sardonicus—it all made a kind of intuitive sense 28 years ago.

(record inventory, 2005-06)

Samoans Leave Home

Worst job I ever had, worse even than my bad imitation of a conscientious office stooge, was a three-week stint back in Georgetown on the Divide and Conquer truck. This was a public works program devised to gather up glass, tin, and newsprint for the purpose of recycling. People left the stuff out with their garbage, and Paul Sargent ("Sarge") and I scooted around in a van and picked it up. No doubt the guy who thought up D&C was some dedicated conservationist who meant to do the world a big favor, but come Judgement Day, he'd have less to answer for had he spent his entire life travelling the country setting random forest fires.

Garbage pick-up, which you might guess is worse, isn't bad—not glamorous and somewhat hellish, but at least it's a one-dimensional kind of hell. You jump off the truck, toss the garbage up, and jump back on. Simple. D&C, on the other hand, is a multi-dimensional, eight-pronged kind of hell, implacable in its ability to invent new and ever more intricate tortures to drive you insane. Literally insane: a week or so before I was transferred to D&C, I witnessed the guy I was about to replace thrashing about in the back of the van, throwing glass and tin every which way, screaming "cocksucker this" and "motherfucker that," eyes aflame and near tears. It was hilarious. Little did I know.

As it turned out, D&C didn't merely entail picking, you had to further jump into the van's cabin and separate as you went along. Eight huge dump bins, four aside, lined the cabin walls for the glass and tin; newspapers were piled down the middle as high as they could go without toppling over. People were supposed to package the glass and tin neatly in plastic bags or bushel baskets, so it could be easily dumped; newspapers were supposed to be firmly tied up so they could be stacked solidly. Good luck on either count.

So picture: you roll up to a house with two bushel baskets of glass, one bag of tin, and three bundles of newspapers; before making it back on the van, one of the bundles breaks; newspaper flies everywhere, you grab as much as you can and climb on; stack the newspaper, then return to the bag of tin and try to break it open. The bag has been tied into the most intricate knot imaginable, though, a real Boy Scout work of art, and you can't get the tin out; you rip and pull and curse until you wind up and rifle the still-bagged tin into the bin; oops, wrong bin—better dig that out; meanwhile the van has been slowly creeping toward the next house, and this one has 12 bundles of newspapers, six little cardboard boxes of tin, and one glass bottle that someone has thoughtfully tied up in a plastic bag; you curse some more, start tossing up the newspapers that have been stockpiled for who-knows-how-long, get your answer when the headline LINDBERGH BABY KIDNAPPED passes before your eyes, miss the van with your toss, get a wave of nausea from the smell of rotting tin, miss the van as you attempt to jump on, sit on the ground as it pulls away.

That's what you do for the first six hours; for the next two, you transfer and stack the bundles of newspaper in a monstrous, cavernous trailer, trying to construct a solid wall as you push further out. Sometimes, after you've piled about a thousand bundles, the wall topples over. You start again. It's ninety degrees, your hands are raw from gripping string, and newspapers engulf you on all sides like the famous promotional still from *Citizen Kane*. After the newspapers are taken care of, the bins inside the van get dumped into bigger bins; attracted by the sweet, gooey smell of residue on the glass and tin, wasps swarm everywhere. The bins are heavy, they have to be lifted well into the air to reach the top of the bigger bins, so sometimes strength gives out and you miss. Oh well, you jump off and manually toss glass and tin up for the next little while. Finally, everything finished, you sit in the lunch room and blank out for 15 minutes before punching out—or, if you're me, you close your eyes and ponder the Angry Samoans: "There's nothing more you can leave behind/So forget about seeing, get into your mind/Everything looks better when the world is black/Grab a fork, make your first attack/LIGHTS OUT, POKE-POKE-POKE YOUR EYES OUT.

(*Nerve*, 1987)

Write about the first record you bought for yourself, why you bought it, what was going on in your life at the time; or write about some other early record, or not-so-early record, or recent record, or something. Or a book or a star or a movie, or anything else.

Rather than having any particular record I can pinpoint as my first, I really had three different kinds of "first records" from three different periods in my life. The first records of the collection I have now—the first records I bought upon consciously deciding to start a record collection, the new innovation being that I'd now make an effort to take care of whatever I owned—I bought around 1975, when I was 14: *The Worst of the Jefferson Airplane* and *Weird Scenes Inside the Goldmine*. From that point forward I've pretty much kept every album that's ever come my way, not just what I bought myself but also all of the dumbest promos and most inappropriate gifts, everything from the Raunch Hands to Skinny Puppy to Ted Nugent's *Weekend Warriors*. I sold about 30 or so art and metal albums from my high school days to a guy I worked with in the mid-'80s (I now regret even that), otherwise I've kept almost everything.

Obviously my contact with records started well before 1975. I can remember occasionally in the late '60s and early '70s pestering my mom to buy a certain album or 45; I'll call these my second set of first records, records that were manhandled voraciously and are now long gone. Among the titles I associate with that time are the Guess Who's *Rockin'* (which I needed for some kind of elementary-school party where we were all supposed to bring something; I badly wanted to bring in a cool and dangerous rock album, and the Guess Who's "Guns, Guns, Guns" was certainly very cool and dangerous), the "American Pie" 45, the first Partridge Family album (I used to set up a home-made drum kit in the corner of my room—pencil crayons for drumsticks, an old radio and books and furniture and the walls as cymbals—and bang away to "Singing My Song," a first-rate percussion workout for one of those Partridge drummers), Mashmakhan's "As the Years Go By" (probably the first record I purchased on my own), and *Ray Stevens' Greatest Hits*, the one that came right after "Everything is Beautiful" and had "Ahab the Arab," "Gitarzan," and Ray's other formative hits. I just loved Ray Stevens when I was 7 or 8, a passion I shared with my English friend Martin Young. What I remember about Martin: he had scruffy blond hair like Brian Jones and a chopped-off finger that he claimed was lost in a meat grinder, and he could make me laugh hysterically by jumping out from behind a corner and yelling "Wolverine!" in a way that sounded like a chainsaw starting up. I guess that helps explain why I found Ray Stevens so funny.

My absolute *first* first records were brought home by my Dad from Dell's Milk, the variety store he owned in the West End of Toronto through the 1960s. There were a couple hundred of these around the house, a mishmash of Nat King Cole, '60s easy-listening, Johnny Cash, popular soundtracks, CHFI's *Candlelight & Wine* series, Vicki Carr and Petula Clark, Harry Belafonte, Elvis soundtracks, and a number of pop and rock albums that were obviously brought home for the sole purpose of clearing some room in the store. Although I never officially claimed ownership of any of these records until much later—once I launched my own collection with the two albums referred to above, I began to incorporate a few of them in with my newer purchases; the entire lot of Dell's Milk records was finally junked sometime in the late '80s—I would regularly poke through them and take back certain titles to play on my portable. There were copies of *Beatles*

VI (accounting for the special significance that "Yes It Is" has for me), *The Best of Herman's Hermits* (ditto "Mrs. Brown You've Got a Lovely Daughter"), *Best of the Beach Boys, Vol. 2*, a Cowsills LP, *A Wild Pair* (a Canadian album shared by the Guess Who and the Staccatos, who later made stirring protest music as the Five Man Electrical Band), the Soul Survivors album with "Expressway to Your Heart" (very psychedelic in presentation, with a story on the back about how the group met during a near-fatal collision on a bridge), a few bubblegum-heavy compilations on the Syndicate label (Andy Kim, the Ohio Express, the Turtles, etc.), *The Who Sell Out* (all I really played from that was the bizarre "Monday-Tuesday" business before "Armenia City in the Sky"), and many others I've forgotten. A couple of the records in there were too weird to hold any interest for me— Love's *Forever Changes* and the Incredible String Band's *The Hangman's Beautiful Daughter*—which meant that they remained in good enough shape to later move into my own collection. There was also an album by the British Modbeats, and if I could have just one of those albums back now, that would be my first choice.

I'm almost positive the British Modbeats were not British—I believe they were Canadian, although they're not indexed in the one history of Canadian pop I have. I do know that their album is worth a small fortune now: at the opening party for a record store I used to work at, I overheard the guy whose label it came out on telling someone that he'd put a few copies aside and was waiting to cash in on them. (There actually are fanatical collectors of obscure '60s Canadian pop. At that same store, I worked with a guy who was one of the country's number-one collectors of Canadiana, Gerry Michaels. I once engineered a three-way deal between myself, Gerry, and the University of Toronto radio station whereby I got the second Chantels album, the station got a Squirrel Bait record, a Misfits record, and an Anthony Braxton record, and Gerry got an album by some people named Reign Ghost, a Canadian band he'd been mad for. It was a very complicated trade—I think one of us may have come away with a Triple-A shortstop as a throw-in.) The Modbeats album came out in '66 or '67 on the Red Leaf label, and the front cover had psychedelic balloon lettering and the group standing against a wall in dramatic pose, each Modbeat wearing flowered pants that (no exaggeration) must have been flared 2-3 feet across. All I remember are two songs: a cover of the McCoys' "Sorrow," and a faster thing called "L.S.D." I probably would have been intimidated by the group on looks alone, but "L.S.D." clinched it; if there was one thing that put the fear of God into me when I was eight, it was drugs. I was absolutely terrified of drugs.

It most likely started with stories I'd heard about some of the older kids from Rosefield Drive who were going down to the creek behind our subdivision and fooling around with drugs. If there was any truth at all to the stories, "older" probably meant 12 or 13 and "drugs" probably meant pot, but being a rather wide-eyed eight-year-old who was afraid of my own shadow to begin with, I was convinced that these drug-addled maniacs were going to abduct me and take me to their hideout down in the darkest recesses of the creek, where they'd shoot me full of hypodermics and have me hooked for life. The creek ran through a large undeveloped field that bordered the back of my own street and two other streets in the neighborhood; after hearing these stories, I would sometimes accompany one of my friends a few yards onto the flat upper part of the field, but I'd never go down below to where the drug people were. (This is not going to turn into a *River's Edge/Stand by Me* story: no dead bodies will turn up at any point.) To the other kids on the street, the creek was a place to go look for stuff or to take your kite out to, and in the winter it was for tobogganing. To me, it meant heroin and evil and death; there was something even grimmer about the image of drug-taking going on in the dead of winter, with everyone all huddled together shivering and strung out.

My drug phobia lasted from grade 3 until I got to middle school. I have three other distinct memories having to do with this. I remember Norm Allen's drug books—little government-type pamphlets that he'd gotten from his older sister, a pamphlet for each different classification of narcotic, with lots of distorted funhouse-mirror photos in the volume on hallucinogenics. Those photos had a tremendous impact on me. Norm lived on Stevens Crescent, and if every kid from your childhood was famous for at least one thing, Norm was famous for his bike: he was the first person any of us knew to get what was an extremely desirable model at the time, a Fastback 100 I think it was called, a low-slung orange thing that was unique in that it had five gears instead of three and a flat L-shaped seat instead of the then-popular banana style. I also remember getting an anti-drug poster I'd made (grade 4?) hung outside the library. It featured a very detailed drawing of Mad's Alfred E. Newman taken from a stencil I had, with the phrase—what else?—"What Me Worry? Me No Take Drugs" written across the bottom. I was definitely Nancy Reagan before my time, doing my part to keep the streets of Georgetown safe from the drug scourge that was sweeping through small-town Ontario in the late 1960s, even though the drug warning on the poster was actually secondary to the amazing drawing of Alfred E. Newman I'd been able to pull off thanks to the stencil. I would have been just as happy to have Alfred issue a stern warning against the dangers of cantaloupes.

rain gray town

The most absurd episode of drug panic I can recall was one time when I was walking home with my best friend John Karolidis. We had just turned the corner at Delrex onto Rosefield, less than a minute away from my house. As we walked along, someone came up behind us and said "Boo!" (I'm not substituting "Boo" for words I've forgotten; "Boo" was exactly what the person said.) It was Bruno Martina, one of the older kids who lived at the other end of Rosefield. I'd never spoken to Bruno, but I knew where he lived, I knew that he was big and bullyish and mean-looking, and in my mind he'd already been pegged as the living embodiment of all my worst drug fears. As soon as I turned around and realized who it was, I lit out for home running faster than I'd ever run in my life. I ran straight up Rosefield for a few more houses, flew around the corner onto Roydon, and never looked back until I was safely on our driveway. I then stood around waiting for John, who sauntered up some 45 seconds later—he had continued walking and talking with Bruno, whom it turned out John sort of knew through his cousin Louie. Can an eight-year-old have a deadpan sense of humour? John came up the driveway without saying a word—he just gave me a look that was the equivalent of wryly rolling one's eyes in disbelief. He later told me that Bruno had asked "What's wrong with him?" to which John shrugged "Beats me."

Beats me, too, but I know that the British Modbeats and "L.S.D." were a part of it, and later on *Go Ask Alice* and *The Marcus-Nelson Murders* would be a part of it (by then, phobia had given way to fascination and the first stirrings of curiosity), and there was just a general drug-scare tenor to the late '60s and early '70s that I was very susceptible to. It was more than enough for my imagination to transform an overgrown field into Needle Park, and 12-year-old Bruno Martina into some monstrous phantasm out of William Burroughs.

(*Why Music Sucks*, 1996)

"Stutter," Elastica

There are other songs I could put in this spot, but I don't have any stories about them; I have two stuttering stories. The first goes back to 1982 or 1983, the time I tagged along with my friend Norm for an interview he was doing with John Hammond Jr. Because I've never had any feeling for blues music, and because I hate the kind of musical snobbishness that holds blues to be somehow purer or more important than pop (a view obviously held by Hammond), and most of all because Norm was writing regularly for *Shades* and I hadn't yet written for anyone, I primarily went along to see what trouble I could cause. I got my chance when Hammond dismissed the Jefferson Airplane as having only played to 13 and 14-year-olds around the time of *Surrealistic Pillow*. What he said may or may not have been true—he was there, I wasn't—but I started to argue the point with him, and I wouldn't let up. Hammond was a stutterer; at one juncture I jumped in too soon with my next harangue, causing him to snap at me viciously that if I'd only let him finish, I might begin to understand the truth of what he was trying to explain to me. It's not a pleasant memory. Neither is the other episode (I'm saving all my happy stuttering stories for a whimsical Calvin Trillin-type collection), although there I was only a witness—the grade 11 health class where Bill Jensen (stutterer) was quietly destroyed by Scott Flaherty (teacher). We were watching one of those bad high-school sex filmstrips, with the usual laughter and unsolicited commentary making its way around the room. As the filmstrip went on, it became clear that Flaherty (then a first or second-year teacher) was losing control of the class. I can't remember if Bill actually said anything himself—not very likely, I'm sure it must have been Jeff Frenette providing most of the comedy—but he was laughing as much as anyone else, maybe even more since he didn't need to stutter when he laughed, and this provided Flaherty with an opening to rein the rest of us back in. He asked Bill what was so funny; Bill tried to answer but couldn't get anything out. Flaherty—a sleepy-eyed late-'70s buddy-buddy type, Joe Walsh as a gym teacher—calmly waited for an answer, and when Bill was finally able to complete the word "Nothing" after a minute or so, Flaherty started to ask him some more questions: where did Bill live, what was his phone number, etc. Flaherty went on for three or four minutes, after which the class was perfectly quiet again. Of course I regarded Flaherty as a fool after that, but I'm not as judgemental now as I was before I started supply teaching. (I'm still a little judgemental; it's hard to relate the story without some of that creeping in.) While I haven't yet taken to seizing on kids' most obvious deficiencies as a means of class control, when I find myself in situations where I'm in over my head—which happens no more than two or three times a day—as often as not I make bad decisions on how to get out.

(#10, year-end ballot, 1995)

rain gray town

Kiss

Whenever I start comparing notes with anyone on the best live shows I've ever seen, the one I'm most inordinately proud of claiming as part of my "heritage" is Kiss, Blue Oyster Cult, and Artful Dodger at Toronto's Varsity Stadium in 1977. Yeah, I guess I should have been listening to the Sex Pistols and the Ramones at the time, but the town I grew up in was still very much operating on standard dazed-and-confused time in 1977; I think a small underground network of Cars and Devo fans might have infiltrated my high school the following year, but that was about it for punk rock. I'm not even totally sure who was with me at Varsity Stadium, other than that there were three of us and my dad wasn't one of them. I saw a lot of great club shows through the '80s, but Kissapalooza '77 was a benchmark, the one show that most makes me feel a part of my favorite musical decade of all. And now, if you don't mind, I'm going to give myself a round of applause. The band says I deserve to.

(record inventory, 2005-06)

Ambulance Fever

My old high-school friend Steve recently e-mailed me the following, with no accompanying words other than a "Too bad no sound" subject heading:

http://www.youtube.com/watch?v=0df4vyeFhEo[2]

By "no sound," I guess he meant actual voices; I think the song that plays overtop for the first half works just fine.

I don't want to write too much here, because if the video should get pulled, anything I say won't mean nearly as much without the visuals. I learned from the Obama blog how tenuous YouTube links are; I think about half the video I embedded has since vanished. (Truthfully, I'm still waiting for YouTube in general to drastically curtail access. I use it regularly in the classroom now, not just for Ed Sullivan clips and the like, but also for science and math—it all seems too good to be true.)

I will say that this gets as close as anything I can think of to what it

---

2   Still up five years later; take a look at it to get a sense of what I'm rambling about here.

was like to be in high school in my hometown of Georgetown in the mid-'70s. *Dazed and Confused*, if you will, except it's not a movie—this is the thing itself. I feel like I should recognize most of the faces, but other than what I think is one of the Bratkin sisters around the 3:20 mark, I don't recognize anybody. I'm about five years younger than the people here. And this wasn't my life in a literal sense, in that my friends and I did our drinking and drugging in our own little universe that mostly ran parallel to the one documented here. (Adam Goldberg's triangle in *Dazed and Confused* makes for a rough analogy.) But in a much deeper sense, I lived this exactly. I've tried to write about that time on many occasions, in *Why Music Sucks* and elsewhere. I think I caught some of what it was like, but I just can't write well enough to put into words what's above. What the Dead Sea Scrolls or a newly unearthed Robert Johnson recording might be to someone else, that's more or less how I feel about this footage. Not to over-dramatize or anything.

Of special interest: right at the five minute mark, two people walk past G&S Television, where 35 years ago I bought the albums that launched my record collection.

(homepage, 2009)

"Theresa's Sound-World," Sonic Youth

I might have this, I honestly don't know—it's obviously Sonic Youth, probably from between *Bad Moon Rising* and *Daydream Nation*. I have both, but except for "Teen Age Riot" I don't know either album at all. (There are three instances on the tape where I don't recognize something but think I might own it anyway. I've decided I won't check these songs until after I mail in my comments.) Or maybe it's from *Sister*, which I don't have. In any case—and in keeping with my humorless-drudge tastes—it's my favorite song on the tape. It brings to mind spooky driving-after-dusk music like "Riders on the Storm" and "Diane"; I think it's even superior to those two great songs. I hear it as the perfect opening for the third part of the three-part film about my hometown that it was my life's ambition to make 15 years ago. Part One, set in 1972, has the kid-like openness of *My Life as a Dog*, but none of the tragedy; the soundtrack consists of Al Green, "Doctor My Eyes," "Hello It's Me," Badfinger's "Day After Day," Bread, the Stylistics, Carole King. Part Two, set five years later, covers the high school period I wrote about two issues ago; music includes Cheap Trick's "Downed," "Rikki Don't Lose That Number," "Sick as a Dog," and lots of Neil Young.

It's like *Dazed and Confused*, but not as funny and twelve times better. In Part Three, ten years later still, there's a return to the town after a lengthy absence. It's the you-can't-go-home-again part, with the Sonic Youth song playing overtop the slow twilight drive through town that opens the film, something like George Amberson's walk through his hometown towards the end of *The Magnificent Ambersons*. Many of the buildings and local landmarks are the same, but everyone's gone and everything looks strange now.

("Blindfold Test," *Why Music Sucks*, 1996)

long journeys wear me out

I was tempted to title this section "Middle-Aged White Guy Tries to Figure Out Things," but I've been trying for a certain allusiveness with the chapter titles, and it didn't feel like that one would fit. The section begins and ends with moments of acute racial self-consciousness, and in between I get caught up in an election and a candidate. Make of that as you will.

One decision I had to mull over in terms of what would go into this book was whether or not to include anything connected to the 2008 or 2012 presidential elections. Almost everything in here having to do with them is transitory of-the-moment stuff—process, conflict, scandal—and such concerns tend to evaporate almost instantly. (I have no illusions about being a serious political writer, or even about being any kind of a political writer at all; I did come out of 2008 with the idea that I might make a good political strategist.) That's one problem; the other, familiar to anyone who got swept up in the excitement of 2008, is how much of a slow-motion ordeal Obama's two terms have been, whether you place the blame on him, on the other side, or somewhere in between. (Still sympathetic, I'll draw the line at least two-thirds of the way towards the other side.) Some of what I wrote in 2008 will seem quaint or naive or worse. Which is fine. That's how I felt at the time, and I'm glad I didn't stand to the side and will myself, in the name of realism or pre-emptive resignation or whatever, into not feeling that way.

So the armchair election-watching stays, and I thought that would go together well with my 30-year attempt (going back to Schoolly-D's first album) to understand why I'm attracted to, and sometimes repelled by—often both simultaneously—a certain kind of hip-hop record. Which I thought (again, rather naively) might become a thing of the past through Obama's presidency. No—even based on my very tiny sampling these days, that story continues.

Alexander O'Neal

Largely against my wishes, I watched this show from a spot very near the stage. I prefer hanging back for a couple of reasons: the simple matter of having space to move and breathe, and the fact that the closer I am to a performer, the more I feel compelled to look like I'm having a good time. The latter particularly came into play with O'Neal, who continually admonished the audience to yell "Party!" and wave their hands in the air. Now, I couldn't have been enjoying his performance more, but not even Gowan could get me to yell "Party!" So I began to feel self-conscious, which, in this context, means conspicuously white. And paranoid: every time I made eye contact with O'Neal, I was sure he was going to stop the show and say, "Hey everybody, we got a guy over here—that guy right there—who's not yellin' or clappin' or anything. He's not doin' dick all—get him the fuck out of here."

(*Nerve*, 1987)

Schoolly-D

Salt-n-Pepa are a perfect example of the way my hip-hop timeline is almost always in a state of permanent erosion. When "Whatta Man" and "Shoop" were on the radio, I remember thinking how much more alive and interesting they seemed than "Push It" or *A Salt with a Deadly Pepa*. A couple of months ago I bought a dollar copy of *Very Necessary*, and "Whatta Man" sounds even more dated to me right now than "Push It" did in 1993. I've made this point already as I work my way through this, but I bring it up again because Schoolly-D is the exception that proves the rule. I hardly ever listen to him anymore, but on the rare occasion when I do go back to his first LP, "P.S.K." and "Gucci Time" sound as weird and as menacing as ever. The slow-motion drugginess of both the production and Schoolly's delivery are primarily what keep those songs vital for me, and the shock-value of what then amounted to a breakthrough in lyrical filth still counts for something too. I'm aware that Schoolly wasn't the first to go down that road, but he did generate a lot of debate at the time by upping the ante significantly. These days, I can listen to 50 Cent celebrate anal sex on mainstream radio while driving to work in the morning. I'm glad to say I still feel a degree of shock when stuff like that is done convincingly enough, which it is in 50 Cent's case. Not appalled—I'm even more glad I haven't reached that stage yet, which'll be a good time to stop paying attention altogether—but still somewhat shocked.

(record inventory, 2005-06)

"Crossover," EPMD

I don't want to rewrite my "Pop Goes the Weasel" comment, but I would like to know who, specifically, they're talking about. (Which, to 3rd Bass's credit, wasn't a problem.) Color Me Badd's name seems to come up; fair enough, I don't like them either, but have Color Me Badd traded in their "hardcore" roots? P.M. Dawn, probably, but I'd ask the same question. Kris Kross? Let's hope not, that'd be silly (it would also be called "Krossover"). So who else, post-Vanilla Ice (I assume they're not reaching back that far for their condemnation), could they be referring to? Can't be Heavy D., because Heavy D.'s down on crossover too. Must be Garth Brooks—that's it, they're a little disturbed about Garth Brooks. There's an excellent song on the first EPMD album, "Get Off the Bandwagon," that could be interpreted as an attack on the same process. It's a weird song: lots of echo, stuttering bassline, and that desultory mumble that first brought EPMD to prominence. "Crossover"'s not bad, but it's basically a more palatable version of the old EPMD cleaned up for radio. That's fine—I'm starting to believe that even at this late date, rap may sometimes be off-limits in even those radio formats that pretend to be inclusive, and that complaints to that effect may be as justified as they are ancient. (The specific example that convinced me: on a "Weekly Top 40" from last month, 38 records were played, none of them rap, while A.L.T. and Kris Kross were merely listed as occupying such-and-such a slot. Kris Kross! I wish I knew how to calculate random chance—as coincidences go, it was pretty coincidental.) So in no way can I fault EPMD for feeling the pinch, especially as they've been around for a while. But as for trying to deflect attention from their own makeover by pinning the blame on others, that's another story. (5.5)

(*Radio On*, 1992)

"Fantastic Voyage," Coolio

I'd never thought of "Hot Fun in the Summertime" as anything but what it sounds like, a blissful celebration of summer, so it was weird for me when I read the entry on it in Dave Marsh's singles book, how it made him and others envision "fire trucks, national guardsmen, rocks, rifles, and Coke bottles refilled with gasoline." It wasn't so much that he suggested this as a possible way to hear the song, it was his matter-of-fact declaration that this was in fact how he heard it. Not to sound naive, but I'd never considered such an interpretation—other songs from the same period, yes, that's sometimes all you hear, but not "Hot Fun in the Summertime." This has to do with age: I was eight when the record came out, and I've continued to hear it as the same eight-year-old ever since. I mention this because I can't see any eight-year-olds of today experiencing a similar disorientation 20 years from now over "Fantastic Voyage"—the lyrics make it pretty clear that the song's mood is one thing and its story another.

In late July, I posted one of my periodic letters to *The Toronto Sun*, a publication which agitates me enough that I'm addicted to it—Ridiculous Newspapers and the Men Who Love to Hate Them. The letter had to do with a George Clinton interview, and an editorial that followed it two days later. In the interview, Clinton said a few words that newspapers don't like to print: "fuck," "motherfucker," "shit," "dicks," and "n_____." (My letter had nothing to do with Clinton, who was funny in context; it was what the newspaper did with his words that caught my attention.) As the interview appeared in print, the first three words were dashed ("f_____"), the fourth turned into "(chests)," and the last was left intact. The follow-up editorial, written by one of the paper's bad movie reviewers, complained about how silly it was to be dashing obscenities, and that the only objectively offensive words in the English language were racial epithets. This I agreed with—except for some reason the editorial never made mention of what was allowed to stand in the Clinton interview, bizarre when you consider that this was precisely what the writer was supposedly addressing. So I wrote them suggesting that they simply print what people say, otherwise their editorial selectivity ends up raising questions about what the *Sun* does and doesn't consider offensive. The letter wasn't published, as has been the case with all but one of my letters to the *Sun*—they like to play little games, they just don't want anyone to figure them out.

I'm trying to adjust to the way "n_____" is just becoming part of the scenery, something else that goes back to childhood—like most kids, I think, I learned very early that it was something you just didn't say. I believe I called the black kid living down the street one when I was five or six, and I have a lingering sensation to this day that I knew—or was made to feel, by my parents or by him or by somebody—that I'd said the worst thing in the world. I can't say for sure that this happened, but I have some kind of memory pertaining to it. I don't want to overdramatize, and I know it's not an uncommon anecdote. In any case, the intense unpleasantness of the word stayed with me; if I force myself, I can say it in order to quote someone else, but even that doesn't come easy. The cruelty of the word aside, it's almost like a deep-seated neurosis with me, one that I think a lot of blacks would find hilarious.

Through sheer inundation, the word seems to be losing its taboo value. Even though that's logically a good thing, it's also what I'm left to grapple with—it's impossible for me to feel that it's a no-big-deal word, so I have to gauge how it affects me according to the circumstances. (Perhaps someone black might say that I don't want it to lose its taboo value, that I want to keep that around in case I ever want to revert to my five-year-old self and use it on someone. All I can say is that wouldn't be true.) If you go back to *The Godfather*, where it turns up once or twice, it's jarring; in *Menace II Society* (an excellent film, with the best opening scene in recent memory), it must account for 5% of the screenplay. It doesn't bother me in *Menace II Society*—I don't think it serves its purpose any better by being there in such quantity, but it is there for a reason. On the first Schoolly-D record—which maybe started all this—it was kind of spooky; on the first N.W.A. record, it was closer to comical. A lot of rap records it's there to impress, and that's just annoying; on some rap records, it hardly makes any kind of an impression at all. On an alternate version of "People Everyday" that I bought, it's all over the place and I can't figure out why; on the radio version of "People Everyday," which I initially misinterpreted until I heard it played without the splice that one local station had inserted, it's used once and used meaningfully. "Fantastic Voyage" is maybe a landmark in that it's the first time I can recall a record this popular making such upfront use of the word: four times I count, plain as day all of them, and the Top 40 station here plays it uncensored (as it should) all through the day. (The dance station and MuchMusic both take it out.) And this is where the whole subject becomes even more complicated for me: in a record like this, where every detail is vivid and the delivery has a force and a confidence (and a casualness) that jump out at you—where you know you're listening to a great record and get carried away by it—the word isn't merely defensible, and it doesn't even do to say that it's necessary (especially because it's not; if it had never been put there in the first place, I wouldn't notice its absence and I wouldn't be writing all of this). It's actually exciting: it excites me, just like I think it excites Coolio. (9.0)

(*Radio On*, 1994)

O.J. Panel

It's almost over. For most of the summer I only watched the trial for minutes at a time, usually dividing my attention with whatever else I was doing at the moment. The peak of interest for me happened early, the week of Fuhrman's testimony, which happened to coincide with my March break. After that the proceedings settled into a steady background hum, always there but not requiring full-time attention, a routine part of the day like any other. (There were occasional flare-ups, the discovery of the tapes being the most obvious example, which were as wild as the Bronco chase, and they'd always have me back watching full-time for a couple of days; like Michael Corleone, I wanted to go straight but they kept pulling me back in) Much as Nicole Simpson and Ronald Goldman were quickly abstracted out of the picture, O.J. himself seemed to disappear before too long: it's all about the lawyers, the labyrinthine array of oddball witnesses, and the small industry of TV analysts which set up shop along the way. Most of the talk I hear comes from three sources: Van Susteren and Cossack on CNN (who *Nightline*/hostage-crisis-style got their own TV show out of the trial), Philibosian and Abramson on *Nightline*, and the once-a-week Larry King group comprised of Jack Tenner (judge), Milton Grimes (defense attorney), Dick Thornburgh (prosecutor), and Gerry Spence (character). Without getting into Larry King himself—I've had a few people tell me they despise him; although there are certain things about him that irritate me, generally I think he's OK—his O.J. panel is excellent. All four are advocates, as is virtually anyone you'll hear talking about the trial on TV, but none of them maddeningly so. Thornburgh argues for the prosecution, Grimes for the defense, and Tenner (prosecution-leaning) and Spence (defense-leaning) are more in the middle, but they're never pushy or abrasive about it, they all concede points to the other side, and you never feel like you're just watching paid surrogates, a feeling that's come over me with more than one supposedly impartial trial observer. Most of all—and I'll skip the standard apology for trivializing murder, as it's long past the point where it's still possible to trivialize anything about this affair—they're entertaining. Tenner and Grimes are the best odd couple this side of Nomo and Lasorda: Tenner's avuncular and Charlie Weaverish, Grimes is intense and soft-spoken, and they play off each other like a Sanford and Son of the lawyering trade. Grimes has a terrific deadpan sense of humour—quoting him doesn't begin to capture how funny he can be—while Tenner's a hoot-and-a-half. When it turned up that one of the defense witnesses was Tenner's former son-in-law, King asked Tenner if he still liked the man: (extra-long pause, wheels turning) "Let me call my daughter and get back to you on that." It took me a while to warm to Spence, but now I enjoy him—if he's not quite Sparky Anderson in the annals of folksy philosophers, he's certainly a lot more fun than Ross Perot's pathetic act. Thornburgh reminds me of Henry Fonda in one of his political roles, with an easygoing manner that provides perfect ballast for the rest of the group. If you're still interested in the trial, but the minutiae of DNA charts and the never-ending procedural slowdowns are much too much for you (as they are for me), then the King panel is a good way to keep up. (I imagine they'll still be on at least through the end of October.) Here I am now, entertain me—I'd make a lousy juror.

(*Radio On*, 1995)

Is prejudice against "poor white trash" the last acceptable prejudice for liberals/progressives? If so, why do you think that is?

The answer is yes, at least as it applies to what I will and won't say myself. "White trash" is the one ugly epithet I'll sometimes let slip out. I feel bad about it afterwards, but then I'll go and say it again two months later. Sometimes I just think it; I use it a lot in imaginary conversations I play out with my noisy neighbour George, who works nightshift and boozes up with his hockey friends and calls everyone "buddy." These conversations always end with me calling him an ignorant white-trash buckethead; when he tells me to go fuck myself, I ask him where he learned the two-syllable word. It's a phrase that goes hand-in-hand with the part of me that's still a pretentious snob.

(*KITSCHener*, 1997)

"You," Lucy Pearl

We've got a new "urban" station in Toronto, FLOW-93.5. (Arty on *The Larry Sanders Show* after being informed by the network that the Wu-Tang Clan are too urban to be booked: "Well, I could call up my good friend Lenny Kravitz—he's only half urban.") They're off to a good start: lots of stuff the other three dance-pop stations don't play, but always accessible enough that it never feels like work. (In other words, lively album tracks from popular dance and hip-hop artists, while I've yet to hear any Disposable Heroes of Hiphoprisy/Me'Shell Ndegeocello nonsense—which explains why *Now* magazine dismissed the station a couple of weeks ago.) One strange thing was that for a while, it seemed like Snoop Doggy Dogg could be heard on every seventh record. I was hearing five or six minimum, either from his own album or in a supporting role like here. "You" is the one that stood out. It was getting a lot of play before it suddenly disappeared, so the rating might be a little low. I don't know how exactly the group arrived at Snoop Doggy Dogg as the logical collaborator on a sweet mid-tempo ballad. They must have gotten drunk and played word-association: "Romance?"—"Snoop Doggy Dogg." "Devotion?"—"Snoop Doggy Dogg." "Time, love, and tenderness?"—"Snoop Doggy Dogg." (7.0)

(rockcritics.com, 2000)

"When the Last Time," Clipse

Most of the hip-hop I hear that's preoccupied with scaring me barely even registers anymore, but these guys really do sound as heedless and as criminal as they set out to. They've got five, ten, fifteen girls jammed into their limo, everyone's all liquored and drugged up, and even though the girls are ready and willing, the nasal vocal and sinister blips make it sound like gang-rape anyway. In the middle of all the chaos, two lovers' eyes meet: "Her head's spinnin' and my head's spinnin'/Mine from juice-and-ginnin', hers from neck-and-chinnin'."

(#6, year-end ballot, 2002)

"99 Problems," Jay-Z/"99 Problems," Danger Mouse

Jay-Z's original was easily the song that most knocked me out this year, and after coming to DJ Danger Mouse's version late and spending a couple of weeks with it, I'd have to say it's every bit as good. (Just to make sure, I got out the Ouija board and consulted with retired Jay-Z scholar George Wallace: "Ain't a dime's worth of difference between them," he concurred.) Of hip-hop's two polarities, socially-minded versus novelty—Public Enemy vs. Tone Lōc, more or less (my points of reference are so up to date)—I've never thought one was inherently better than the other. There's stuff I love and hate at both extremes, and anyway, Public Enemy had jokes, and Tone Lōc had some very philosophical—well, Public Enemy had jokes. Having said that, at a time when 97% of the hip-hop I hear is in-the-club-this and in-the-club-that, and every video I see has the same Bluto Blutarsky surrounded by the same six gyrating Pam Griers, "99 Problems" probably would have caught my attention just by virtue of having a narrative and some connection to the actual world the rest of us live in. But it's so much more than just what-it's-not—it has the authority and mastery of "Ohio," and the Rick Rubin original is the hardest hip-hop I've ever heard on mainstream radio. (Almost too much so: past a certain volume that's lower than what I usually like to play my favorite radio hits at, it simply becomes too distorted and I have to turn it down). Jay-Z's complaints about radio stations not playing him are a little melodramatic—he's all over Toronto's 93.5, and really, who cares anyway—but his confrontation with the MFL is brilliant, a high-wire act pitched somewhere between mock-Stepin Fetchit and Johnnie Cochran, conjuring up the Coasters (the cop is pure "Charlie Brown") and Sammy Hagar (bet *he* wouldn't have been pulled over, and he'd have been clipping along at well over 60) along the way, with a spectacularly withering "uh-huh" from Jay-Z buried somewhere in the back-and-forth. The verse that sends him to jail, well, I'm still trying to negotiate my way through that one. I wore out "Helter Skelter" in high school, but DJ Danger Mouse jolts it back to life like he's John Travolta resuscitating Uma Thurman in *Pulp Fiction*. If only he'd overdubbed one line, just to fuck with the head of one very old Beatles fan sitting in jail: "You crazy for this one, Charlie!"

(#1, year-end ballot, 2004)

"Was a Time," Whigfield (2004)

All the melancholy white people, where do they all come from? All the melancholy white people, where do they all belong? Not on—well, I guess I can't say "radio," since radio barely exists anymore (my Jay-Z comment notwithstanding, even I've started to burn my own music, and I always figured I was one of the last people participating in these polls who got his new music from the car radio), so I'll call it the "pop consciousness" instead, which is just a pretentious way of saying what-people-pay-attention-to. Whigfield had a big hit 10 years ago with "Saturday Night," but now they're relegated to the fastest-growing genre in pop music, That Which Is Insufficiently Hip-Hop. They must still be newsworthy somewhere if this managed (via a friend) to reach me, but Saturday Night for music like this, for the time being at least, seems to have given way to a somber, very uncelebratory Sunday Morning. Watch out, Whigfield, the world's behind you.

(#7, year-end ballot, 2004)

"George Bush Doesn't Care About Black People," Legendary K.O./ Gold Digger," Kanye West

The timing of the Kanye West single—if I remember correctly, it was starting to get a lot of play in the couple of weeks leading up to Katrina—had to have been the most politically serendipitous since the release of *The China Syndrome* right before Three Mile Island 25 years ago. I specifically mean West's chorus, which was just waiting there for anyone who wanted to do something with it after Katrina (hinging on a word I'm always reluctant to quote), and also, of course, his televised condemnation of Bush in the immediate aftermath. I only caught it on replay, but it was something to see how nervous and agitated West was as he forced himself to say what he wanted to say; it felt like the only such instance since Sinead O'Connor's *SNL* debacle where a pop star had actually departed from the script for a vertiginous leap into no-man's land. (If nothing else, I hope we're at least in agreeance that West's ambush was more surprising than Fred Durst's war-is-bad bombshell a few years ago.) Legendary K.O. takes the template of a great record and some controversy and fills in all the details, with his first order of business (title notwithstanding) to change West's "George Bush doesn't care about black people" to "George Bush don't like black people," a much harsher indictment that happens to scan much better in a song. Funniest line easy is "Five long days, five long days, and at the end of the fifth, you're walkin' in like *'Heyyyyyyyy,'*" and "He would have been up in Connecticut twice as fast" is pretty great too. I don't know if we'll ever hear from Legendary K.O. again or not. Senator Bobby had a cover of "Mellow Yellow" out within two months of "Wild Thing" in 1967, but the moment has already passed for a "Brownie, You're Doin' a Heckuva Job" follow-up.

(#2, year-end ballot, 2005)

"Mr. Me Too," Clipse

I don't know if Michael Richards' meltdown will be good or bad for charmers like Clipse: the ugliest word in the English language has regained its taboo value after years as ho-hum-part-of-the-scenery, and sure enough, I got a listener complaint when I played this on the radio two weeks ago. I'm 95% sure the caller was black, and seeing as he asked if I'd play some Captain Beefheart or Frank Zappa instead, I'm assuming he was bothered by "Mr. Me Too"'s barrage of N's rather than all the F's. (Or maybe not even that—his specific complaint was that his kids were listening.) Which is fine—it's a word that should upset people, and if black comedians and black hip-hop artists are being put on alert by Al Sharpton, that's a good thing. But, for better or worse, when all the hate comes packaged in something as musically arresting as "Mr. Me Too," it'll always have a strong pull on me—and now that the taboo's back in place, the pull is that much more visceral. Additionally, there are some great bits between all the N's and the F's. I love "Bof'us laughin'" when the singer and P-Diddy deplane in Aspen, and nobody comes up with better verbs than these guys—"juice-and-ginnin'" and "neck-and-chinnin'" on "When the Last Time" a few years ago, "dunce-cappin' and kazooin'" on "Mr. Me Too."

(#4, year-end ballot, 2006)

"Upgrade U," Lil Wayne

Snoop used to wear a Maple Leafs sweater during his "Gin and Juice" heyday, but, as far as I know, "Upgrade U"'s the first time Toronto's resident sports institution—as mythical around here as the Yankees or Packers, the difference being we've been in a 40-year slump—has made it into actual hip-hop rhyme (setting up my favorite line of the year: "But I'm a champion/Where's the fuckin' *Rocky* theme?"). Every year, I revisit this same place: I continue to be fascinated with my fascination with this sludge. I'm tempted to say that with something like "Upgrade U," hip-hop is officially into its *Exile/Riot* phase, all that Christgau stuff about anomie and layers of murk, except that that probably already happened 20 years ago on Schoolly-D's first album. The layers get uglier and druggier all the time, though, and to that end, I can hear the appeal the schlocky horror-show sample from Beyonce's original might have had for Lil Wayne. It almost functions like Elvis's "Let's get real, real gone for a change," except here the invitation reads "How low? This low."

(#5, year-end ballot, 2007)

March, 2008

CNN's playing some footage of Clinton in Mississippi the other day. She's addressing a presumably mostly black audience, the two men standing on either side of her black, and she's acknowledging that Obama has a lot of support in the state—"As he should!" She pays tribute to Medgar Evans. There's some obvious uncertainty as she speaks, a hesitation, as she tries to find the words that will finesse her way around...what?

(election blog, 2008)

Hillary Mash-Up/Jeremiah Wright

I sometimes ask Scott Woods to put together audio for my radio show, and he always exceeds expectations. Here's a Hillary mash-up he's pieced together from some horror-film sound files. It's a perfect summary of where the campaign is at right now—waiting, waiting, waiting, peeking warily through splayed fingers, wondering what's about to jump out of nowhere. NAFTA, Samantha Power, Michigan/Florida, Rezko, and now Elmer Griff, Friendly Neighbourhood Preacher. This one's worrisome.

It doesn't really matter if Wright is more or less saying things that have been said many times before, just more stridently and theatrically. A reasoned analysis won't be enough to put the story to rest. Obama's post on Huffington's site yesterday, and his television one-on-ones last night, were all perfectly rational responses to the situation, but I've still got a bad feeling. The Fox interview is an omen of where I fear this may be headed. The interviewer was very insistent about getting one thing on the record: if Obama had been subjected to similar sermons from Wright on an ongoing basis over the past few years (as opposed to one or two isolated examples, as Obama argues), would he have left Trinity church? After a couple of attempts, he got what he was looking for: Yes, Obama assured him, he would have left the church if that had been the case.

You don't have to be a genius to see what's coming next: countless reporters combing over every single Wright sermon since 1990, and matching what was said against recorded evidence of Obama's presence or non-attendance. If a pattern emerges, watch out.

Jesus, I hate religion.

(election blog, 2008)

long journeys wear me out

Sirius

My sister and her fiancée bought me a subscription to Sirius for Christmas, and I've basically parked myself on Patriot; it's like eavesdropping on some parallel universe that you've heard lots about but never really experienced up close. (I could maybe extend the rationale to *Godfather* territory, the idea of keeping your friends close and your enemies closer, but I'm just not passionately political enough to make such a dramatic claim.) In the early part of the campaign, when I think it was generally assumed Clinton would eventually prevail—up to and including Super Tuesday, let's say, before Obama took 11 in a row—all the focus on Patriot was on her, and whatever was said about Obama was neutral at worst, with occasional hints even of being caught up a bit in the swoon. No more: Mike Church (the "King Dude" or some such thing) repeatedly referred to Obama as a clown yesterday, in between affecting a "Negro accent" as he did a bit where he read fairy tales as delivered by Wright. Quite disgusting. Sean Hannity and Mark Levin haven't, from what I've heard, devolved that far, but they have gone full-tilt on the hysteria front. If it does end up Obama and McCain, there will be the usual two campaigns being waged. There'll be the largely high-minded one for public consumption, the one where they shake hands at debates, reiterate again and again how much they admire one another's public service, and pick over details of the war and the economy. And then there'll be the shadow campaign, the subterranean one that exists on Patriot, and I couldn't even begin to guess how ugly that one will get.

(election blog, 2008)

Scrabble

I was playing online Scrabble yesterday—don't ask—and my opponent laid *cling*. "Lol," I typed into the chat window, "Barack's word." (Shameful confession: when playing Scrabble or backgammon online, I will, on occasion, use the "lol" acronym, usually on the heels of a tepid attempt at humour. It's a lot quicker than typing in "That was sort of clever, but you'll have to do a lot better before I actually laugh.") As soon as I did, I wondered if the response would make me regret doing so. It's a site where the person you're playing could be from anywhere in the world: England, Australia, Israel, South Carolina, or 15 minutes up the road from where I live. If it is someone from South Carolina, I thought, it might be someone who likes Obama, and takes my comment one way, or it might be someone who doesn't, and takes it very differently—and if that's the case, brace yourself for the worst. Thankfully, after first expressing confusion, the person related she was from Canada and not completely up on the election. Close call. I should have immediately abandoned any thought of winning the game, and just tried to get "bitter," "lapel," "sniper," "pastor," and "elitist" onto the board. Especially "elitist," a 50+-point word I've never played; the letters are so common, I've probably had it sitting on my rack dozens of times.

I lost the game on the final play: *insole*, with two blanks.

(election blog, 2008)

Wright's NAACP Address

And then there's the good Reverend, who I'm convinced will turn up on *The Surreal Life* five years from now, after America has learned to love him as the crazy uncle Obama dubbed him as a few weeks ago. When I turned on CNN last night, after Wright had finished delivering his NAACP address, the news people were gushing, calling the speech funny and wise and demonstrably unthreatening. Well...I think I caught about 15 or 20 minutes' worth on replay. Really, the totality and the specifics of the speech don't matter; all that matters is what the media choose to extract from the speech, which will probably be collapsed into four or five clips. If Wright's educational theories—primarily that black children learn differently from white children—get a lot of play, that's going to be a problem. I don't think his Kennedy and Johnson imitations will be a big hit either. It's not so much that there was any meanness behind Wright's mimicry, it was more on aesthetic grounds that I object—the imitations were kind of inept. It will be pretty funny, though, to see conservatives get all indignant over JFK and LBJ being mocked.

A caller on Hannity today mistakenly referred to Wright as "Reverend White." That's not a Freudian slip, I don't think. I'm not sure what it is.

(election blog, 2008)

Wright/Thomas

I'm somewhat encouraged by today's big Clinton defection—could be an anomaly, or could be looked back upon as a major turning point when all of this finishes. I've also been thinking about Clarence Thomas. In a post above, I mentioned that I had no great emotional investment in the Thomas-Hill showdown 17 years ago (17—amazing). But I was definitely riveted by the proceedings, and I also had a strong opinion as to who was telling the truth: Hill. I based my opinion on a) her credibility as a witness, and b) a logic matrix I worked out with regards to Thomas's contention that he didn't watch Hill's testimony.

I don't know of any compelling reason to revise my conclusion today, least of all Thomas's bizarre record of never actually speaking up in session; I forget the exact time-frame, but he hasn't offered an oral argument, or even a question, for a number of years, behaviour that to me would be consistent with a man who knows he doesn't belong there. Nevertheless, Thomas's famous charge of a "high-tech lynching" has been in the back of my mind these past few days. There are two clear points of intersection with Obama-Wright. In both cases, it was one African-American being trotted out from the past to bring down another African-American; if you're one who suspects nefarious orchestration, you can almost hear the words "But the act of betrayal must be by somebody black, too much suspicion will be raised otherwise" whispered in the background. And each case plays to one of the two great boogeymen that have always driven white America's fear of black America: black sexuality in Thomas's case, angry black militancy in Obama's.

I really don't like talking about this stuff, and rarely do. But I think I have some (perhaps unwarranted) new-found respect for Thomas after the events of last week.

(election blog, 2008)

Conundrum

For all the battering Obama's been subjected to since that breakthrough night in South Carolina when he was still walking on water, I think one thing remains more or less as true today as it was then: the Republicans really aren't sure how to run against him. Sometimes Wright/Ayers/San Francisco seems to be the way to go, but then something like that congressional race in Mississippi will strongly suggest otherwise. So there they were yesterday, flailing away on three different fronts: Bush in Israel, an anti-Michelle (!) ad in Tennessee, and Karl Rove addressing the NRA. (I'll give Huckabee a pass on his lead balloon at what I assume was the same NRA event. He earned some markers for his sanity and civility over Wright.) I suspect the Republicans are going to have a real fat-kid-in-a-candy-store problem from now until November: they're going to be running against the first black presidential candidate ever, a deliberative intellectual with an unconventional background, a young guy with big ears and a name that's allusive in all the wrong ways, and even though they know they ought to tread lightly around all that stuff and "stick to the issues," they just won't be able to help themselves. One after another—the President today, some mid-level advisor tomorrow, the candidate himself next week—they're going to dive right in and self-destruct.

(election blog, 2008)

Jesse Helms

He may have gotten his wish: he didn't live long enough to see the one thing he never wanted to see happen. You can never be sure with politicians. Maybe Jesse Helms believed very little of what he publicly pronounced, at least with regards to race; maybe he just clung to an opening that would always ensure he got one more vote than the other guy (apparently about his normal margin of victory for his five senatorial wins). A quote from David Broder upon Helms' retirement in 2001 suggests otherwise: "What really sets Jesse Helms apart is that he is the last prominent unabashed white racist politician in this country—a title that one hopes will now be permanently retired."

In any event, the world was passing him by. After Iowa, North Carolina was Obama's single most crucial win. And he got it, if you remember, by winning not just 90% of the black vote, but also a not-insignificant 35% of whites. Still a large disparity, but one that is moving in the right direction. Helms' infamous "Hands" ad from 1990 is being mentioned up-front in a lot of today's coverage. I don't find it as creepy as Bush I's Willie Horton ad, insofar as the Horton spot appealed to voters through insinuation and code; the argument posited by "Hands" is right out in the open, and you either reject it or accept it. Which might be a convenient moment to bring up what I believe is really one of the taboo subjects of Obama's candidacy: why does he have such consistently strong support among university-educated voters? One theory is that this dovetails with his supposed elitism, and another is that, because educated voters are presumably better off financially, they're less reluctant to hand over the economy to someone with minimal experience. What you're not allowed to say: Obama is the smarter, more forward-looking vote, and educated voters as an aggregate are smarter than those who aren't.

The guy behind the "Hands" ad, Alex Castellanos, has been a regular commentator on CNN the past few months. He seems affable enough, but his résumé is worth remembering.

(election blog, 2008)

Half a World Away

There's a new McCain ad that's been the subject of some back-and-forth on Sullivan's site. I think it's pretty effective, but then I find almost anything that evokes the chaos and antagonisms of the late-'60s inherently dramatic. I suspect it falls woefully short of actually bringing any voters over to McCain, though. It parallels, in a way, today's weird Jesse Jackson flare-up. I had to go online to find out exactly what Jackson had said; Wolf Blitzer was stepping so lightly around specifics, you'd have thought he gave a full recitation of George Carlin's "Seven Words You Can Never Say on Television." Pretty mild, in actuality, so seeing Jackson have to immediately embark on the Grovelling-Apology Tour was a little depressing. How so? I had the distinct feeling that the apology was less over what was said than a symbolic acknowledgement by Jackson that he's well aware he is no longer the most important black public-policy voice in America; Barack's the guy, nobody wants to hear what I have to say right now, and I need to remember to stay out of the way. Even his son said as much: "His divisive and demeaning comments about the presumptive Democratic nominee—and I believe the next president of the United States—contradict [my father's] inspiring and courageous career." Rough translation, right out of *The Godfather*: "My father's way of doing things is over—it's finished. Even he knows that."

I think McCain and Jackson are both confronting something I experience all the time with my students (not to mention a lot of younger teachers) when I start talking about anything from the '60s or '70s. Excepting one or two of them (if I'm lucky), nobody cares—not at all, not in the least. Or as Steely Dan put it, those days are gone forever, over a long time ago.

This is one of the reasons Obama looks to be headed for a sizeable victory, and all in all, that's a good thing. And installing someone as president who's still fighting the Viet Nam War in some (understandably large) corner of his mind—installing Travis Bickle, to exaggerate for effect—is obviously not desirable. Still, I don't like the idea that all that old footage of marching hippies and National Guardsmen is now viewed as politically quaint, or the thought that it will induce widespread yawns in a large segment of the electorate. Something gained, something lost.

(election blog, 2008)

New Yorker cover

Best controversy since Jeremiah Wright—first really good one of the general.

I think it's a brilliant cover: *Dr. Strangelove* comes to mind, Country Joe's "I-Feel-Like-I'm-Fixin'-to-Die Rag," *The Manchurian Candidate*, anything where somebody said, "Let's take everything that's floating around out there and follow it to its logical conclusion—this is what we're all thinking about, right?" (David Remnick was on CNN today—he'll be everywhere in the next few days—and drew the more immediate parallels with Stewart and Colbert.) I realize there's a broad spectrum there as to the objectives of the creators: Kubrick's ridiculing what's on the screen, *The New Yorker*'s ridiculing not what's on their cover but the paranoid mindset that fantasized it into existence.

I've already heard a couple of Obama operatives express their dismay, one calling for (yawn) a boycott of *The New Yorker*. They seem to be worried about the part of America that's not going to get the joke. It must be news to them that they probably won't be getting many of those votes anyway.

(I've only looked at online scans of the cover so far—I'll buy a copy when it hits Canadian newsstands. I get the feeling it's like Dylan's *Bringing It All Back Home* cover, where you want to comb over it really closely for additional clues. I want to see if there are titles for those books sitting on the left-hand shelf. I'm hoping Barry Blitt, the artist, made one of them *Favorite Sermons of the Reverend Jeremiah Wright* or something like that.)

Two days later, and, having barely sampled the fallout, I'm even more convinced of the sublimity of Blitt's *New Yorker* cover. I really wanted to hear Hannity's reaction—and believe me, no one's been peddling some of

Blitt's iconography harder than Hannity the past few months; not the Muslim angle, but the flag-burning and Michelle-as-secret-Angela-Davis have been just below the surface of a lot of his ranting—but didn't feel like sitting in my driveway in a parked car at four in the afternoon. Anyway, what could he possibly say? I bet he's somewhere close to Mark Hemingway's petulance in *The National Review* yesterday, which to me translates as "How dare you make fun of us making fun of you." Obama's response on Larry King last night was appropriate; he expressed guarded appreciation of *The New Yorker* as an institution, then more or less shrugged off the cover. That so many of his supporters are indignant, though, that baffles me. (One thing that makes this such a good controversy is that it's actually controversial: over 6,000 posts on Huffington's site, which is amazing using the rest of the comment-counters as a barometer.)

(election blog, 2008)

Celebrity

This must be an especially gratifying election for American Muslims. It's like one long *Seinfeld* episode: "Let me state categorically and unequivocally that I am NOT of the Muslim faith—not that there's anything wrong with that..." I don't blame Obama for this.

Let me backtrack a bit on my last post. I think I'm usually pretty aware of possible subtexts in how Obama has been portrayed these past few months—by Hillary, by the media, and now by McCain. When Karl Rove called him "arrogant" a few months ago, the meaning behind his words seemed obvious to me, and I wrote about it. But until I took in some of the fallout from Thursday's race-card flare-up on CNN, the connection between Obama's remarks and the Britney/Paris ad hadn't occurred to me. The ad was so inane on the face of it, the possibility of it conveying anything beyond McCain's petulance flew right past me. But Donna Brazile, Roland Martin, and probably a whole lot of other people are raising the question: why Britney Spears and Paris Hilton rather than Tom Cruise and Brad Pitt (or Oprah Winfrey and Tiger Woods)?

Hmmmm...worth considering. Obviously, the ubiquitous tagline "I'm X and I approved this ad" doesn't mean that X also conceptually engineered the ad, so I wouldn't even doubt that in McCain's eyes, it's strictly an ad about celebrity and nothing more, but that whoever dreamed up the ad in the first place had a dual purpose in mind. I'll stand by what I wrote about how Obama should handle the issue, though—stay clear. If the subtext is indeed there, whoever notices will either be appalled or will buy into it, and if it's the latter, it's not a vote that was going to be won anyway. If it's not there, or if the viewer is oblivious to it (like I was), then you're just creating problems for yourself for no reason by bringing the subject up.

I don't know if this is a blip or an opening shot. Mr. Yes We Can, meet Mr. Yes I Can and Mr. Yes He Did[3].

(election blog, 2008)

Obama Embraces Elitism

I've come to the conclusion that Obama is fighting a losing battle on the elitist-celebrity front, and that the time has come to adopt a Britt strategy of brazenly transforming perceived vulnerability into unabashed celebration: "This is who I am, America, now love me." (And in the final analysis, America does love celebrities, right?) In that spirit, his arrival in Denver needs to be choreographed like the greatest Busby Berkley musical ever. He descends onto the stage from above, a stunning blonde on each arm, 75,000 chanting groupies in sway, Joe Walsh's "Life's Been Good" blaring from the sound system: "My Masarati does one-eighty-five/I lost my license, now I don't drive/I have a limo, ride in the back/I lock the doors in case I'm attacked." And just to drive the point home, the Republicans can relocate their convention to that neighbourhood supermarket where McCain knocked over all the applesauce, bringing them ever closer to the common folks.

(election blog, 2008)

Bike Ride

Posts will slow down until Obama's numbers pick up. Standing watch over this death-by-a-thousand-paper-cuts phase of the campaign isn't much fun.

I took a bike ride down the Lakeshore into Port Credit earlier today. I stopped for a hot dog, and the vendor, noticing my Obama hat, pounced. The guy was somewhere in my own age range, early 40s maybe; he looked a little like Charles Napier, the guy from all those Russ Meyer movies...I mean, the guy from *Silence of the Lambs*. His complaints began with Obama's inexperience, and the fact that he isn't smart enough to handle the presiden-

---

3   Mr. Yes I Can = Sammy Davis, Jr.; Mr. Yes He Did = O.J. Simpson. The original post had accompanying photos.

cy. I countered, completely off the cuff, that he probably stood alongside Clinton as the smartest guy to run for president in a long time. What was my evidence, he wanted to know. Well...He was a Harvard law instructor; that would seem to suggest a certain level of intellectual facility. (Got that one wrong—Obama was a law student at Harvard, but it was the University of Chicago where he taught.) Doesn't mean anything, I was told, especially seeing as he got there because of preferential treatment. We kicked that around for a while, then Obama's other shortcomings began to make their way into the conversation. He brought up the subject of "bro' culture" two or three times (including the charge that Obama had sold crack, which is news to me), and also something about "the family" that would follow Obama into the White House—he wasn't clear on that one, but he seemed to be referring to some rumoured extended family that was part of the package. He especially disliked Michelle Obama, and would be more amenable to Barack if he were married to a white woman. I pointed out that he'd be politically dead if his wife were white, and that seemed to amuse him.

The guy was very politically engaged—he knew a lot about American politics over the past 40 years—and he was especially fixated on the recent developments in Russia. I think I've accurately conveyed about 30 minutes' worth of back-and-forth.

As I suggested yesterday—and even though it's tiresome and counter-productive to talk about it—race is still the unknown factor in all these polls, just as it will be the unknown factor in November. What percentage of the American electorate shares a mindset somewhat close to this guy's—5%? 15%? More? (If he's giving voice to some percentage of the Canadian viewpoint, it ain't gonna be better Stateside.) If it's even 10%, that means Obama would have to draw his winning 50.1% of the vote (forgetting about the electoral college for a moment) from the remaining 90% of voters—which would mean, essentially, winning 55% of the vote among people who are open to voting for him in the first place. I guess you could say that if 10% of the electorate is black, that more or less neutralizes the write-off 10%, except that now Obama would have to win better than half the remaining 80%, and he'd have to do so without the African-American base that was so crucial throughout the primaries. I'm just picking these numbers out of the air, but I sure hope they get out the white university vote when it counts.

(election blog, 2008)

Mark Levin

Hell-hath-no-fury department: Mark Levin was something to behold on Patriot tonight. I caught about 10 minutes' worth, consecutive calls from what seemed to be Obama supporters. (On right-wing radio, anything less than total deference to the host pretty much indicates you've infiltrated from the other side.) The first guy, black, had "stupid" and "moron" thrown at him, the second (pronounced New York accent) was treated to "dummy," "moron" (popular, that one), "dope," and "lowlife"; both were cut off. And Obama? An "idiot," whose acceptance into an Ivy League school mystifies Levin in view of his "drugged-up" high school years. If you find such stuff weirdly compelling, and subscribe to the Vito Corleone theory of keeping your friends close and your enemies closer, there are podcasts online.

(election blog, 2008)

From the Hills of Wasilla

It was good...and it was weird. I took a quick look around, and Tracy Flick seems to be the most common comparison among the dread Angry Left; I kept thinking of Edith Prickley. More tomorrow. One thing's for sure—they've totally blown the community-organizer vote.

My favorite moment early in the evening (I missed Huckabee and Romney) was when Carly Fiorina promised that McCain was going to prepare a full evaluation of all government programs and post his findings on the internet. This is identical to a promise he made 10 weeks ago, just before he discovered the existence of the internet, except I believe the original idea was to disseminate the information via carrier pigeons.

The strangest disconnect of all, something I've been fixated on the past few weeks: education, education, education. Better schools. School choice. School vouchers. Charter schools. Education, education, education. Standards. Accountability. Merit Pay. Global competitiveness. Education, education, education. Children are entitled to the very best education we can give them. Education means everything. Education, education, education. Go out and get an education—it makes us whole. We mean it. We really do.

Just make sure you don't get an education from Harvard. That doesn't mean shit—it's about as low as a human being can sink.

(election blog, 2008)

Muslims

I should say, by the way, that Obama's pig-in-lipstick line doesn't bother me much; Palin continues to seem so uber-silly to me that, on the merits, they're entitled to put her down as sarcastically as they wish. (The tactical wisdom of doing so is another issue.) I winced more at Obama's Mohammed-the-cab-driver line, which, not so surprisingly, hasn't generated any indignation at all. I've come to the conclusion over the last few years that in Canada and in the U.S., the last group you're allowed to make fun of with virtually no repercussions is Indians, Arabs, and (more generally) brown people from the Middle East. That's more than one group...I don't know of a term that links them all together, so I hope that's clear enough. Letterman will make the most tasteless jokes about cab drivers, turbans, and personal hygiene—often it's a three-for-one—and it's no big deal. Or when Mujibur and Sirajul used to come on the show in a running bit, or Apu from *The Simpsons*. Mujibur was really funny, and so is Apu, but could you get away with either if their ethnicity were something else? I doubt it. Obviously, Obama wasn't making fun of his hypothetical Mohammed—he was aiming for the complete opposite—but the contrast of Bad Muslim = Terrorist/Good Muslim = Cab Driver was awfully clumsy, to say the least. He seemed to be a lot more focused in the clip I saw today.

(election blog, 2008)

Post-Palin/Biden Debate

Fourth quarter, clock ticking down: "Our opponent...is someone who sees America, it seems, as being so imperfect, imperfect enough, that he's palling around with terrorists who would target their own country." (I lifted that from a news report; I assume as originally delivered it was "pallin' around," perhaps even "gall darn it pallin' around.") Oh, man...Just for fun, I hope someone gets a chance to follow up: "Tell us what you know about the Weathermen, Governor, or what you know about 1968. Tell us a little bit about John Carlos, Curtis LeMay, or Creedence Clearwater. Tell us a little bit about something. Tell us a little bit about anything." The response from Obama's campaign yesterday was too tepid to bother quoting, but I'll again defer to their strategic discipline. If I'd been in charge, I would have blown the whole election.

(election blog, 2008)

Right Side of History

When Ichiro was chasing the single-season hits record a few years ago, a friend of mine didn't want him to break it. Why? Because George Sisler, who'd held the record for 70-some years, was a much better player than Ichiro, and records should only be held by superior players.

I agreed with him up to a point—if it had been Joe Shlabotnik threatening the record, a player of absolutely zero distinction having a historically fluky year, I would have been rooting for the record to stay with Sisler. But Ichiro, a few years into his career by that point (many years, if you counted his time in Japan), was clearly a great hitter. Overrated a bit, almost certainly, but great nonetheless. From there, it came down to one simple question for me: would you rather witness history, or would you rather read about it in a book?

One of my favorite clichés is "the right side of history"—it has a nice ring to it, and I think it describes a meaningful distinction. Unless something stunning unfolds on Tuesday, Barack Obama will make history. I can't vote for him, but I share something with all the people who will: I'll feel very good if he wins, and, yes—and I realize how self-righteous this sounds—I'll feel like I was on the right side of history in rooting for him.

Some people rooting against him have acquitted themselves well—if you've been following closely, you already know who they are. Others haven't, and if Obama wins, I hope the full weight of their reaction to Obama's candidacy stays with them for a long time. If nothing else, lots of video and audio evidence will linger.

"History? I was there, and I wasn't there. Basically I spent 10 months yelling and screaming like a scared little child."

(election blog, 2008)

The Best Man

Withdrawal: I'm sitting at the computer today, checking Huffington and Real Clear Politics and all the other sites that have become part of my life the last few months, and I catch myself wondering, "Why am I doing this?" The handful of people who've been looking in on this page regularly will soon be asking yourself the same question, if you aren't already.

The most exciting moment of Tuesday night happened Wednesday morning for me. As an Obama win became certain, I arranged for my overworked and underpaid engineering staff to grab a network call off YouTube and e-mail it to me as an mp3, which I then burned onto a CD that I brought into school to lead off the morning announcements. I posted the front page of *The Toronto Star* outside my classroom, and for the rest of the day I had one kid after another coming up to me to say, "Mr. Dellio, Obama won!" It's my hat, and the fact that I bored last year's class silly going on and on about the primaries—I'm Obama Guy around Huttonville P.S.

Just as I imagine Obama looking at David Axelrod Tuesday night and re-enacting *The Candidate* ("What do we do now?"), I'm not sure where I go with this. I may continue to observe the Obama presidency, I may veer off into a more conventional blog, or I may just stop until something else captures my attention. The Palin freak show doesn't appear to be going away anytime soon, so maybe that'll be enough to keep me connected.

I finally finished the Goldwater book. Arizona Senator gets trounced in a landslide, party in complete disarray—perfect timing. On to *Nixonland*.

(election blog, 2008)

"You Can Vote However You Like," Ron Clark Academy (2008)

Much more than anything McCain himself did during the campaign, it took a bunch of middle-school black kids from Atlanta to bestow upon him some of the dignity and honor that were supposed to be his currency. Simply by allowing that there was a case to be made for the wrinkly old white guy, a generosity they had no earthly reason to summon, they rescued the campaign from the slime pit of Wright, Ayers, Hannity, Limbaugh, Ferraro, Lynn Westmoreland (Mr. Uppity, in case you missed that one), Joe the Populist Prop, and all the other sundry phantasmagoria conspiring to hijack history. Discovering, via Andrew Sullivan, "You Can Vote However You Like" sometime in the waning days of October ranked right alongside Iowa and South Carolina as my purest moment of joy in an election I followed obsessively but ultimately didn't enjoy enough because I spent too much time waiting for the bottom to fall out. These kids, seemingly oblivious to the slime pit, enjoyed the moment as much as humanly possible.

(#3, year-end ballot, 2008)

Book Report

A girl in my grade 6 class submitted her book report this morning. Title: *The Jeffersons*. First sentence: "This biography is about how the person Thomas Jefferson was a president, and his family."

(ILX, 2009)

"Number 33," Jan & Lorraine (1969)

Another pick directly attributable to the radio show. Scott joined me on air the Sunday before the 2008 election, and we began with "Number 33," which at that point I'd only just recently discovered. (The rest of Jan & Lorraine's album made no impression on me.) For reasons that are as elusive as the song itself, it seemed to capture perfectly the strangeness that marked those last few weeks leading up to Obama's election—that palling-around-with-terrorists, Joe-the-Plumber moment, when stuff that had been lurking just below the surface began to spill all over the place. The insanity has never really stopped, if you ask me, it just continues to take on new and different forms. Strangeness: they often went off the rails, but if there's one thing hippies had a gift for, it was strange.

(#84, Facebook Top 100, 2010-11)

Obama's negotiation skills

That to me was the flaw in the analogy the other day about selling the apple pie: you need someone who wants to buy it to work the back and forth. If you want to sell a pie, and the other side wants to buy it, then yeah, you go through the process (which both sides are well aware of) of meeting somewhere in the middle. With Obama trying to get through health care, it was more like:

> *Obama: "I want to sell you an apple pie for $5.00. What are you willing to pay?"*
> *Republicans: "Beluga Whale."*
> *Obama: "Come again? What will you pay for this apple pie?"*
> *Republicans: "Don Knotts."*
> *Obama: "You don't really want this apple pie, do you."*
> *Republicans: "Socialist!"*

If the pie analogy was targeted at the three or four Democrats who were a problem, though, that makes more sense. And I agree Obama could have handled those folks better.

(ILX, 2011)

Obama's wars

This'll be a waste of time, and will be answered by a one-sentence dismissal by somebody—and doesn't belong on a Watergate thread besides—but, as briefly as possible, here's why I think Obama doesn't end the wars. 40% of the country will be with Obama no matter what; 30-35% is going to attack him no matter what. That leaves everyone else, and I think you could probably start chopping them up into little groups too. Somewhere in there, I think there's 10-15% of the electorate who had an unspoken deal with Obama: we'll vote for you, but please don't do stuff that's going to remind us that you're black, and no sudden movements, please, because sudden movements will remind us that you're black. Yes, I know—post-racial world, Obama's just the president, not the black president, etc., etc. I don't believe that, and I doubt that Obama does either. On top of that, you can throw in the usual Democratic skittishness when it comes to appearing weak on foreign policy, something that's defined the party since Reagan.

So, I believe, he does the crassly political thing and keeps two wars going, and, tentatively, sort of half-starts a new one. He does this because he has it in his mind that everything will unravel if he doesn't—he'll lose that 10-15% who has been keeping his approval ratings somewhere close to 50%, and from there, no legislation and no re-election. That's not a defense of the wars, and maybe I'm completely wrong. I'm just trying to explain my interpretation of what's happening.

(ILX, 2011)

Morning Coffee

This is unusual for Toronto. I realize that it's way on the mild end of the spectrum Stateside.

In the coffee shop this morning (fairly empty), some woman three tables over ripped out her earpiece and announced, "That's it—I can't stand listening to him." Her friend, sitting at the counter where I was seated: "Who's that?" Woman: "Ignatieff." (For anyone oblivious to Canadian politics, that would be our mushy, eggheaded John Kerry-type liberal-centrist.) Friend: "He looks like a faggot." He then amended this to say he looks like Frankenstein. Woman: "Hey, you know who's running for president? Donald Trump." After they both agreed that Trump understood money, the woman said, "I saw him on TV, and he said he's going to get rid of OPEC." This is big news: Donald Trump is going to fire OPEC if elected. Woman: "They need someone in there who understands what to do. Mr. *Obama* (she said it like Senator Geary says "Corleone" in *Godfather II*), who says he's not a Muslim..." At this point, yes, I turned my head around and gave her my most pointed look of contempt. Woman (smiling): "Never mind—you just read your paper, we'll be quiet."

They were both in their late-50s, early-60s. Again: one-tenth of one percent of what I'm sure I'd overhear in almost any American coffee shop. But unusual here. The last time I encountered something similar was when I spent half-an-hour arguing with a hot dog vendor in 2008. No mention of Muslims, but he was concerned that Obama was going to run a 24-hour house party out of the White House.

(ILX, 2011)

Evolving Door

The din on Obama's gay-marriage about-face—as in CNN, the message board, and Sullivan; I don't go anywhere near Tweeterville—was in full force today, so I'll keep this relatively brief. I'll be listening and skim-reading a lot in the next few days, more than at any time since the halcyon days of Newt Surge #1.

Obama's proclamation was political, of course. If you're someone who doesn't believe it lives up to the purity of Kennedy's and Johnson's push for Civil Rights legislation, a timeline might be instructive. They (and Eisenhower) dithered when it was convenient, moved forward when they had to, or when they could. Not sure there's much difference—if anything, I'd say Kennedy and Johnson were even less justified in stalling.

So politically, I'd say Obama goes two for three:

- On the downside, demographics and the electoral map. According to CNN, every single swing state (as defined by whomever defines such things) has struck down gay marriage already; those that are already wobbly for Obama will presumably move in Romney's direction now. And Catholic Hispanics are supposedly very unhappy.

Maybe Obama's side feels that reinvigorated young voters will neutralize all of that. I doubt it.

- The substance: it's always, I believe, politically smart at some level to do the right thing, regardless of motives. So that's a plus.
- Romney wants to keep the focus almost solely on the economy, with a little bit of sabre-rattling mixed in, but now, for the next few weeks at least and maybe all through the summer, he'll have to contend with an endless procession of people like the guy Piers Morgan had on tonight yelling, "Should we allow brothers and sisters to marry? Should we, huh?" For Santorum or Gingrich, this would have been a prayer answered. For Romney, I've got to believe he's mortified by today's events.

(Managing the Decay, 2012)

If You Come to a Fork in the Road, Take It

I'd better post something about the Supreme Court's Health Care ruling before Friday's jobs report, when it'll probably be back to hand-wringing and panic and "Are we actually going to elect this guy president?"

I was sitting in my class when I checked the computer sometime before noon on Thursday. (I usually would have checked right at 10:00, but the end of the year can be a little chaotic.) Can't remember what the kids were doing, but a few looked over when they heard me say "Wow" or "Whoah" or something like that. I explained what was going on, and what a surprise it was.

I felt great then, and still feel great today, after a week of absorbing every analysis, counter-analysis, diatribe, and conspiracy theory out there. As I posted on the message board, I don't pretend to understand the intricacies (or even some of the basics) of the actual legislation. I don't even totally understand how our own health-care system works. Rarely getting sick, and never seriously so, has a lot to do with that. I'll probably start learning more about our system than I care to know within the next 10-15 years.

I felt great instead because it was a rare chance to feel great. If you rooted for Obama in 2008, this has been a brutal first term. Insanity from the right, disappointment (or something much fiercer) from the left, and an economy that just crawls along. No exaggeration: there have maybe four or five opportunities to feel good. There was the initial passage of HCR, the occasional jobs report that exceeded expectations, gay marriage*, and then I start to come up blank. Osama bin Laden, somewhat—more for how silly it made the other side look than for the event itself.

Here again, Republican reaction to Roberts' about-face is part of what makes last week's events so satisfying. Primarily the shock—the complete perplexity that what was a foregone conclusion did not come to pass. I also love that one way or another, this forces Romney's hand. It was an awful feeling that he was going to get a pass on this—that the Supreme Court was going to take care of his "repeal on day one" bluster for him. Maybe the theory that his repeal promise, in the eyes of Republican voters, now takes on added urgency is correct, and that the law being upheld will be a net win for him in terms of motivating turnout. But really: imagine the symbolism or optics or whatever if HCR had gone down. As another theory goes (I've been reading a lot of theories the past week), there goes the election in a single commercial: "As you were struggling to stay afloat the past four years, the president was busy passing unconstitutional legislation." That would have been it, I'm positive.

Obama may still well lose. But if he does, the ACA will still be there. And if Romney wants to overturn it, he'll have to do it himself. And if he does, then he'll have to live with the consequences.

*This slipped my mind when I first posted, I guess because it was so ephemeral, if that's the right word. No legislation, not even something as concrete as numbers on a jobs report—it was a television interview. But that interview may outlast everything else, as words can't be legislated away.

(Managing the Decay, 2012)

I Dropped by to Pick Up a Reason

Good controversies are as rare as good news (for Obama) this campaign, so again, I'd better not let this one go by without comment. I'm talking about Romney at the NAACP—Bain is still evolving, so I'll put that one aside for the moment, other than to say my guess is that it will gradually give way to the Read My Lips: No New Tax Returns issue.

I'm going to give myself a pat on the back: when the initial reading of what had happened was still at the Romney-embarrassed stage on Wednesday afternoon, I and a couple of other people were on the message board calling him out for the transparent political calculation involved. This was a couple of hours before the usual din made its way online, most of which reached the same conclusion as us: far from an unexpected ambush, Romney came away with exactly the clip/sound bite he had set out to get.

I try not to assume the worst in these situations—I'd actually commended Romney a few days earlier for his decision to go—and I wasn't implying the very worst interpretation here, either: that the intent was to rabble-rouse the racist element of the Tea Party right. To point out the obvious, those people are motivated enough right now to want Obama out, and to make sure they make it happen by getting out to vote. All Romney would have done is alienate some part of the middle.

Instead, the objective seemed to be three-fold: 1) Mr. Etch-a-Sketch stays consistent, in a context where you might have expected him to pander; 2) Hey, base, look at me standing up to the NAACP—told you I was really one of you; 3) Get people feeling sorry for him. Sounds far-fetched, I know, but I watched Wolf Blitzer later that night, and there he was feeling sorry for Romney.

A couple of points I raised on the message board:

- When politicians get booed, they usually respond with an awkward attempt to smooth things over. They might raise their hands and say something like "Now, now…", they may quickly move to another subject, they may throw out a rhetorical question ("You mean you'd rather…") meant to logically reason with the audience. What I can't remember is somebody just standing there and basking in the booing. I find that really odd.

- The smile (frozen in plaster, to quote Neil Young) Romney has as he looks out at the crowd. My own interpretation is that it's an embarrassed, almost apologetic smile: "I'm sorry I have to do this; this is the business we've chosen." In other words, I don't think he did it with much enthusiasm.

It'll all be forgotten by yesterday, of course. Obama was going to get 95% of the African-American vote a week ago, and that's what he stands to get today. But the whole episode was revealing in trying to figure out what's going on with the other side.

(Managing the Decay, 2012)

Puzzlement Value

So strange, my first-ever quote of a Tweet: "This is a perfect representation of the campaign: an old white man arguing with an imaginary Barack Obama."

Eastwood actually started off really well: "Save some for Mitt" made me laugh, as did the line about not hot-dogging it. He seemed completely at ease, unscripted (I got that one right), and a better choice than the rumoured surprise I thought would hurt Obama the most, Colin Powell. The first sign of trouble was when he said he cried watching the celebration in Hyde Park four years ago, and that he hadn't cried like that since he realized there were 23 million people out of work. Which doesn't really make sense, because that's, you know, now, and the other thing was then. It was one of those reverse time-travel things, like in the *Terminator* movies. After that he started in on the chair, and he didn't even seem especially upset with Obama; the tone was wry and almost apologetic. I agree with something someone said on the message board: that the rambling was less a function of age than of not really having his heart into whatever it was that he was trying to say. Except for the gesture where he slit his throat. That didn't come across well for different reasons.

I'm not kidding when I say that Eastwood may have accidentally done Romney a favour anyway by deflecting all the attention onto himself—such a nothing acceptance speech. There was maybe one line I can imagine getting some play over the next few weeks: the contrast between Obama wanting to quell the oceans with Mitt wanting to help families. It feeds into that early caricature of Obama, the Greek columns and such, and it's suitably pithy. Otherwise, I wish I knew how to edit and repost YouTube clips; SCTV's *Goin' Down the Road* parody, where John Candy promises Joe Flaherty a Toronto filled with "doctorin' jobs and lawyerin' jobs—lots of jobs!" pretty much captures the "granular" (Paul Ryan's word) specificity of Romney's five-point recovery program.

Once again: I don't think any of it will matter as much as the next couple of jobs reports, or suddenly worsening gas prices, but a collective shrug of the shoulders is now officially the best Romney's going to do in the likeability department heading into November.

(Managing the Decay, 2012)

long journeys wear me out

Tina Fey's Palin

The music network here plays *SNL* reruns during the week. This morning, they had the sketch from '08 where Ferrell/Bush was in the Oval Office, ready to endorse McCain, and Fey/Palin walks in. I don't think you can say this enough: Fey's Palin was something beyond genius. "John and I have just been out travellin' around this great country of ours, talkin' about change and energy independence and William Ayers." The way she says it, the way they're all just words divorced from any meaning—she doesn't know what any of it means, she's just overjoyed to be there. Fey was so integral to why that election was so memorable.

(ILX, 2012)

Free Angela Davis and All Political Prisoners

I saw the documentary this afternoon. Can't find a thread, and she should have one. I knew some of the basic story, but learned lots. I want to track down a copy of the 1970 *Life* with her on the cover. There's a clip in the film where I recognized the interviewer but couldn't place him, and turns out it's Barry Callaghan, Morley's son, who used to be all over Canadian TV—I'll post an excerpt from the interview below. One of Davis's three lawyers, Leo Branton, Jr., not only sounded exactly like the famous baseball broadcaster Red Barber, he even looked like him—somewhat amazing, as Barber was a Southern white (who in the Ken Burns baseball film talks movingly about how Jackie Robinson forced him to grow up) and Branton a light-skinned African-American. There's probably a good film to be made about Rodger McAfee, the white farmer from California who put up Davis's bail money just before the trial began. Nixon provides the film's postscript as only Nixon can. Looked online for a reasonably priced Free Angela Davis button and was quickly disabused of that notion.

(ILX, 2012)

Reflections

Sullivan posted the video for Randy Newman's "Dreaming" during the evening; I'd stumbled over it on *Slate* a little earlier, where they had a short interview with Newman. I wasn't sure at first if the song was brand new, or if it had been around for a few weeks (or maybe even months).

I in turn posted the video on the message board, a couple of people pounced, and I soon found myself in the odd position of defending Randy Newman, someone whose music I've had very little affinity for over the years. Most of it, I haven't even heard—I've got *Sail Away* and *Good Old Boys* on vinyl, and a couple of more early ones on CD. I did like "It's Money That Matters" when it was a video hit.

Purely as music, "I'm Dreaming" is no easier for me to like than Randy Newman ever is. It's slow and stately, but his idea of beauty is rooted in Tin Pan Alley and Irving Berlin, whereas mine comes out of hippie folk music and stuff even more ephemeral than that. (That's what threw me about *Sail Away* when I bought it in high school: I thought I was buying a singer-songwriter album that would sound like *After the Gold Rush* and "Fire and Rain.") The other thing is, Newman's voice seems to be shot. I often complain about what Dylan and Lou Reed have lost as singers over the years, and the vocal on "I'm Dreaming" is no less off-putting.

It made an impression on me anyway. It gets at something tangible about Obama's 27% (or thereabouts—take that, Mitt), that part of the electorate that hates him and seems to have experienced a complete loss of control the past four years, a loss of what the Supremes once called The Way Life Used to Be. Newman does not sound sarcastic to me, which would ruin the song. (Going back to that *Slate* interview, I'm apparently wrong about that, at least in terms of his intentions; it was indeed meant as a sarcastic song.) He sounds a little out of sorts, sad but still hopeful, talking to himself. "Someone who we can understand/Someone who knows where we're coming from"—that contains a lot. Obvious or not, has anyone else written a song like this since Obama took office? I must have missed it if someone has. And if someone hasn't, maybe it's not so obvious after all.

(Managing the Decay, 2012)

Fiscal Cliff

It's funny how Wolf Blitzer always says "so-called fiscal cliff." Presumably he's trying to reassure people who think it's a real cliff, and who are worried about falling into a giant chasm like all the Egyptians in *The Ten Commandments*.

(ILX, 2012)

"Blessed," Schoolboy Q/"Ima Read," Zebra Katz

    I won't embarrass myself trying to grapple with these two songs the way I used to with "Fantastic Voyage" and "People Everyday"—if you're a middle-aged white guy who's out of the loop on this stuff, that would surely amount to high comedy in 2012. I did do a little reading on "Ima Read"'s backstory, and of course (I suspected as much) it's not at all what it seems; it's also the only song I think I've ever heard that mentions proofreading, and, having once spent two years proofreading Woolco-Woolworth's advertising flyers, I'm very excited about that. "Blessed" has that beautifully forlorn little keyboard flourish (or sample, or something—I never know) the whole way through, so I whistle along with that and leave the words to Schoolboy Q. "Last of a dying breed," says Schoolboy Q—perhaps. But I won't put my Top 10 on the blackboard this year the way I sometimes do. Eleven-year-olds do not gravitate towards backstories, and I don't really want any parent phone-calls.

                                                         (#8/9, year-end ballot, 2012)

Anita

    I saw Freida Mock's documentary on Hill this afternoon. I've always said that the three most riveting events I've ever watched unfold were the O.J. saga, the Thomas confirmation hearings, and the Obama/Clinton nomination fight. (I was 12 during the Watergate hearings, so my memories are almost non-existent.) The timelines were very different—days vs. months vs. a couple of years—but it felt so precarious through all three, like no matter how much was said publicly, you were always on the precipice of something much worse and much more calamitous.

    The last 20 minutes of the film is all uplift and the next generation and such, and I generally squirm through that kind of thing. But most of the rest is footage from the hearings, and I found all that just as compelling 20+ years later. The film's about Hill, but the cast of characters making up the Judiciary Committee is amazing. You'll never see a group of old white men spend so much time furrowing their brows and sighing. I'll never forget Alan Simpson hissing, "and they all told me, *watch out for this woman*," while he pretends to search his pockets for all the telegrams he's received—that's in there. Lots of Biden and Heflin and Specter, a little Kennedy, no praise for anyone. No Thurmond, surprisingly (he's there, but you don't hear from him). Even a bit of *SNL*, though I wished they'd gotten Farley-as-Heflin in there: "Judge Thomas, do you think that *po-no* is the way to go?"

The most electric moment was the semi-surprise introduction of Hill after the film. (We'd been told that the filmmaker and a "surprise guest" would take questions afterwards—c'mon, there was a chance Thomas would be there...) She told a really funny story about running into Specter at an airport, where he cheerfully suggested they should "work together" some day.

(ILX, 2013)

"Echelon," Angel Haze (2013)

I'm so enamored of this song, I want to quit my life and go help her out in all these feuds she's having with record companies and rivals. "These bitches is awful"—such a great line; I hate them all. The Mary-Kate and Ashley clones, I hate them too. (I thought it was Mary J. clones until I checked a lyrics page.) I'm starting to get worked up just thinking about these people. I'm starting to get aggy. The anomalous celestial-choir voices that pop up initially threw me, but I've come to love the way Angel Haze cuts across them, followed by my favorite part of the record, the "killing those motherfuckers" chorus that sounds like, I don't know, the Go! Team or something else I can't quite figure out. Listening to this young black woman curse and fulminate probably amounts to the same illicit thrill that's been placing profane hip-hop songs on my year-end lists since Schoolly-D in 1986. I'm so white, it's awful.

(#2, year-end ballot, 2013)

fragments falling everywhere

My favorite chapter title from before I actually had chapter titles belonged to this part of the book: "General Music section." I'm not sure that Flipper, Public Image, or the Pet Shop Boys could have come up with anything so perfectly eloquent. And that indeed is the concept—if it's about music and it doesn't make sense anywhere else, here's where it goes.

I was initially going to give power-pop a section of its own, but in the end whatever was slotted for that has been relocated here. At issue: 1) Too much (too many?) Shoes. I needed to include two pieces on the Shoes to make such a section even possible, and there was too much overlap between them. Now I can cut one out. 2) Not enough besides the Shoes. Even though power-pop has been my main musical interest for at least the past decade, turns out I hadn't actually written as much about the genre ("genre"—try to get anyone to agree on what belongs) as I thought. Part of the reason for that is, 3) I haven't yet abandoned the idea of one day attempting the power-pop book I sometimes tell myself I was meant to write. I've probably been consciously holding back a little, in the event that ever comes to pass.

More than any other section, the writing that follows is drawn from numerous sources, with a concentration on the Facebook Top 100 and non-record-collecting entries from the inventory. There are even a couple of actual record reviews, a form I rarely ever took up again after my *Nerve/Graffiti* days, plus a photo showdown between Elvis and my dad. Please don't sue me, Elvis estate, I'm at your mercy.

"Passing the Time," Cream (1968)

I don't really have any sense of where Cream stand (if at all) with younger critics today. To maybe shed some light on this, I did something I don't know that I've ever done before; I headed over to *Pitchfork*, specifically to their list (poll?) of the Top 200 songs of the '60s. No Cream. If it were an album list, maybe they'd be on there, but speaking as someone who came to them via a compilation—*Heavy Cream*, probably one of my first dozen LPs when I started to build my collection around '74 or '75—to me they're a song band before an album band. I didn't buy my first album proper till 20 years later (*Fresh Cream*), and I still don't own *Wheels of Fire* or *Disraeli Gears*. But that compilation had a huge effect on me in high school.

Especially "Passing the Time," a most peculiar song. Or two songs: drony, druid-like frame, an echo of the Yardbirds, with a childlike, impressionistic tone poem housed within, complete with cello, calliope, and glockenspiel. (Needed some online help in naming those last two.) It may have been the first time I ever observed of a rock song—not a Top 40 hit, but a certified older-brother rock song, buried away on an album no one in my high school could possibly have known about except me—"Wow, is that ever beautiful." Still feel the same way today.

(#29, Facebook Top 100, 2010-11)

It's Ivan!

I thought it would be a good idea to begin an interview with Ivan, singer for Montreal's Men without Hats, by asking him about his reputed distaste for the trappings of rock stardom (which led him to balk at playing *Solid Gold* in 1983, and proceed to take an extended leave of absence from making records). Leading innocuously enough with "It basically has to do with the male ego," Ivan's quickly off on a 10-minute jag that takes in his upbringing, the pressures that attended "Safety Dance"'s world-wide success, the changes his lifestyle underwent during the hiatus, the radical black feminist poetry he's been reading and learning from, a little bit about witchcraft, a momentary return to rock stars, the notion of *Pop Goes the World* as a concept album, and the media barrage that he feels is controlling our lives. All of it fascinating, but too elaborate to condense here. So after Ivan rapped me on the forehead three times, we commenced with the second question: now that you're back and doing interviews with everyone, where do you draw the line with regards to industry protocol?

(*Graffiti*, 1988)

"Hey Gyp," Keith Shields (1967)

Genre permutations have exploded exponentially the past decade. Everyone has his favorite: mine's Post-Rockist Grimecore, but tomorrow that may change. Keeping track of genres used to be much easier—time was that five was enough to cover everybody, but now even the '60s and '70s have undergone a posthumous genre makeover. I can think of at least three that have been excavated and officially named fairly recently: Psych Folk (which may actually have been referred to as such during its lifetime, although I'd never heard the term myself until five or ten years ago); Sunshine Pop, which corrals a bunch of stuff I've always loved, from the Association to the *Mary Tyler Moore* Theme; and Freakbeat, home to Keith Shields, the Creation, and others. British garage, basically, but I guess that conjures up frat houses and the Kingsmen and matching Nehru jackets, so Freakbeat had to be pressed into duty.

(#90, Facebook Top 100, 2010-11)

The Move

"Message from the Country" was among the songs I included on "Beatlesque," a mix-tape I once compiled for a teacher (and Beatles lover) who was leaving my school. The idea was pretty self-explanatory, with a fluid enough interpretation of Beatlesque to guide me that, along with obvious things like the Knickerbockers and Big Star and Traffic's "Hole in My Shoe," I had "Take the Skinheads Bowling" and Hüsker Dü's "Books About UFOs"—songs that don't sound like the Beatles at all, but which seem to me to capture something fundamental about what they might have been doing had they existed in a different time and different set of circumstances. "Message from the Country" is more of a straightforward soundalike, although I can't point to any one specific period it aligns itself with—*White Album*-Beatles would be the closest match, I guess. As a warm-up for their Beatles flirtation, "Wave Your Flag and Stop the Train" joins the Five Americans' "Western Union" in a surreal mini-genre I've mentioned before: the Imitation Monkees Genre. I don't know if there was ever an Imitation *Electric*-era Cult Genre, but that's about the only possible parallel I can conceive of.

(record inventory, 2005-06)

Beat Farmers

The Beat Farmers belong to a group of default punch lines I keep handy in case of emergency. I've got Right Said Fred from the early '90s, Wishbone Ash for the early '70s, Doctor & the Medics and the Beat Farmers for the mid-'80s. Whatever the joke, insert the applicable name and you can't go wrong:

1. Q: Why did the chicken cross the road?
A: Wishbone Ash.

interrupting my train of thought

2. Q: How many lawyers does it take to screw in a light bulb?
A: The Beat Farmers.

See?

(record inventory, 2005-06)

Pushin' Less Hard

In the Offspring's "Self Esteem," my favorite hard-rock single of the '90s, a hapless pincushion contemplates registering a complaint with his girlfriend. Her various transgressions include spending his money, abusing him, sleeping around with his friends, and making house calls at two in the morning. "I guess I should stick up for myself," he courageously equivocates, but he instead takes her home and makes her dessert. "I really think it's better this way."

If you get a kick out of the way pop songs seem to speak to each other years and sometimes decades apart, the "Self Esteem" guy made a return appearance a couple of years later on Matchbox 20's "Push." He wasn't so obliging this time. "I wanna push you around," the new version declared. "I wanna take you for granted."

It was undoubtedly the pushing-around that got Matchbox 20 a foothold on the radio. ("Push"'s ubiquity over the next few months points to it as having touched a nerve; if there were people who interpreted the threat of physical violence literally and were offended, there wasn't much controversy to speak of.) But it was the taking-for-granted part that was meaner, more sinister, and, for better or worse, inspirational. This was the purest, most casually insidious kind of vindictiveness, the carefully worked-out manipulations of a passive-aggressive tyrant. (The kind of thing I instantly recognize because, um, I've read books about such people.) Anchored by a spare, lyrical guitar line, singer Rob Thomas's vocal came from the same place as Tom Cruise's best line in *Magnolia*: "I'm quietly judging you." "Back 2 Good," a later single, was a worthy reprise.

Matchbox 20 is now Matchbox Twenty (the most enigmatic fine-tuning of a name since Ce Ce Peniston suddenly woke up and turned into Cece Peniston one day), and "Push" is no longer what most people know them for. Thomas's between-albums turn on Carlos Santana's multi-everything "Smooth" ensured that Matchbox Twenty's new *Mad Season* LP would get an immense amount of attention, and a quick look at newsstands verifies that it has. True, I spent the first month of "Smooth"'s chart run disinterestedly switching it off, thinking it was the singer from the Dave Matthews Band (whose name may or may not be Dave Matthews). You might not think it possible to confuse Matchbox Twenty with the Dave Matthews Band, but it is. Anyway, Thomas is much more credible as a humorless scold than a would-be Ricky Martin. (Though for some of us, even Ricky Martin doesn't make for a credible Ricky Martin.)

Thomas generally stays clear of both extremes on *Mad Season*, which is probably not named in honor of the Seattle one-off supergroup responsible for 1995's great "River of Deceit" single. Maybe Matchbox Twenty did get some grief over "Push," and as recompense there's a conscious effort on the new album to lighten up on the finger-wagging, or at least to disguise it better. On "Last Beautiful Girl," for instance, Thomas is in standard lecture mode, but the airy harmonizing of the rest of the group is played against him—if lyrics just function as shapeless background for you, it's a song about beautiful girls. Elsewhere there are a couple of stately ballads ("If You're Gone," "Bed of Lies"), an agreeably loopy title song that would be fine on the radio, and a horn-driven thing about "the Technicolor dreams of black-and-white people" that isn't nearly as gruesome as it sounds. Even songs bearing titles that are presumably meant to be stark and ominous ("Angry," "Crutch," "Bent") are delivered as modestly as an Oppressively Emoting White Guy like Thomas is capable of. In short, what lots of people loved about "Push" isn't much in evidence here, but neither is what lots of people hated about it.

There's an obvious problem, though. *Mad Season* runs over an hour (including a hidden epilogue), and excepting the aforementioned "Black and White People," the other 55 minutes pick over the minutiae of relationships, primarily failed ones. Relationships aren't uninteresting—in fact, they're sort of interesting. Except they're also sort of all the same. The Guess Who, to name a very contemporary example, took care of relationships in a single line from "New Mother Nature"—"She hasn't got the faith or the guts to leave him when they're standing in each other's way"—and that left them lots of room to sing about rain dances, bus riders, Wolfman Jack, and lots of other world-important matters. That's what Rob Thomas needs to do at this point: write a song about a rain dance.

(*Village Voice*, 2000)

interrupting my train of thought

Ralph Vaughan Williams

"The Lark Ascending" is the first thing I'd play for somebody if it were a really windy person who was in the habit of saying things like "Play something majestic for me." Like "My Favorite Things" and "Cowgirl in the Sand," it's an epic that dissolves the world around you. Some of it soars, some is balanced precariously between a sustained note and silence, mountains come out of the sky, the muses dance and sing, they make the children really ring, you stand to lose all time. I get the same feeling from the background score heard in some of Spike Lee's movies; my guess is that Lee's father (*Malcolm X*) and Aaron Copland (*He Got Game*) were heavily influenced by Williams. "The Lark Ascending" is waiting for some director to lay it overtop the most stunningly contemplative 10-minute nature passage ever filmed. A few seconds of it were actually used in *24-Hour Party People*, of all things. If I remember correctly, Williams turned up during the big "Pastoral Rave" sequence.

(record inventory, 2005-06)

"Alabama Bound," Charlatans

I bet no one ever makes reference to this group anymore without immediately appending, "the hippie Charlatans, not the British ones." So, just to keep that tradition alive: "Alabama Bound" is by the hippie Charlatans, not the British ones, a distinction seemingly lost on even some of the people who download them—when I tried to get confirmation from one file-sharer that his "San Francisco Charlatans" folder was indeed as advertised, it turned out that most of it was in fact comprised of the other guys. "Oops," he explained... This version of "Alabama Bound," recorded for the Kama Sutra label in early 1966 but not released until anthologized years later, is close to ground zero in the evolution of west-coast psychedelia; there's a little bit that predates it, but not much, and as with such other blueprints as the Jefferson Airplane's "Come Up the Years" (1966) and the 1964 Byrds demos later collected on *Preflyte*, I don't think you can find a purer, more visionary exemplar of that somewhat amorphous term. There's jangle and there's swirl in "Alabama Bound," but the deep, drony, almost zombie-like incantation of the chorus—"I'm Alabama bound, I'm Alabama bound"—gives voice to a kind of dread every bit as disquieting as that which the Velvet Underground was exploring on "Heroin" at the time. It's a song that has little connection to almost everything else the Charlatans would go on to record, much of which could be described as genial novelty music, and while a longer version included in the band's one official album release, 1969's *The Charlatans*, retains some of the original's mystery and presence, the sense of listening in on something altogether new and momentous is lost.

(*Stylus*, 2005)

"Field of Stars," Oliver Schroer (2006)

I tentatively penciled in something stridently political for this spot a couple of nights ago, but in light of what's going on in Arizona, I'll hold off on that for the time being.

A friend introduced me to "Field of Stars" on a mix-CD of Canadian stuff. I'd never heard of Oliver Schroer before that; by the time I did, he'd been dead for a couple of years. Not really sure where you'd file something like "Field of Stars" in a record store—Celtic or folk, I guess, but classical or new age or ambient would seem just as appropriate. Much like the Arvo Pärt piece I listed way back at the beginning of this, it's out there waiting for the right film director to lay it overtop eight minutes of stunningly beautiful images where nothing much happens at all: *The Piano*, *McCabe & Mrs. Miller*, *Paris, Texas*, something in that tradition. But no matter how beautiful the images, I need the music for such films to work. If it's there, I'm a complete pushover. Take it away, and I'm trapped inside Tarkovsky's *Stalker*, counting the days and the weeks till it's over.

(#56, Facebook Top 100, 2010-11)

Favorite Albums

It's been ten years since I thought about music first and foremost in terms of albums. I have lots of them—about 3,000—and two or three times a year I'll find a good used sale and buy a bunch more, but for the most part my record habit is a thing of the past. Obviously I can't buy newer music on vinyl anymore, and that's a big factor. I buy maybe 15 or 20 used CDs a year. But all of that is almost incidental to the real reason albums-as-albums don't define music for me anymore: I just stopped kidding myself that albums, even my very favorite ones, are as important to me as the best songs on those albums, or that they're as important as many other songs from albums that aren't even particularly good. The idea of the truly great album says that from start to finish you get nothing but pleasure from it—every song counts, it's all of a piece (even if a greatest-hits album), the whole is greater than the parts, so on and so forth. I can't speak for anybody else, but I finally came to the conclusion that I would always have to lie a little to myself to make that happen. Albums just aren't made up of twelve perfect songs that you like equally; you always like some more others. The greater the album, the greater its best songs, in which case the greater the gap between what you love about the album and what you merely abide by in order to get to what you love. These secondary songs may be OK or even pretty good—on a great album they usually are—and I can think of lots of albums that are without any outright bad songs, but that's not really the point. A part of the album still ends up being an intrusion, and those two or three songs are diminished even more by the greatness of what's around them.

Ten years ago I could have listed 40 favorite albums easily; it's a struggle for me to make it up to ten now. The ones I've picked are there because of how much their best parts mean to me, which in most cases accounts for upwards of 2/3 of the album. That's about as high as I go these days, and in keeping with all that I've written above, I'll mention the couple of songs in each case that get in the way of how much I enjoy even these albums. "Ticket to Ride," "I Need You," and "Tell Me What You See" are perfection; *Help!*, as great as it is, is not.

1. Neil Young with Crazy Horse: *Everybody Knows This Is Nowhere* (1969) — I guess "The Losing End" is my least favorite song, but as #1 this obviously has special significance for me. It might be better if I start to apply my crackpot theories to album #2.

2. The Beatles: *Help!* (British version, 1965) — "Dizzy Miss Lizzy," "Yesterday," "Act Naturally."

3. Dionne Warwick: *My Greatest Hits* (1975) — "Alfie," "I Just Don't Know What To Do With Myself."

4. Shoes: *Black Vinyl Shoes* (1978) — "Fire for Awhile," "Tragedy."

5. *The Velvet Underground* (1969) — I don't like "Candy Says" and "Pale Blue Eyes" as much as most people who love this album do—strange, because they're probably the album's two most famous songs.

6. *Jefferson Airplane Takes Off* (1966) — All three blues songs: "Tobacco Road," "Chauffeur Blues," "And I Like It."

7. *The Who Sell Out* (1967) — I don't like "Silas Stingy" at all— that counts as a double deduction. Another problem is that my favorite song, "I Can't Reach You," is on the side I consider weaker.

8. *The Best of the Stylistics* (1975) — It's not so much that I dislike "Rockin' Roll Baby"—I'm not crazy about it, but on a different album it would be OK—it's just that it's too much of an anomaly stuck in the middle of all these amazing ballads. Same with "Heavy Fallin' Out," though somewhat less so.

9. The Byrds: *Preflyte* (1969) — "Mr. Tambourine Man" (a pre-hit version) does not belong on this album—too familiar. Otherwise, "The Airport Song."

10. *Al Green's Greatest Hits* (1975) — "I Can't Get Next to You," "Here I Am (Come and Take Me)," "Let's Get Married." I lose interest in Al Green as he starts to get bluesier; I would love to replace those three songs with "Sha-La-La (Make Me Happy)," "Hangin' On," and "Have You Been Making Out O.K."

Nitpicking about what are supposed to be my ten favorite albums must seem rather bizarre, but as Madonna might say, put it down to human nature ("Oops, I didn't know I couldn't nitpick about my ten favorite albums")—the imposition of impossible standards on what you love. Take what I've written as a roundabout expression of how brilliant the rest of each of these albums is.

(*Tapeworm*, 1995)

Minor Threat

I actually wrote to Ian MacKaye sometime after the group's "Salad Days" single with a rather amorphous idea for a book that would have involved his own band, the Shoes, and the Chantels. I'm sure I wouldn't have explained the connection very well (I couldn't explain it very well today; I was just kind of, uh, feeling it...), I think I'd done about six record reviews for *Nerve* at that point, and all things considered he wouldn't have been out of line to take a deep breath and count back from ten and maybe I'd go away. But he replied with a postcard gracious enough that I didn't at all feel like I'd just made the most harebrained proposal in the world, a gesture for which I've always felt some gratitude, coming as it did when I was just starting out. (I've had nobody-editors make me feel smaller.) I never followed any of MacKaye's post-Minor Threat projects—I think I occasionally played Fugazi when I was at CIUT—but I'll support the idea that he's one of the genuine good guys out there.

(record inventory, 2005-06)

"Fear Is a Man's Best Friend," John Cale (1974)

I've been going back to this for years whenever I'm in a certain frame of mind. It's a mood that I'm not sure I could describe, as elusive and as fragmentary as the song itself. The fear that you're asked to embrace is amorphous too, and also inescapable: an unnamed man, your eye on the door, waiting, waiting, waiting. You know it makes sense, don't even think about it. Have a good time even—there's a certain music-hall jauntiness in the piano playing, and it's a fun song to sing along with. An obvious zero-sum, yin-yang observation: the music that John Cale made in the early '70s—*Paris 1919* has songs I like almost as much as "Fear Is a Man's Best Friend"—holds up much better than what Lou Reed was doing at the time. The only thing that survives from either one of them on the radio is "Walk on the Wild Side," which for reasons I can't quite figure out still gets played regularly on Q-107 (even heard it on the way to work this morning). Not a knock on the song, which I actually find kind of moving these days, now that I know who all the characters are. Just that its enduring place in Q-107's version of the world makes no sense.

(#55, Facebook Top 100, 2010-11)

A Sex Pistols Symposium

This is the second symposium I've been involved in this summer; the other consisted of me, my neighbour, and my landlord, and the subject at hand was whether my neighbour was too noisy or whether I was a nitpicking crank. I had lots to say in that one, but I'm less sure how much I have to say about the Sex Pistols. Even though I was in the middle of high school when they came along, I didn't hear a Sex Pistols record until my friend Peter got me interested in punk in 1979 (a landmark year for both me and Billy Corgan). Their album had a tremendous impact on me at the time, but I don't think it's the kind of record that you keep playing for years afterwards. Hüsker Dü had an even bigger impact on me, and I don't even play their records any more.

My initial reaction to the news that the Sex Pistols were getting back together was the obvious one, that it was a ridiculous idea, but it wasn't a reaction that registered very deeply. I can't imagine getting upset or even disappointed about it. It's not like John Lydon is someone who has all this carefully preserved mystique still intact—great baseball players are better at that than pop musicians, and Lydon's been pretty hard to take for a while now. Of course, if I were to ever have the impact that he had with the Sex Pistols, I wouldn't know what to do for a second act either. (A third act, actually; his second one, the *Second Edition* album, was great.) So I just watch his coming and goings from a distance and don't hold too much of what he does against him.

When I'd drive over to the mall for lunch this past winter, I would sometimes hear Lydon's syndicated spot on CFNY, "Rotten Day," where he does really outrageous things like make fun of A Flock of Seagulls. I never quite knew what to make of that, either, though I'd often find myself laughing (along?) anyway. I had an argument with a friend as to whether it's really Lydon or not. My friend thinks the whole thing is so absurd that it has to be a put-on by the station. I agreed with his premise, but I told him I'm still convinced it's the real Lydon. There are probably people who have the same argument at these reunion concerts.

(*Eye Weekly*, 1996)

Doo-wop

My immersion into doo-wop dates to the second half of the '80s, especially my time at CIUT; it became the core of my all-night show's second incarnation, an all-ballad format I adopted partly as a joke, and partly as a pre-emptive overreaction to a bit of CRTC trouble I got into during the show's first incarnation. I think it was a combination of *Mean Streets* and Greil Marcus's occasional writings on the genre that first got me interested in doo-wop, with *American Graffiti* and *American How Wax* also playing a role. I learned very quickly that this was a body of work that was locked into the time frame it came out of (the very end of the '40s to the early '60s, approximately; I'm not sure exactly when the name doo-wop came into general usage, but I know it didn't happen for at least a few years), and that trying to drag the genre into the present-day—New Edition's *Under the Blue Moon* was one version of how that might be done; those PBS revue-type specials that periodically air are another—is invariably a bad idea. That faraway, almost secretive world that my favorite doo-wop conjures up was very appealing to me, with a beauty and a stillness in songs like the Sonics' "This Broken Heart" and Dee (Clark) & the Kool Gents' "When I Call on You" comparable to what I hear in "Norwegian Wood," the Velvet Underground's "Jesus," and the best parts of *Kind of Blue*. The closest I've ever seen anyone come to capturing the dreamier end of the doo-wop spectrum on film is Kenneth Anger in *Rabbit's Moon*. The intensity of my feelings for the genre began to subside over time (a process hastened along by a few too many starry-eyed mix-tapes for another CIUT D.J.), and when I play any doo-wop on my current show, it's usually of a wilder variety: the Chips' "Rubber Biscuit," the Cellos' "Rang Tang Ding Dong (I Am the Japanese Sandman)," and Sheriff & the Ravels' "Shombalor" are my current favorites. But that world contained in the ballads will always have a spot somewhere in my imagination.

(record inventory, 2005-06)

"Airborne," Wussy (2005)

I've been listening to their (relatively) new album the past couple of days, and I think they might be my favorite band in the world right now. This is the first of what will be two appearances by Chuck Cleaver on my list—of the handful of people who are going to make it twice, he provides the most in the way of "Um...who?" puzzlement value. He looks like an ancient hillbilly, has a quavering voice to match, and he and his wife Lisa rank with Ira & Georgia, Grace & Paul, Dick & Dee Dee, and all my other favorite rock and roll couples. (Neil & Chris, too, if they were to ever tie the knot.) Two lines from "Airborne" kill me: "Well, it was just another Thursday/Like any other Thursday" (what does a generic Thursday feel like? I'm not sure...), and "You went off like Frankenstein." I've lost it a few times in my life, but I don't know that I've ever gone off like Frankenstein. That sounds real bad.

(#76, Facebook Top 100, 2010-11)

"Survivor," Destiny's Child

If I could choose anyone right now to enlist a long-dead cliché (Greil Marcus was making fun of survivor-songs 20 years ago) in the service of an overwrought "diva" anthem, Destiny's Child would be my first choice. Whatever it is they survived, they definitely came out looking none the worse for wear. I wish they'd picked up on a mini-genre that turned up in an early *Radio On*, Songs-That-Make-False-Claims-About-Your-Résumé (like Elton John saying he used to be a Rolling Stone), and written this as a tribute to the early '80s instead: "I'm in Survivor/Eye of the tiger/Mr. Roboto/Don't forget Toto." (3.0)

(rockcritics.com, 2001)

"Levi Stubbs' Tears," Billy Bragg (1986)

The '90s are Scott's black hole; for me, it's the '80s. There was Haysi Fantayzee, of course. Everybody knows Haysi Fantayzee—except Mrs. Haysi Fantayzee. (Hi, Rob!) Squirrel Bait had a couple of great songs, Billy Ocean had it going on for a while, and that was about it. There'll be a little less from the '80s on my list than from any other decade; if I expanded to 200 songs, there'd be a lot less. But "Levi Stubbs' Tears" still gets to me. It has a contender for the most perfect line ever written: "When the world falls apart, some things stay in place." You could, as the saying goes—I think there's a saying—retire on that line. Also, Billy Bragg inspired my greatest joke ever, written back in 1991 for the first-ever edition of the now unfortunately defunct *Eye Weekly* year-end poll. You'll have to hunt it down yourself—the punch line had to do with Elf Insurance.

(#74, Facebook Top 100, 2010-11)

X

Many people count *Wild Gift* as the single greatest achievement of American punk. I loved it then, it still sounds great as I listen to it right now, but for me, it ended up being a prelude to Hüsker Dü and the Replacements. There's an inclination to wonder if you have to be married to get the full effect of *Wild Gift*, but when it was my favorite record in the world in 1981, I wasn't any more married then than I am now, so I'm not sure if that explains why I went on to become (and remain) a bigger fan of Hüsker Dü. More pertinent to my own biases, Hüsker Dü were rooted in the Beatles and the Byrds, X in some weird amalgam of rockabilly and the Doors (having said that, I'm surprised that it's two of the most Doors-like vocals on *Wild Gift* that I count as the album's highlights); also, my favorite music tends to reach me through sound and mood much more than words and themes, and *Wild Gift* is a narrative before it's anything—a compelling one, but lacking that visionary whoosh I would hear on *Metal Circus*. (Which might also explain why *Zen Arcade* is my least favorite LP from Hüsker Dü's magisterial '83-85 run—they got so caught up in the narrative, they lost a bit of that whoosh.) I don't want to overstate the comparison—when it came time to review *Ain't Love Grand* for *Nerve* (my start there), I still considered X one of my three or four favorite groups. The album was so-so; really, although there were still some good songs scattered here and there (from memory, "Around My Heart," "4th of July," and "See How We Are," though I don't know how they'd hold up today), X didn't make a good LP after *Under the Big Black Sun*, and through the middle part of the decade, they seemed more lost than the Ramones. I saw them play the El Mocambo around the time of *More Fun in the New World*, which was a little too late; what I remember most about the show is Billy Zoom's schtick, that transparently contemptuous grin he had frozen in place the whole night, just to make sure you knew that he rather would have been off playing with Crazy Cavan or somebody. Too bad they didn't make it into Michael Azerrad's *Our Band Could Be Your Life* (something to do with Slash's distribution, I think, or maybe their early signing to Elektra)—they've never been name-checked nearly as religiously as Sonic Youth or Hüsker Dü or Minor Threat, and for a group that was such a locus of attention for a couple of years, they seem somewhat forgotten.

(record inventory, 2005-06)

"Any Other Way," Posies (1990)

I've written elsewhere—on the message board, and in a piece I once did on pop music in movies—how interesting a year 1990 is to me. Interesting in retrospect; at the time I thought things had sunk to a new low. I was also paying less attention than at any other time in my life, so it becomes something of who-made-who question: was I not paying attention because things were so bad, or did I mistakenly think things were so bad because I wasn't paying attention? A bit of both, I'd say. It was the year that fell between what I considered a great year for crossover hip-hop and R&B—Soul II Soul, Young MC, Neneh Cherry, Ten City, De La Soul, Tone-Lōc, Inner City, etc.—and the year of *Nevermind*'s release, which marked the beginning of *Radio On* and a half-decade where I was very interested in chart music. 1990 was a complete blank to me. I went off to Windsor to attend teachers college, where I closely followed Cecil Fielder's quest for 50 home runs across the river, but didn't even bother buying *Ragged Glory*. I have a vague memory of sending a year-end list to Scott (in Vancouver?) that consisted of "Around the Way Girl," maybe "Nothing Compares 2 U," and a Ninja Turtle song. I still think it was a relatively weak transitional year, but, needless to say, I've since discovered stuff I missed. Some of which is obvious—"Bonita Applebum," "Getting Away with It"—some less so. Altogether, I've got two-and-a-half hours of music from 1990 on my hard drive—at the lower end of the spectrum for the '90s, but basically a year like any other.

Above all else, I missed a couple of things—"Any Other Way" and a more obscure record still to come—that I'd put forth as possible templates of the hypothetically perfect power-pop song I've been pursuing for years. Alfred Hitchcock spent his career trying to find the perfect blonde. If the perfect blonde comes my way tomorrow, I won't send her away, but truthfully I've devoted more time and energy to trying to track down the perfect power-pop song. It's an elusive hall of mirrors that you find yourself lost in—power-pop is built upon a foundation of seeking and never finding—where the most marginal gestures take on great significance. (The Shoes: "There is so much at stake/With every word I say.") "Any Other Way," which may have been conceived as nothing more than a nice Hollies tribute, encompasses all that I love about an essentially amorphous genre—people tend to have very different interpretations of what constitutes power-pop. In my version, it's got jangle, it tells a story, someone averts his eyes, it soars, it gets quiet. And, returning to 1990, the fact that "Any Other Way" appeared in the middle of nowhere (or, if you'd prefer, "Hammer Time") makes it that much more poignant to me.

(#26, Facebook Top 100, 2010-11)

Five Poppiest Art Rock Songs

1) "Roundabout," Yes (1971)
2) "Teacher," Jethro Tull (1970)
3) "Can't Get It Out of My Head," Electric Light Orchestra (1974)
4) "Tubular Bells," Mike Oldfield (1973)
5) "Back in N.Y.C.," Genesis (1974)

I was going over candidates for this list a couple of weeks ago with my friend Brent, one of seven people in the world who owns the Kansas album from last year (assuming everyone in Kansas has a copy too). Of course, right away you have to contend with the age-old problem of what does and doesn't count as art rock. We were very inclusive: "Yeah, that's sort of art-wave." "I guess you'd call that art glam." "The Feelies? They're art-jangle." In the end, we decided that everyone who's ever made a record counts as art rock, with the possible exception of Freddie & the Dreamers and Pink Floyd. There may still be a few bugs to work out in the eight-step screening process we used...#1's easy, although the chorus of "I've Seen All Good People" might even be better (dragged down by the "Your Move" prologue). Picking one Jethro Tull entry is difficult: "Fat Man," "Living in the Past," "Nothing Is Easy," they're all castaways from some medieval version of *The Fabulous Bubblegum Years*. I limited myself to pre-*A New World Record* for Electric Light Orchestra, after which it's like shooting giant hogweeds in a barrel. With "Tubular Bells," I'm voting for the last five minutes or so of side one—the part where Mike Oldfield does his roll-call of instruments, a surprising homage to Sly & the Family Stone. And I hadn't intended to vote for Genesis until the list below reactivated long-dormant memories of that synthesizer...Which still leaves lots of also-rans unacknowledged, so let me hereby issue history's first-ever shout-out to Gentle Giant.

(rockcritics.com, 2002)

Jesus & Mary Chain/Jethro Tull

Something just died inside me: going by the mixworthy list, I would appear to like Jethro Tull twice as much as the Jesus and Mary Chain...The funniest thing about *Psychocandy* to me right now is thinking about how I used to get upset at staff who'd get upset whenever I played it in the record store. I put "Never Understand" on a CD-700 this past summer, and as I listened to it in the car, I was just shaking my head: what were they thinking when they recorded that, and what was I thinking when I assumed people who'd come in to browse through albums would want it playing in the background? Full credit for audaciousness, then and now, but what a bizarre, ear-splitting din. My *Psychocandy* review for *Nerve* was almost as over-the-top as the album itself—an accurate enough expression of how I felt at the time, that here was something I'd unknowingly been waiting forever to hear, but if I tried to read it right now, I wouldn't be able to make it through two sentences...I don't know *Living in the Past* nearly as well as *M.U.*—*M.U.* goes back to high school, *Living in the Past* I bought a few years ago—but it's the earlier compilation that seems to be more highly regarded (you know, among people who regard Jethro Tull albums at all), so there's probably a song or two I could add from there. I'm listing "Fat Man" for the same reason I listed "Best of My Love" earlier: *Boogie Nights*. Nothing captures the apocalyptic decadence of disco, pornography, and cocaine like a crazy-mad Ian Anderson flute solo.

(record inventory, 2005-06)

Elvis Presley

My Elvis Problem is my most conspicuous blind spot of all in a lifetime of listening, much more so than my Otis Problem or James Brown Problem or any of the other gaps I've talked about herein. (In stature, he actually pairs up well with my great literary blind spot: all my early attempts at Shakespeare were miserable failures—only university course I flunked, although I'll defensively add that it's more accurate to say I gave up, which amounts to the same in the end anyway and I've never gone back for another try.) I know how bizarre and maddening it would be to anyone who counts Elvis as his frame of reference for everything to see the entirety of his discography collapsed into a couple of Sun recordings, a late-'60s comeback hit, and a bit of throwaway soundtrack fluff. The handful of times in my life where I've had people tell me they didn't have any use for the Beatles, it was like an invisible but meaningful barrier between us had instantaneously appeared; "How can anyone feel that way?" So I wish I liked Elvis more, and I'm not at all sure why I don't. Neither am I sure to what extent I was aware of him when pop music first started to matter to me. Through the mid-to-late '60s, when I was listening from the back seat of the family car, I don't recall him being much of a presence; he was back on the radio with "Burning Love" when I really started turning into a radio junkie in 1972, but it was far from one of my favorite songs. (I liked the imitation-Elvis via imitation-CCR "Long Cool Woman" much more.) I definitely got hooked on the wave of '50s nostalgia then taking hold, but, possibly because of protective licensing, Elvis didn't seem a part of that—none of his music was used in *American Graffiti*, and he never turned up on any of the Jukebox-Revival compilations popular at the time. Getting *The Sun Collection* early in university led to a brief period where I listened to more Elvis than I ever had before, and once that ended, that was it; I loved Marcus's *Dead Elvis*, but I'm not sure that it inspired me to take a single Elvis record off the shelf. I read somewhere last year—it may have been Marcus himself who said it—speculation that Elvis's hold on the popular imagination was finally beginning to wane, and that 50 years from now, he'd be no different than Robert Johnson or Bing Crosby or any other important but historically remote figure. I think that maybe already happened with me quite a while ago. (It may be my own bias speaking here, but, if that does turn out to be true, I don't think the same fate awaits the Beatles, not anytime soon, anyway. To me, there's something intrinsic in the music of the Beatles that makes it accessible and likeable to virtually anyone; I always sense that of all the music I play for my students, they're able to connect more easily and more immediately with the Beatles than with anyone.) In an odd sort of way, I think my most tangible connection with Elvis is a picture I have of my dad taken sometime in the '50s. It's pretty obvious who carried the rock-star-glamour gene in my family. It must skip a generation; I apparently inherited the gene associated with the other Elvis, the rock-critic-with-glasses gene, from my mom.

(record inventory, 2005-06)

 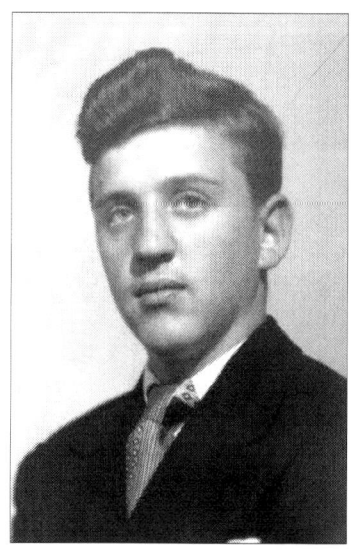

fragments falling everywhere

"Panic," Smiths (1986)

Scott and Dave will be very surprised to see me listing the Smiths—listing them at all, much less this high. I was a Hüsker Dü/Replacements/Meat Puppets guy straight down the line for my first couple of years at *Nerve*, so the Smiths were who you made fun of. They were all guitar bands, of course, but the Smiths were British, they were writerly and precious (no, those are not euphemisms for gay), and they replaced the Jam in my mind as the kind of band Toronto's silly new-wave station at the time, CFNY, and people who (snobbishly, I believed) preferred British to American music in general, wildly overrated. I'm still far from being a fan, but I'm not so oblivious to the flaws (and sometimes complete uselessness) of the bands I gravitated to instead, or to my own forms of snobbishness.

"Panic," though, I've come to regard as one of the most moving songs ever recorded. I was trying to explain why on the message board a while back, and didn't do a great job of it. It's not necessarily what the song's about, my understanding of which amounts to this: British radio stations and/or club DJs were playing a surfeit of dance music at the time (a lot of Loose Ends-type stuff, I would imagine), and Morrissey didn't like dance music, so he wrote a short little song that made hanging the DJ sound like a fun and joyous thing to do. It got him into some trouble: "hang the DJ," when directed at primarily black dance music, was uncomfortably close to lynch-mob imagery. I understand that—I think it has as much validity as the Stephin Merritt charge, but I understand the connection.

What I find so moving is...somebody saying exactly what he wants to say, and saying it so perfectly that he never needed to say anything before, and he'll never need to say anything ever again. Obviously he did, and obviously he has. And there's no rational reason why I'd get that out of "Panic" any more than out of a million other songs. But I do. And I blissfully sing along, even though I like mid-'80s Loose Ends-type music. I'm exacting some kind of revenge where none is needed. *"Hang the DJ! Hang the DJ!"* It feels like something that must be done, right away.

(#21, Facebook Top 100, 2010-11)

Thesaurus in My Pocket

Exhibit A: "I'm the kind of person that will say 'a person that I've been spending time with in a romantic way' rather than saying 'my boyfriend.' "

Exhibit B: "I'm a man who likes talking to a man who likes to talk."

Exhibit C: "That particular month we needed time to marinate in what 'us' meant."

So which one is (a) Alanis Morissette singing? (b) Alanis Morissette talking? (c) Sydney Greenstreet in *The Maltese Falcon*? The Greenstreet quote's obvious (especially as it was Peter Lorre who had the boyfriend in *The Maltese Falcon*), but sorting out the other two's tricky—depending upon your fondness for circular doublespeak, it's either heartening or alarming how much Alanis talks exactly like she writes. For the record, Exhibit C is lifted from "That Particular Time" off Alanis's new *Under Rug Swept*, making her the first singer-songwriter since Hasil Adkins to examine a failed relationship in terms of culinary technique. Exhibit A, from a recent interview with *The New York Times*, finds Alanis sounding very much like a woman who likes talking like a woman who talks like Alanis Morissette.

Good try, Jon Voight, John Turturro, and Dennis Miller, but the closest thing we've got to Howard Cosell right now is Alanis. Much like even non-football fans used to be mesmerized by Cosell's genius for never using two words when 23 would do, you don't have to be a love-damaged 17-year-old girl to find *Under Rug Swept*'s dense verbiage a trip. Words tumble forth and arrange themselves kaleidoscopically into all sorts of unusual categories. Multi-Syllable We-Can't-Even-Think-of-a-Word-That-Rhymes Words: "communicative," "connectedness," "reciprocity," "vacillated." D-Verbs That Nobody Ever Really Uses: "derive," "divulge," "dispel," "disarm," "discern" (what, no "delineate"?). Support-Group Thanks-for-Sharing Words: "engage in dialogue," "provide forums," "conflict resolution," "playing the victim," "survival mode," "midlife crisis." Ambivalence-Is-Maybe-Possibly-a-Sign-of-Wisdom Words: "not necessarily," "supposed," "so-called," "essentially," "conditional." Alanis-Must've-Made-These-Up Words: "ungood," "arms-lengthing." Perfectly useful, a lot of them, and the point definitely isn't that dumb is better or purer than smart. I'm just not sure that pop music should come out of a thesaurus. "(I Can't Derive No) Satisfaction," "Thank You for Engaging in Dialogue with Me Africa," "A Person I've Been Spending Time With in a Romantic Way's Back"—the world's a better place without them.

Under Rug Swept is being sold and written about as Alanis's psychic excavation of a bad love affair dating back to when she was a teenager. This is news? Hasn't she been writing about, for, and mostly at this same guy since "You Oughta Know"? (Still a distressing song for me, personally, being someone who can't even abide occasional whispering in a movie theatre.) Alanis was really coy about his identity then, too, suggesting that the blueprint for her whole career resides more in "You're So Vain" than anything by Joni Mitchell or Patti Smith.

But for all of *Under Rug Swept*'s mood of coming-to-terms-and-moving-on, there are still blind spots in Alanis's latest indictment big enough to drive Saskatchewan through. On "Narcissus," she ridicules her former partner as a self-centered egoist; meanwhile, *Under Rug Swept* might just as well be called *11 More Songs Detailing the Emotional Complexity of Me* (or at least *Nine More, Plus a Couple Where I Pretend I'm a Man*). In "21 Things I Want in a Lover," self-deprecation is held up as one of Alanis's ideal virtues; about the closest she herself ever gets on *Under Rug Swept* is the not exactly damning "I can feel so unsexy for someone so beautiful." Come on, girl, you're supposed to be Canadian—we invented self-deprecation. Alanis's talk of "selflessness" or "working at this" sends her straw man "running for the door." Maybe—or maybe it was "I bet you're wondering when my conditional police will force you to cough up" that scared him off.

If I'm treating *Under Rug Swept* (even the title's an unwieldy echo of Kubrick's *Eyes Wide Shut*) as if it were a lyric sheet rather than a collection of songs, well, the music's an afterthought for Alanis, too. Greil Marcus, writing about the Pet Shop Boys' "Rent": "I wonder where the melody came from—did they happen on it, say, My god, we've got an all-time pop melody here, what words can we write that could live up to it, or did they derive that all-time pop melody out of a serious lyric, sardonic wit, etc.?" It's not a question that jumps to mind listening to *Under Rug Swept*, not when you catch vocal contortionist Alanis squeezing in phrases like "capital punishment" at the end of a line. Of the 21 things I look for in even the most confessional singer-songwriters, a serendipitous gift for the all-time pop melody takes up spots one through seven. That's what makes "Sugar Mountain," "Both Sides Now," "Fire and Rain," and "Fuck and Run" so indelible—check out their melodies. Alanis has gotten, and continues to get, most of the way there sometimes: "Ironic," "Hand in My Pocket," "Unsent," and now "Surrendering," *Under Rug Swept*'s best song. But mostly you get the feeling that her songwriting process goes something like this: "'Post-obstacle'—my god, I've got a truly abstruse and daunting word here; what music can I dash off that could live up to it?"

There's a lot of well-intentioned autobiography pouring out of *Under Rug Swept*, but I wish it were the work of Thora Birch's character in

Ghost World instead—same level of confusion and venting, but with a sense of humor, some Don Knotts, and lots of sexy mischief-making thrown in. As is, it's more like the secret diaries of Thora's draggy art teacher.

(*Village Voice*, 2002)

"Another Girl, Another Planet," Only Ones (1978)

I've never compared notes on this song with anyone who doesn't love it. It's more likely that you don't know it at all, although in the context of the group following this countdown, most will know it very well. (I shouldn't be so quick to make broad assertions. I used to believe that there wasn't a human being alive who disliked Creedence Clearwater Revival, until I scrolled through a thread on the message board devoted to that very question, and of course a few people had jumped on to declare that yes, they disliked CCR. If you build it, they will come.) I'm not exactly sure at what point in my own life it became something more than just another new-wave song I liked. I bought a remaindered copy of *Special View* at Cheapies in either late '79 or '80. I'm pretty sure I didn't have "Another Girl" on either the CIUT or *Radio On* lists (too lazy to check right now), but it was very high on the CKLN list. So sometime between 1992 and 2005, it began to occupy a place apart from "Life Begins at the Hop," "The Day My Baby Gave Me a Surprise," "(What's So Funny 'Bout) Peace, Love and Understanding," and other songs from that moment I still like a lot. Some days, it's my favorite song ever.

It's a great song if you enjoy testing out your best fake-British accent; when I sing "You get under my skin/I don't find it irritating," I'm immediately transformed into this wan, skinny British kid with Johnny Thunders hair and a thrift-shop wardrobe. (I checked the car mirror once, and this transformation actually does take place—it's quite amazing.) I feel silly about this, but until about six months ago, when something prompted me to do some reading on Peter Perrett, I had always taken the song literally: it's about a girl, and he's so in love with her that finds himself on another planet whenever he's with her. Duh—it's about Perrett's love affair with heroin, something the lyrics make eminently clear if you give them two seconds' worth of thought. Cluing into this has not really affected my relationship with the song one way or the other—it still gets under my skin, and I still sing along like I'm on *Top of the Pops*. I have started to rethink "White Rabbit" and "Puff the Magic Dragon," though.

(#18, Facebook Top 100, 2010-11)

fragments falling everywhere

There's a Lot of '70s

"Beautiful Second-Hand Man," Ginette Reno/"Get Down To," Mainline: Canadiana. Ginette Reno—who had absolutely nothing to do with what happened at Waco—was a popular Québécois singer in the early '70s, the Celine Dion of another time, although Celine never has and probably never will come up with anything as good as "Beautiful Second Hand Man." It was Reno's one English crossover success, and it's the most amazing 5th Dimension imitation (specifically, "Wedding Bell Blues") you'll ever hear... well, I can't really think of any others, so I guess it wins by default. Mainline was a country-bluesy Toronto bar band led by Joe Mendelson; in the winter of '72, when I paid closer attention to AM radio than at any other time in my life, they had this terrific steel-guitar hit on CHUM called "Get Down To." Many years later, Mendelson flip-flopped his name and became Mendelson Joe, a local artist who's famous for bombarding Toronto's daily and weekly papers with letters ranging from borderline-crackpot to tell-me-something-else-l-don't-know. It's really something—he's been turning up every few weeks for at least a decade now, and he seems to have a free pass when it comes to getting his letters into print. I write a fair number of letters myself, though not nearly as many as Joe, and only a small percentage of mine are published. So Joe's kind of a role model for me: if I ever completely flip out, I plan to be just like him.

"Glass of Champagne," Sailor/"Sweet Thing," Goddo: Short of K-Tel, these are the real dregs of the '70s—I can't even include Sweet in this group, they were just too highbrow. Sailor was modern-rock circa the Bicentennial (literally—the only station that played them here was CFNY, thus placing them in the great Ultravox-OMD-Nine Inch Nails tradition that CFNY has kept alive over the years), a quasi-Roxy Music that actually did dress in sailor suits when they played live; they were in the navy before the Village People had even finished basic training. Goddo was a Toronto band that made it into *Stairway to Hell* for 1977's *Goddo*, a record I don't know. Speaking as a Canadian first and a heavy-metal fan 97th, I'm sure Chuck has the wrong album—it's *Who Cares* they're remembered for here, especially 'Sweet Thing" and "Oh Carole (Kiss My Whip)," a fan letter to Rough Trade's Carole Pope. In ways I can't describe, one of the highlights of my summer was having Tim Powis— a friend of mine who saw Rush open for the New York Dolls at a Toronto strip-club in 1973—recite key lyrics from "Sweet Thing" whilst air-guitaring in the middle of a trendy Queen St. cafe: "You like the fact I'm in the Goddo band/You're aware of a one-night stand/ That don't bother a girl like you/You get your cake and you eat it too." (Rob

Sheffield and Renée Crist were visiting at the time, so I know they'll back me up on this.) You can spend the rest of your life working variations on those lines: "You like the fact I'm in the Dogg Pound band." "You like the fact I'm in the Frente! band." "You like the fact I'm in the Blowfish band."

"Always Something There to Remind Me," R.B. Greaves/"Kooks," David Bowie: "Always Something There to Remind Me" is Bacharach/David, and it's one of those foolproof songs—this version, Dionne Warwick's, Naked Eyes', they're all great (haven't heard Sandi Shaw's, but I'm sure it's great too). I was surprised to find out that Greaves's rendition, his follow-up to "Take a Letter Maria," made it into the Top 30—don't think I've ever heard it on the radio. The Bacharach/David influence turns up in the oddest places, chief among them for me "Kooks" and Neil Young's "Till the Morning Comes." There's a lilt to both of them that's pure B&D. I completely lost interest in David Bowie after high school, and the last few years I've tended to knock him every chance I get: he's just so pompous, and looks so bad when he's out of step with the times, that I have a hard time detaching even his best '70s music from how I feel about him now. Except for "Kooks"—"Kooks" is three minutes of absolute genius, I think, a once-in-a-lifetime fluke that single-handedly makes me thankful for David Bowie. The melody is bliss, every swishy affectation makes you beam, it's generous beyond words, it talks about the bullies and the cads (and the Dads of the bullies and the cads) and makes them likeable, and it builds to a small moment of perfect joy: "And if the homework brings you down/Then we'll throw it on the fire and take the car downtown." It's Bacharach/David, it's Donovan, it's Noel Coward, yet it's also something new. It's a song I'd always loved whenever I was able to hear it on the radio, and now that I have *Hunky Dory*, I may have revised my thinking on what song I'd single out as the most emblematic—the most surprising, the most miraculous—of the '70s. I thought it was "Surrender," but it might be "Kooks."

"All Day Long," New Order/"Crystal Blue Persuasion," Tommy James & the Shondells: More from *Stranded*: Marcus calls Tommy James the Elton John of his day, citing "Crimson and Clover" as "a statement of utter abstraction and a natural number one." Those words might just as well have been written about "All Day Long." Being something of an Anglophobe during the Hüsker Dü/Replacements mid-'80s (I still am, I suppose, though not nearly as knee-jerk as I used to be), I didn't pay any attention to New Order between "Temptation" and the *Brotherhood* album—it was hearing "All Day Long" and "Every Little Counts" in the record store I used to work at that made me realize how good they could be. Listening to "All

Day Long" and "Crystal Blue Persuasion" back-to-back, it seems so obvious to me that New Order was the Tommy James & the Shondells of *their* day.

(*Tapeworm*, 1996)

Undertones

I saw the Undertones live in 1979, opening for the Clash at the O'Keefe Centre, one of the more famous Toronto shows ever because the crowd got out of hand and started ripping up the place. I was the ringleader... well, not really, but I was an enthusiastic onlooker; it's all a blur at this point. Anyway, it wasn't until a few years later that I turned into a big Undertones fan, possibly triggered by picking up *Hypnotised* as a delete and for at least a few weeks thinking the title track was the greatest song ever. All of this is backdrop to reviewing Feargal Sharkey's solo record for *Nerve* and feeling—there's no other way to say it—deeply betrayed. The only other time that jumps to mind where I felt the same way was with *Trans*. What usually happened with me then when it came to my favorite performers, or somebody following up an album I liked a lot, was that I'd listen and listen and eventually convince myself that it was a pretty good record—maybe not what I was hoping for, but good enough. Examples: X's *Under the Big Black Sun*, the Cramps' *Psychedelic Jungle*, the Gun Club's *Miami*. I was a total fan; I wanted to believe, usually worked hard enough that I was able to, and when that wasn't enough, I took it personally. Without going into a lengthy, convoluted explanation of what happened between here and there—the short version is I got older—I can't imagine ever working hard to like something now, and even less getting overly upset because somebody I like puts out a bad album. Too bad—feeling that passionate about something is a good thing. (I'm still passionate about music I love, just not so protective when it comes to specific artists. It's much more a matter of stumbling onto things blindly now.) The strange thing is, I'm still inclined to get that way with certain filmmakers. On the heels of *Boogie Nights* and *Rushmore*, *Punch Drunk Love* and *The Royal Tennenbaums* were huge disappointments (*Magnolia* was bizarre enough to get a pass initially, but I don't think much of that one now either). I wrongly felt the same about *Lost in Translation* the first time I saw it, until a second viewing turned me around. I'm at a point now where I'm prepared to be disappointed by the two Andersons, but there are two directors, Sofia Coppola and Terry Zwigoff, who still have a clean slate with me; the first time either one puts out a mediocre film, I suspect I'll feel like I did with Feargal Sharkey. (This is kind of funny—I've been anxiously waiting for Zwigoff's follow-up to *Ghost World*, and I find out just this morning, reading Andrew Sarris's review of *The Bad News Bears*, that *Bad Santa* was Zwigoff's. I had no idea. I'll rent it out soon. I'm not optimistic.)

(record inventory, 2005-06)

Genesis

It's useful to remember that no matter how strange or obsessive one's own pursuits may seem, there are always people out there who make you look like the picture of mental health by comparison. When I was looking around for an image of one of the Family albums I own, I came across Andy Thompson's "Mellotron Albums List": an extensive index, with reviews and ratings, of what is apparently every pop album of the past 35 years to feature a mellotron on one or more of its tracks. Loads of mid-'70s art rock, of course—including lots of German bands with names like Alma Alta and Embryo—more recent things like Oasis and Pavement and the Flaming Lips, and also a number of people I do not associate with mellotrons: Jose Feliciano, Jimmy Cliff, David Lee Roth, etc. I don't see Schoolly-D anywhere, but there are definitely some striking anomalies in there. *The Lamb Lies Down on Broadway* gets four-and-a-half out of five stars: "Banks used his 'tron on less than half of the album's tracks, and many of those sparingly, but there's several grade-A Mellotron classics..." (The way mellotron is routinely shortened to "'tron" is one of the things I most love about the site.) "Back in N.Y.C." isn't mentioned as being one of those classics, which surprises me, but then I don't know a mellotron from a synthesizer from a harmonica. You could spend several lifetimes trying to track down all the music indexed by Andy, so if that's your idea of a good time, this is where to start. You'll have 'tron, 'tron, 'tron till your daddy takes the Magma away.

(record inventory, 2005-06)

"Girlwish," Fudge (1991)

I have to be careful—as I did in my Posies entry, I tend to go a little off the rails when I try to put into words what I hear in my favorite power-pop songs. Of my remaining 16 picks, three of them are sort of power-pop—i.e., only if your definition casts as wide a net as mine. So: as most people understand the term, "Girlwish" is my nomination for the greatest power-pop song ever recorded. Greater than "Shake Some Action," greater than "September Gurls," greater than anything by the Shoes, or Cheap Trick, or Badfinger, or anybody. As Alan Garfield says in *The Conversation*, "The best, bar none."

Start with the title, which sums up the entire genre very well: not the girl herself, just a wish for said girl. It's just under four minutes long, and it builds like a symphony; there are distinct sections, and each one takes the song somewhere new. There's some genuinely smart wordplay: "I want to find a little bit of me in you." (One of power-pop's weaknesses is an addiction to wordplay that rarely rises above clever in the pejorative sense. You find this all over the Shoes' LPs: e.g. "Trying to feed the hand that used to bite you" from "Now and Then." Not terrible or anything, and the Shoes have lots else going for them to compensate, but such lines always make me wince a little.) There's a rudimentary guitar solo, a little bit of feedback, and loud parts; I'm too partial to the pop side of the power/pop equation, but "Girlwish" splits the difference perfectly. And there's a line that (unintentionally, I'm sure) speaks to this song's ambitions: "She wants everything, she wants it all."

Fudge put out two LPs in the early '90s, neither of which I have. They shared a label with Pussy Galore, and wrote a song about Patty Hearst—not sure how "Girlwish" emerged out of that. I like this user-comment on the Amazon page for one of their LPs: "My cousin Kenny used to be in this band! I was sorry to see them break up!"

(#17, Facebook Top 100, 2010-11)

Five Favorite Moments in Canadian Musical History

1) *Everybody Know This Is Nowhere* (1969) and *After the Gold Rush* (1970), Neil Young (tie)
2) "Rain Dance," the Guess Who (1971)
3) "Big Town Boy," Shirley Matthews (1964) and "Beautiful Second Hand Man," Ginette Reno (1970) (tie)
4) "Get Up, Get Out and Move On," Fludd (1972)
5) "Attack of the 50 Ft. Teletubbies," Galaxy Twins (1999) and "Chariots of Foam," Surfin' Tapeworms from Venus (1983) (tie)

1) The "nowhere" that Neil sings about is obviously L.A., which must also be where he is when he wires mom for money in "Cinnamon Girl." He's wishing he were back in Winnipeg, forgetting that he got out of there as quickly as he could just a few years earlier. If you're a teenager growing up in a small Canadian town, you intuitively understand what he's really singing about: nowhere is nowhere else except where you are. 2) The lament of the Cherokee Reservation Indian, as performed by a bunch of schlubs from Winnipeg under the direction of Burton Cummings. As enigmatic to me today as when I first heard it on 1050 CHUM as a 10-year-old. Part of the post-*Little Big Man* cycle of early-'70s Native American radio novelties—"Indian Reservation," "Half Breed," Redbone, Buffy Saint-Marie—but who's John and, my sentiments exactly, where'd he get the gun? It's more like an echo of Charles Whitman, or an omen of that guy who opened fire in a San Diego McDonald's a few years later. There's also some stuff about a bakery, and it all sounds as poppy as the Osmonds. Summing up: ??? 3) The first can hold its own against anything by the Ronettes or the Shangri-Las—there's a Canadian band from the mid-'60s named after it whom I don't think I've ever heard, although they charted four songs on CHUM. "Beautiful Second Hand Man" is an amazing "Wedding Bell Blues" rip that I'd take over anything by the (quite good) Michel Pagliaro, Quebec's big rock star of the era. 4) There's stuff on Tim's and Scott's lists that could just as easily go here, but for the sake of avoiding repetition I'll go with another *Dazed And Canadian* favorite, a one-of-a kind extravaganza by a group that had just located the wah-wah pedal on their amplifier and got a little carried away. 5) I only know three rock stars in the world personally, and two of them are behind these records. (I also occasionally play darts with Charlie Watts.) For reasons of security, I can't reveal their identities. But "Chariots of Foam" is just what you think it is, done up Ventures-style, and it once served as bumper music for my overnight campus radio show. "Teletubbies" measures the cost of Mike Harris's "Common Sense Revolution" as subtly as Our Lady Peace's "Naveed" exposed the nihilism of SCTV's "Maudlin's Eleven" sketch. (If anybody's interested in decoding this really annoying in-joke, please e-mail me for footnotes.)

(rockcritics.com, 2002)

Stooges

There was an early *Seinfeld* where Jerry and his bombshell Spanish neighbour are flirting, and she says, "Please, Jerry—tell me about these Stooges." She meant the eye-poking ones, but the line crossed my mind as I mulled over what to say about the other Stooges. Not surprisingly, I don't think I've played any of the first three LPs for at least a decade. At least I hope that wouldn't be surprising—I turn 44 this year. Is there anyone my age who still plays their Stooges records with any regularity? *Funhouse* was always my favorite, and if you want to hear something purely and unrelentingly chaotic, it has no equal. *White Light/White Heat* and *Album Generic* are in the same general vicinity, but both are on the dronier, dirgier end of the spectrum for long stretches; the Stooges are still basically playing a variation on heavy metal, and as such, there's never any mistaking it for trance-out music—they just pound and flail away for the duration. (Almost, anyway—"Dirt" stops everything dead for seven minutes.) There's something extremely physical about *Funhouse*—it was always one of the first albums I'd throw on whenever I came home drunk, and I'd kind of lurch around the room in a manner that vaguely resembled what is often referred to as "dancing"—whereas the other two seem more cerebral/conceptual. I'm contradicting comments I made earlier about Led Zeppelin, where I said it was the Stooges who were more self-conscious about what they did. It's all relative—as self-consciousness goes, I guess I'd put the Velvet Underground and Flipper at the more deliberate end of the spectrum, the Stooges somewhere in the middle, and Led Zeppelin as the most intuitive of the four. Seeing as I like both the Velvet Underground and Led Zeppelin more than the Stooges, I don't consider self-consciousness to be inherently good or bad. Yeah, that's what I think. (Note to self: don't try to theorize, you're not very good at it.) By the way, I still experience my fair share of amorphous anger at times, but I rarely turn to music anymore when I'm in that frame of my mind. Don't ask me what's replaced it—online Scrabble arguments, sometimes.

(record inventory, 2005-06)

"The Warning," Hot Chip (2006)

Probably half or more of you are getting ready right now for the same storm as I am. This storm—well, it's not just going to be any storm. CFTR's been hyping it all day as nothing less than the apocalypse. I told my students before they left today that, even though I'm generally a pessimist when it comes to these things—that if you go home and sit waiting by the window, *snow will not appear*—this one was a sure thing: there will be no school tomorrow. (And if there is, I was thinking, their teacher's not going to be very pleasant.)

Apocalyptic snowstorm music: I'll have to give it some thought, but for now, "The Warning" will do nicely. Snowstorms are majestic, so I want something pretty; snowstorms are easy to get lost in, so I want a song about getting lost; snowstorms are dangerous, so I want something called "The Warning." As with many songs on my list, there are a couple of lines I dwell on where I feel like they're trying to give voice to something very elusive: "There's nothing in a world where the melody's broken/There's always some way to make a silence be spoken." Something to do with the transformative sway of (pop) music, I think, in a lyric worthy of Pete Townshend or the Velvets' "Rock and Roll."

(#36, Facebook Top 100, 2010-11)

"Jaded," Aerosmith

Aerosmith has gotten more mileage out of a handful of amazing songs—my own list stops at "Sweet Emotion," "Toys in the Attic," and "Sick as a Dog," but I know most people would add "Walk This Way" and a couple more—than just about anybody I can think of. Now that they're in the Rock and Roll Hall of Fame, I move that the following be immediately voted into Cooperstown: Fred Lynn (a perfect analogy extending to geography and timeline; Fred was nice enough to bow out around the time of "Janie's Got a Gun"), George Foster, Cesar Cedeno, Frank Tanana, Will Clark, Gary Templeton, Willie Wilson, Fernando Valenzuela, Orel Hershiser, Wally Joyner, Lance Parrish. They were all pretty great for two or three years too. Or John Olerud, now into his 17th season of prolonged, Aerosmith-like drift. (5.0)

(rockcritics.com, 2001)

"I Am Trying to Break Your Heart," Wilco (2002)

More than just being a song that could have been #1, something I said was true of my entire Top 20 or so, I actually did have this slated for #1 soon after we began. Somewhere along the way, I decided that making people wait three months for a Wilco song at #1 might be deemed cruel and unusual punishment in some jurisdictions. It would have been just like the opening scene in *Help!* where everybody starts throwing darts at the screen. I would have been the screen.

I'm not a big Wilco fan. The last couple of years, I've started to take a casual interest in them—saw both films, put a song from their last album on my year-end list, and next time they come through Toronto, I may consider seeing them. My friend Steve made me a couple of CD-700s years ago, and they went right past me. To paraphrase Christgau on Elvis Costello's first album, "they suffer from Jackson Browne's syndrome—that is, they're a little boring." "I Am Trying to Break Your Heart" wasn't on either CD.

It's a song that occupies the same space in my life as "How Some Jellyfish Are Born": I'll play it three or four times in a row on the way to work some mornings, and then I'll do it all over again for the next day or two. It'll be the only song I can tolerate on such mornings. I sing along, I drive, and I try to think about nothing. Except maybe that some of the angular instrumental noodling reminds me of "Rikki, Don't Lose That Number."

It's not what you'd call a serene song like "How Some Jellyfish Are Born," or Arvo Pärt and Grachan Moncur III earlier. The title should be taken literally: it's about an "American aquarium drinker" who's made it his mission in life to disappoint everyone he knows, time and time and time again. Films and music are always blurring into each other in my mind, and "I Am Trying to Break Your Heart" makes me think of Bruce Weber's Chet Baker documentary *Let's Get Lost*. That film and this song are one and the same.

One of the main reasons I was ready to put it at #1, besides the fact I had been playing it so obsessively when we began, was discovering the accompanying video clip around the same time. According to the person who put it up, "I done gone and made this fer my film class." I guess so—it's so bracingly perfect, and such an inspired distillation of the song, I'm skeptical of that, but there's not really any other explanation for its origin that would make sense. I hope Nonesuch stepped in and bought it for use as the "official music video" without the question mark. And I wish somebody would give the creator lots of money to make a real film.

(#4, Facebook Top 100, 2010-11)

"Consider Me Gone," Jellystone Park (1991)

I feel like at least half my remaining songs are going to be a big letdown. And as far as trying to guess them, forget it. My #1 is giveaway (the artist, though not necessarily the song), another artist should be easy if you've been paying attention, and another one or two you might have an outside shot at. Four of them, including this one, are non-starters. In all honesty, I'd be happier posting a Top 10 where I felt confident I was connecting with most everyone, but, well, that's just not going to be the case.

Here's another one—still not the last—from the *I Wish I Was a Flexidisc* site. I first got hold of it just before November of 2009. It's an easy date to trace, as it's a song that will always have an inescapable link for me to my mom's death that month ("Big Blue Bus" also, listed earlier). No need to get panicky—this won't be an especially long entry, and the song itself is not morbid or depressing. It's actually quite sprightly; it sounds a lot like the English Beat's "Save It for Later" (something I briefly considered for this list), speeded up a bit and with atmospherically muffled vocals. I'd been playing it constantly for a few weeks after downloading it, and when I went back on the radio after a couple of weeks off, I knew it was the song I wanted to end with. It was the right choice. Later, I even thought about trying to assemble a YouTube video of my own, with a photo collage and some completely unauthorized use of Jellystone Park's song—maybe, 10 or 20 years from now, it would have been used for somebody's Top 100 countdown on Facebook ("Neat video—no idea who the woman is")—but didn't get much past the point of figuring out how to set up an account and log on. I haven't yet abandoned the idea altogether.

(#9, Facebook Top 100, 2010-11)

Disco

To repeat something I've said elsewhere—and which was probably made clear as I worked through the alphabetical section—I'm hardly the world's most passionate disco lover, but neither am I anywhere close to those people my age who came out of the '70s with a lifelong vendetta against the genre. (The funniest of which are Q-107 programmers and listeners who I swear remain oblivious to the fact that "Miss You" and "I Was Made for Lovin' You" and "Another Brick in the Wall" might just have one or two similarities to disco. Hate on, you crazy diamonds, hate on.) There were certain songs that sounded great to me then and continue to sound great (Thelma Houston, Maxine Nightingale, "I Feel Love"), a few masterpieces I only really ever paid attention to after the fact ("I Love Music," "Good Times"), a lot of famous hits that have never been here nor there to me, and a small amount of stuff I do loathe, some of it more now than then—as my first-year roommate once said about I forget what, given the choice between dancing to "Y.M.C.A." at a staff party and castration, I'd choose castration. (No one actually forced me to choose at last Christmas's staff party, so I just quietly remained seated.) I have no memory at all of any special animus towards disco at my own high school, which strikes me as odd, seeing as my school was as small-town and as lilywhite as it got, and seeing as my years there (1974-1979) perfectly bracketed disco's heyday. Either the memory's faulty, or we were so behind the times that the backlash arrived late too—it may have hit Georgetown sometime in the mid-to-late '80s. Anyway, the collection I'd take first from those listed above would be *Disco Gold* ("Ronco Presents..."), which has eight songs I've listed at some point in this inventory. *Disco Hustle*'s a TeeVee International double I found sealed, so tucked away somewhere around here I've got a "Disco Hustle Instruction Booklet" that I do plan to make extensive use of one of these summers.

(record inventory, 2005-06)

Sonic Youth

"Teen Age Riot" is perfect: all those weird tunings they invented may as well have been brought into existence for that one song and that one moment, an eloquent and fortuitously timed farewell to something that had been plugging along for 10+ years at that point (or 20, or 35—depends whether you hear the farewell as being for punk, guitar-rock, or rock and roll in general) and appeared to be dying with a whimper just as hip-hop was beginning its ascendancy. Which is a very simplistic equation, of course: a) the song seemed to have been intended more as an "All the Young Dudes" rallying cry than as an elegy, b) much of that hip-hop was harder than the standard guitar-rock of the mid-to-late '80s—i.e., was more rock and roll than the rock and roll it was replacing, and c) Guns N' Roses was situated on one side of the song, Nirvana on the other (the relative merits of which I won't get into, because it's 2005 and who could possibly be interested in continuing to argue about such stuff?). In any case, it felt like an elegy then, and still does today, and they carried it off brilliantly.

(record inventory, 2005-06)

"Africa," Thundermug

A record I feel comfortable in calling legendary, insofar as if you're of a certain age and grew up listening to Canadian Top 40 radio, you'll get talking to someone of similar background and invariably one of you will ask, "Do you remember this really weird song about Africa, or North Africa, or something having to do with Africa? I think the group was Canadian." If the other has a sharp memory and comes up with "Africa" by Thundermug, this will instantly be greeted by "THUNDERMUG! That was it, Thundermug!" Among other things—bongos, kazoos, bird-tweets, silly Mungo Jerry accent—"Africa" has a line that sounds to me like "Live off the land-a/Smoke mashmakhan-a," which would help explain the name of another drecky Canadian group from the same era, Quebec's Mashmakhan ("As the Years Go By," 1970). Or maybe the two bands had a big rivalry, and Thundermug was promising to "smoke Mashmakhan" by selling more records than them.

(*Tapeworm*, 1995)

K-Tel/Ronco

I've been looking for a sensible place to link to Scott Woods' recently launched *Blender/Rolling Stone* showdown, and, in a way, the strange worlds of K-Tel and Ronco provide one. As an undertaking like this album inventory should make clear, I'm a thousand percent in favour of lists; I've been making them for approximately 30 years, and, to paraphrase Bob in *Twin Peaks*, I will...list...again! I also don't have any particular problem with the idea that *Blender*'s list is intended as an alternative to *Rolling Stone*'s. Everybody knows what's maddening/ frustrating/mildly annoying (you can choose the intensity of your own reaction) about *Rolling Stone*'s version of pop-music history, and every time they try to manufacture interest in their latest reshuffling of the same old standbys, they're just asking to be ridiculed—as I'm sure they're aware by now, ridicule actually seems to be the most sure-fire way of guaranteeing that such lists are noticed. What strikes me as phony about *Blender*'s own list, though, is the "since you were born" premise, and the arbitrary cut-off date of 1980 that goes along with it. It reminds me so much of the old political joke about strictly enforced balanced-budget bills: "Stop me before I spend again." *Blender* would say that their 25-year window is meant to reflect their readership, and there's obviously truth to that, but any list that starts with Michael Jackson and follows with Outkast, Guns N' Roses (eye-catching on *Spin*'s 1988 Top 100, as doctrinaire as *What's Going On* in 2005), U2, Nirvana, Madonna, Joy Division, and Run-D.M.C. is hardly an affront to *Rolling Stone*; it basically *is* a *Rolling Stone* list, right? (I stopped at #9, the dismal Britney Spears, although judging from all the plaudits for last year's "Toxic," she too is headed for canonization one day.) Looking at *Blender*'s Top 10, I swear that "since you were born" is really just somebody's—one editor or a group of writers, I don't know—way of pleading, "Stop me before I vote for 'Good Vibrations' again." But do you really need the 1980 rule to avoid overlap with *Rolling Stone*? Speaking as someone who's fairly doctrinaire myself, even I can tell you that there's no shortage of fantastic pre-1980 pop music that has no place on *Rolling Stone*'s list. So instead of wasting space on the many useless songs I see all over *Blender*'s list, all for the sake of filling some artificially imposed calendar quota, what about Edison Lighthouse and Mungo Jerry and Alive & Kicking, or "Magnet and Steel" and "Draggin' the Line" and "To Sir With Love," or all the lesser known doo-wop and garage and early-'70s soul that always gets bypassed by *Rolling Stone*? There's even some hippie music they've forgotten about—do you really need to rule great songs by the Charlatans, the Fugs, Hot Tuna, and Quicksilver Messenger Service as ineligible for the sake of "No Diggity" and Duran Duran? (I'm being disingenuous: the Hot Tuna and Quicksilver Messenger songs I have in mind I've discovered just within the past month.) So I get the basic thrust of the *Blender* argument: *Rolling Stone*'s version of what is and isn't worth preserving from the history of pop music never changes, or at least only changes incrementally and at a glacial pace, and we've got 500 songs that prove how out of touch they really are. But the safety net they then set up—and just to make sure we don't mess up, we're going to knock all the stuff that supposedly bothers us so much right off the ballot before we even start—is bizarre. Take a cue from K-Tel and Ronco: open the door to everything and let God sort it all out later. If you're sick of "Whole Lotta Love," that'll take care of itself, and if you sincerely believe that the Backstreet Boys made a better record than Al Green ever put his name to, that'll take care of itself too, but you won't close the door on the Mungo Jerrys and Edison Lighthouses of the world in the process. I realize that carping about these lists is the only thing more predictable than the lists themselves, so I'll stop before I seem more passionate about all of this than I really am—I'm much closer to the mildly annoyed end of the spectrum when it comes to both the *Blender* and *Rolling Stone* Top 500s. It'll be great following Scott as he tracks each list song-by-song; he's got lots of statistical comparisons either up and running or in the works for the Bill James crowd ("listometrics," I believe this newest branch of data analysis is called), and, in much the same way that Michael Moore's creepy self-aggrandizement in *Bowling for Columbine* had me feeling sympathy for Charlton Heston that he didn't deserve, I even have a rooting interest in which list comes out on top...I just wrote a special little poem that I'm calling "Ronco Haiku":

> "The guy who did 'Magnet and Steel,' does this character have a name?"
> "His name is Walter Egan."
> "That's a great name!"

(record inventory, 2005-06)

"Mandarinerna," Kim Hiorthøy (2004)

I've posted two videos of people driving thus far; this one needs its own driving video too. My whole aesthetic when it comes to music can be explained much more simply than all that obscure rambling in the Posies entry, and it's been pretty consistent since the late '70s: all of my deepest listening takes place in the car. Whatever I connect with in there, those are my favorite songs. There's daytime music and there's nighttime music. "Mandarinerna" (and Arvo Pärt, and Oliver Schroer) is the kind of nighttime music that has replaced the doo-wop that was all over my CIUT and *Radio On* lists. I was listening to it on the way home tonight, a CD-700 I made for someone at work. Ambient would describe most of what's on there, but I put the Grachan Moncur song I listed earlier on there too, so I'll just call it nighttime driving music. It empties your mind of everything.

(#25, Facebook Top 100, 2010-11)

Fugs: "Carpe Diem," "Frenzy," "Dirty Old Man"

The school board I work for is always telling me that teachers are supposed to be lifelong learners, so I'm always trying to acquire new knowledge. This summer the most useful bit of wisdom I came across was from an old Fugs song, "Carpe Diem": "You can't outfuck the angel of death." I'm going to try to remember that. Maybe I'll write it on the blackboard next September, and keep it there all year.

fragments falling everywhere

For the longest time, the little bit I knew about the Fugs came from the entry for them in Lillian Roxon's old *The Rock Encyclopedia*, which I used to pore over obsessively when I discovered a copy in my middle-school library 30 years ago. Lillian's first sentence: "Who could start to describe the Fugs?" That was more than enough to get me hooked, but I was never able to fill in that blank, as the only albums of theirs I'd ever see were prohibitively-priced wall copies at used stores. Thanks to somebody out there, however, I was recently able to download semi-recent reissues of *The Fugs First Album* (1965) and *The Fugs* (1966). I don't think the Fugs would have minded—if they were around today, they'd probably even be celebrating the joys of frenzied group file-sharing rather than bohemian orgies.

"Carpe Diem," which turns up on both albums in different versions, is one side of the Fugs, the nihilistic folkies who undoubtedly knew the Smithsonian and Harry Smith (name-dropped on album #1's "Nothing") catalogues front to back. "Carpe Diem" reminds me of one of those scary Carter Family deathwatch songs like "There's No Hiding Place Down Here," another variation on the truism that we're all doomed in the end. The earlier version is drony and hypnotic, the second go-around prettier and more elegiac, notwithstanding its introduction of the "outfuck" lyric quoted earlier. Hearing a pop musician sing "fuck" in 1966 would be noteworthy in almost any context; hearing it sung sweetly and mournfully is thrilling.

On "Frenzy" and "Dirty Old Man," Lenny Bruce and *Mad* magazine take over. What surprises me most about these songs (and "Slum Goddess," "Group Grope," and a few others) is not the words, which, as great they often are, are pretty much what I anticipated, but how good the Fugs were at flailing their way through rudimentary garage rock at a time when everyone was still making it up on the spot. You get the feeling they loved corny three-chord rock and roll (and especially loved that it was miraculously within their grasp to play it), unlike their obvious parallel, the Mothers of Invention, where you're sometimes not sure where the residual teenage affection ends and the condescending aesthete takes over. "Frenzy" provides exactly what its title promises, a hyperdriven two-minute invitation to the band's new army of groupies to join them after the show for "baskets of love." Ed Sanders was nearing 30 when the Fugs first got together, while co-founder Tuli Kupferberg was 42(!); on "Frenzy" they sound like kids let loose in a candy store, overwhelmed by the possibilities. I mean, I'm sure there's some distance and irony in there somewhere, but those baskets of love carry the day. "Dirty Old Man" whizzes by in a kind of drill-sergeant call-and-response, and I suspect anyone who remembers Arte Johnson's old park-bench lecher from *Laugh-In* ("Do you believe in the hereafter? Then you know what I'm here after...") will love it as much as I do. It's probably redundant at this point to speculate on who they're *really* singing about.

(*Stylus*, 2004)

"The Boy Who Crossed the Street," St. James Infirmary (1989)

I better warn you from the start: a real "Huh?" pick, but my last one, promise. And a final thank-you to the people who run the *I Wish I Was a Flexidisc*, *Jangle Pop Boutique*, *Take the Pills!* and *Wilfully Obscure* blogs, whoever you are. I don't know how these sites will viewed 10 or 20 years from now—I understand the argument that they're the scourge of the music industry—but to me, the kind of obsessiveness that informs *I Wish I Was a Flexidisc* isn't any different from what Harry Smith or Lenny Kaye used to do. I'm pretty sure I wasn't going to discover St. James Infirmary for myself wading through eBay or MusicStack, and on the one in ten thousand chance that I had, I'm not one to move on to the cheque-writing stage. First thing I love about "The Boy Who Crossed the Street" is the title. It's mundane above and beyond the outer reaches of mundane. Here's one of my favorite *Radio On* reviews ever, New Zealand's Andrew Palmer writing about "How Bizarre" (before any of the rest of us had heard it yet) in the Monty Burns issue:

> *"This is the biggest song out of New Zealand in years...for a couple of months everyone was saying 'How bizarre' at the slightest prompting. Someone would drop a pen on the floor and you'd say 'How bizarre.' They'd bend over to pick it up and you'd say 'How bizarre.'"*

"The Boy Who Crossed the Street" is like that.

> *"Hey, you've got to hear this amazing song by St. James Infirmary."*
> *"What's it called?"*
> *"'The Boy Who Crossed the Street.'"*
> *"What's it about?"*
> *"It's about a boy who crossed the street."*
> *"Hmmm...Okay, I'll bite: why did the boy cross the street."*
> *"To get to—actually I don't know, I can't make out the lyrics."*

fragments falling everywhere

Making out the lyrics is something I need to sit down and do. This is the fourth song we plan to play at my school assembly—very fast but very simple; it's actually "Take the Skinheads Bowling" upside down—and the lyrics can't be found anywhere online (the seventh and final level of complete obscurity in today's world). I've decided I'm going to transcribe what I can and just make up something reasonably close for what I can't—maybe I'll even throw in a "how bizarre" or two. I'm all over the background "do-do do-do/do-do do-do"s; by my count, 118 of them.

Who were St. James Infirmary? Don't know.
Where did they go? Don't know.
How did they ever come up with something as perfect as "The Boy Who Crossed the Street"? Don't know.
Why isn't it famous? I'm trying.

(#5, Facebook Top 100, 2010-11)

Long Ryders

Here's a story I've told many times. It's from Dave Bookman, a local DJ/musician who used to be on CIUT the same time I was. Dave's band once opened for the Long Ryders. Dave: "I love how on *State of Our Union* there's a liner note saying 'The Long Ryders wish success and happiness to all bands.' The only thing they said to us the whole night was, 'Hey, buddy, can you get your van out of the way?'"

(record inventory, 2005-06)

What's My Age Again?

Love my people. Love them madly. Well, sort of. From a distance. Teenagers, I mean—aggressively whiny ones, especially when they temper their ill will with a devout belief in the redemptive powers of pretty guitars. I feel a pang of recognition when Blink 182 open their new *Take Off Your Pants and Jacket* by proclaiming in "Anthem Part Two" that "teenage rules, they're fucked and boring." But 25 years removed from adolescence, my lingering kinship isn't attributable to the lyrics. Truthfully, I don't remember a lot of the rules I was expected to follow beyond the age of 15 or so. Once I got my driver's license, there was the one about Not Smashing Up the Family Car, but I can see now that there were sound philosophical underpinnings and a clear line of logic at work there. Otherwise, it's more or less come and go as you please, and, as long as you keep up your grades, be as disagreeable or uncommunicative as you want.

Not a problem, because even in Blink 182's us-against-them and you're-to-blame songs, they do their best work between the lines anyway. "Anthem Part Two" proceeds with a list of grievances interchangeable with standard-issue Korn or Rage Against the Machine: school, politicians, corporate leaders (always a major concern among teenagers). But the carping is intercut with elegiac little pauses that align Blink 182 with a branch of punk rock you could trace through the Replacements and *Ramones Leave Home* back to the more ethereal of early Who songs. So is *Take Off Your Pants* "emo-core"? There's probably too much emo and not enough core, but I still bet there's at least somebody in this group who gets all choked up over misfit-for-life Wes Bentley's soliloquy about the wafting plastic bag in *American Beauty*.

The first time I really took notice of Blink 182 was at an end-of-year party for the sixth grade class I was teaching last year. Elegiac is ideal for the last day of school, and as the sad story of a kid apologizing to his mom before checking out for good played in the background, I asked Adam Pugsley ("Pugs"), the CD's owner, what was playing. "'Adam's Song' by Blink 182." Lou Barlow once said that the pinnacle of human experience is being 17 and in a hardcore band. Maybe—but being 13 and having the punk-rock version of "It Was a Very Good Year" named after you has to be close. I was a little jealous of Adam and a lot smitten with the song, and seeing the group romp through their mini-masterpiece "All the Small Things" on *SNL* a few weeks later made me a fan.

Take Off Your Pants' release was timed nicely with the end of the school year, too—Blink 182 is the perfect band for white adolescent boys graduating from Shaggy and Britney Spears to what I've come to think of as "older-brother music." That's not a value judgement, just a fact of life. I went through it in the mid-'70s with the move from K-Tel novelties to art rock and heavy metal, and I've seen it happen to my students with Nirvana, Metallica, Green Day, Limp Bizkit, and others. It can't be the illicit thrill of Blink 182's strict five-"fuck"s-per-song quota that's the main attraction, not at this late date—surely that's part of the scenery to kids raised on hip-hop. It's something deeper and more psychological that draws you in at that age. The little girls don't know, but the older brothers understand.

Oh yeah, girls—they're Blink 182's number-one favorite subject and "source of most frustration." *Take Off Your Pants* tells of nervous phone calls, hand holding, first kisses, a prom, even some wishing upon a star. (With time out for ejaculation into a sock—I'll get to those songs in a minute.) When the guitars are clipping along and lifting the melodies into a state of near purity—"Roller Coaster" and "Everytime I Look for You" are my favorites—it's like you're listening to the Mark Ratner Story from *Fast Times at Ridgemont High*. This *is* a value judgement: I'd much rather hear puppy-love woe from these guys than the Backstreet Boys. Not that Blink 182's is any more real; it's just that ringing guitars are God's intended Greek chorus for lonely teenage boys, and the Backstreet Boys don't have any.

Punks and pranksters that they are, Blink 182 also want to be G.G. Allin and the Meatmen. There's some gross stuff on *Take Off Your Pants*, but it's all quite corny and more than a little redundant. The Angry Samoans were the one group that ever did that kind of thing consistently well, and even with 20 years of accumulated wisdom on their side, there are only so many fresh insights Blink 182 can bring to the subject of anal sex with dogs. Happily, the most egregious offender on this count is hidden away as a bonus track, safely out of view.

Take Off Your Pants really ends, as it should, with two songs about home—leaving it, as the Ramones (or Hüsker Dü on *Zen Arcade*) once did, and then just as quickly wanting to come back. I wish the order were reversed and they'd gone out on "Shut Up," where halfway through the music drops away to a couple of strummed chords and there's a plaintive, almost lullaby-like declaration that "I think it's time that I should leave." (A live-in relationship, that is, but that's not what a 15-year-old heart's going to hear.) It's these few seconds that have been running through my mind for days. If you're somebody who left long ago, it's nice to be transported back to a time when the idea first started to take shape.

For anyone right in the middle of it all, "Shut Up" must feel like a bittersweet graduation gift written just for you.

(*Village Voice*, 2001)

"Georgy Girl," Seekers (1966)

Rootsy guy that I am, let me begin with a bold statement: here are the roots of Sunshine Pop, right here, right now. (Guarantee that some scholarly type will jump on to say that it really begins with the Association and

"Windy" a few months later, and I wouldn't argue the point. I think Alan Lomax may have done some field recordings with the Cowsills in the 1930s, but I'm leaving them out of the conversation altogether.) I've loved "Georgy Girl" forever—can't remember a time when I didn't love it. It's the ultimate in what I think of as backseat-of-my-parents-car music (not to be confused with older-brother music, an important genre even if you don't have an older brother), like "Downtown" and "Dizzy" and lots else from the late '60s. As Jerry Seinfeld once said about Sue Ellen Mischke, I'm crazy about it—I love its whole free-swinging, free-wheeling attitude.

(#75, Facebook Top 100, 2010-11)

"Janis," Country Joe & the Fish (1967)

My favorite fan letter ever. "It's not very often that something special happens/And you happened to be that something special for me"; if someone had sang that in 2009, or even in 1972, I don't think such a sentiment would have been especially noteworthy. But "Janis" appeared in November of 1967, and, according to Wikipedia's timeline, would have been written in either 1966 or early 1967—i.e., would have been written when comparatively few people had even heard of Janis Joplin. I've got to make passing reference to Godard for the second time in three entries: I can't think of a better, or prettier, or more prescient example of nostalgia for the present than what Joe McDonald summons forth here. "The sound of her voice/We once were there"—wow.

(#86, Facebook Top 100, 2010-11)

if anything should happen

In 1984, as I spent inordinate amounts of time listening to Manuel Göttsching's "Quiet Nervousness" (it was either that or R.E.M.'s *Reckoning*, I can't quite remember), I emerged from university with what was essentially a double-major, even if it wasn't officially designated as such: the English major I signed on for at the start, and the "cinema specialist" I upgraded to along the way. The course load wasn't quite split equally—there were slightly more courses on the film side of things, along with a couple of philosophy courses, plus an extra year for good luck. The English half was largely a waste, with the exception of a course I took in biography. My fault entirely—I just wasn't a reader then, something that happened, as it probably does for a lot of people, after I left school. The film half...was not. That's a very emphatic ellipsis there; it's not like I'm trying, 30 years later, to convince myself of the truth of this assertion.

Trying to explain what I got out of such an impractical (to put it charitably) degree isn't easy—there's an explanation of sorts towards the end of the *Sight & Sound* piece that follows, and "Anticipation of *La Notte*," a remembrance of Philip Lopate's a couple of decades removed from my own experience, does a fantastic job of capturing that time. It was something like an awareness that I would be a film student for the rest of my life, a default reverence for the directors and films I first learned about as a teenager. Not reverence in the sense of blindly liking everything I saw—far from that; a lot of what I saw then I initially hated—but a patience, a willingness to put in time that I don't always have when it comes to music. With my musical blind spots, I tend to move on and never look back once I give somebody a reasonable hearing. The Band and Otis Redding and lots else was lost to me years ago, for good. But I still dutifully haul myself back to *L'Avventura* every five years, hoping it will finally click. It still hasn't, but I'm happy to put in the effort.

In other words: I've never been a film critic, but I've written a fair amount about the subject over the years, and going to the movies still hasn't lost that sense of adventure I felt when I drove into the city at 17 to see *Belle de Jour* at the long-gone Fine Arts Cinema up at Yonge and Eglinton. (Full disclosure: there was a healthy amount of Bart Simpson and his friends setting out to see "*Bar-ton Fink*! *Bar-ton Fink*!" mixed in there.) My time studying film, and the couple of years leading up to that, was where that all began.

The Heartbreak Kid (Elaine May, 1972)

The Maddening Objectification of an Impossibly Perfect Blonde for Mary, a Carpenters cover for Steven, Neil Simon for everybody. Don't lose heart—we've only just begun. (Maybe Elaine May behind the camera is enough to get me a pass on the first transgression.)

The Heartbreak Kid played constantly on TV when I was a teenager—I must have seen it at least 10 times before I headed off to university. It's a surprisingly key film from a time in my life when some of my basic attitudes about movies began to take shape: feelings about how music should be used, a certain kind of mood I gravitated towards (whatever the filmic equivalent of Sunshine Pop is, that's the mood I responded most deeply to as a 15-year-old), and a central character who stood just enough in opposition to "conventional society" (whatever that meant to me at the time) that he met with my approval. I know, I know—Charles Grodin makes for a very poor Che Guevara. But the way he bamboozled those fur-loving football players was more than enough for me.

Kael liked it a lot, Kauffmann and Simon, not so much. (Double-checking, I'm surprised to find out that Simon praised the performances—I figured he'd be especially merciless.) Especially in the lower reaches of my list, I'll have a few picks that no one's going to mistake for art. Like Jeff says, I'm going to try as much as possible to go with those films that made a lasting impression on me for one reason or another, allowing the necessary room for more recent favorites where there hasn't been enough time for lasting impressions. *The Heartbreak Kid* clears that bar with room to spare. And I haven't even dwelled on the Impossibly Perfect Blonde, the Maddening Objectification of whom is played off against the (almost cruel at times) reduction to caricature of Jeannie Berlin. It worked on me. I still hang around ocean-side beaches, waiting to hear a disembodied "That's my spot" whispered from up above one day.

(#50, Facebook Top 50, 2011)

Library Films

When Martina first wrote to me about *Big Secrets*, I thought it was going to be devoted to library-related topics. So, as a possible contribution, I started a list of films that had library scenes in them. It seemed like a good combination: Libraries and movie theatres are two of the most obvious places in the world where you're not supposed to talk, and if you do you're likely going to be *ssshhh*-ed by somebody like me. (Actually, I'm not a *ssshhh*-er, but I do glare without much provocation—including glares directed at this one librarian in my local branch who's incredibly loud when giving assistance.) Soon after, I was told by Martina that *Big Secrets* was going to be more like a Russ Meyer film than anything else. I'd already started my list, however, so I just continued with that.

Eight of the films that follow I'm writing about strictly from memory, two I double-checked against written descriptions, and five I rented out to confirm what I thought I remembered. The rentals were partly because I can be obsessive about fact-checking, also because I'm forever in search of the sorriest single thing a person can do with his leisure time: "What did you do on Friday night?" "Rented out five films I'd already seen so I could fast-forward to all the library scenes."

Part I: Miscellaneous

Citizen Kane (1941): Thompson, the reporter assigned to investigate Kane's life, is granted 20 minutes to sit in an empty room inside the Thatcher Memorial Library and peruse Walter Thatcher's private journal. The room is dramatically illuminated by a shaft of light from above, and there's a frumpy attendant who recites a litany of rules Thompson must abide by during his stay.

Philadelphia (1993): An obviously sick Tom Hanks is asked by a librarian if he'd be more comfortable working in another room; Denzel Washington witnesses the incident, and agrees (having declined earlier) to represent Hanks in a lawsuit. The only other library scene I can recall with such heavy gay content is in *The Simpsons*, the episode where Lisa's flipping through index cards and comes across "homoeroticism."

It's a Wonderful Life (1946): It's hard to say what the message is here: In the nightmare version of Bedford Falls without George Bailey, Vi Bick is a prostitute, Uncle Billy's insane, brother Harry's dead, and Mary Hatch is an owl-eyed spinster seen locking up at the local library. Unmarried old librarians were obviously held in great esteem in 1946.

Goodbye Columbus (1969): Ali MacGraw's mother is contemptuous of Richard Benjamin's job in a library, and it's soon revealed that Ali isn't too happy about it either. There's a well-handled subplot involving a young black kid who hides out in the stacks and looks at art books; Benjamin befriends him, but there's an awkwardness in their conversations that's a little sad to watch.

Breakfast at Tiffany's (1961): Two important library scenes, one happy and one tragic, tying it with *Goodbye, Columbus* as the most library-intensive fictional film on this list: (1) As part of Paul and Holly's day-long romp where they take turns doing things that they've never done before, they visit a library and sign out Paul's book of short stories; (2) The next day, after they've spent the night together, Paul finds Holly in the library making plans to move to Brazil so she can marry one of the world's richest men. They have a nasty argument and part ways for a few months.

The Spy Who Came in from the Cold (1965): Richard Burton takes a job in a library, part of an elaborate scheme to make himself available for Communist counter-intelligence recruitment. He meets Claire Bloom there, also employed under false pretenses. There's a second woman who's their superior, and she's a real librarian. I have reason to believe that something equally sinister is going on inside the Georgetown library, and I think that guy who talks too loud is the ringleader.

Carrie (1976): Carrie is doing some research into what it is that allows her to flip over ashtrays and kids—there's a huge close-up of her finger moving across the word "telekinesis" as she phonetically says it aloud—when Tommy Ross tracks her down among the stacks and asks her to the prom. As soon as he gets the question out, Carrie flees.

Toute la Memoire du Monde (1956): I barely remember this, but I must have seen it because I instinctively checked books on Alain Resnais and Michelangelo Antonioni to see if either had directed a documentary about a library. I was right, it's by Resnais, and I think I saw it in class together with *Night and Fog*. It's probably worth seeing, but I'm reminded of something John Waters once wrote for a "Guilty Pleasures" column in *Film Comment*, how foreign films should be hyped by Hollywood-style trailers: "This summer, the director of *Hiroshima, Mon Amour* will take you for the ride of your life—a non-fiction extravaganza set entirely in a library!"

Night of the Demon (1958): Another entry that dates back to university for me—I wrote a paper on this for a big horror film study I did in my final year. Here's a quote from that paper that I'm especially proud of: "The long, high-angle shot of Holden entering the public library, dwarfed by countless books on all sides, is central to the film's movement away from language, as the limitations of this mass assemblage of recorded knowledge are quickly highlighted by the absence of a single volume. That the witchcraft volume and the runic formula are, indeed, potent examples of written discourse presents a dual level of interpretation, one level in conformance with the 'distrust of language' reading, one moving beyond such a reading." I'm a little surprised that nobody thought to shoot me in those days, or at least slap me silly for a couple of hours.

Part II: Ivy League Spotlight

The Paper Chase (1973): Harvard law student Hart (I don't think his first name is ever given) discovers that his contract law professor's undergraduate notes are kept in a special collection not accessible to students. Hart is obsessed with Professor Kingsfield, so one night he and another student break in and sit high above the shelves reading Kingsfield's notes by flashlight. It's a good enough scene—Hart is amazed to learn that Kingsfield doodled—that you don't take too much notice of how lax security must be.

Love Story (1970): After the opening shot of Oliver Barrett sitting alone on a rinkside bench, he and Jenny Cavilleri are shown in flashback meeting for the first time inside the Radcliffe library. She's working on the desk, giving Oliver a hard time because he's from Harvard and wants to sign out books from a much smaller library, really just trying to get him to invite her for coffee. Ali MacGraw had starred in two films at this point in her career, both of them with library scenes, after which she became more vehicle-oriented with *The Getaway* and *Convoy*.

Chances Are (1989): Robert Downey works at the Yale library, where he intervenes on Mary Stuart Masterson's behalf so she won't have to pay some $80 in overdue fines. The two of them then make a pact to go on a cross-country killing spree—not really, what actually happens is they fall in love. It's a funny scene, and a pretty good film.

Part III: Lifetime Achievement Award: Dustin Hoffman

The Graduate (1967): Ben and Elaine are in limbo: He's following her around Berkeley, trying to get her to commit to marriage, but Elaine's confused about whether she should stick to her original plans and marry Carl Smith, her Aryan-looking fiancée from med school. Sitting in the library one afternoon, Ben grills Elaine on various details about Carl, like what it was he said when he proposed—"He said he thought we'd make a pretty good team." Ben gets *ssshhh*-ed twice in this scene.

Marathon Man (1976): Dustin shares a table inside the Columbia library with Marthe Keller (also could have gone in Ivy League section); he hides one of her books so he can run after her and return it, but really it's she who's entrapping him. When he catches up with her at her doorstep, they have a thoughtful discussion on the ins and outs of library romance. "So why do you pursue people who sit at your library table?" asks Marthe; "You won't meet another thief like me in the library again," says Dustin, trying to sweet-talk her into a date.

*All the President's Me*n (1976): It was a banner year for our greatest of library-film actors...Early in the Watergate investigation, Woodward and Bernstein are following a lead that Howard Hunt's been gathering information on Teddy Kennedy. After two failed attempts at confirmation—one librarian fudges her story over the phone, another tells them that all White House transactions are confidential—they are handed a mammoth stack of transaction slips by a Library of Congress clerk, followed by a towering overhead shot of the two of them working away at a table. (*Straw Dogs* should also be mentioned here—no library scenes that I can remember, but Hoffman plays a mathematics professor who looks like he spends much of his time in libraries.)

There are no doubt a hundred other films that could be listed, but those are the ones I know for sure. I think there's a prison library scene in *Malcolm X*, an SAT-related library scene in *Boys n the Hood*, and there are a few films where I have a vague feeling they belong: *Born Yesterday*, *Dead Poets Society*, *Sixteen Candles*, *Ordinary People*, some others. My mom says *Teacher's Pet*, but I haven't seen it and she can't be trusted. There are a number of films I can think of which have no library scenes whatsoever: *The Ten Commandments*, *The Wild Bunch*, *Alien*, and *The Bridge on the River Kwai* immediately spring to mind.

(*Martina & Kay's Big Secrets*, 1994)

if anything should happen

The Sugarland Express (Steven Spielberg, 1974)

I'm again making my picks as I go along, working from a loose master list of about 75 films. I decided on *The Sugarland Express* Thursday night, before Jeff posted his *Close Encounters* entry. Thought about switching to something else, but the serendipity must mean something, so I'll go ahead as planned.

There are a few Spielberg films where you can legitimately ask, "I wonder how many people have actually seen this?"—*Empire of the Sun*, *Always*, the airport movie—but I'm willing to bet that *The Sugarland Express* is still his most underseen great film. If it weren't for *Jaws* (which I'll probably bypass; the fatigue factor discussed in the music countdown is still operable), I'd say it's his greatest film by any yardstick. I know that's hard to accept if you think his pinnacle was *Schindler's List* or *Saving Private Ryan*, and it's probably just as baffling to anyone who gives that designation to *E.T.* or *Close Encounters*.

With *Jaws* and *The Sugarland Express*, I feel like I'm watching the work of a runaway talent who's still completely immersed in the telling of great stories, without any of the stuff that will creep into Spielberg's more ambitious films. I don't want to start knocking what comes later—I like *Close Encounters* a lot, and I understand why the other three benchmarks I've mentioned are famous—but I'm just not as interested in the box-office behemoths (*Jaws* made a ton of money, but it wasn't a preordained event like Spielberg's other biggest money-makers), in watching Spielberg work through his various father issues, or especially in Spielberg the Award-Winning Artist. None of that is even on the horizon in *The Sugarland Express* (well, there's maybe a trace of the father issues): it's just stunning camerawork from Vilmos Zsigmond, Goldie Hawn's best performance ever, a key work in a lineage of New Hollywood outlaw films that runs through *Bonnie and Clyde*, *Easy Rider*, *Thieves Like Us*, and *Dog Day Afternoon* (among others), and a 28-year-old prodigy unleashed.

And music, of course—I'll be guilty throughout this list of giving disproportionate weight to music in arriving at my picks. John Williams does the score, but it's Toots Thielmans' evocative little harmonica bits that convey the film's mood best (and capture how much feeling Spielberg has for the four principals, all of whom inhabit worlds far removed from his own). My favorite moment, and probably one of my favorite shots in any film: when the screen splits in half horizontally as Thielmans' theme plays, and Hawn and Ben Johnson make eye contact in a car mirror and smile back at each other.

(#49, Facebook Top 50, 2011)

interrupting my train of thought

Il Posto (Ermanno Olmi, 1961)

If nothing else, this one gets in on the Neil Young Rule: "I fell in love with the actress/She was playing a part that I could understand." The stuff about playing a part that you can understand isn't even all that important.

My list will be woefully short on non-English language films. I'm guessing two or three; another 10 would be in my second tier of favorites—a Top 150, maybe—but there just aren't that many that have ever hit me with the force that my American favorites from the '60s and '70s did. The number of silent films on my list will be even more pathetic: zero. For a guy with a film degree, I make a very poor cinephile.

I've seen *Il Posto* three times now—most recently a week ago, when I rented it out, which is why I want to comment on it while it's still fresh in my mind—and I'm confident that it belongs here. Steven gave it a very middling write-up in his weekly round-up a few months ago, and while I can't say I sharply disagree with anything he said, I love some of the very same things that left him cold. He wrote that the story never really goes anywhere; it may in fact be somewhat generous to credit *Il Posto* with a story at all. (Plot summary, more or less: teenage boy applies for an office job, hangs around for a few hours with another girl who has applied, both are hired, boy goes to company Christmas party, girl doesn't show, next day at work, the end.) Sometimes I respond to such minimal narratives, sometimes I'm bored silly—*Il Posto* is one where I respond. Steven mentioned Sandro Panseri's "big dark eyes," and said they hint at something deeper than the otherwise blank expression he wears throughout the film; for me, the combination is richly expressive—of uncertainty, of loneliness, maybe even of a deep sadness, although there doesn't seem to be any particular reason he'd be so sad at such a young age.

Steven also made note of how the ending suggests "a lifetime of alienation," but didn't seem particularly convinced that the film went any deeper than the suggestion. I think *Il Posto*'s final shot sets up the life-of-quiet-desperation thing as completely and as depressingly as any movie I know. (The film appeared around the same time as Billy Wilder's *The Apartment*, and both seem to come out of the *Man in the Gray Flannel Suit* anxiety of the mid-'50s.)

I've used Steven's write-up to set my own—see *Il Posto*, and you may well find yourself just as indifferent and unmoved as he was. Steven didn't mention Loredana Detto, the girl who catches Panseri's eye as he waits to be interviewed. They go for coffee afterwards in the clip below (sorry, no subtitles). I didn't know she was also Olmi's wife until I went looking for some information about her. She's part of my own life now, having replaced Nico in *The Chelsea Girls* as my new screen-saver.

(#46, Facebook Top 50, 2011)

Nightmare in Chicago

Robert Altman made this for television in 1964. I don't know if it's available on video, but after being interested in it for years, I finally got to see it last month when a Toronto station ran it at 2:30 in the morning one Saturday. I'm wondering if it was the first film ever made about a modern-day serial killer—*Peeping Tom* came earlier, but that's something different, and I don't remember *M* at all from when I saw it 15 years ago (nothing except the ball rolling away, anyway). I'm not sure if I can explain this, but *Nightmare* looked much more like a 1969 film to me than one from '64. It looked like something that came after *Bonnie and Clyde* and *The Graduate*, not before—clean, hard, precise. The guy who plays the killer ("Georgie Porgie" is his colorful serial-killer nickname) is great, especially near the end when he's hiding out in a truck with a girl he's taken hostage. Ted Knight plays the police commissioner, so for a while you keep waiting for Murray or Sue Anne Nivens to pop up out of nowhere; eventually I adjusted, and you will too. Good film, and good background for *Natural Born Killers*, which looks like it's going to be a mess-and-a-half and wildly entertaining (and which, because it'll be my first Woody Harrelson film, will probably require a similar adjustment—I'm sure my eyes will gravitate to the edge of the screen as I search for Cliff, Paul, and Lilith). (7.5)

(*Radio On*, 1994)

The Straight Story (David Lynch, 1999)

If it weren't for three films—well, two films and a TV project—the career of David Lynch would be pretty much without interest for me. *Mulholland Dr.* and *Inland Empire* are my two personal *bete noires*, and I jump on the message board every chance I get to assail them with derision. The former was so universally acclaimed, and topped so many decade-end polls,

I'm willing to grant that there's something there I'm just not getting; God himself could declare *Inland Empire* a work of genius, and I'd still roll my eyes. Most everything else Lynch has done goes right past me, *Eraserhead* included. I'll give a pass to *The Elephant Man*—I know Scott loves that one, and I probably need to watch it a second time.

So what *do* I like? On one hand, the two most obvious candidates—*Blue Velvet* and *Twin Peaks*—and on the other, the least obvious, which would be this. I can't think of a more anomalous movie in anyone's filmography than *The Straight Story* within Lynch's. It's not just a departure, the way something like *The Age of Innocence* was for Scorsese; on closer inspection, such departures often turn out to be a director's signature film in disguise, with the same themes and the same stylistic flourishes. And maybe someone else could make the same case for *The Straight Story*. I couldn't—I find it as disconnected from *Blue Velvet* as Neil Young's *Trans* was from *Everybody Knows This Is Nowhere*. (But a disconnect in the right direction with Lynch.)

The Straight Story is surely one of the best films ever made about getting old, deserving of a privileged place alongside *Wild Strawberries*, *Tokyo Story*, *The Leopard*, and a few others that always get listed at the front of that line. Among brother films, it's up there with *On the Waterfront* and *Raging Bull*. It's one of my favorite road movies ever; here, the road goes by very, very slowly. It's a work of such subtlety and such feeling, and so completely* free of all the stream-of-consciousness weirdness that marks Lynch's career—a weirdness that's sometimes stunning, but more often forced and juvenile—that I'm not at all surprised it seems to be little more than a footnote among Lynch's cult. On one of the threads devoted to him on the message board, a couple of people list their Lynch Top 10s: one puts *The Straight Story* 7th, the other has it 9th. (A few posters do praise it.) My default Lynch putdown is an ominous voiceover on a trailer announcing, "Coming soon, from the mind of David Lynch…" You wouldn't find that voiceover on any trailer for *The Straight Story*.

This was Richard Farnsworth's last film; he died a little less than a year after its release. I've been meaning to see *The Grey Fox* for years, but just haven't gotten around to it. Ending your career with *The Straight Story* is like Sandy Koufax in 1966, or the Velvet Underground with *Loaded*. As for the plot…Farnsworth plays a guy who travels across four or five states on a tractor to visit his estranged brother. It takes a while, and things happen along the way.

* (Not completely true: there's a roadside scene with a distraught woman that feels like it was parachuted in from some other Lynch film—for me, the movie's only misstep.)

(#41, Facebook Top 50, 2011)

North Dallas Forty (Ted Kotcheff, 1979)

I'm sticking with the musicals. This one has some music—Chic's "Good Times," to be precise.

A baseball fan for as long as I can remember, I dislike baseball films almost without exception; football I haven't paid attention to since the days of Roger Staubach and Lynn Swann, but my favorite sports film is about football. (Favorite non-documentary sports film, anyway—and that may even be true if you count *Raging Bull* as a sports movie.) *North Dallas Forty* came out the summer after I finished high school, a point in my life where my feelings about sports—playing sports, as opposed to fandom—were at their most jaundiced ever. All thanks to my high school basketball coach there. So the timing was perfect: Kotcheff's film (I haven't read Peter Gent's novel) gave voice to those feelings almost as witheringly as Jim Bouton's *Ball Four*, which I had discovered a year or two earlier, and watching Nick Nolte and Mac Davis flash "Can you believe this nonsense?" looks at each other during team meetings was pretty much the story of my high school basketball career, such as it was.

The accompanying clip is a mish-mash of various scenes from the film, some of them key. I love John Matuszak going off on Charles Durning's weasly assistant coach: "Every time I call it a game, you call it a business, and every time I call it a business, you call it a game." Most of the final scene is included, where Nolte gets hauled before management on a trumped-up charge meant to corner him into quitting. Which he does, after delivering the film's key line: "We're not the team—*they're* [motions towards management] the team." A lot of *North Dallas Forty* makes more sense in the context of a pre-free agency world, when management still held the upper hand and professional athletes were basically cattle to be bought and sold on a whim. Baseball was a few years into that system being overturned by 1979; I'm not sure, but I think football was slower to change. In the world of LeBron James and Alex Rodriguez, Matuszak's speech and Nolte's righteous outrage seem quaint. But I'm enough of a fan to believe that there's still fundamental truth in some of what they say.

Nolte, Davis, G.D. Spradlin, Dabney Coleman, a bunch of people in smaller roles, they're all terrific. Spradlin especially interests me: between this, Senator Geary in *Godfather II*, and his spooky military guy in *Apocalypse Now*, I count him as one of the decade's great forgotten supporting players. I'm not putting forth *North Dallas Forty* as film art. Visually, it's nothing to look it—it's probably interchangeable with *Firepower*, *Force 10 from Navarone*, and all the other crummy late-'70s fare that played at the theatre where I ushered—and there's one terrible performance from Dayle Haddon. But it's a movie that appeared as manna to me in 1979—I felt like I too had just finished putting away childish things—and I love it to this day.

(#39, Facebook Top 50, 2011)

2002 Films

#1: *Pornstar: The Legend of Ron Jeremy*: Automatically of interest to me, being the story of a man who started out as a teacher and ended up a porn star; I, on the other hand, spent many years working as a porn star before switching over to teaching. (If there's anyone connected to my school or my board who has stumbled onto this page, please, don't panic—I'm kidding.) Not a major work like *Crumb*, this was still one of the few times at the movies where I didn't feel cheated or let down last year. Whatever reviews I looked at when it passed through town early in the winter seemed to indicate that Ron Jeremy was a rather sad and forlorn figure, a lowly schlub with delusions of grandeur as oversized as his fabled "hedgehog." Maybe I misunderstood, I skim reviews quickly, but I didn't come away with the same impression at all—Jeremy seemed modest, admittedly ambitious but more or less comfortable with himself and his lot in life, and altogether likeable. I think those reviewers *wanted* him to be sad and frustrated, much as it angered some people that the characters in *Boogie Nights* were so caring and supportive of each other—the desperate, hateful pornographic worlds common to *Hardcore*, *Star 80*, *Auto Focus*, and the like are obviously easier to process. You'll have to judge for yourself. I do know that the obsessively detailed scrapbook that Jeremy totes around wherever he goes is a modern-day version of Joe Gould's *An Oral History of Our Time*, no pun intended. (7.5)

#2: *As I Was Moving Ahead Occasionally I Saw Brief Glimpses of Beauty*: Maybe you could take a lifetime of home movies drawn from anyone's life and come up with something worth preserving, something that feels like art; that's essentially what Jonas Mekas has done here (it's like a test case for the old question of whether there's a good novel waiting to be written about anyone's life). I was never bored for the five-hour duration, and although the deep nostalgia of Mekas's childlike voiceover passages is wearing at times, it's more often engaging and moving. It helps too that every now and again a famous face flashes by. Buried somewhere in the sprawl, the most thrilling use of pop music I came across all year: Mekas's daughter learns to walk, and underneath footage of her scampering about the room, the Velvet Underground's "Run Run Run" plays full-blast. (7.0)

#10: *Bowling for Columbine*: Always pleased with itself, shamelessly so on at least two occasions, consistently interesting anyway. The two segments that are beyond the pale, the K-Mart sojourn and the Heston interview, have been adequately ridiculed, so I don't have much to add there. (Priceless: Heston saying, "You want *me* to apologize to Flint?")* The blatant dishonesty that Kael attacked in *Roger & Me* sneaks into *Bowling* in a one-second clip of Chuck Eddy among a chorus of people that supposedly lays the blame for Columbine on Marilyn Manson (to be included, Moore requires footage of the person saying "Marilyn Manson"). Anyone who knows or has read Chuck will realize how laughable his inclusion is—my guess is that the full body of his quote went something like, "Marilyn Manson? Um, he reminds me a lot of the DeFranco Family, minus the horns—musical horns, not the Satanic kind." Completely inconsequential, but once you catch that, and compound it with Moore's Twilight-Zone notion that in Toronto we all keep our doors unlocked at night, you of course start wondering how much else is a fabrication. So there's a lot of frivolous stuff to wade through, some of which I enjoyed: the too-easy but funny anyway bit about "African" vs. "European" bees, the *South Park* cartoon, the great punch line to Toronto's unlocked-door policy, and, best of all, Camper Van Beethoven over the opening credits. Moore's most cogent argument, related to but more insidious than the gun issue, is laid out convincingly: that the American media treat every corner of life as a spin-off of *The Texas Chainsaw Massacre*. (5.5)

* (A line that I later found out I interpreted very differently than a friend did. He heard the voice of Heston today, the NRA spokesman and right-wing moralist: "You want *me* to apologize to Flint? Don't you know I was Moses and Ben Hur?" I heard the echo of an earlier version of Heston, the long-gone movie star who once got to do pretty much whatever he wanted: "You

want *me* to apologize to Flint? Don't you know I used to drink with Bogart and fuck starlets?")

(homepage, 2002)

Straight Time (Ulu Grosbard, 1978)

1977 and '78 was right around the time when my interest in film started to deepen—or, more precisely, when certain movies started to affect me more than movies had ever affected me previously. I was 17 in '78, so my timeline won't match everybody's; I think for many people, the most formative movie experiences of your life happen earlier, sometimes much earlier. I still have a vague memory of *Straight Time* being in theatres, and I remember that it looked like something I'd want to see. I'm going to guess that at that point in my life, I would have seen *All the President's Men* and *Lenny* at the drive-in with my parents, and possibly *The Graduate* on TV. Don't think I yet knew who Pauline Kael was, so I wouldn't have known that she called Dustin Hoffman's performance in *Straight Time* "daring, stretching, self-testing." That was an aside in her review of *Agatha* a year later; she didn't write about Ulu Grosbard's film at length until *5001 Nights at the Movies*, where she said "Hoffman gives what is possibly his finest (and most demanding) performance." In any event, it would be another 20 years or so until I finally caught up with *Straight Time* myself. I'm not sure why there was such a gap between taking an interest in the film and actually seeing it.

Performances aside, Kael didn't seem to think much of *Straight Time*. Couldn't disagree more. That first time I saw it 10 years ago, I was surprised by just how good it was; watching it for the third or fourth time last night, I started thinking that it's pretty much a perfect film. I find myself drawn into its world almost immediately, when newly-released ex-con Max Dembo (Hoffman) checks in with his parole officer (M. Emmet Walsh) for the first time. It's a most unpleasant scene to watch: you experience Hoffman's embarrassment and humiliation acutely. I can't think of another movie character who gets you to hate him quicker than Walsh's parole officer, and he manages to do it with a smile. Max Dembo, meanwhile, is worlds away from Benjamin Braddock in *The Graduate*, but like Ben, Max plays it very close to the vest—he chooses his words carefully.

Straight Time is a good heist film in the tradition of *The Killing*, *The Asphalt Jungle*, *Reservoir Dogs*, *Heat*, and many others. But it's great film about the recidivist mindset of the career criminal, and while I'm sure there's **also a** tradition it belongs to there, I can't start rhyming off titles as easily. Something else it shares with *The Killing* is a devastatingly bleak last line, with a few final images to match.

I've written about character actors in the '70s before, and *Straight Time*'s one of those films like *The Godfather* or *Nashville* where they're all over the place. Walsh, Gary Busey, Sandy Baron (Jack Klompus on *Seinfeld*: "Take the pen!"), Kathy Bates, Eddie Bunker (also in *Reservoir Dogs*), they all make an indelible impression in their two or five or ten minutes of screen time. And Harry Dean Stanton, one of the key character actors of the '70s, has never been better. He gets off a line in his first scene that might be the highlight of the film, and he even plays some guitar and sings a little bit.

The only other Ulu Grosbard film I've ever seen is *True Confessions* with De Niro and Duvall. It was quite tedious, and I've forgotten it completely.

(#34, Facebook Top 50, 2011)

Two-Lane Blacktop/The Panic in Needle Park

For a movie about a car race, *Blacktop* is slow, slow, slow—if it were double-billed with *Panic*, which I also saw recently (*Panic* I'd seen before, first time for *Blacktop*), you'd need some kind of stimulant pumped into you intravenously to stay awake through both. But my whole way of looking at movies was so shaped by my initial exposure many years ago to the great American films of the early '70s, I can look at almost anything from that era today and get much more out of it than I would from a contemporary equivalent—the mood, the look, the familiar actors, they all click in and reawaken that initial sense of discovery. (*Panic* and *Two-Lane Blacktop*, for instance, share a completely forgotten actor who must have looked like he had a future the equal of Hoffman or Redford at the time: Alan Vint, a cop in the first and a redneck in the second, even though he looks more like someone who should have been taking over campus buildings in *The Strawberry Statement*. "Whatever became of Alan Vint?" I started wondering after he turned up in *Two-Lane Blacktop*.) *Panic* has great NYC cinematography by Adam Holender (who had earlier shot *Midnight Cowboy*), a good supporting performance from Richard Bright (Al Neri in the first two *Godfathers*), about a minute of a very young Paul Sorvino, and an already hammy but generally likeable Al Pacino; it stumbles around aimlessly, but as drug films go I'll take it over *Trainspotting*, which by coincidence I happened to see the very next day. (It's also the only film I think I've ever seen without a solitary second of recorded music, soundtrack or incidental or otherwise; very disorienting.) In *Two-Lane Blacktop* you get close-up after close-up of James Taylor behind the wheel of a large automobile (at times looking like he just fell off Mount Rushmore), Dennis Wilson anticipating Richard Edson in *Stranger Than Paradise*, lots of obvious *Easy Rider* parallels to mull over, a strikingly arty and obscure ending, and (the one thing the film's most remembered for) Warren Oates making bent small talk with anyone who'll lend him an ear. He's not oblivious to what's happening to him: says Warren to one of his many hitchhiker passengers, "If I don't get myself grounded soon...I'm going to go into orbit." (*Two-Lane Blacktop*, 7.0 for sheer weirdness; *The Panic in Needle Park*, 5.5)

(*Radio On*, 1996)

Comfort and Joy (Bill Forsyth, 1984)

This is the Bill Forsyth film that flew under the radar back when he was getting a fair amount of attention in the '80s. It started with *Local Hero*, which I like almost as much as *Comfort and Joy*; I would have been okay with including that somewhere near the beginning of my list. I think we got *Gregory's Girl* next over here, even though in Scotland it was made and released earlier. I didn't much care for that one, although I know it has a following. Critical enthusiasm for Forsyth reached critical mass a few years later with *Housekeeping*, which came after *Comfort and Joy*: some ecstatic reviews upon release (Sarris might have had it as his favorite film of '87), yet it's now something of a forgotten film. I've been meaning to rewatch it for years. I found it ponderously slow at the time, but I'm guessing I'd be more open to it today. A few years after that, there was a doomed star vehicle (*Being Human* with Robin Williams) that essentially killed off his career. Haven't seen it—few have.

Comfort and Joy, like *Shoot the Piano Player* and *Il Posto*, is a low-key examination of one man's melancholia, in this case a popular morning drive-time DJ in Scotland who feels he's deep-down a serious person with serious things to say. The melancholia experienced by Alan "Dickie" Bird is less cosmic than what you find in the Truffaut and Olmi films—he seems like a basically happy guy until the mundane circumstance of his girlfriend walking out on him intrudes. Their break-up scene as the film starts is probably the most genial of its kind that you'll ever see; Bird is even seen reluctantly assisting the vacating girlfriend's helpers as they remove all the furniture from his apartment.

Where the film goes from there is summed up perfectly by the expression on Bird's face towards the end of the accompanying clip: fanciful to the point that you don't quite believe what you're seeing, yet so deftly rendered that you accept it all and go along with it anyway. (The story is actually based on real-life events, I seem to recall, the Ice Cream Wars or something like that.) The improbable intrigue that Bird finds himself caught up in is just backdrop to the real story anyway, which finds its resolution in a throwaway scene in a hospital where Bird hears first-hand the real value of his unserious work telling jokes and affecting funny voices on the radio.

Three reasons I love this film so much, all of them found in the clip: 1) lots of driving scenes, many of them at night (all the drivers are sitting on the wrong side of the car, but that's okay); 2) Claire Grogan from the band Altered Images; 3) jokes that leave me smiling for days—"Give us an autograph, Dickie." My favorite in the entire film has to do with Mr. Softy.

(#30, Facebook Top 50, 2011)

In the Company of Men

Great premise, mostly well handled, but surprisingly (considering all the controversy) it goes conventionally soft the last half-hour. I don't think the basic plot would have unfolded any differently had this been made in the '40s—someone would have fallen in love, someone would have suffered pangs of guilt, lessons would have been learned—and I wish the director had followed through on the unremitting nastiness of Chad (Aaron Eckhart), which is really *In the Company of Men*'s main reason for being. Critics who love the film seem to view Matt Malloy's Howard as a necessary foil to Chad, a moral compass of sorts; I'm not saying Howard needed to be as malignant as Chad, and I'm not sure how the film would play out if he were, but as is, Howard's doddering around feels like a hangover from some other movie, the anomalous Martin Milner character from *Sweet Smell of Success*. I liked the film's abrasive, skronky soundtrack music a lot, normally not my type of thing—it felt threatening in a way that the movie ultimately doesn't, and every time it reappeared in one of the chapter lead-ins, my heart would start to race a bit. My favorite scene by far was Chad sitting at the conference table, sizing up his coworkers: "I despise that fuck. He's just the worst...it's like he's some totally new breed of fuck." That's what makes Chad so exciting: he really does seem like a totally new breed of fuck. (6.5)

(*Radio On*, 1997)

Welfare (Frederick Wiseman, 1975)

This should more accurately be placed a little higher on my list, but I've just finished watching a rental copy, and I want to write about it right away. Like *Comfort and Joy*, it's probably about as close as you can get to "not all that easy to see" in this day and age. (Frederick Wiseman sells expensive copies on his website.) I've seen it three times now.

If I had to pick one single film to encapsulate (from a distance—I was only a teenager at the time) my sense of what the mid-'70s felt like, *Welfare* would be on my short list with two or three others. What I mean is, my sense of the mid-'70s then was the same as any teenager's would have been, and I was preoccupied with the same things that a teenager would be preoccupied with today. The lives of welfare recipients were not on that list. But when I piece the story together retroactively, with an adult's understanding of Nixon's resignation, the Patty Hearst story, the assassination attempts on Gerald Ford, Ford's "drop dead" to New York City, and all the other stuff that was happening at the time, *Welfare* speaks to all of that in ways that are amazingly prescient and resonant. Prescient because it was actually filmed in 1972, before any of that happened; resonant because, in short, it's a cinéma vérité plunge into a country on the brink of collapse. You can date the beginning of that collapse to the JFK assassination, escalation in Vietnam, 1968, or wherever you choose, but *Welfare* really does feel like the end of the road.

Wiseman famously directs films about social institutions: high schools, hospitals, courts, boxing gyms, etc. *Welfare* is exactly as advertised (Wiseman's knack for intentionally mundane titles is as dryly precise as the Pet Shop Boys'): he takes his camera into a New York welfare agency, and you spend almost three hours watching people argue, plead, and hiss invective at each other as clients and agents try to negotiate their way through the Byzantine rules and regulations that govern eligibility for government assistance. "At each other" is misleading—most of the time, people talk past each other in *Welfare*. The clients are caught in this (the cliché applies) Kafkaesque cycle of getting bounced from government agency to government agency, and one after another, they seem to be delivering a tale of misery they know by heart by now. The government employees who try to process them, who try to piece together their stories and set them straight on what they need to do to get a cheque (or maybe just an appointment, or something called a "fair hearing"), seem to be asking a lot of questions that circle around each other and lead nowhere. Nothing much ever seems to get accomplished. I'll quote the exact words (dutifully transcribed by yours truly) of a woman I count as the film's most unforgettable client, an apoplectic middle-aged black woman with a weirdly menacing black streak down her forehead. She's trying to sort out her mother's situation:

Welfare Agent: "You're making it sound like it's my fault."
Woman: "It's not my fault, either. It's not his [*her father's*] fault, he's in the hospital. It's not her [*points at her mother*] fault, she's sick. Whose fault is it?"

It's a question that is never answered in *Welfare*—and, what's so perfect about Wiseman's technique, I'm not sure the film even tries. Wiseman just recedes into the background and watches it all happen.

(#26, Facebook Top 50, 2011)

I Shot Andy Warhol

The best moment in Mary Harron's *I Shot Andy Warhol* is a quiet one: as the Lovin' Spoonful's "Do You Believe in Magic" plays, Valerie Solanas (Lili Taylor) and Andy Warhol (Jared Harris) stare warily at each other across a roomful of frugging and monkeying Factory-types. It's Warhol's party and Warhol's world; he's peering out as Solanas peers in, and neither one can make sense of the other. The gulf between them reminded me of Dustin Hoffman's mismatched presence at *Midnight Cowboy*'s Factory-styled party, appropriate because Taylor sometimes seems to closely model her portrayal of Solanas on Hoffman's Ratso Rizzo. When she finally commits the movie's title act, it's not really convincing as presented; up to that point, she seems like someone who's more disdainfully amused by men than actually enraged by them. Not carrying around a lot of female rage myself, this basic hollowness wasn't a big problem for me. There's a good feeling throughout for period atmosphere, lots of great music used intelligently (other highlights are "Walk On By," "Grazing in the Grass," Blue Cheer and the MC5, and a pretty version of "I'll Keep It with Mine" by Bettie Serveert), and two performances I'll remember longer than the more acclaimed work by Taylor and Stephen Dorff (as Candy Darling). Michael Imperioli, my favorite actor right now, is perfectly nasty as Ondine, and Harris's Warhol is sublime. Looking over Solanas's *S.C.U.M. Manifesto*, he gushes, "Oh, gee, did you type this yourself? You should come type for us." You just know that it wouldn't have mattered if it had been the Bible or the phone book, his reaction would have been identical.

(*Real Groove*, 1997)

Elephant (Gus Van Sant, 2003)

I had planned on reluctantly bypassing this, but last week it was viciously attacked in the comments section—viciously, I say—and now I have no choice but to put it on my list.

I originally came to *Elephant* with little interest in Gus Van Sant, and even less in Columbine. There's a real arbitrariness to the big news stories I get caught up in. I was obsessed with the O.J. case, but hardly paid attention to Phil Spector or Robert Blake. The Japan earthquake, the hurricane in Haiti, and even 9/11 felt remote (I know that sounds terrible), while Katrina couldn't have felt any more immediate. A few sex scandals I've been hugely interested in, most not at all. I don't know what it is that connects me to some stories while the rest slip away. As a teacher, especially, Columbine should have felt very close.

There was that barrier to get past, and then there was Van Sant's methodical, seemingly detached way of depicting an event that on the face of it suggests exactly the opposite approach. Instead of chaos, much of the film involves watching kids walk through school hallways—sometimes the same kids and the same hallways more than once. I mentioned on the song countdown how integral music is to me when I'm required to have the necessary patience to watch languorous, long-take filmmaking (Tarkovsky, Béla Tarr, etc.). Give me some beautiful music, like the Arvo Pärt song I listed on the countdown, and suddenly Matt Damon driving a car in the middle of nowhere for six minutes—*Gerry*, also by Van Sant—is as good as it gets. But *Elephant* does not rely on music to do its work; I think there's some music here and there, but after seeing the film five or six times, I couldn't tell you a thing about it.

So the first time I saw *Elephant*, I had the same reaction that I've used to describe other films that threw me: I knew I'd seen something, I just wasn't sure what. When I wrote about it for Scott's site (listing it as my 6th favorite film of 2003), I hemmed and hawed, praising it for what it wasn't—sensationalistic, sentimental—but not quite sure how to address what it was. I thought it came up short on the thing that mattered most: feeling devastated when kids started getting killed.

Eventually, though, the film's rhythm made perfect sense. The sheer ordinariness of the world that the killers shatter is rendered dreamlike by Van Sant, and it slowly draws you in. One boy snaps pictures in a park, a girl scurries off to her library job, another boy puts up a front for his girlfriend. There's one passage around which everything else seems to arrange itself, and it's repeated two or three times from different vantage points: the photographer, the boy, and the girl pass each other in the hallway (the two boys stop and talk for a minute) as they make their appointed rounds. Once you have a feeling for this world, once you retrieve it from memory, when the deaths do start coming they're indeed devastating. Which is why I say "seemingly detached."

Two clips, both of which foreground the killers. (Everything that's prelude to the killings is lightly represented on YouTube in the way of shorter clips; the whole film seems to be on there, though.) The first is the massacre—just awful. The other is from a user, a slow-motion assemblage of bits and pieces set to Tears for Fears' "Mad World," the *Donnie Darko* song. I think it gets at what I love about the film very, very well. Don't bother with the comments—I took a look and couldn't get past the second one.

(#24, Facebook Top 50, 2011)

Crumb (Terry Zwigoff, 1994)

I'd have to do some detective work to reconstruct the exact timeline, but I think *Crumb* was the film that kicked off a window of 10-plus years where documentaries gradually started to account for at least half of the new films I saw. There were a few before *Crumb* that opened my eyes to how great a doc could be—*28 Up* and *Let's Get Lost* come to mind; *The Thin Blue Line* I didn't care for, and *Hoop Dreams* took a second viewing—but starting in '94, the number of documentaries out there that interested me seemed to multiply exponentially from year to year. That window hasn't exactly closed—I'm still seeing a lot of good ones (most recent: *Bobby Fischer Against the World*)—but, as Jeff says, a certain predictability of style and tone crept in somewhere along the way. Just as an example, I wasn't nearly as big on *Inside Job* or *Client 9* as everybody else was.

Crumb startled me the first time I saw it, and I still find it fascinating. I knew very little about Robert Crumb going in. There was a Toronto outfit called Crazy David's that used to sell "Keep on Truckin'" T-shirts back in the '70s, and I think I knew that Crumb was behind those; I'd owned *Cheap Thrills* for years, and probably knew he'd done the cover; I hadn't read a comic book by anyone in years, much less any of his. More often than not, my favorite documentaries are those where I know very little about the subject matter going in.

You can approach *Crumb* from a few different directions. It's a film about an artist making art; even though Crumb mostly laughs off any attempts to explain his objectives or themes, he does, somewhat sheepishly, reveal a lot about what he does and how he does it. More specifically, *Crumb* is about "outsider" or "transgressive" art (hate clichés, but sometimes I relent), with a detour or two into the phenomenon—not exactly new at the time, but newer then than now—of political correctness; one of the highlights is Robert Hughes practically hissing the words "Well, what do you do with anybody who doesn't conform to the standards of Berkeley?" There's a little bit about Haight-Ashbury and the hippie moment, even though Crumb is adamant that he despised all of that—he does tell a funny Janis Joplin story, though.

But more than anything—and why Jeff picking *Capturing the Friedmans* makes for a perfect set-up—*Crumb* chronicles (or maybe, like *Capturing the Friedmans*, inadvertently stumbles onto) the most nightmarish family unit imaginable. When I was watching *Crumb* again last night, I thought of *The Tree of Life*. They'd make a weirdly great double-bill; I've already made it clear I wasn't all that fond of Malick's film, but if you wanted to set two versions of life in the '50s under a domineering father side-by-side, they'd do nicely. Sean Penn wanders around in *The Tree of Life*'s contemporary scenes heavy with memories of his childhood. Next to Charles or Maxon Crumb, Robert's two brothers who are so integral to the story Terry Zwigoff tells, Penn is the very picture of a well-adjusted adult.

I couldn't find any clips of Charles on YouTube, which is not surprising—it'd be nice to suppose that the sensitivity of YouTube users decided that, but more likely Robert intervened. Charles is why the film was so startling the first time; he's quite probably the single most compelling figure I've ever seen in a documentary.

I've seen two of the three films Zwigoff's made since *Crumb*: *Ghost World*, which I liked a lot (had it on my decade-end Top 10), and *Art School Confidential*, which I thought was pretty good. When I wrote up the decade-end list, I said I'd make an effort to see *Bad Santa*. Still haven't.

(#21, Facebook Top 50, 2011)

The Agony and the Ecstasy of Phil Spector

I saw the Spector documentary tonight. The two or three reviews I glanced at beforehand were middling. I don't get that at all—I thought it was fantastic. Two medium-sized quibbles: 1) barely any mention of the Christmas album, and no mention of its doomed release date (Nov. 22, '63); 2) use of a big flashy concert clip of "River Deep" from '70 or so, immediately prior to hearing the record for real. If you like that Las Vegas-y side of Tina Turner, you'll like this segment; I don't, so it was pointless. One relatively minor omission: no mention of *End of the Century*. One omission that's so gaping, there has to be some kind of legal injunction behind it: the name Ronnie Spector is not uttered once. Past that, I wouldn't change a thing. You could go to the film as kind of a *Capturing the Friedmans/Thin Blue Line* exercise, and get caught up in questions of guilt or innocence; there's a good film there. For me—and not to diminish the life of the woman who may or may not have been murdered by Spector—that was almost backdrop to 90 minutes of Spector holding court. He seems to be in the early stages of Parkinson's, and seems to have a touch of dyslexia, too, but he's just so incredibly smart and funny about so many things. I know; he's in jail for murder. But hearing him talk about what drove Duke Ellington and Miles Davis, or the phoniness of his high school graduating class, or this mob guy from New York named "Skeezy" who stole "Be My Baby" for his movie, or working on "God" and "My Sweet Lord" back-to-back, all of it was amazing. He even finds Tony Bennett's elevation to MTV icon as amusing as I do. Actually, he's obsessed with Tony Bennett to a degree that's comical. Can't wait to see this again.

(ILX, 2011)

No Country for Old Men (Ethan & Joel Coen, 2007)

I'm about 50 pages into Bill James's *Popular Crime*. I like this quote from Nate Silver on the book jacket: "It's sabermetrics meets the Coen Brothers." Having once written a sabermetric defense of Milli Vanilli, I can vouch for the endless flexibility of sabermetrics. (So far the book has been largely formula-free, but I've just gotten to James's 100-point evidentiary scale as applied to the Lizzie Borden case, so the math is picking up.)

More than any film I've ever seen, I needed a second viewing of *No Country for Old Men*. (I'm up to about eight now.) I watched at least three-quarters of the film through splayed fingers the first time. It wasn't so much the violence itself, which is both graphic and plentiful—I've seen lots of films that can match *No Country* in the quantity and ferocity of its violence. What most unnerved me about Anton Chigurh's various killings was the *sound* of that violence; whether done with that horrific contraption he carries around or by some other means, every act was accompanied by a loud, sharp, crystalline *whoosh* or *thomp* that cut through the silence and made me jump out of my chair. Didn't even have to be a killing—as one of the YouTube commentators points out, the phone in the accompanying clip is lethal.

We're into the Top 20 now, so I wouldn't be listing *No Country for Old Men* if its big accomplishment was a lot of expertly choreographed violence, even expertly soundtracked violence. Every third American film since *Bonnie and Clyde* can lay claim to expertly choreographed violence, and most of the time I can't think of anything that causes my mind to shut down quicker. It's worth going back to Marge Gunderson's "And for what? For a little bit of money?" from *Fargo* at this point, and also to a line from Kael's famous *Bonnie and Clyde* review: "During the first part of the picture, a woman in my row was gleefully assuring her companions, 'It's a comedy. It's a comedy.' After a while, she didn't say anything." (I always wonder whether people like this woman actually existed when I read Kael, but we'll put that aside.) *No Country for Old Men* for me is an incredibly sad film. The world that Tommy Lee Jones's sheriff is drawn into is several degrees more brutal and inexplicable than the one that Marge Gunderson has to contend with. Marge solves the case and restores order in the end; Jones is left to turn his back and walk away, with the suggestion that he'll be forever revisiting what he's just experienced in obscure, fragmentary dreams.

No Country for Old Men was released in close proximity to *There Will Be Blood* (November of 2007, just under two months earlier than P.T. Anderson's film, according to IMDB), and the two are closely connected in my mind. Above all else, and for all their obvious differences, they both feel like George W. Bush films to me, large-scale reveries in which people get swallowed up by the landscape and by lawlessness and go a little insane. I know it's tenuous when you start linking movies to presidential administrations—J. Hoberman pulls it off in *The Dream Life*—but they share a mood that captures the waning months of the W. era well as everything began to ground down to a halt. I'm about to do something I've never done and will never do again, which is to quote Bruce Springsteen: "Well, sir, I guess there's just a meanness in this world."

I'll mention one caveat about the Chighur character I've made before, something that I don't think makes him any less of an unforgettable creation: he's basically an American art-film version of Freddie Kruger or Jason Voorhees, the indestructible monster that can't be killed. (Bardem's hair belongs in some kind of hall of fame alongside Joe Pesci's in *JFK* and Sean Penn's in *Carlito's Way*.) No slight to Bardem or Jones, but I think the most subtle performance in *No Country* is given by Josh Brolin, who's got a foot in each of their worlds. He ended up playing both W. and Dan White within the year; both felt like hollow mimicry.

(#20, Facebook Top 50, 2011)

The Candidate (Michael Ritchie, 1972)

I might be forgetting something, but there are three political films I love. I'll first qualify that statement the same way I did on the song countdown, which is to say that by political I mean overtly so, not just in the sense that you can read politics, either a little or a lot, into most any film if you want to. (And a second qualification: documentaries excluded. *The War Room* comes to mind, and there are probably others.)

The first is slated for my Top 10, although it's really more about journalism than politics. Not hard to guess what that one is. The second would be Otto Preminger's *Advise and Consent*, which I first saw two or three years ago and gets better each time I go back. It's far from perfect—it's got some of that slickness you'd expect from a big-budget early-'60s film, and the performances are all over the place—but I find it quite compelling nonetheless. And then there's *The Candidate*. *Advise and Consent* details the day-to-day maneuvering involved in getting a controversial nomination through the Senate; *The Candidate* takes a step back and details the day-to-day maneuvering involved in getting yourself to the Senate in the first place. The film's central theme, that getting elected is no different than successfully packaging and marketing any product, will hardly startle anyone in this day and age, and Michael Ritchie and writer Jeremy Larner obviously owed a lot to Joe McGinniss's *The Selling of the President 1968*, which got there first. The film didn't even necessarily startle in 1972; Stanley Kauffmann's review basically amounted to "Well done, but tell me something I don't know."

Point conceded, to a degree. What continues to amaze me about *The Candidate* is how unerringly right every last detail is, and how little has changed in the intervening years. I've read the McGinniss book, and I think *The Candidate* is a much more atmospheric, meticulous, and free-wheeling reconstruction of a political campaign. It's been a while, but McGinniss specifically focused on the advertising wing of Nixon's '68 campaign, as I recall; that's only one of many elements in Ritchie's film. Especially in 2008, as I obsessed over first the Obama-Clinton contest, and then Obama-McCain, things would pop up that seemed right out of *The Candidate*. One example among many: when Hillary dismissed Obama's qualifications at one point with a brusque "And Senator Obama gave a good speech," it perfectly matched the Crocker Jarman spot that dismisses Robert Redford's Bill MacKay with a brusque "And what are Bill MacKay's qualifications? His father *was* senator." So maybe Kauffmann felt the film was yesterday's news by '72, but to me it feels more and more prophetic with each passing year. (Obama. I don't want to get into a big political thing here…I get tired of it on the message board…so I'll just say that it was a little sobering watching *The Candidate* again last night at a moment when Obama's presidency seems more adrift than ever.)

Kael called *Nashville* an orgy for movie lovers, so I'll echo her and call *The Candidate* an orgy for political junkies—those like me who are addicted to the drama and the spectacle, not to the minutiae of policy. The film is an accumulation of great moments out on the trail: a summit with a labour leader that anticipates the closed-door meeting between Michael and Senator Geary in *Godfather II*; some unusable ad footage of Redford trying to interact with overwrought mothers at a health clinic (I swear these few seconds planted the idea for *Welfare* in Frederick Wiseman's head, and they also set up my favorite line in the film, Allen Garfield's "Grim scene, baby, grim scene"); an editorial from the real Howard K. Smith, who'd do it all over again in *Nashville* (and a roving reporter who's always addressing "Walter" in his spots—nice touch); a great running joke with a groupie; so forth and so on. And Peter Boyle, who steals the film.

Choosing a clip was easy. If a semi-famous film (at best) can have a famous ending, this is it—I hear political commentators make reference to it regularly. I especially like how Redford's question is voiced almost silently the second time.

(#19, Facebook Top 50, 2011)

The Social Network

I'll see this a second time before the year's out, but I'm positive I won't ever think as highly of it as *Zodiac*. After seeing *Zodiac* six times, I had a hard time pinpointing why I loved it so much when I wrote about it on my page; *The Social Network* is good, it held my interest, but I don't think I'd find it any easier trying to pinpoint why it felt a little hollow to me. Twice I thought it was great: the look on Eduardo's face after Brenda Song flirted with him at the Bill Gates lecture (I've got the same problem as Eduardo, so that's not what you'd call enlightened analysis), and the Beatles at the end. I give Fincher all the credit in the world for choosing "Baby You're a Rich Man"; it was the perfect song for those last couple of minutes, and if you put your images up against the Beatles, you lay yourself open to people like me thinking "God, the Beatles were great—they got at so much of *The Social Network* into a five-minute song almost fifty years ago." One thing I'm pretty sure is missing is any feel for period, which may not be a fair complaint for any film set so recently; nonetheless, this could have been 1987, or 1996, or 2010. (*Zodiac* has an *unusual* sense of period—it doesn't feel like any other recreation of the '60s or '70s I can think of—but it is there.) Justin Timberlake is really good.

I've been thinking about the film for a couple of days, and one thing I think it misses is something it actually got at quite well in the trailer with the slowed-down "Creep": what is it that's so psychologically addictive for people about Facebook? As I mentioned on the which-technologies-do-you-own? thread, I've been on Facebook for about a year-and-a-half and it's barely a blip in my life—it's about as important to me as the Weather Channel. (Not trying to be condescending; I've got other addictions even sillier, like online Scrabble.) But for millions of people (I hesitate to say "a generation," since those millions probably cover a wide age demographic), Facebook is inordinately important. The film doesn't venture into any kind of an explanation, and in fact doesn't even try—which is fine, but based on that great trailer, I think that was something I was hoping for. A character or two mentions the addictiveness in passing, like Parker's one-night stand: "It's so addictive." But the film goes no deeper than that. (I thought the time-lapsed panorama was more effective in *Zodiac*.)

I can't wade through every post on this thread to double-check, but I'm pretty sure everyone has treated Zuckerberg's character, and how we're supposed to perceive him, as a function of Fincher's and Sorkin's intentions. I'm a huge fan of *The Squid & the Whale*; if you compare Jesse Eisenberg's performance in that with what he does in *The Social Network*, you're going to see a lot of similarities. (One apprehension I had going into *TSN* was that he was too narrow an actor to carry such a film; I'm not sure I've changed my mind on that.) I think Eisenberg has as great a hand as either Fincher or Sorkin, maybe even greater, in the conception of Zuckerberg. He's a really unusual actor.

Something I remembered in connection to Eisenberg's importance in how you view Zuckerberg. I remember an interview with Spike Lee soon after *Jungle Fever* came out, in which he talked about Annabella Sciorra's character in very schematic terms: she symbolized this, she symbolized that, she was everything except an actual human being. And I remember thinking that maybe that's what you intended, but she's so good and so humane in that film, none of that comes across. Same with Eisenberg: however Fincher and Sorkin see him, I personally find him such an off-putting performer, that's the single biggest factor in how I perceive him (which is as not very likeable).

I waited a few weeks, and saw this a second time last night. Glad I did—not that I didn't more or less like it the first time, but it got a little better. My interest didn't flag for a second, and for a long film second time through, that's an achievement. There's not a performance that I don't think is good. There were about a half-dozen times where I thought, "That's a really great moment." And sometimes I'd think that of whole scenes, like Parker's first lunch with Zuckerberg and Eduardo. (Timberlake blows into that scene like he's Moe Greene.) I think one of the film's worst moments and maybe its best happen back-to-back, right at the end. Worst: the lawyer does not need to verbalize her oft-quoted thoughts about Zuckerberg. She may be right, she may not be—I'd much rather be left to figure out that stuff on my own. (Again with *The Godfather*, but it's like when Kay verbalizes things about Michael in the second film that we've already figured out.) The best: the final image as the Beatles come up. That's just so good: don't mean to sound like a dork, but (I assume you've seen it by now if you're on this thread; if not, etc., etc.) Zuckerberg staring blankly as he hits refresh over and over is—takes deep breath, ducks oncoming fire—a pretty great metaphor for the world today.

In general, I think one thing the film lacks—one of the reasons I know I prefer *Zodiac*, and also *Carlos*—is music. There's a little bit—besides the Beatles, there's a good song playing when Parker and Zuckerberg are in the nightclub. But I place more far importance on music than most filmgoers, so I don't expect anyone to agree.

Also: picked out Wallace Langham—totally missed that that was him first time.

There is the soundtrack music, yes; it didn't make much of an impression on me, but it must have done its job, because I never felt like it was intrusive. I meant music more in the Scorsese/Tarantino/the two Andersons/*Carlos* sense. Someone said on another thread somewhere that it's not a director's job to be DJ. That's something I strongly disagree with. Or at least with specific directors, I disagree. If you're talking about Sidney Lumet and 99% of the directors who've ever made a movie, sure. But if I see a Wes Anderson film, or a Sofia Coppola film, I'm very cognizant of what they're doing with music—*Rushmore* and *The Virgin Suicides* would not, for me, be half the films they are without the pop music. I wouldn't have put Fincher in that group before *Zodiac*, but I thought "Hurdy Gurdy Man" and Three Dog Night and Santana were used memorably. And I would like to have seen more of that in *The Social Network*.

I liked Andrew Garfield a lot. I think the tension between Eduardo and Parker is one of the best things in the film—during that first lunch, when Eduardo arrives at the Palo Alto house, the final confrontation with Parker after they pull the rug out from under him. The look on his face when he chides Parker about making him feel tough is perfect.

Glad you've come around on Garfield a bit. Of the three principals (I'll leave the twins out of this), I think his is easily the most challenging role. Eisenberg plays the sarcastic, sullen, (mostly) amoral genius, Timberlake the vainglorious, playing-the-room, amoral wheeler-dealer; they're both really good, but those are roles that actors love and thrive in. (I've also seen Eisenberg in three films now, and he's really no different than he was in the other two; I'm not yet sure he has a second part in him.) Whenever you have to play the stodgy, cautious straight arrow with some kind of a moral compass matched up against such types, if you don't strike the right balance (like Martin Milner in *Sweet Smell of Success*), you stop the movie dead every time you're on screen. It's like the Bridges brothers in *The Fabulous Baker Boys*: Jeff is very good in the glamorous role, like he always is, but for me, Beau gives the great performance. Garfield also provides maybe my three favorite moments in the film, two of which I mention upthread: 1) the look of I-can't-believe-this-is-happening bliss when Brenda Strong flirts with him at the Gates lecture; 2) The way he says "You?" in response to Parker's "You know what's cool?"; and 3) again to Parker, after he gets him to flinch near the end: "I like standing next to you, Sean—you make me look tough in comparison." He's got this terrifically smug smile on his face, like he knows he's lost, but it was worth it for these few seconds of shattering Parker's facade of cool.

I agree that the one Winkleheimer (not so much the other) is the extreme pillar of virtue in the film, so much so that it's played for laughs. To the actor's credit, he adds enough shading to the character that he avoids the Martin Milner problem. But I do think Eduardo fits that general description too. He's stuck in that old business model of wanting to put ads up on the site, something that Zuckerberg sees beyond, and for which Parker contemptuously ridicules him. If Eduardo isn't quite as obvious a cautious, straight-arrow type as Winkleberry, I think it's because the character is more complex.

We see the character differently. To me, Eduardo's only a chump in outline—in two of the three scenes I listed above, he's got Parker figured out exactly. He signs away his fortune, yes, but—and this is definitely where people are going to view him differently—I don't see him as a chump there, just a guy who's again operating in a universe different than the one Zuckerberg and Parker are in. (This admission won't make me sound especially complex, but I think I'd put up with a lot of psychotic behaviour from Brenda Song to have her climbing all over me.)

The Social Network (5/5—initial misgivings are gone; I completely love this now).

(ILX, 2010-11)

if anything should happen

The Squid and the Whale (Noel Baumbach, 2005)

Strange, unsettling, and a different kind of claustrophobic. Autobiographical, clearly, but my guess is that it's the kind of autobiography that (unlike *Rushmore*) invents the bare minimum—changes someone's name from Gary to Jerry, makes the next-door neighbour a dentist instead of a doctor, that kind of thing. But it really does feel like Noah Baumbach is recounting his upbringing very precisely here.

It's an upbringing that I half recognize. In broad outline, it couldn't be more dissimilar to my own. The two boys here—teenager Walt Berkman (Jesse Eisenberg from *The Social Network*) and his younger brother Frank—live in a fairly rarefied world, less economically (although that too) than culturally. That's what I mean about fudging the details just enough: the Berkman parents both write fiction, the mom for *The New Yorker*, whereas Baumbach's mom was a film critic for *The Village Voice* (Georgia Brown—I think I used check her reviews for a time), and his dad is listed in Wikipedia as a novelist/film critic. The boys have a private tennis instructor, their father's idea of small-talk consists of authoritative dismissals of Dickens and Fitzgerald—always a big topic of conversation around my own family's dinner table—and they just generally comport themselves in the detached, eccentric manner of kids privileged enough to be a beat or three removed from the mundane concerns of less privileged kids their age. When their parents split up, they take sides. It's the world of Wes Anderson and Whit Stillman—"the upper-class WASPs of the U.S. socio-cultural elite," Wikipedia calls it, also linking the three directors together. None of that applies to me.

What I do recognize, though, and what I'm sure most people will recognize, is a family dynamic where a lot gets left unsaid. It's a common theme: it's there in *Long Day's Journey Into Night*, which is great, and it's there in *Ordinary People*, which, based on dim memories from 30 years ago, is ordinary. (Not a film for a 20-year-old, least of all one horrified to see it beat *Raging Bull* for best film—I should see it again.) Big things get left unsaid—maybe we shouldn't talk about mom's morphine addiction—and little things. One by one they accumulate, and after a while everyone knows the trap doors. When someone opens one up accidentally, or with the intent of antagonizing someone else—*The Squid and the Whale* is very much about those deliberate acts of provocation—the carefully constructed house of cards starts to teeter. In the Berkman family, everything pivots off the father. I don't think I've ever encountered another cinematic father like the one Jeff Daniels creates here. To say he takes up a lot of oxygen would miss the mark significantly. There no oxygen at all when he's around. Maybe that's why the younger Berkman son seems beyond just detached and eccentric at times. It's more like he's brain-damaged.

I don't know where Daniels' frightening performance comes from—prior to this, he was just the genial doofus in *Something Wild* to me. Laura Linney is as real as the mother as she was in *You Can Count on Me*. Seems like I've seen a lot of memorably weird kids in American movies the past decade, and Eisenberg and Owen Kline would head the list. I like *The Social Network* a lot, but the strength of Eisenberg's performance in *The Squid and the Whale* creates some interference for me.

Here's the final scene, one of the most elliptically perfect I've ever seen. The movie follows with Bert Jansch's "Counting Blues" over the end credits, something I wrote about in the song countdown (Jansch's "Running from Home" was my #4—I may still have never heard it if not for Baumbach). I'll repeat the key line from "Counting Blues" here: "Don't be afraid."

(#17, Facebook Top 50, 2011)

To Sir with Love (James Clavell, 1967)

I had something really *Sight & Sound*y slated for #16, but I've flip-flopped a couple of picks so I can bring Steven and Jeff's canonical reign of terror to a momentary end. Be forewarned: I'm a great believer in the infinite powers of nostalgia, and can be very protective about the most cherished objects of my misty-eyed reveries, so if you're someone who dismisses such a mindset—not naming any names here—just take three steps back and be very, very careful.

We talked a bit about Mark Harris's *Pictures at a Revolution* earlier, in conjunction with *Midnight Cowboy*. The not-so-secret star of the book is Sidney Poitier. He made three hugely successful films in 1967, two of which vied, deservedly or not, for Best Picture, and inadvertently found himself caught up squarely in the politics of the day. As cities rioted, he was #1 on the list of 1968 box-office stars (#7 on the '67 list—there must be a year's lag in measuring that). All three of his '67 films put race front and center—pretty much impossible not to at the time if your lead actor was African-American. (Even in *Night of the Living Dead* a year later, race is weirdly front and center because of George Romero's inspired decision to avoid any mention or even awareness that his lead character happened to be African-American.) American film in 1967 meant *Bonnie and Clyde*, *The Graduate*, and Sidney Poitier.

A brief word on the other two Poitier films that year. I don't know that anyone would argue for *In the Heat of the Night* as being great art, but it's well done, and watching Poitier and Steiger go at it is very entertaining. I think Poitier should have won Best Actor that year for the sum of his performances, but Steiger was otherwise a fine choice. As for *Guess Who's Coming to Dinner*, well, it's not without merit, and not as hopelessly dated as you might expect. That's about the best I can say—it's been a while since I last saw it.

To Sir with Love was the least consequential of the three at the time, and has probably been seen by far fewer people (although it's hardly obscure—I find that most people anywhere close to my own age have seen it). If you're puzzled by my inclusion of it here, you likely find it no less cloying, sentimental, or naïve than *Guess Who's Coming to Dinner*. And indeed, Sarris simultaneously praises and dismisses it as "super-Kramer" in *The American Cinema*.

Where to begin conveying what I love about it? I'm sure every teacher can point to a film or two as the idealization of what kind of teacher you want to be and too rarely are. Mine is split between a few films (there's even a part of me that likes being the supercilious Kingsfield in *The Paper Chase*), but *To Sir with Love* wins that one walking away. Ending up as a teacher wasn't even on my radar through my 20s (I remember ridiculing a friend who went straight from university to teachers college), but when I did finally apply at the age of 28, I know that somewhere in the deepest recesses of my mind was the moment in *To Sir with Love* when Poitier turns the corner on the final day, pauses, and there's everyone all lined up looking as angelic as can be. Once Poitier gets past the moment early in the film when he justifiably flips out and has the (convenient, yes) light bulb go off in his head as to how he needs to handle the class, he's a model of temperance, good judgement, and deep concern the rest of the way. I have my moments where I stumble onto one or another of those elevated states of being, but mostly I'm just making it up blindly as I go along, so I really fall for that part of the movie.

The rest of my attachment is where nostalgia takes over. I saw *To Sir with Love* at a very young age (probably at a drive-in), and the music, the dinginess of East London, Judy Geeson and Lulu, Christian Roberts as Brando/Dean, the period details, the incredible field trip to the museum, Poitier's dramatic gesture at the end, it all made a deep impression on me. Poitier and Geeson dancing to "It's Getting Harder All the Time" at the graduation party is in the running for my single favorite scene ever. I even love how it subverts one of the polite racial stereotypes of its day: as Poitier lurches around preposterously, it's Geeson who turns out to be the fantastic dancer. Actually, I'd say that *To Sir with Love* is more nuanced in its treatment of race than *In the Heat of the Night*. The crotchety old teacher who baits Poitier casually slips in a couple of especially venal lines.

Remember now: be very, very careful.

(#16, Facebook Top 50, 2011)

Welcome to L.A.

Finally saw *Welcome to L.A.*—I wanted to see it in 1976, but got sidetracked. The DVD has a warning up-front about "best available transfer," which isn't really necessary; it's a good-looking film, and the slightly faded quality only adds to that. Richard Baskin's songs are everywhere, even more than in *Nashville*. You have to be able to put them to the side somehow to get through the movie—don't think I've ever heard a more iconically awful version of a mid-'70s singer-songwriter. (I've always liked *Nashville*'s music fine in context, some of it even out of context.) Besides Baskin and Keith Carradine and Geraldine Chaplin, there's also Allan Nicholls, who played Bill in *Nashville*. I'm always fascinated by the conception of female beauty that held sway in the '70s: Chaplin, Sissy Spacek, Lauren Hutton, Sally Kellerman—I'm not sure if they'd have made sense at any other time. (Spacek went on, I know, but the '70s Spacek is like a person apart for me.) Carradine has dalliances with all of them, of course, Diane Abbott too. His callowness and silences and fedora overwhelm every woman who comes into his orbit—he's gone through three of them within 10 minutes of showing up. Mostly I liked this. Many would be repulsed.

(ILX, 2012)

Pather Panchali/Aparajito/Apur Sansar (Satyajit Ray, 1955/1956/1959)

I was whining and cajoling and instigating about being too deferential to the canon the other day. It's my turn now, so different rules.

I'm exceptionally lucky to have seen these at the Cinematheque back-to-back-to-back in a single sitting something like 15 years ago—a little under six hours, plus a short break between each film. I saw them again on consecutive days a few years after that, and last week I watched them all at home over the course of four or five days. But it's still that first encounter I think back to. There are certain screenings in my life that I carry around in my head the way

if anything should happen

you might remember famous bands you saw in your 20s, and seeing *The Apu Trilogy* (as it's generally called) shown as the one long movie it essentially is occupies a place at or near the top of that list. I want to call it a time-lapse version of a human life lived, but that's just what it feel likes when it's all over; in actual fact, *Pather Panchali* begins before Apu is born, and Apur Sansar only takes him up to about the age of 30.

I could have limited myself to just *Pather Panchali*, which I think most people would agree is closer to perfection than the two later installments. (There's one moment that doesn't hit me right—the father's reaction to Durga's death—otherwise I'd say it is perfection.) Chunibala Devi as the old aunt is like Charles Crumb: you will literally never encounter anyone else remotely like her in any other film. I'll again link to the montage of Ravi Shankar music I used for the song countdown, which is basically *Pather Panchali* in miniature. You get our introduction to the boy Apu (a moment as joyous as anything I can think of), some nature footage that ranks with the riverboat sequence in *Night of the Hunter*, Durga's otherworldly communion with the monsoon, and the lingering sadness of the film's final image. On its own, *Pather Panchali* just barely snuck into *Sight & Sound*'s Top 10 list in 1992—the year of Ray's death, although I don't know if there's any connection; he died in April, and I thought the poll was published early in the year—but dropped out again last time.

I'm voting for the trilogy, though, because there are moments in *Aparajito* and *Apur Sansar* I simply would not want to be without. I'm thinking especially of Apu in *Aparajito* after his teacher gives him the books, and he starts breathlessly sharing his discoveries about eclipses and Africa with his mother. Again, joyous—the simplest, most joyous expression of opening one's eyes to the world that you'll ever see. (A sly echo of the first film, but this time a metaphorical opening of one's eyes rather than literal.) Or the scene where the children watch the puppet show, clearly the inspiration for a similar scene in *The 400 Blows*. And more death, of course, a part of Apu's journey in every film; in *Aparajito*, he loses both parents.

Apur Sansar belongs to Sharmila Tagore, Apu's accidental wife as he struggles to find his place in the world as an adult, and to Alok Chakravarty as Apu's estranged son Kajal. You can't find a speck of information about him online (*Apur Sansar* was his only film), but the sequence of him running around with that silly mask on, or his cat-and-mouse maneuvering with his father at the end of the film, brings everything full circle back to the young Apu in *Pather Panchali*. He's amazing.

(#15, Facebook Top 50, 2011)

The Heart of the Game (Ward Serrill, 2005)

It may turn out otherwise, but I'm fairly sure this will be the most obscure pick by any of us from this point forward. Relatively obscure; it's been rated by 669 people on IMDB (for purposes of comparison, *Pulp Fiction* has been rated by just under half a million, *Welfare* by 124), and you can link to 51 external reviews, including Ebert, the *Voice*, and *Rolling Stone*. So it's not exactly an experimental film from the '60s, or one of those Ukrainian silents from the '20s that were once all the rage with film undergrads. But I figure my yearly screenings in class have single-handedly accounted for 17% of this film's viewership over the past half-decade.

I don't think I've provided many plot summaries (or maybe just descriptions—this is a documentary) during this countdown so far, but as briefly as possible: *The Heart of the Game* follows Darnellia Russell, a high school basketball player, and Bill Resler, her coach, for a period that begins with the season before Darnellia arrives as a freshman at Seattle's Roosevelt High, and carries through to her graduation five years later. Yes—it's basically *Hoop Dreams*, which Steven listed earlier. I like *Hoop Dreams* a lot. I absolutely love *The Heart of the Game*.

Darnellia and Resler are one of my favorite screen couples of all time. (It would seem as wrong to call her by her last name as it would to call him by his first.) Not in that way, no—nothing unseemly here, although we do learn that one of Darnellia's teammates is indeed being sexually preyed upon by her private basketball instructor, a brief but powerful detour. They're like a template for one of those opposites-attract romantic comedies: Darnellia an intense, quiet, intimidating, mercurial black teenager, Resler a disheveled, philosophical, avuncular, wildly outgoing white 50-something who's also—much to the amusement of Darnellia and her teammates—slightly unhinged. Or at least that's the image he cultivates in order to get the most out of his players. They even "meet cute" when Resler sidles up anonymously to Darnellia the day tryouts begin:

> "They tell me you play some basketball."
> "Who are you?"
> "I'm the coach."
> "Oh."

Add long pauses and an appropriate level of disdain for full effect. I won't detail the ups and downs of Darnellia's time at Roosevelt, other than to say (just like *Hoop Dreams*) the film encompasses so much above and beyond basketball—and the basketball stuff is thrilling. Somewhere, I think it may have been one of those annual *Time Out* guides, I read a reviewer who brushed off *The Heart of the Game* to the effect of "nothing you haven't seen before." It struck me as just a supremely stupid comment. I mean, if you reduce the film to its basic trial-tribulation-big game arc, sure. Just like if you reduce *Citizen Kane* to "guy who has everything loses it all," it looks kind of ordinary on paper too.

I had my students this year write fan letters just as school was ending, and I posted them using whatever addresses we could track down online. One of my girls wrote to Darnellia. We couldn't find anything for her, so I actually sent her a short message via Facebook explaining what we'd done, and would she mind providing an address where I could send my student's letter. Never heard back—she undoubtedly thought I was a nut. The letter's still sitting in my car. I just found the film's website, though, and there looks to be a couple of options there.

(#13, Facebook Top 50, 2011)

Night of the Living Dead

Went to see this with Romero introducing yesterday. Very likeable guy—in his 70s, still wears a ponytail.

Although it doesn't have the same impact on me now as when I first saw it (early '80s, I think)—horror films had a much greater effect on me when I was young and, to quote *Night*, all messed up—I still think it's amazing. Romero says that Duane Jones was cast simply because he was the best actor available—the part was originally assumed to be a white character—and that he was oblivious to the race angle that critics picked up on (and that Jones himself was very conscious of). I'm sure the casting was indeed spontaneous, but once Jones got the role, Romero must have been either weirdly oblivious to resonances that most anyone would pick up on, or else he's fibbing a little. When you've got Jones barricaded inside the farmhouse at the end, and a search party with police dogs on leashes, how can you not think of those photos from Birmingham not five years earlier?

As far as the other most common reading of the film goes, as a comment on Vietnam (or even societal breakdown in general), I honestly think it belongs alongside something like *Weekend*. When Barbara, in a daze, keeps asking "What's happening? What's happening" near the beginning, it reminded me of "This is not a dream, this is really happening" from *Rosemary's Baby* (also '68). I was wondering if the TV anchor was meant to evoke Cronkite breaking the news of JFK's assassination—at one point, he says something in a way that is very similar to Cronkite's delivery.

(Nothing to do with anything: two of the three women in the film are extremely attractive.)

(ILX, 2012)

Five Easy Pieces (Bob Rafelson, 1970)

Bert Schneider, 1969: "If I could find a no-name American director who had the Bergman look and the Bergman feel, I could make a billion dollars." I'm just making that up, of course, and I'm not even sure if, beyond an obvious *Wild Strawberries* homage, *Five Easy Pieces* has much to do with Bergman ("Of course, the people are all wrong for Bergman"—Geraldine Chaplin in *Nashville*). It's probably got more of an Antonioni feel. In any event, it's very definitely an American attempt as the '70s got underway to make a European-style art film of the 1960s. Continuing on from *The Graduate*, *Bonnie and Clyde*, *Easy Rider*, and few others that set the stage, I imagine *Five Easy Pieces* felt like something new at the time.

I can only guess—my own history with *FEP* is blurrier to me than most of what I've listed. I remember seeing it with my first-year roommate at university, and how much he loved it—this would have been '79 or '80—and while I'm positive I'd seen it a time or two on television before that, that was probably when it permanently lodged itself in my own imagination too. That Tom would have gravitated towards such a film doesn't surprise me; he may have been the most Bobby Dupea-like person I've ever known, an incredibly bright guy who lasted all of one year at UT before heading back home to Indiana, and then drifting (back to Toronto, for a while) for a few years after that. He was similar in broad outline, anyway—maybe I just want to say I've known a Bobby Dupea, since I'm not much of a Dupea myself.

Director Bob Rafelson turned into such a cipher after a couple of more films, I'm not sure how to explain the almost perfect pitch he achieves in *Five Easy Pieces*. Only once, when he has Nicholson tell off a pompous writer, does he (badly) telegraph anything. Rafelson quickly redeems himself, though, first in the incredible scene I'll link to below, Nicholson trying to explain his whole life in a few halting sentences to his paralyzed, unresponsive father, then again in the how-could-it-end-otherwise? final scene. Nicholson's monologue with his father contravenes a rule I think films are generally wise to observe: show, don't tell. Nicholson tries to tell—very poorly—and it works. (The Dupea family reminds me somewhat of the Berkmans in *The Squid and the Whale*.) Watching *Five Easy Pieces* tonight, the ending seemed very much in line with those lingering, unresolved endings already discussed from *The Graduate, The Heartbreak Kid,* and *The Candidate*; just like in the latter, the third time Nicholson says "I'm fine" he does so silently.

What else…László Kovács' cinematography: even a decades-old VHS on a 17" screen looks painterly in the best sense. Some of my favorite shots are when Nicholson wanders around town the night after he hops on that truck with the piano. Try to imagine *The Last Picture Show* in colour—no less desolate, but a vivid wash of neon rather than dust. Karen Black and Susan Anspach are a couple of iconic actresses of their day who only make sense in the context of the '70s. Black, especially—she's got to be up there with Shelly Duvall as the decade's most unconventional conception of female beauty. The expression on Nicholson's face when she starts counting sheep as a come-on to sex defies description. Billy Green Bush, Lois Smith, Fannie Flagg, they're all great.

I will, of course, provide a second link, the diner scene. I've played it for my students many times, and always tell them it's the key scene of the decade. May be true, may not be—it sounds dramatic, and I don't think it's an indefensible statement. I wonder sometimes whether actors have any idea that they're doing a scene that will become famous. There's a brief shot near the beginning of the diner scene, just after the waitress says "No substitutions," of Helena Kallianiotes and Toni Basil looking on in such a way that it almost feels like they're bracing for something historic. I also love the punch-line to the scene back in the car, which is easy to forget after Nicholson's show of bravado: "Yeah, well I didn't get it, did I?" His toast, that is. New decade.

(#12, Facebook Top 50, 2011)

Les Quatre Cents Coups (François Truffaut, 1959)

Just this past Sunday, I was at the Jays game where they retired Roberto Alomar's number. First time the club has ever done that; my guess is it'll happen again 15 years from now with Roy Halladay. So what does that have to do with a half-century old French film? Well, *Taxi Driver* was slated for this spot a few weeks ago, before Steven listed it as his #30. I knew it'd be a tough one for me to drop, but that's what I'm doing. Which is fine: it's a film that I've seen too many times, thought about too much, quoted too often, and written about enough. So if you can direct your attention over to the scoreboard in centerfield, you'll see that I'm retiring *Taxi Driver*'s number. That also drops Scorsese from my list. *C'est la vie*, say the old folks, etc.

This will also give me a chance to amend something I think I was wrong about earlier, when I listed *Shoot the Piano Player*: "I could have gone with *The 400 Blows*...but I still feel closer to *Tirez sur le pianiste*." And indeed, such was true for years and years—through my 20s and 30s, *The 400 Blows* was just one of those canonical, good-for-you films that I'd see periodically, enjoy, and never give a second thought to. But the last two or three times, including another look soon after I listed *Shoot the Piano Player*, it has deepened in ways I wasn't expecting. It's a film about a kid, but it took me a few decades to really see it.

The first change was something I briefly mentioned in my *Piano Player* comment: the idea that I now experience *The 400 Blows* from the other side of a divide that I crossed somewhere along the way. Through my 20s and into my early 30s, even though I wasn't all that close to Antoine chronologically anymore, I retained enough of his adolescent sense of aggrievement that I still saw *The 400 Blows* more or less through Antoine's eyes. It wasn't teachers and parents giving me grief, but it was still me against the world, and I still felt put-upon and crowded from all sides, much like Antoine. Today, it's different. Watching Antoine now, I think of all the time I spend nagging at kids—getting on them about unfinished homework, telling them to turn around or stop talking or get back to work, making sure at every turn that they don't do the kind of silly things 12-year-olds do for fear of having the class slide off into something resembling the anarchic pillow fight in *Zéro de conduite*. I embody the drudgery that's there waiting for kids when they come back from the weekend or summer vacation. I'm no longer Antoine, or even someone who can relate to Antoine tangentially; I'm now one of the people who makes Antoine's life miserable. As a teacher, and a pretty strict one by disposition—a control freak, essentially—I feel all of this acutely, but maybe I would have ended up on the other side of that divide anyway, I don't know.

There's something else I find tremendously moving about *The 400 Blows* now, specifically having to do with the famous ending, something more elusive and harder to explain. If you watch a lot of films, and know something about film history—enough that you're able to step back and take a longer view than whatever you're watching at any given moment—certain images acquire the power to resonate far above and beyond their function within a film itself. I don't know if there's an equivalent as far as music goes; songs are songs, and I hear them whole. But I remember sitting in a rep theatre three or four years ago, watching Antoine running along the beach as if for the first time, and when the camera swooped in and locked on that famous freeze-frame, I felt myself suddenly caught up in an awareness that film history was never going to be the same after this shot—that Truffaut had, in a single image, opened the door to all the New Wave films of the '60s, and more generally to the European art films of the '60s, which in turn would lead to all the American films of the '70s that mean so much to me, so on and so forth. No matter how much of a simplification that is, that's exactly how it felt, and I still remember that flash of awareness vividly.

So here's the ending, plus the puppet show Antoine and his friend happen upon during one of their truancy adventures around the streets of Paris. You can clearly see the influence of a similar puppet show in *Pather Panchali* there, and Ray can also be felt in the way Truffaut presents Antoine's parents: an ineffectual, somewhat bumbling but well-meaning father, and a mother who's resigned and businesslike to the point of seeming aloof at times. Wish I could add a third clip of Antoine on the gravity-defying carnival ride, but no luck.

(#11, Facebook Top 50, 2011)

2004 Top 10

#1: *Mayor of the Sunset Strip*: I really didn't know a lot about Rodney Bingenheimer before seeing this, even though he comes out of a world I know very well. I've had his *Rodney on the ROQ* compilation for years, which is mostly pretty useless from what I remember. (I'm looking at it right now: the Crowd, David Microwave, the Simpletones, the Vidiots, the Wigglers...who are these people?) Other than that, he's always been first and foremost the guy who the Angry Samoans vilified in their great "Get Off the Air": "Glitter rock and Bowie's cock/Are his idea of new-wave rock!" (The Samoans' Mike Saunders, an occasional contributor to *Radio On*, still ridicules Bingenheimer every chance he gets.) So I had Bingenheimer fixed to a specific moment in time, and was completely unaware of his rather amazing Rupert Pupkin/Zelig-like presence through three decades of pop history. I didn't like *Eternal Sunshine of the Spotless Mind* nearly as much as everybody else, in part because I find Charlie Kaufman's weirdness a little forced. I don't think Kaufman could ever come up with a more bizarre concept than Bingenheimer's entry-point into show business: he served as Davy Jones's double in *The Monkees*, which is kind of like signing on to play the shadow of a shadow. (Later on in the film, Kato Kaelin turns up—it's a movie filled with Zeligs.) The sequence where Bingenheimer starts popping up in the background of all these iconic '60s clips, singled out by a little superimposed arrow each time, was the funniest, most inexplicably sublime thing I saw all year. I loved the music throughout, and (the trickier part) loved how director George Hickenlooper made use of the songs he chose. The last 10 minutes was somewhat pat—Bingenheimer travels to England to spread his mother's ashes—but his mom's centrality to the kind of person he was had been established earlier, so I thought the sequence was justified. I wouldn't say I came away from the film exactly liking Bingenheimer, but neither did I find him sad or creepy. I'm not sure what I think of him, which is not a bad place for a documentary to leave you.

#8: A League of Ordinary Gentlemen: A perfect triangle: Walter Ray Williams, Jr., the unflappable square who does nothing of interest except win (anyone who watched the PBA in the '70s will remember Earl Anthony; that's Walter Ray); Pete Weber, the mercurial flake who doesn't seem unnerved by anything, except Walter Ray; and Wayne Webb, the sad-sack introspective who's barely hanging on. Bill James once wrote something about flaky baseball players—Joe Charboneau, Joaquin Andujar—that I won't even try to find, but essentially he said that flakes are fun for a while, and then they're gone; flakes don't end up in the Hall of Fame. Well, Weber's in the PBA Hall of Fame, with almost as many tour wins throughout his career as Williams, but when he gets the one thing he's been dying for, a shot at Walter Ray in the newly created "PBA World Championship," James's theory flashed across my mind and I felt like I knew exactly how it would all turn out. The five minutes of film that provided the answer was the most exciting thing I saw all year.

#9: *Word Wars*: Anyone who reviewed this treated it as *Spellbound* for maladjusted adults, and that describes it pretty well. I'm only going to write a little here, because otherwise I'd need to write 10,000 words. It's loosely based on Stefan Fatsis's *Word Freak*, which starts by following around a handful of circuit Scrabble players from tournament to tournament, and quickly shifts to Fatsis himself becoming enmeshed in this world, a severe addict with a borderline-expert rating. Amazing book. You'd think I would have paid heed to Fatsis's cautionary message, but soon after reading it, I stumbled onto the Internet Scrabble Club (where some of the same people who figure prominently in both book and film can be found playing), and within a matter of weeks I developed a consuming addiction of my own. And I do mean addiction in the fullest sense of the word—Ray Milland in *The Lost Weekend*, Jack Lemmon in *Days of Wine and Roses*, Lou Reed in "Waiting for My Man," the whole nine yards. I'd sit in front of the computer at work till the custodians kicked me out at 11:00 p.m., then I'd stop at an internet café on the way home. After buying a computer last summer (I'd been without for a couple of years), I began the school year by playing till 4:30 in the morning, getting an hour of sleep, then heading off to work. (Ten hours later, I'd periodically drift off for a second or two driving home—scary). The hook was the rating; I got up near 1400 at one point, far from expert (1800-2000) but still good. I was able to stop when everything got so out of hand, I started embarrassing myself—berating and arguing with other players, resigning if I didn't like the way somebody played, demanding rematches over and over till I was able to beat someone who was beating me. (Losing is the best thing that can happen to you when you start to think you've got anything of a competitive nature figured out.) It was a bizarre six-month episode[4] in my life that I still can't fully explain. Happily, I've forgotten a lot of the words that became second-nature to me during that time. "Atonies"—I seemed to lay that one every other game for 50+ points, so there's one I remember. The film...*Word Wars* gets at some of what I've just described, but it's too genial to go as deep as *Word Freak* does. Marlon Hill steals the movie; if you can re-imagine Malcolm X as a world-class Scrabble player, you've got a good idea of Marlon.

(rockcritics.com, 2004)

Zodiac

I think with everything I've listed so far, and everything I'll be listing after this, I'm able to quickly zero in on what it is I love about a particular film. (In my mind, I mean—how well I'm then able to explain myself is a separate issue.) Not so easy with *Zodiac*, least of all why I've got it in my Top 10. It's a serial-killer movie—an unusually long one (almost three hours), but superficially it has more in common with *The Bone Collector* or *The Eyes of Laura Mars* (or David Fincher's own *Se7en*) than with *Citizen Kane* or *The Seven Samurai* or what more typically ends up near the top of these lists. The easiest explanation is that the ranking is simply a reflection of how often I've watched *Zodiac* since it came out: after another look yesterday, I'm probably closing in on my 10th viewing. Eventually I'll wear it out, the mistake I always make with my favorite films, but for now, based solely on what sabermetricians derisively call counting stats, it belongs in my Top 10.

---

[4] Since writing those words 10 years ago, I've only relapsed 783 times. I'd doing just fine.

The less easy explanation is something I hinted at weeks ago: *This is important. This means something.* You've heard that already during this countdown. It's the mantra voiced by two or three characters in *Close Encounters of the Third Kind*—by Dreyfuss, by Truffaut, and I think (not sure) by Melinda Dillon, too. You never hear the exact same words in *Zodiac*—Jake Gyllenhaal speaks a variation on them a couple of times when cornered as to why he's so obsessed with solving a case others have abandoned—but they're the foundation upon which a film that fascinates and puzzles me like no other the past few years is built. And, just as with *Close Encounters*, the something that is so important is a blank canvas left for you to fill in yourself. Steven and I had a bit of back-and-forth about this on his blog a while back. He thinks the failure (intentional or otherwise) to provide some sort of explanation for Gyllenhaal's obsession is a weakness of the film; for me, it's one of *Zodiac*'s major strengths.

Because of its length, *Zodiac* is a serial-killer movie like no other. There's time enough for it to be a meticulously detailed procedural—theories and facts and criss-crossing timelines accumulate inexorably (in the space of a minute or two, subtitles will hurl you forward hours, then weeks, then months)—but that largeness also begins to take on a dreamlike quality as the film progresses, creating space to wander around in and get lost. So you get sequences like the time-lapse construction of a skyscraper (with Marvin Gaye's "Inner City" playing underneath), or the what-we-do-is-secret "Hurdy Gurdy Man" opening, where the visuals have a beauty and an intensity that belie the gruesome subject matter; a narrative where the killer will disappear for long stretches of time, becoming more amorphous and elusive with each passing year, almost to the point of abstraction; and a feeling for period that seems both unreal (I've never seen a recreation of the late-'60s and '70s that looks or feels anything like this) and absolutely right.

One of the things I love most about *Zodiac* is the way the three leads play off of each other. There's something very classical and very satisfying about the way they're triangulated. Gyllenhaal, a veritable Boy Scout—Eagle Scout, to get technical—is on one side, Robert Downey's sardonic drunk is on the other, and caught somewhere between them is Ruffalo, the Hawksian cop who just wants to be left alone to do his job with as little fanfare as possible. That's not really a triangle...I think Ruffalo's especially great. Downey is showy, as always, but I like him fine here, and Gyllenhaal projects wide-eyed befuddlement as credibly as the kid in *Il Posto*. Ruffalo, though—I think he's my favorite movie cop ever, and the way he interacts with his partner, played by Anthony Edwards, reminds me of Cooper and Truman in *Twin*

Peaks. (Stuff you learn checking IMDB: Edwards was also in *Fast Times at Ridgemont High* and *Heart Like a Wheel*, where he was Shirley Muldowney's son. Hadn't a clue.) I could single out another dozen performances, but I'll limit myself to one: Chloë Sevigny makes a great hippychick circa 1970.

In the end, Gyllenhaal's obsession is never explained and the killer is never caught. But as defined by Gyllenhaal earlier in the film, we are left to believe that, in a single instant, closure has come for him. It's an amazing moment—perversely religious in a way, like Moses looking upon the burning bush up on Mount Sinai.

(#10, Facebook Top 50, 2011)

On the Waterfront (Elia Kazan, 1954)

Steven's #9 caught me by surprise—he's been saying that his Top 10 is "pretty standard," and while *Streetcar* is indeed a venerated, highly-awarded film, it's not to my mind something that turns up on those *Sight & Sound* lists we keep talking about. And, as I'm sure I've made clear by now, for me that's a good thing. (Which is not to say that the films that do turn up on those lists are a bad thing...geez, here I am heading down that same dead-end road again.) Anyway, since he's got Brando at #9, I'll drop my #8 one spot so I can have him there too.

Here's a brief history of three decades of American film that's simplified to the point of being meaningless: the '30s were stylish people in evening dress exchanging barbed witticisms; the '40s brought shadowy dread and film noir; and the '50s were wide open and epic—the films that come to mind when I think about the '50s are *East of Eden* and *Shane*, *The Searchers* and *From Here to Eternity*, *The Ten Commandments* and *The Bridge on the River Kwai*. The advent of Cinemascope obviously had something to do with that; for all I know, maybe Eisenhower did too. (He seemed like kind of a wide open and epic guy.) There are a few thousand examples to the contrary, but I don't want to undermine my theory with facts—*The Night of the Hunter*, to name one, has got enough shadowy dread for a half-dozen film noirs.

On the Waterfront was not shot in Cinemascope, and its running time is a fairly modest 108 minutes. It certainly feels epic, though, especially in memory—its emotions and ambitions are large. I almost want to quote two words from Steven's *Streetcar* comment—"But Brando..."—and leave it at that, but when I first saw and fell in love with the film some 25 years ago, I discovered that there really was a lot more here than just him. For starters, we've got a director who's already placed two different films in our Top 10s—he was no slouch. Boris Kaufman's cinematography, Leonard Bernstein's music, Rod Steiger and Eva Marie Saint and Lee J. Cobb, there's landmark work all over *Waterfront*. (Karl Malden, a little less so.) And if you're so inclined, it's also a film that dives right into the great political issue of its day, McCarthyism and the ethical calculus of turning state's evidence when cornered. But not exactly objectively: *Waterfront* is widely perceived as Kazan's self-exculpatory parable for his own role in the HUAC hearings of the early '50s. (I should mention here that *Waterfront*'s script was actually written by Budd Schulberg.)

I read Richard Schickel's biography of Kazan, and without detouring into specifics, most of which I don't remember anyway, Schickel (a Kazan advocate) says it's a gray area. People still have very strong feelings about Kazan's testimony (and, as a consequence, *Waterfront*'s alleged role in excusing that testimony), on full display when Kazan was given his honorary Academy Award a few years ago, just prior to his death. I don't know—as presented in the film, detached from the events of Kazan's own life, Terry Malloy's testimony against the mob racketeers who control the docks is difficult to question. But I can see why the very clarity of Malloy's situation, and the fact that he's made to nobly agonize over his decision, infuriates Kazan's critics.

The first scene I'd show from *Waterfront* to illustrate Brando at work is not the cab ride he shares with Rod Steiger. The cab scene is tremendous—I'll provide a link to that too. (Ideally, I could set this up so you could look at a triptych of Brando and Steiger alongside De Niro's quotation in *Raging Bull*, next to Mark Wahlberg's quotation in *Boogie Nights* of De Niro quoting Brando.) But my absolute favorite scene is Brando and Eva Marie Saint in the park. I can't think of a more perfectly acted scene in the whole history of movies—by both of them—or one that's more romantic. It also has one of those moments that steps outside the film and seems to reach into the future: at 2:20, when Brando touches his nose and then says, "Well, some people just got faces that stick in your mind." On cue, Bernstein's music reappears. Brilliant—absolutely brilliant.

(#9, Facebook Top 50, 2011)

Sweet Smell of Success (Alexander Mackendrick, 1957)

Here's another film set in a universe parallel to the one I inhabit. The people speak something resembling English, but it's a language unto itself. I think so, anyway—I may have just dreamed it in a dream.

if anything should happen

As memorable first screenings go, *Sweet Smell of Success* is way up there for me. The film seemed to be completely out of circulation for a time in the '80s—it was almost certainly Kael who first got me interested, and there was also the kid in *Diner* (a film I otherwise hated at the time—it looks okay now) who wandered around in a daze quoting lengthy sections of dialogue verbatim. Anyway, one day it suddenly showed up at 3:00 in the morning on CFMT, a local station that was primarily given over to a variety of ethnic programming. They sometimes ran movies deep into the morning, though, and whoever was picking them did not seem to have anyone looking over his shoulder; I'd caught *The Texas Chainsaw Massacre* and *Repulsion* on there at a similar hour. *Sweet Smell of Success* was everything Kael promised and more—it just completely knocked me out, and when I was finally able to see it on a big screen a few years later, and able to appreciate James Wong Howe's noirish cinematography, it was that much better.

Like *On the Waterfront*, it's a film that is bound up with the McCarthyism of its day. Burt Lancaster's J.J. Hunsecker is a gloss on Walter Winchell, and he's also a stand-in for McCarthy himself—he's in the business of destroying lives, possessed of an absolute power that corrupts and disfigures him absolutely. (Winchell was a McCarthy supporter.) Tony Curtis's Sidney Falco is sort of Roy Cohn, Hunsecker's lapdog underling, although Cohn did not seem to be terribly conflicted over his actions in the way that Falco is. The political allegory is there, and it does deepen the film, but people like me don't obsess over *Sweet Smell of Success* because of its political subtleties. As brilliant as Lancaster and Curtis are (if someone had wired up Nixon like they wire up Vincent D'Onofrio in *The Cell*, I think his id would have manifested itself as a monster on the order of Hunsecker), they're not the main attraction either. *Sweet Smell of Success* is about Clifford Odets' words—a torrent of them, so caustic and acerbic and insanely funny that you'll be quoting them for the rest of your life.

> *Now you take Sidney here. If Sidney ever got anywhere near Susie, I'd take a baseball bat and break it over his head.*
>
> *J.J., you've got such contempt for people, it makes you stupid.*
>
> *You're dead, son. Get yourself buried.*
>
> *Son, I don't relish shooting a mosquito with an elephant gun, so why don't you just shuffle along?*

Just a sampling, skipping the Manny Davis line I've already made reference to three or four times during these countdowns. The dialogue in *Sweet Smell of Success* mesmerizes—while you're dimly aware that nobody you've ever met or ever will meet in your life actually talks like that, you enter the film's world and it washes over you. I know that I've been waiting years for just the right moment to drop the elephant gun line on someone who especially crosses me.

There's one glaring weakness in *Sweet Smell of Success* (the fact that I have it at #6 anyway tells you something about its strengths): the Martin Milner/Susan Harrison relationship on which Lancaster and Curtis's machinations pivot. They're just so wholesome and earnest that they seem to have been parachuted in from some other film. Their time on screen is relatively brief. The best that I can say about them is that their dragginess brings the corrosive rot of Hunsecker and Falco into sharper relief—and when Milner is required to confront them directly, he's actually not that bad.

The rest of the supporting cast is fantastic. There's David White from *Bewitched* as Otis Elwell ("I can't even think of a bad reason"), Joe Frisco as Herbie Temple ("You tell him I stutter"), Barbara Nichols as Rita the Cigarette Girl ("I don't know, it's a big apartment"), and, my favorite, Emile Meyer as the fat cop Kello ("Sidney, I want to *chastise you*"). There I am quoting dialogue again. Can't help it.

For a clip, here's the film's most famous scene, a companion of sorts to *Waterfront*'s cab ride—they even both make reference to the Polo Grounds. Listen to Lancaster's voice when he says "I want that boy taken apart." His voice doesn't rise above a whisper. And like they say about Hannibal Lecter in *The Silence of the Lambs*, I bet his pulse never rises above 85.

(#6, Facebook Top 50, 2011)

2003 Top 10

#1: *Spellbound*: For me, the one unassailably great film of the past two years. The biggest obstacle in advocating for it (something I've been doing all year) is that anyone who hasn't seen it probably assumes it's good, but good in the most earnest, studied kind of way—good for you. To be honest, that's how I felt about *Hoop Dreams*. I dutifully sat through it when it came out, aware that I was seeing something important and ambitious and observant, and I have never once felt the urge to revisit it. *Spellbound* I've seen four times, most recently with my grade 6 class, and the initial thrill hasn't waned a bit. For a film about something as staid as a spelling bee, where requests for a word origin count as major plot twists, it's as sly and disarming as can be—even, thanks to iconic wingnut Harry Altman, anarchic at times.

It's also the first film I can think of since *Nashville* to throw an American flag up there in huge close-up (done twice) and make it count—audacious, imposing, an austere blank, it registers in all kinds of contradictory ways. That's one of the things I most love about *Spellbound*: either of the two political parties could lay claim to it in order to beat the other one over the head, and they'd both be right. (Or, if you'd rather, they'd both be wrong.) Arguing from the left, you might see vindication for the public school system, which, for all of its shortcomings, still manages to produce its share of minor miracles like the eight kids under scrutiny here. (Or at least they appear to be publicly educated—there's no direct mention of it either way, and although Neil and Emily might possibly attend private schools, with the other six of more modest means, anything but the public system seems out of the question.) From the right, you'd zero in on the musings of Neil's father, an Indian immigrant who comes across like a Republican shill for the superfluousness of affirmative action: "If there's one thing I've learned about this country, it's that it's impossible to fail if you work hard." Those are words that should feel empty and false, but they don't. As he stands there inside the palatial Orange County home that he and his brother built from scratch, it's hard to argue with him.

Class and race are integral to *Spellbound* (self-consciously so: the kids seem as carefully handpicked as a test-marketed sitcom), but if that's all there were, there'd be a ceiling on how much I could like it. The eight participants are so indelible and alive above and beyond all that, though, you'll probably find yourself doing as I did, projecting where their personalities and quirks will take each one of them down the road. (In that respect, *Spellbound*'s very much like an American *21 Up*.) Nupur, Angela, and Emily are funny and well-adjusted and will never have a neurotic thought in their lives, while April and Ted will have nothing but. Ashley's cheery disposition and strong sense of self will take her far away from her neighbourhood, unless they're not enough and they don't. Neil's head will explode one day, at which point he'll pick up the pieces and start over. And Harry, he's a force of nature—he's Joseph Wiseman in *Detective Story*, he's Michael Richards in *Seinfeld*, he's Mark Fidrych stalking around the mound and lecturing the baseball in 1976. There are always two or three Harrys bouncing off the walls in my own school at any given time, and you're always reminding them of one thing: that just because you have a thought, you're not obligated to speak it aloud. I haven't a clue what will become of Harry, but the strategic placement of the last shot we get of him is *Spellbound*'s most sublime joke. (I love how Georgie, a ninth character, is suddenly introduced three-quarters of the way through as some phantom Godzilla waiting in the wings.)

When *Bowling for Columbine* won the Academy Award for best documentary last year, I didn't think it was a bad choice. I even wanted it to win, notwithstanding its preciousness and other obvious faults—I wanted to, you know, see what kind of a spectacle Michael Moore would make of himself. I hadn't seen *Spellbound* at the time, wasn't even aware of any of the other four nominees. It absolutely floors me in hindsight that anyone who'd seen both films could choose *Columbine* as the best documentary of the year. For an institution with no shortage of monumentally stupid gaffes, that has to rank near the top.

(rockcritics.com, 2003)

Double Indemnity (Billy Wilder, 1944)

I cannot hide from myself any longer; for the first time, I have no choice but to pull the trigger on something already listed (by Jeff, back at #33).

There are movies throughout the course of film history that serve as benchmarks, with very much of a before-and-after feel about them. *The Birth of a Nation* is an obvious one, and so are *Breathless* and *Bonnie and Clyde*. It's debatable whether you can point to anything more recent that deserves that designation, but *Pulp Fiction* might be viewed as a dividing line of sorts, at least in terms of how many imitations followed in its wake. The clearest before-and-after film of all, of course, is *Citizen Kane*.

In terms of my own movie timeline, *Double Indemnity* is a benchmark—it divides film history in half the way *Citizen Kane* does in pretty much every official version of events. It's no accident that it's the earliest film on my list; for me, *Double Indemnity* is the first film that feels completely modern to me, that establishes a tone—fatalistic, weary, caustic, sometimes mean—perfectly aligned with titles all over my list, from *Sweet Smell of Success* to the American stuff from the '70s right up to *No Country for Old Men*. That's in no way meant as a knock on *Citizen Kane*, and I'm sure there's lots of stuff from before *Double Indemnity* that caught the same tone—I think there were French gangster films from the '30s that get written about in those terms. I'm speaking 100% subjectively here: *Double Indemnity* has a look and a language that feels completely new to me, and it points the way forward.

My favorite moment along those lines—to me, the emblematic moment in any film noir—is when MacMurray's Walter Neff gets home the night of the murder, double-checks that he dotted every last *i* and crossed every last *t*, and as soon as he realizes that yes, he's in the clear, that he's just conspired to commit the perfect murder he always fantasized about, he has a sudden moment of clarity:

That was all there was to it. Nothing had slipped, nothing had been overlooked, there was nothing to give us away. And yet, Keyes, as I was walking down the street to the drug store, suddenly it came over me that everything would go wrong. It sounds crazy, Keyes, but it's true, so help me: I couldn't hear my own footsteps. It was the walk of a dead man.

No idea whether that's found in Cain's original novel or whether it's an invention of the film, but it's such an amazingly vivid articulation of formless dread; it's another one of those moments that leaves the film behind and, I think, says something very profound about...I hesitate to say "the modern world," because I'm quite sure people have been experiencing various kinds of formless dread since the beginning of time, so I'll just say life in general instead. "Suddenly it came over me that everything would go wrong"—that's good enough for Camus and all those French philosophy guys. (The two-way street between existentialism and film noir has been analyzed plenty.)

I don't think I could pick a favorite performance from among *Double Indemnity*'s three principals. Two of them are archetypes. MacMurray is the forerunner of such noir patsies as Edward G. Robinson in *Scarlet Street*, Kirk Douglas in *The Strange Love of Martha Ivers*, and Elisha Cook Jr. in *The Killing*—not as pathetic as someone like Robinson, he nominally takes charge at times, but there's never any question as to who's yanking whose chain (so to speak). I like Barbara Stanwyck a lot in *Meet John Doe*, but her Phyllis Dietrichson is a different creature altogether—she ought to sprout razor-sharp tentacles every now and again, like those femme fatale monsters in movies like *Species* or *Splice*. And as great as they both are, Edward G. Robinson's Barton Keyes is a complete original. His whirlwind monologue on all the different ways one can commit suicide—"suicide by leaps, subdivided by leaps from high places, under wheels of trains, under wheels of trucks..."—is a masterpiece.

Some of the back-and-forth in *Double Indemnity* is, like in *Sweet Smell Success*, somebody's fevered invention of a whole new language. (When I showed the climactic confrontation between Neff and Dietrichson to my class last year—yeah, I know, probably not advisable—one of my students asked, "Why do they talk like that?") My favorite exchange among many:

> *"I wonder if I know what you mean?"*
> *"I wonder if you wonder."*

I think Billy Wilder is the third director to place two films on my list, with one more to go. *The Apartment* and *Sunset Boulevard* are famously dark films, but for me, *Double Indemnity* is even darker. Like *Sunset Boulevard*, it's (almost) narrated by a dead man. The film begins with you knowing that, yet somehow there's still this paradoxically awful feeling throughout that things will get even worse.

(#4, Facebook Top 50, 2011)

Rosemary's Baby (Roman Polanski, 1968)

Come—come see the child.

When I did a Top 10 for *Radio On* in the mid-'90s, this was my #1; same thing on my ballot for the aforementioned Lightbox poll, and same again for a list or two I posted on the message board. No special reason why it's not #1 this time. I guess I just wanted something different there.

Rosemary's Baby has something elemental in common with *The Godfather* and *Jaws*, albeit on a smaller scale: it was critically acclaimed (even more now than then), made a ton of money, and was a cultural phenomenon of sorts. The first time I saw it was around '73 or '74 on TV; it was a "network premiere," a big deal when they used to do that sort of thing, and I think I even remember the network—NBC. I managed to Google some online corroboration in the way of a user comment:

> *"I also remember how much they hyped the network TV premieres of movies back in the seventies. It seems like they publicized Rosemary's Baby for weeks before it ran one Saturday night on (I think) ABC. The commercials were so ubiquitous that CBS countered with one of their own, showing a baby carriage on a mountaintop, just like the Rosemary's Baby logo. Lightning flashed and thunder roared as the camera moved in to show Mary Tyler Moore, Bob Newhart and Carol Burnett inside the carriage, dressed as babies and shouting 'Watch us instead!'"*

if anything should happen

We disagree on the network, but we both remember it as a certified event. (That commercial sounds great!)

Thirteen or 14 at the time, I watched most of the film through splayed fingers, except for the ending, where the fingers were no longer splayed. Which is pretty funny when you think about how comparatively mild *Rosemary's Baby* is when placed alongside its progeny, most obviously *The Exorcist*. Mild in terms of what you actually see, that is—in terms of mood, it's got as much foreboding and dread as anything I can think of. Unless you experience it as a really good comedy, like Pauline Kael did. It's what you might call a hybrid.

Let me completely contradict my *Godfather* comment and point to something thematic that I love about *Rosemary's Baby*. (Maybe I sidestep themes when they're in plain view, and only like the ones I invent myself.) In a weird way, Polanski's film accidentally speaks to what was probably the most chaotic year of the past half-century better than numerous other films that self-consciously aspired to something similar. Accidentally, because it would have of course been filmed in 1967, and also because it's a film about a bunch of seemingly harmless octogenarians who keep active by trying to conjure up the living Satan so he can impregnate a mortal woman and begat a son—it doesn't directly address the issues of the day. And yet, and yet...it's also about something unseen and awful, something beyond comprehension. It's about betrayal, and helplessness, and malevolent plots. And, appearing six days after Robert Kennedy's assassination, and a couple of months after Martin Luther King Jr.'s—with the Democratic convention just around the corner, not to mention everything else that was going on around the world—it has a line that, once again, leaves the film behind: "This is no dream—*this is really happening*." I hear that line as a bookend: there's the close-up of Janet Leigh's eye in *Psycho* at one end of the shelf, and "This is no dream—*this is really happening*" at the other.

The first performance that people recall from *Rosemary's Baby* is the one that won the Academy Award, Ruth Gordon as Minnie Castavet. I love her, of course—hearing her bray "The carpet...the carpet!" is music to my ears. Mia Farrow should have won every award out there. She's winsome and beautiful (aside from that Vidal Sassoon monstrosity and all the chalky make-up), and you're so much on her side at every point along the way that it's basically a first-person narrative. I just finished a John Cassavetes (not to be confused with Roman Castavet) series at the Lightbox, which included *Rosemary's Baby* among all the films he directed himself. I like him fine here, although I find him a little blander than everyone else. (Not just the character—him.) I think the two old British guys, Sidney Blackmer and Maurice Evans, are great, though. Stanley Kauffmann called Evans "an elocutionary dud" for lines like "Well, we'll assume Dr. Sapirstein knows whereof he speaks," but I think he's missing all the magical *Bewitched* goodness in such rhetoric.

Polanski's direction needs a book, not a comment. If I had to pick a favorite moment, I'd probably go with the way the camera glides up and away from Cassavetes and Farrow the first time they hear the chanting through the wall. Or the entire impregnation sequence, a disturbing and masterful assemblage of dreamlike fragments. Or Laura-Louise sticking out her tongue right near the end—it really is a great comedy.

(#2, Facebook Top 50, 2011)

Logorrhea (Top 10 of the 2000s)

#10: *Andy Warhol: A Documentary Film*: In an almost identical version of this list I submitted to an ILX poll a few weeks ago, I had this at #11 and *Wendy and Lucy* at #10. I've only seen *Wendy and Lucy* once, though, and just don't remember enough specifics to write about it, so I'll go with the Warhol documentary. I liked Chuck Workman's *Superstar: The Life and Times of Andy Warhol* from a few years ago, but Burns's PBS-sponsored version dwarfs it. (Stuff you find out when checking credits: Workman released a documentary last year on Jonas Mekas. Hadn't heard a word about it—can't wait till it makes its way here.) I don't know if this is as dense as *No Direction Home* (also of PBS origin—I think both were part of American Masters), but clocking in at an extra 40 minutes, you can bet there's quite a morass to lose yourself in here, too. There's a section on the JFK assassination right at the end of part one that I'd probably name as my single favorite sequence of the decade. You see the assassination through Warhol's eyes; he's still feeling his way at the time, still trying to get his name out there, and the '60s—and everything that that phrase has come to encapsulate—have begun but haven't begun. He hears the news, goes back to his studio ("What does this mean?" he keeps asking anyone within earshot), and before long is furiously painting those now-iconic images of the grieving widow. As one of the interviewees explains it: "He understood instantaneously the second Liz turned into 'Liz'—which was with her tracheotomy, and her sexual scandals in the early '60s—and with Jackie, the second JFK was shot, just to understand that immediately they were...incomprehensible spectacles that would make one speechless to contemplate. And he got that immediately." Melodramatic? Maybe—give me some evocative music in the background, and my defenses against such rhetoric crumble away. Not only do I buy it, I want to live inside those quotation marks; my new greatest aspiration in life is to become an incomprehensible spectacle that would make one speechless to contemplate.

(homepage, 2010)

Nashville (Robert Altman, 1975)

Odd place to begin: unlike many of the films I've listed—more than half, I'd say—I don't remember the first time I saw *Nashville*. I dimly remember that it was indeed in a theatre, but there's part of me that thinks it would have been a strange film for a 14- or 15-year-old to be seeing first-run. Yet that must have been the case; I doubt that it would have showed up on network TV until the end of the decade, and I'm positive I thought of it as being among my favorite films as I began university in '79 (underscored by the fact that I wrote about *The Long Goodbye* later that first year).

About 15 years ago, Scott had someone interview David Edelstein for rockcritics.com., after Edelstein (who I think is excellent) had just written a piece in *GQ* or somewhere about how he didn't think *Nashville* had held up that well. I started to write a long response, kept getting hopelessly bogged down as I tried to refute the objections he raised, and when I finally got about three thousand words (of mostly preamble, I remember) into it, my old Mac conked out. The disk where I had the piece couldn't be converted, and it ended up being the only big piece of writing I've ever lost. To help me avoid the same fate, let me take the easy way out and compile a list, like Jeff did for one of his picks. *Nashville* is like a perfect storm of so many things that I've been fixated on throughout this countdown:

1) The '70s. Go back to early in the countdown where we tried to place films like *Bonnie and Clyde* and *Close Encounters* on a timeline of "New American Cinema." Well, *Nashville* is the middle of the middle. I think it's fair to say that for a lot of people who consider the '70s the greatest decade ever for American film, *Nashville* is the exact midpoint of a line that stretches from *Bonnie and Clyde* to *Heaven's Gate*—maybe not the literal apex of that line, but squarely in the middle chronologically and, at the very worst, pretty close artistically. (Maybe I need to diagram that out…See what I mean about getting bogged down?)

2) Nixon. Yes, it's another Nixon film, another one where he's hovering there invisibly the whole way. When Carradine contemptuously says, "Kill anyone today, Sarge?" that's a Nixon moment through and through; when the Tennessee Twirlers meet Barbara Jean at the airport, that's Nixon too. Haven Hamilton's Nixon ("his eyes flashing with paranoid gleam as he keeps the audience under surveillance"—yes, I've got Kael close by my side), Allen Garfield's slobbishness and Ned Beatty's hapless everyman always make me think of Nixon, and Hal Philip Walker is Nixon in that he just blathers on and on, and probably even accidentally makes sense now and again. Finally, the film's it-don't-worry-me conclusion is such a perfect punch line to the Nixon presidency in a dozen mysterious ways that I don't think I've ever even tried to clarify in my mind why I think that. And I won't make the attempt here.

3) Kael. Her pre-emptive review of *Nashville* is her signature piece—more even than her reviews of *Bonnie and Clyde*, *Last Tango*, the *Godfather*s, *The Sound of Music*, *Shoah*, or anything else that invariably gets mentioned whenever she's under discussion. To go along with my favorite movie, that's my favorite movie review ever. I can't think of another instance where a film critic was so hard-wired to the moment, to the director, and to the film. *Nashville* and Kael are inseparable for me.

4) Supporting performances. I've probably talked more about supporting players than leads during this countdown, and *Nashville* is comprised of nothing but—in a way, the term has no meaning here. Only Tomlin and Blakley were nominated—vote-splitting is the only explanation for how Lee Grant managed to win for *Shampoo*—but I'm ready to hand out another seven or eight right here, starting with Henry Gibson. I don't know that there's a single performer from among *Nashville*'s ensemble of 24 who I don't enjoy when they're on screen…I don't even mind Shelly Duvall. I also look forward to some of the really small parts that support the ensemble. The Smokey Mountain Laurels, the bartender at the Demon's Den, the guy at the lunch counter who engages Keenan Wynn, Frog, I love them all.

5) Music. If there's a main complaint about *Nashville*, one I've addressed before, it's that Altman has contempt for country music, or, at the very least, condescends insufferably to it. I think there was a time when I would argue that point, but now I'd just say yeah, probably—some condescension for sure. It still doesn't bother me, though, for the simple reason that I like most of the songs too much. I can think of one case where I read someone who loved the film but thought some of the songs were horrible. I don't know—a couple, sure (discounting Gwen Welles' stuff), but there's

so much music throughout, I think you've got to like a decent percentage of it *as music* to really love the film. My favorites: "Dues" (of course), "Since You've Gone," "Trouble in the U.S.A.," "Memphis," and "It Don't Worry Me." And, in context, I'd add "I'm Easy."

See if I can keep this to 1,000 words. The whole film's on YouTube, and anyone who chooses to watch it that way for the first time will disappoint me greatly. Ned Beatty joins Brando, Balsam, and Curtis in making his second appearance in my top 10; newscaster Howard K. Smith has the unusual distinction of playing himself for the second time in my top 20. I'll link to the same clip I used for the song countdown. I bet I've said this at least a dozen times already, but now I'm telling the truth: my favorite scene ever.

Thanks to everyone who read along, and to Steven and Jeff for signing up. Before we started, I told them some lie about why it would be helpful to me to post Wednesdays and Saturdays. In actual fact, I just wanted to make sure I was in a position to do this:

End of countdown.
End of cinema.

(#1, Facebook Top 50, 2011)

Downgrade

The list is out. Yes, that one—*the* list.

I recounted my own history with *Sight & Sound*'s once-a-decade survey of the greatest films ever made in an e-mail exchange with Andrew LaPointe when the 2002 list came out. (In a weird way, one of my favorite things I've ever participated in; the whole thing was set up by Scott Woods, and I didn't know until we'd basically finished that Andrew was 17. Still makes me laugh.) As indicated by the title of our exchange, "Kill the Headlights and Put It in Neutral," 2002's list represented something of a holding pattern. This year's, less so—because the thing that many people thought might come to pass actually did, the 2012 list will make some news.

I'm basically indifferent to *Vertigo*'s ascension to #1. Given the choice between the two leading contenders, I'd much rather *Citizen Kane* had held down the top spot once again—for one thing, I'd still be able to announce to my students with a great dramatic flourish *Kane*'s half-century domination of the poll when I talk about Welles on his birthday next year— but seeing as I've made up many favorite-film lists of varying lengths over the years and not once put *Kane* on any of them, it'd be silly to get indignant. I've come to think of *Vertigo* as the *On the Beach* (Neil Young version) of the film canon; I'm convinced its stature owes at least something to the fact that it was long out of circulation, but I can also appreciate why its particular mood connects with people so deeply, even if I don't share that connection myself.

The Godfather(s), which last time looked like they might make a bid for #1, are out (say the beginning and end of that sentence in your best Michael Corleone voice). Mostly that's due to an accounting decision: last time, votes for the first two were added together, this time *I* and *II* were counted as separate films. If they'd stayed with their initial decision, the combined vote total for the two would have grazed the lower reaches of the Top 10, down from #4 in 2002. I started out very much in favour of treating the first two as a single film (which is how they come together in my own head), but now I'm closer to being on the fence. I can easily explain why I think it makes much more sense to combine votes for the first two *Godfathers* than for Kieślowski's *Three Colors Trilogy*. I'd have a much tougher time trying to rationalize why it makes any more sense than to combine votes for all three Apu films, something I wouldn't agree with.

So what makes me happy about this year's results? I like that most—most, not all—of the hallowed names going back to when I was a film student 30 years ago still find their way into the Top 50 with at least one film. I'm like John McGiver in *Breakfast at Tiffany's*: even though there are films on there I don't personally get much out of (*8-1/2* is always the first example I point to), it gives one a feeling of solidarity, almost of continuity with the past, that sort of thing. I like that *The 400 Blows*, which has become one of my favorite films the past few years, still does pretty well (33 votes, good for 39th), and that *Persona* is still hanging on. *Taxi Driver* tied for 31st (with *Godfather II*, coincidentally)—if I had to settle on one of the core Scorsese films to push ahead of the others, that'd be the one. And I like seeing films like *Jeanne Dielman, 23 quai du Commerce 1080 Bruxelles*, *Histoire(s) du cinema* and *Andrei Rublev* on there—strange films I would have once brushed aside with jokes and exasperation, but that now interest me a great deal. I still have a few more of those to catch up with. (*Stalker*, at #29, still inspires jokes and exasperation.)

My biggest disappointment would be the absence of *Nashville* in the Top 50. Altman's the kind of director who splits votes among a few films, and my guess is that, in total, he exceeded the 29 votes necessary to finish 50th. But I'm surprised that *Nashville* still hasn't emerged as the consensus choice, and surprised that Altman's death, as death sometimes seems to, didn't give it a little extra push. And, in keeping with my great interest in documentaries the past few years (on the wane somewhat), I guess I would have liked to have seen one or two of my favorites show up somewhere towards the bottom of the Top 50...well, that just wasn't going to happen; thinking about the ones that mean the most to me, I'd be surprised if any of them got a single vote.

I may have some more to say when individual lists are printed (not until the print issue in September, it appears). I've refrained thus far from saying anything about *Mulholland Dr.* at #28. Let's keep it that way.

(homepage, 2012)

Two for the Road: Reinventing the Double-Bill

Inside every rock critic, there's supposedly a frustrated musician. Those who can, do, and those who can't, write about it. This commonly held view is buoyed by the number of critics who made the transition from writing to performing: Patti Smith, Chrissie Hynde, Ira Kaplan, Neil Tennant, etc. Greil Marcus once addressed the issue by pointing out that far from wanting to be a musician, his own secret ambition was to be a DJ. What Marcus was saying, I think, was that given the choice, he would rather test his ideas and his tastes by choosing and organizing music made by others—setting up juxtapositions that would highlight surface connections and, the real attraction, uncover hidden ones—than by trying to create his own.

Speaking as someone who used to host an all-night radio show on the University of Toronto station, it *is* a rush when you discover one of those perfect matches, even if accidentally. I remember a show where, in the midst of counting down my favorite 100 songs, the lingering last note of Frank Sinatra's "It Was a Very Good Year" gave way to Guns N' Roses' "Sweet Child O' Mine," then still new and climbing the charts. Their proximity wasn't planned, but as one blended into the other, it immediately occurred to me that they were essentially the same song separated by 20 years. Thinking about that segue 15 years later, I now realize that their singers, in some rather unattractive ways, were also essentially the same person.

There's an obvious parallel that can be drawn between rock critic-turned-musician and film critic-turned-filmmaker, again supported by a number of real-life examples who travelled in the same direction (most prominently from various French and British film journals of the late '50s: Truffaut, Godard, Rohmer, Anderson, Reisz, etc). And again, an intermediate alternative presents itself, one that affords almost as much room for self-expression and mischief-making as filmmaking itself: programming a repertory cinema.

The independent repertory house, whether a neighborhood theatre running a Pam Grier festival or a museum-sponsored program resurrecting forgotten Soviet films from the early '60s, is the last outpost for that long-ago saviour of the film industry, the double-bill. A product of the depression ("It was the Depression-era moviegoer who first insisted on a complete three-hour plus program for his or her money," according to Todd McCarthy and Charles Flynn's *Kings of the Bs*), by 1935 double-bills were the standard at 85% of America's motion picture houses. For the next decade-plus, until television and anti-trust legislation killed them, double-bills were paired according to a strict economic hierarchy: an "A" movie at the top of the bill, bearing the imprimatur of a major studio and featuring name stars, and a cheaply produced genre picture to fill out the program. Unlike the main feature, where box-office receipts were split between the distributor and the theatre, "B"s were rented out at a fixed rate; this built-in ceiling on profits kept the majors away and left production of "B" s to such "Poverty Row" studios as Monogram and Republic. In retrospect, many of those "B" space-fillers were later re-evaluated by auteurist-leaning critics as being superior to their "A" counterparts, but at the time, putting a double-bill together was simply a matter of cut-and-paste overseen by management. Freed from any obligations beyond the simple fact of availability, however, programming a double-bill can be an exercise in film criticism in and of itself—a chance, as with the creative DJ, to construct a dialogue between films, genres, and eras. But any good repertory programmer needs to be able to answer one basic question—What makes a good double-bill?—and answer it in a variety of different ways.

Far and away the most common pairings favored by today's rep houses are those chosen according to director or leading player (often, as with the collaborations of Ford/Wayne or Wilder/Lemmon, both). *Raging Bull* and *Taxi Driver*, *Psycho* and *The Birds*, *The 400 Blows* and *Shoot the Piano Player*—such double-bills are staples of repertory houses, and for good reason. It would be welcome if a little more attention were paid to second-echelon stars and role players: a night of Patricia Neal (*A Face in the Crowd* and *Hud*), Piper Laurie (*The Hustler* and *Carrie*), Murray Hamilton (*The Graduate* and *Jaws*), or even John McGiver (approximately three unforgettable minutes in each of *Breakfast at Tiffany's* and *Midnight Cowboy*) would be a welcome departure from the standard Brando/Dean/Eastwood fare. My favorite bit of acting lore is Anthony Hopkins' claim

if anything should happen

that he based the cadences of Hannibal Lecter's voice on Katherine Hepburn, intriguing rationale for a *Silence of the Lambs*/Hepburn double-bill. Happily, *Guess Who's Coming to Dinner*"'s clunky mediocrity excuses it from consideration.

The other most common programming strategy is genre, and again, such double-bills require little explanation: *The Big Sleep* and *Double Indemnity*, *Casualties of War* and *Full Metal Jacket*, *Rock 'n' Roll High School* and *Fast Times at Ridgemont High*. Genre pairings generally bring together films of comparable vintage, with a window of ten years or so. My own ideal rep theatre would loosen the parameters of chronology. *Sexy Beast* looks well past *Reservoir Dogs* for its antecedents to various heist films of the '50s (*The Asphalt Jungle*, *The Killing*), while every metaphorical death-of-the-western of the post-*Wild Bunch* era, from the elegiac (*The Shootist*) to the murky (*McCabe & Mrs. Miller*) to the perverse (*Dead Man*), makes a good match for the much earlier stirrings of genre self-consciousness found in *The Gunfighter*, *High Noon*, and *Shane*. (Just as *Red River*'s stirring cattle drive—"Take 'em to Missouri, Matt"—has its nightmarish companion 15 years later in *Hud*'s wholesale cattle massacre.) A programmer can do almost anything within the realm of genre, especially subvert it altogether. David Cronenberg's *The Brood* finds its ideal complement a quarter-century earlier in *Forbidden Planet*, but only within the boundaries of horror/sci-fi; as Cronenberg himself has pointed out, however, *The Brood* was really his version of *Kramer vs. Kramer*, a fascinating contrast in the mechanics of domestic disintegration.

Moving beyond director/performer/genre, unexpected points of narrative intersection make for some offbeat pairings. Bergman's *Wild Strawberries* is an obvious partner for either *Harry and Tonto* or *The Straight Story*, but when Victor Sjöström and his entourage give a bickering middle-aged couple a lift, one is immediately reminded of Helena Kallianiotes ("I've seen filth that you wouldn't *believe*") and Toni Basil in *Five Easy Pieces*—taken together, a cautionary double-bill about why it's not a good idea to give rides to strangers. (Or, to take the point even further, a double-bill of *Wild Strawberries* and *The Texas Chainsaw Massacre*.) Pairing an art-house favorite with its low-rent shadow is almost invariably a good idea waiting to happen. Besides *Wild Strawberries*, *The Texas Chainsaw Massacre* also matches up well with either Godard's *Weekend* or Kon Ichikawa's *Fires on the Plain*: to paraphrase Barbara Streisand, people who get eaten by people are the unluckiest people in the world. And instead of *The Seventh Seal* alongside a Bresson or Dreyer, why not Herk Harvey's *Carnival of Souls*, in which Candace Hilligoss is stalked by a grinning, malevolent spectre not unlike Bergman's corporeal Death figure? All that's missing from Harvey's ultra-creepy shocker are the chess boards.

Bob Rafelson's lesbian hitchhikers in *Five Easy Pieces* were likely an explicit homage to Bergman, another illuminating means of pairing films that cut across time and geography. When Gene Hackman observes in Arthur Penn's *Night Moves* that the Eric Rohmer film he once saw "was like watching paint dry," an opening is created for a double-bill with *My Night at Maud's*. Likewise Ozu's *Tokyo Story* and Jim Jarmusch's *Stranger Than Paradise*, wherein Richard Edson assures John Lurie that Tokyo Story is "a good one" (took me a half-dozen viewings to realize he's referring to a race horse). In the case of *On the Waterfront, Raging Bull*, and *Boogie Nights*, homage is passed from one film to another like a relay baton: first Scorsese has De Niro recite Brando's famous could-have-been-a-contender soliloquy, then Paul Thomas Anderson pays tribute to Scorsese by having Mark Wahlberg re-enact De Niro's recitation. So *Raging Bull* works well with either film; the more esoteric approach would be to take Scorsese out of the equation altogether.

Boogie Nights is also a natural partner for Mikhail Kalatozov's *I Am Cuba*, thanks to Anderson's meticulous recreation of the latter's elaborate poolside tracking shot; Kalatozov looked to Lenin for inspiration, Anderson found his in Eric Burdon. A few other double-bills suggested by the duplication of specific shots or images: Robert Altman's *The Long Goodbye* finishes with a variation on *The Third Man*'s final shot; Warren Beatty's dreamy, snow-entombed death in *McCabe & Mrs. Miller* echoes Charles Anzavour's similar end in *Shoot the Piano Player*; there's a strong evocation of *Jules and Jim* in Billy Wilder's *The Private Life of Sherlock Holmes* when the three principals go bike-riding; both *The Shining* and *Barton Fink* (maybe even Michael Snow's *Wavelength*) pair well with Polanski's *Repulsion*, all of them ending on a slow zoom into a photograph or painting; and Spielberg clearly had *Vertigo* in mind when devising his spectacular zoom-in/track-out on Roy Scheider during the second shark attack in *Jaws*. *Vertigo* also makes an excellent match for Michael Powell's *The Life and Death of Colonel Blimp*, where the casting of Deborah Kerr in three different roles—an elusive image of beauty that haunts the film's two principals though three wars—anticipates Hitchcock's use of Kim Novak 15 years later.

Sometimes points of overlap that are almost certainly accidental open up other affinities between two films. In Wilder's *Fedora* (at first glance, an obvious partner for either his own *Sunset Boulevard* or Fassbinder's *Veronika Voss*), pages and pages of manuscript are discovered on which the putative title character has written "I am Fedora" over and over again. It's an image that had me automatically thinking ahead to Nicholson's "All work and no play" breakdown in *The Shining*, at which point the way that both films play around with notions of identity, isolation, and madness came into focus. Kubrick, working from Stephen King's novel, may not have been thinking of *Fedora* when he had Shelly Duvall discover Nicholson's demented handiwork, but the scene serves as a gateway into a meaningful double-bill.

Not surprisingly, remakes and sequels are routinely paired together at rep houses. There are also films that match up so well they function as *de facto* remakes in disguise. *The Sweet Smell of Success*, Alexander Mackendrick and screenwriter Clifford Odets' corrosive expose of Walter Winchell, has its perfect companion in *Wall Street*, Oliver Stone's liveliest and least heavy-handed film. Each is anchored by its era's iconic symbol of greed, ruthlessness, and the rot of power (Burt Lancaster's J.J. Hunsecker, Michael Douglas's Gordon Gekko); both tyrants have lapdog apprentices in tow (Tony Curtis and Charlie Sheen) who eventually become dismayed enough to strike back at their masters; and both films waver between fetishizing and shrinking back in revulsion from the material trappings of success within their respective worlds (a table at 21 in *Success*, overpriced art and a DIY blood-pressure gadget in *Wall Street*). There's a temptation to want to pair *Success* with *Diner*, in which a zombie-like teenager recites Lancaster and Curtis's climactic showdown word-for-word, but Levinson's mild nostalgia piece would evaporate alongside Mackendrick and Odets's bile. Allowing for a few nuances of language, however, Hunsecker ("I want that boy taken apart") and Gekko ("Ollie, I want every orifice in his fucking body flowin' red") were made for each other.

Trying to find the ultimate pair of movie villains is subject enough to keep any rep theatre going for a year. My own pick would be a double-bill of *Marathon Man* and *Blue Velvet*. Much was made last year of Ben Kingsley in *Sexy Beast*, especially the way his entrance was preceded by a grand build-up like the one given Hopkins' first appearance in *The Silence of the Lambs*. The unannounced arrivals of Laurence Olivier in *Marathon Man* and Dennis Hopper in *Blue Velvet* are much more disturbing, however—Olivier and Hopper take over the proceedings so suddenly and inexplicably, their first scenes leave you numb and disoriented. Each character even comes equipped with his own unfathomable mantra: Olivier's "Is it safe?", Hopper's "Don't you fuckin' look at me."

interrupting my train of thought

George C. Scott would be on my short-list of greatest movie villains for his work in *The Hustler*, which has, besides a few surface similarities to *Raging Bull*, a more esoteric link to Scorsese's film: the real Jake La Motta has a 15-second cameo (and one line: "Check") in *The Hustler* as a bartender. Any Sam Peckinpah film makes a good double-bill with the original *Invasion of the Body Snatchers*, in which the then-obscure director appears briefly as a meter reader. And Joe Dante's *Matinee*, a fictionalized account of gimmicky shock-director William Castle, would play well with *Rosemary's Baby*: besides producing Polanski's film, Castle has a cameo as the man outside the telephone booth whom Mia Farrow initially mistakes for Ralph Bellamy, one of the film's tensest moments.

I'd also pay close attention as a programmer to the much harder-to-quantify subject of mood. Within a few years, Wes Anderson's *Rushmore* will probably become a staple of rep houses, invariably finding itself double-billed with *The Graduate*. A sensible match—there are numerous points of intersection between them narratively, visually, and musically—but *Rushmore* takes even more in terms of its wistful ambience from some lesser-known films of the same vintage: *The Sterile Cuckoo, Goodbye, Columbus, The Heartbreak Kid*. A program of Anderson's film and *The Sterile Cuckoo* would capture the lingering influence of a side of American cinema in the 1960s existing far outside the *Bonnie and Clyde*/Scorsese/Tarantino lineage. *American Beauty* and *The Piano*, which both won major awards while simultaneously becoming targets of critical backlash, would make an odd but compelling double-bill. Seemingly worlds apart, the two films converge in the mysticism of voice-over soliloquies by Kevin Spacey and Holly Hunter in their final scenes, impressionistic reveries on beauty, acceptance, and the great beyond (from where Spacey is definitely speaking; there's some ambiguity whether Hunter is alive or dead). Ambiguity itself is a mood that suggests certain pairings. With both *Last Year at Marienbad* and *In the Mood for Love*, I found myself completely mystified as to whether the principals had an affair or not—if you're someone who likes to leave a theatre befuddled, such a double-bill would be nirvana. (I think it was Richard C. Walls who once observed in *Creem* that "ambiguous," "delirious," and "claustrophobic" were the highest forms of praise from an auteur critic, and that the ideal auteurist film would be the story of a schizophrenic miner told from an uncertain point of view.)

I'd like to see a double-bill of Joseph Losey's *Eve* and either Fritz Lang's *Scarlet Street* or Kubrick's *The Killing*—Stanley Baker's abject subservience to Jeanne Moreau in *Eve* puts him very much in the tradition of such hopeless pushovers as *Scarlet Street*'s Edward G. Robinson and *The Killing*'s Elisha Cook Jr. (Losey also makes expressive use of Billie Holiday's music in a manner that anticipates the post-Scorsese soundtrack, marking it as a good match for Sidney J. Furie's workmanlike Holiday biography *Lady Sings the Blues*.) In Michael Ritchie's *The Candidate*, a few seconds of chaotic footage inside a daycare centre, shot and rejected for a political ad, is played for laughs; Frederick Wiseman's riveting (and at times blackly humorous) three-hour documentary *Welfare* would pair well with Ritchie's film. I mentioned *The Straight Story* earlier in connection to *Wild Strawberries*; Lynch's film has another logical partner in Ichikawa's *Alone on the Pacific*, two versions of improbable journeys undertaken by obsessive, troubled outsiders. Jonathan Demme's *Melvin and Howard* belongs with Max Ophuls' *Caught*, a noirish treatment of a millionaire recluse modeled after Howard Hughes, while *Breakfast at Tiffany's* and *Darling* mirror each other uncannily, right down to their *La Dolce Vita* parties and the appearance in each of Jose Luis de Villalonga as the epitome of diplomatic elegance. Terrence Malick's *Days of Heaven* and Michael Cimino's *Heaven's Gate*, which appeared within two years of each other, would make an instructive pairing. Matters of budget notwithstanding, I've never been able to figure out why Malick's film was (and remains) widely admired, whereas *Heaven's Gate* led to Cimino being virtually run out of the industry—they're basically the same big, empty pretty picture of obscure corners of American history 20 years removed from each other. Finally, some double-bills should almost defy explanation. I'd love to program Spike Jonze's *Being John Malkovich* with the aforementioned *Fedora*, a bizarre house of mirrors that could be subtitled *Being Michael York*. You'll just have to see the Wilder film yourself to understand why.

My own nomination for the ideal double-bill goes to a couple of personal favorites that dovetail perfectly on a number of levels: Martin Ritt's *The Spy Who Came in From the Cold* and Michael Radford's *Nineteen Eighty-Four*. First off, they're two of the most unjustly overlooked films of their eras. *Spy* appeared in 1965, a time when the influence of Andrew Sarris's auteurist writings was starting to take hold; Sarris had already relegated Ritt to the lower reaches of his hierarchy (inexplicably so, on the basis of *Hud* alone), and although Ritt developed a critical champion in Pauline Kael, he never had anything close to the cachet of such '60s auteurist favorites as Sergio Leone or John Boorman. *Nineteen Eighty-Four* had the unfortunate burden of its gimmicky release date, and it was also a second attempt (following a by-then-unavailable 1956 adaptation starring

Edmond O'Brien) to film a novel that many critics considered unfilmmable in the first place. Ritt's and Radford's films did garner good reviews upon release, but they've since been shunted to the margins of official film history.

Although *Spy* is in black-and-white and *Nineteen Eighty-Four* in colour, they aspire to and achieve a common texture—visually, they're among the bleakest films ever made. Ritt's director of photography, Oswald Morris, captured perfectly the dreary Cold War landscape of John Le Carre's novel, a clandestine commute between London and Berlin navigated by aging, shabby, worn-out spies, while Roger Deakins (later to become the Coen brothers' favorite cinematographer) brought to George Orwell's vision of post-war London a blanched, bombed-out decay redolent of privation and hopelessness. The look of each film is eloquent expression of their shared descent into worlds ruled by faceless tyranny: in *Nineteen Eighty-Four*, of course, in the guise of Big Brother (ubiquitous throughout as a fixed, oversized visage staring out from whatever monitor happens to be nearby), and in *Spy* represented by the duplicitous loyalties and meaningless allegiances of mid-level espionage flunkies doing the bidding for higher-ups well out of view (a shadowy arrangement that must have had special resonance for Ritt, who spent part of his career on Hollywood's blacklist). Indeed, as the many about-faces of *Spy*'s labyrinth narrative start to accumulate, one is reminded of *Nineteen Eighty-Four*'s darkly comical "We have *always* been at war with Eurasia" bromide. There's even a kind of parallelism between the Berlin Wall in *Spy* and Room 101 in *Nineteen Eighty-Four*, implacable symbols of oppression and control, where Agent Leamas (literally) and Winston Smith (spiritually) are ultimately killed.

There are other points of similarity—a doomed love affair, the numbing routine of nine-to-five drudgework, the presence of Cyril Cusack—but above all else there is Richard Burton, cast as Leamas in *Spy* and O'Brien in *Nineteen Eighty-Four*. *Spy* catches Burton entering mid-career at the peak of his talents—a year before *Who's Afraid of Virginia Woolf* would elevate him to a new level of public visibility, but well after he first established himself in 1959 with *Look Back in Anger*—while *Nineteen Eighty-Four* was his final film, a grace note on the heels of an alcoholic wilderness marked by such lowlights as *The Medusa Touch* and *Circle of Two*. Burton already had the disgust of middle-age attached to him playing young Jimmy Porter in *Look Back in Anger*, and in Leamas and O'Brien he gives that side of himself (was there any other with Burton?) full rein. The two characters supposedly carry out their maneuvers at opposite ends of the moral spectrum—Leamas fighting the good fight, O'Brien the bureaucratic arm of totalitarianism—but Burton so naturally exudes resignation and self-loathing in any context, both convey the same message in the end: "This is all a corrupt, meaningless charade, but it is what it is and I'll play out my part till the sorry conclusion." (The O'Brien of Orwell's novel comes across as more of a true believer than in Burton's shaded portrayal.) The subtlety and authority of both performances are astonishing. Screened together, *The Spy Who Came in From the Cold* and *Nineteen Eighty-Four* serve as bookends to a career that, although largely squandered, had moments of brilliance on par with the best work of Olivier or Brando.

The multiplicity of connections between *The Spy Who Came in From the Cold* and *Nineteen Eighty-Four* would be my ideal as a repertory programmer, a seamless blend of the visual, the thematic, and the art of performance. *Every* dedicated filmgoer finds his or her thoughts overtaken on occasion by the backlog of fragments and half-formulated theories one accumulates from a lifetime of watching movies. It's like carrying a rep theatre around in your head, just waiting for someone to give you the go-ahead and make it real.

(*Cinemascope*, 2002)

Jeff

The documentary festival here ends tomorrow. I saw *Jeff* last night, about Dahmer—thought it was very ordinary for such an incendiary topic. (Not a fan of re-enactment scenes, but *Jeff*'s were low-key and pretty good.) I felt like people were warily eyeing each other in line beforehand, trying to figure out which of us were practicing and/or aspiring serial killers. I was one of only a few people who wasn't with anybody, so I'm sure a number of people guessed me.

(ILX, 2012)

always window shopping

I've been making up year-end lists of my favorite records going back to 1985. The first two were done for *Nerve*, the next two for *Graffiti* (the second coinciding with the magazine's bankruptcy in 1988, so unpublished—"It Takes Two" was probably my #1), in '89 I did an on-air countdown for CIUT-FM (the University of Toronto station), and then in '91 the annual *Eye Weekly* year-end poll was launched, which eventually overlapped for me with the *Village Voice*'s Pazz & Jop poll, where I started voting in '98. The *Eye* poll disappeared a few years ago, just before *Eye* itself disappeared; I continue, for now at least, as a Pazz & Jop voter. You may have noticed no mention of 1990. I took a break that year, for teachers college and to try to figure out what Roxette was all about.

I think for most people who vote in year-end polls, whether music or film, the list is the thing, a way to take a snapshot of the year and have an impact on the final results. (Maybe I'm wrong—there are undoubtedly lots of different reasons for voting in a year-end poll.) I can't remember back to the beginning, but for me, though, the year-end ritual gradually—especially after I stopped doing *Radio On*, which is when I lost the impetus to keep up with new music (rekindled, somewhat, when I started doing a radio show at another Toronto college station, CKLN, in the mid 2000s)—became a starting, not an end-point: an organizing nudge for me to catch up with some of what I'd missed that year, and then incentive to write about some of it for the very first time. That's not the way you're supposed to do it, and I imagine voters who care about the integrity (sounds a little lofty—let's say the meaningfulness, then) of the results would question me even participating. (Arty on *The Larry Sanders Show*: "Some of the things you do, Hank...they're not quite right.") But I've always told myself that I'd stop submitting ballots as soon as I didn't find anything out there that caught my ear and that I wanted to write about. The *how* and the *when* of it doesn't matter to me, just the *if* and the *whether*.

So far, I'm still at it.

What Publications Do You Write For?

I authored a number of excellent e-mails in 2004. Highlights included my "Curious lack of excitement over John Kerry's New Year's

Plans" e-mail of 11/18/04; a "New Kansas CD sparks furor within the hip-hop community" e-mail that went out a week earlier; September's "Accept this e-mail as a gift on my daughter's wedding day"; 10/03's "Reassessing the Kogan oeuvre"; late July's "I'm Phil Dellio and I approved this e-mail"; "Re: your e-mail" all the way back in February; and, best of all, May's "Crouching Sarthak, Hidden Rachel." I've been busy.

(year-end ballot, 2004)

"Tomorrow," Morrissey

I'm almost sure this belongs on my singles list, but because I've only seen it three or four times I'll pass. Besides making room for St. Etienne, there's a chance that if I heard it some more I'd start second-guessing myself; there's a much better chance it'd end up near the top. "Tomorrow"'s video was unquestionably the one I thought about most last year. It's so simple: one long tracking shot of Morrissey and his friends walking through city streets, Morrissey in front and his friends following. Halfway through, Morrissey starts looking over his shoulder. He'll take a sidelong glance, walk some more, take another look; he slows down a bit, they slow down a bit, he looks again, he keeps walking. Are they still there? Every time he looks it's like he's sure they won't be.

(#1 video, year-end ballot, 1992)

"Man on the Moon," R.E.M.

This came out at an awkward time as far as year-end lists go—I picked it as a video last ballot—but I have to vote for it again, as it was easily the song that meant the most to me in 1993. I listened to it over and over again through January and February, and hearing it months later I have nothing but good feelings about it. The first line is "Mott the Hoople and the game of Life," and then, continuing in an allusive fashion, it expresses a deep nostalgia for something lost—not any one thing in particular, and nothing necessarily connected to the names in the song, but I do experience an overwhelming (and unphony) sense of nostalgia when I hear this. When CNN was providing live coverage of the repair mission in space last month—live coverage—I hardly gave it a second glance; the space program doesn't hold any interest for me anymore, hasn't in years. Compare that with grade four, 1970, how Norm Allen, Bobby Selmer, and Rich Schepaniak held me and the entire class spellbound when they brought in an enormous model they'd constructed of the Apollo 11 craft, the one Neil Armstrong took to the moon a few months earlier. Whenever I give it any thought, which is more often than anybody should, I cannot believe that that kid and the person writing this are one and the same.

(#1, year-end ballot, 1993)

"Right Here," SWV

Whatever the outcome of the Michael Jackson story—and if he's cleared, I'll feel ashamed for having concluded otherwise—his personal and professional breakdown continues to be obliquely soundtracked on amazing records by other people. Taken together, they strike me as an outpouring of gratitude by younger artists who grew up in awe of Michael Jackson—Naughty by Nature, Kris Kross, Mariah Carey, and now SWV. Especially "Right Here," where just having him in the background elevates the same three girls who did the sub-mediocre "Weak" to some place you never would have dreamed they could go. When Michael needs to hear a reassuring voice, someone to remind him of who he is, he should forget about the people he surrounds himself with and turn to Mariah Carey and SWV.

(#3, year-end ballot, 1993)

"Nothing Has Been Proved," Strings of Love

Dusty Springfield's original, played over the end credits of *Scandal*, was one of 1989's best singles; this 1990 cover is ambient Italian house, keeping the music and getting rid of most of the lyrics—all that remain are the key lines, "it's a scandal" and "it may be false, it may be true/but nothing has been proved," whispered again and again over the course of seven minutes. The last thing I expect (or want) music to do is take me outside of my own life, but occasionally a record does make me think that yes, that's what's going on out there. The timing of "Let's Talk About Sex" made me feel that way two years ago, and discovering this in 1993 has done the same. It should be used as the theme music for a *Current Affair*-type show, or could even be the foundation for an entire network, the Nothing Has Been Proved Channel. It would broadcast 24 hours a day as part of your basic cable subscription, just the Strings of Love over an endless loop of silent footage: Michael Jackson, Bob Packwood, Gennifer Flowers, Zoe Baird, John and Lorena Bobbitt, Heidi Fleiss, Amy Fisher, Burt Reynolds and Loni Anderson, Ted Danson and Whoopi Goldberg, Ed Rollins, whoever has the floor for that particular day.

(#1 reissue[5], year-end ballot, 1993)

"Kiss from a Rose," Seal

Another voice trailing off into thought: "There's so much I meant to tell you...", only a vague explanation of what that was. I'm sitting in the New Toronto Library as I write this, and there's some obvious madman at the table across from me scribbling away in his notebook, violently flipping back and forth across page after page, making word changes here and new additions there. He's got two huge volumes of the Oxford Dictionary beside him that he made a point of retrieving and hasn't used since, he keeps scowling and knocking over duo-tangs and papers, and he's been making so much noise that a guy at his table has moved over to mine. He also likes to unbuckle and buckle his belt. Normally I'd glare at someone like this because of all the noise, but I'm a little afraid to, and too fascinated besides. He seems to have something on his mind that he wanted to tell someone once, and he's getting it all down now.

(#4, year-end ballot, 1995)

Caveat Emptor

A few ballots back, I singled out "You Got the Silver" as one of the reasons I was voting for *Wild Palms*; it was actually "No Expectations." The following year I cast a half-vote for the opening credits of *Crooklyn*, even though "I didn't recognize the Chi-Lites song at all"—possibly because it

---

5   Not actually a reissue; my votes in this category used to go whatever older music I was obsessing over at the time, regardless of whether or not it had been reissued. It didn't even have to be especially old.

was a Stylistics song, "People Make the World Go Round." Last year I voted for an HBO commercial featuring Dian Fossey and gorillas; an American friend tells me that it's in fact Jane Goodall and chimps, Dian Fossey's deadness having removed her from consideration for the part. (On the plus side, I noticed that the commercial went on to win some award.) My number-one video pick last year was "Buona Sera" in *Big Night*, my description of which had to do with a scene that uses Rosemary Clooney's "Mambo Italiano." I don't know what's wrong—I certainly try hard for a casual air that's supposed to indicate I know what I'm talking about. I'm calling for an independent counsel to investigate myself, try to find out what the story is.

(year-end ballot, 1997)

"Doo-Wop," Lauryn Hill

A moralistic, almost mean rewrite of "Let's Talk About Sex" from seven years ago, and that's OK—there's so much sweetness and light in the chorus and the two notes that carry the lecture along, I don't mind the badgering and hectoring a bit. A lot of what she says seems reasonable, too, though I can't say I follow it all. "That thing" is a good name for that thing. That thing uses up an incredible amount of time, energy, and creativity. It brings down sportscasters, pop stars, football heroes, film directors, and presidents, and if I haven't yet had my own life fall apart because of it, it's not for lack of trying. Even as I sit in the library writing this, I'm noticing every little movement around me and turning my thoughts over to that thing.

(#1, year-end ballot, 1998)

"We Like to Party!" Vengaboys

Of the countless Mariah Carey/Jay-Z-type superstar duets, this mysterious collaboration between the Teletubbies and the Pikachus is far and away my favorite. It should be made into a kid's TV show modelled after the old Hanna-Barbera cartoon *Wacky Races* (Dick Dastardly, Penelope Pitstop, the Creepy Coupe—the Cartoon Network still plays it, else I never would have remembered). Each week, iconic buses manned by the Partridge Family, the Merry Pranksters, the Who, the Hollies, the Beatles, Jackie Gleason,

Keanu Reeves, Reg Varney, Otto from *The Simpsons*, and the Vengaboys go at it (Kris Kross is still waiting for theirs), with Burton Cummings over on the sidelines supplying caustic commentary: "Hey, Vengaboys—I'm so awful goddamn glad I'm not in your shoes!" Strangely enough, when it comes to partying, I'm very lukewarm on the whole idea.

(#2, year-end ballot, 1999)

"Sour Girl," Stone Temple Pilots

After a false start, Stone Temple Pilots' junky Nirvana imitation has become much livelier and more unpredictable than Pearl Jam's ever-more lugubrious one. (The radio agrees: Toronto stations continue to play "Even Flow" and "Alive," the two Pearl Jam songs with some forward momentum, to death, more or less ignoring everything else.) Actually, on "Vaseline" and "Interstate Love Song" and "Trippin' on a Hole," there wasn't much of an attempt at all to mimic Nirvana—"Interstate Love Song" is a title that belongs on a Marshall Tucker Band album, and the song itself has some of that group's same feel for wide-open spaces. Having said all that, even those songs seem clumsy next to "Sour Girl," whose free-floating weightlessness is touched by pop genius. As with Alice Deejay below, the lyrics function mostly as mantra: the subtle inversion around the title—sour the day she meets him, happy the day she leaves—and the stalker-like suggestiveness of "What would you do if I followed you?" And in the middle break, a line that should have provoked more offense than any of the Eminem singles: "The girl got reasons/They all got reasons." In a very casual, offhanded way, that's a lot of ill-will squeezed into eight words: hostile, patronizing, infantile, dismissive, kind of hateful even. It's the purest, most unguarded bit of male smugness I've come across since my favorite moment of the Simpson trial, the one time when I felt like cheering Johnnie Cochran: (looking askance at Judge Ito after waiting out one of Marcia Clark's worst-abuse-of-the-criminal-justice-system-ever harangues) "Is she finished yet?"

(#1, year-end ballot, 2000)

"Around the World," ATC

This stood in stark relief to everything else on pop radio in 2001, the only music to satisfy my new rule that the best song in any given year must be touched by the hand of "You Showed Me" by the Byrds: mysterious, luminous, melancholy, evanescent, serene. ATC's singer spends much of the time explaining her inability to explain anything ("I don't know what to say—oh not another word, just *la-la-la-la-la*..."), but precipitating her speechlessness is one of the greatest subjects of all for pop music, a disruptive but liberating encounter with "the radio playing songs that I have never heard." In the first verse she hears them, in the second she sits in an empty room waiting to hear them again. No matter how cataclysmic the effect, there's never explicit verbalization of what is better left to the *la-la-la-la-las* and their matching Europop synthesizer flourish. Even the big Martha Wash/ Robin S voice that pops up at the end, which 10 years ago would have been front and center, is mixed way into the background. A deceptively complicated record that is as pure in its way as the Velvet Underground's "Rock and Roll" or the Modern Lovers' "Roadrunner."

(#1, year-end ballot, 2001)

"Work It," Missy Elliott

The heroic weirdness of this leaves me awestruck, bringing to mind Greil Marcus's entry in *Stranded* for *Moldy Goldies: Colonel Jubilation B. Johnston and His Mystic Knights Band and Street Singers Attack the Hits*, a record I've never even laid eyes on: "Cut right after the sessions for 'Get Ur Freak On,' when Missy and her pals were still glued to the ceiling." It's hard to know even where to begin trying to unravel it, other than to observe that all the backwards looping and oh-yessa-massas ("NO!") and gadun-ka-dunk-dunks/toing-tanga-tang-tangs share something else with mid-'60s Dylan, a supreme confidence that amounts to getting away with anything and everything you care to try. Like all my favorite hip-hop, some of it just confuses me: "If you got a big _____, let me search it"—um, website? In the wake of "Work It," "Get Ur Freak On" sounded somewhat conventional the last couple of times I heard it, and "Get Ur Freak On" is not a conventional record. I love discombobulating kids at my school by throwing out anomalous "Work It" quotes:

interrupting my train of thought

"Can I go in and get my hat?"
"That depends—don't I look like a Halle Berry poster?"

(#1, year-end ballot, 2002)

"Sugar," Imperial Teen

"Work It" notwithstanding, the most pleasure I got from music this year was catching up with all three Imperial Teen albums. When they get it right, they're an even better Yo La Tengo than Yo La Tengo (whom I recently saw alphabetized in an Indigo store as "Tengo, Yo La," which is obviously Yo-Yo Ma's fault). And, allowing for the fact that I've taken a crash course, they seem to get it right more and more often every time out: twice on *Seasick* ("You're One"—still maybe their best song, though very different from where they're at six years later—and "Pig Latin"), almost half the time on *What Is Not to Love* ("Lipstick," "Crucible," and the great "Seven"/"Hooray"/"Beauty" finale), and just about everywhere on this year's *On*. I checked and there doesn't seem to be an actual single from *On* ("Ivanka," one of the two or three songs I don't care for, came out four years ago), so I'll narrow it down to "Sugar," "Millions & Man," "Captain," "Undone," and "My Spy," and give the nod to "Sugar" because I always felt that "sugar, sugar" would make a good pop-song lyric and now someone has finally put that to the test. Besides their inexhaustible inventiveness when it comes to reconfiguring the same perfect melody again and again, I think the two things that characterize Imperial Teen are 1) strategic delay (the way the drums tend not to kick in until 30 seconds into their best songs, and also how each album doesn't start peaking until the third or fourth song) and 2) a sixth sense for idiom: "catch me while you can," "can I have a show of hands," "the only game in town," "partners in crime," "we like the cars that go boom," ordinary little everyday phrases they rejuvenate in context. I'm voting for "Sugar," but the best line they've ever written comes in "Undone": "Put your ear up to the radio/You know more than you think you know." I have my own interpretation of what that means, but it's such a beautifully allusive thought, better just to leave it there to linger.

(#4, year-end ballot, 2002)

"Without Me," Eminem

"It feels so empty without me"—I've been trying and trying my hardest to remember what the world was like without Eminem, back to the early months of 2002, and I'm sorry, it's just not possible anymore...All I do is make fun of or complain about Eminem, but this is the third time I've voted for him, so obviously he gets to me (and just as obviously, I have some new jokes and complaints). Unless I missed something, the self-proclaimed King of Controversy was AWOL during the months after Sept. 11, so I don't know if putting Osama bin Laden in a video at a safe remove quite ranks with John Lennon or Sinead O'Connor in the annals of pop-star heresy. Which is fine, I get a charge out of "Without Me"'s Pied Piper-like invitation to "follow me" anyway, the little history lesson about Elvis and black music is ingenious, and "Fuck you, Debbie" is a great way to reintroduce yourself and shift your lead single into overdrive. Even the wildly misplaced attack on Moby is hilarious—I don't have strong feelings about Moby one way or the other, but I do know that middle-school kids, who make up a sizeable part of Eminem's core audience, have never even heard of Moby! He may as well have gone after Klaus Voormann or Edgar Froese. The story's been kind of gruesome since "Without Me," though. "Cleanin' Out My Closet" was just awful, and "Lose Yourself" is a synthesis of at least three different kinds of bad ideas: the Eagles on the travails of stardom, Destiny's Child on surviving, too many to name on the importance of believing in yourself. If it had something going for it in the vocal or the music it could maybe get a pass on such banality, but it has nothing—it's a lead-footed white elephant as oversized as Frank Howard. So at the precise moment when Eminem seems clunkier and less vital than ever, he's half the world's number-one concern. He's the Madonna of "Justify My Love" and *Sex* all over again.

(#10, year-end ballot, 2002)

"21 Questions," 50 Cent

Grade 6 kids take their musical heroes at face value, oblivious to what is, if not absurd, at least a little bit funny about a 50 Cent ballad. Me: "Does he actually ask 21 questions? Has anyone bothered to count? I'm pretty sure he only asks 18." Class: general befuddlement. That's why the music you love when you're 11 stays with you the rest of your life, why "Let's Stay

Together" and "Rainy Days and Mondays" are still of a piece for me, pure and mysterious and unmediated by anything: they are what they are.

(#10, year-end ballot, 2003)

"Outta Control," 50 Cent & Mobb Deep

In my comment on "99 Problems" last year, I did something I try to avoid: I started generalizing about the state of music, specifically the kind of hip-hop that knows of no world beyond some ubiquitous club that may or may not be fictitious, but which is of minimal relevance to the life of a white middle-aged grade-school teacher in any case. Even as I wrote, though, there was a part of me that thought about tacking on a disclaimer at the end based on a lifetime of listening to the radio and being surprised: "My favorite record of next year could very well be set in that same club, which is why it's stupid to start generalizing about the state of music." What I get from "Outta Control" is the same thing I once got from Naughty by Nature's "Hip Hop Hooray": a pause, a celebration, a record so beautiful in all that happens between the words that I'm tempted to call it something lofty like a meditation on the club, even though those words primarily consist of the usual stuff about getting your drink on and swallowing (um, not the drink) and gunning you all up. (Also, if I call it a meditation on the club, that would make it a club meditation, which sounds too much like Club Med.) A week after a 15-year-old shopper was randomly shot and killed on Boxing Day outside the same Toronto record store I used to rush down to on Boxing Day when I was 15, the gunning-you-up line suddenly seems real in a way I wouldn't have expected it to; fantasyland or not—and I usually don't have any difficulty separating the music I love from its real-life implications—I wouldn't want to have to explain to that girl's family why this is my record of the year and that not to worry, it's all showmanship. In a way, 50 Cent takes care of that himself in my single favorite moment of 2005, when the piano comes in for the first time on the line "Trust me, man, it's okay." Again, I'd have a hard time explaining why, but those two or three seconds seem incomparably wise and serene to me.

(#1, year-end ballot, 2005)

"Pimpin' All Over the World," Ludacris

Travelogue pop in the tradition of Chuck Berry's "Back in the U.S.A." and the B-52's "Roam"—not as good, but good enough. The big attraction for me, of course, is the pit stop in Toronto, alerting the rest of the world to something I've been telling everyone for years: the pimpin' here is top-notch, absolutely first-rate.

(#8, year-end ballot, 2005)

"Sexyback," Justin Timberlake

How exactly does one twerk? Not a masterpiece like "Rock Your Body," but it's got a hypnotic pull of its own thanks to the frantic "Take 'em to the bridge" guy and the hardest production white money can buy, and, for me, it also has some high comedy value—specifically, the "Them other fuckers don't know how to act" line. I don't know if that's supposed to be a bid for thug credibility, or if thug credibility is something Justin Timberlake already has among teenagers, but it's as if Carol Brady had walked into the kitchen one morning and said, "Fix your own fuckin' breakfast, Mike, I'm spent."

(#9, year-end ballot, 2006)

"You! Me! Dancing!" Los Campesinos

The first thing with live guitars that I've voted #1 since "Sour Girl" in 2000; I can't tell you how proud I am to reconnect with the tradition of guitar-based rock and roll that the Stone Temple Pilots exemplified so well. High on the list of things I love about "You! Me! Dancing!" is how it feels like two songs circling around each other, and in the one it's the girl who harbors the deep dark secret about her own lead-footedness, while in the other the guy's off in his own stratosphere blithely frugging here, there, and everywhere. (Or maybe he's doing the Freddie—nothing specific is ever named, but the kinetic energy here has a pronounced Freddie/frug feel to it.) It's a subversion of expectations as gratifying as the climactic graduation dance in *To Sir with Love*, where Sidney Poitier lurches around like the Incredible

Hulk while Judy Geeson makes like Ginger Rogers. I wish I could decipher the guy's motormouth ramblings towards the end—online lyric pages don't provide anything. I've been playing this so often the last while, I'm sure I'll wear it out before long. For now, it's "Roadrunner," it's "Every Picture Tells a Story," it's you, it's me, and it's dancing.

(#1, year-end ballot, 2007)

"Icky Thump," White Stripes

"Led Zeppelin reunion" doesn't compute: one guy remains very much dead, and while a few deaths don't preclude a high school reunion from advertising itself as such, one in a four-piece rock group is one over the limit. I bet "Icky Thump" does a better job of honoring the original anyway—such an impressive wall of galumph that, at 46 years of age, I had to reteach myself how to air-guitar before I was fully able to commune with it. Turns out it's not like riding a bike at all—you forget everything if you haven't done it for a while, and my timing and mechanics were so completely off, I'm scheduled for Tommy John surgery come May.

(#6, year-end ballot, 2007)

"House of Cards," Radiohead

This is the group that did "Creep," right? Wow—where they been? I'm 83% kidding. We reviewed "Creep" in *Radio On* 14 years ago (reaction was all over the place; very high controversy-rating, as I recall), and then I somehow managed not to acquire a single Radiohead album, or even hear more than a handful of Radiohead songs, between here and there. So that's my first order of business for 2008: investigate this Radiohead phenomenon. For the longest time, I was mishearing a key line here: "forget about your house of cards" as "forget about your house and car" (comical in view of the title—duh), and from there, taking notice also of the bit about collapsing infrastructure, I figured they were warning me not to become too attached to the material possessions that fill up my life, because at any given moment they could all disappear. Seeing as that's something I think about on a regular basis to begin with, I guess you'd call that a willfully creative misinterpretation. The words are just window dressing anyway, as they basically are on any great pop song; it's the exquisite coloration of everything enveloping those words that draws me in, not whatever lesson may or may not be there. When Thom Yorke's voice leaps up the register right after "forget about your house and car"—I mean, "forget about your house of cards"—I'm 12 years old again and swooning over Badfinger's "Day After Day," and that's more than enough for me.

(#7, year-end ballot, 2007)

"I Believe in Nothing," Vivian Girls

I put together my nine zillionth history-of-punk compilation for someone recently, and ended with this. I think I started anthologizing punk for other people sometime around Flipper's "Get Away": you can make a good argument that it's a story that ended ages ago, but you can make an equally good argument, the Greil Marcus argument, that as long as there's somebody out there who sounds like they heard their first punk-rock record yesterday, it's a story that inches forward in fits and starts, across many years. I hadn't made one of these compilations for a while, and the thing that jumped out at me this time is how virtually everything I put on there post-Nirvana was female: outside of Pavement and "Fell in Love with a Girl" (which is half-female, come to think of it), it was Scrawl, L7, Bikini Kill, Bratmobile, Hole, Sleater-Kinney, Ladybug, She Mob, and the Vivian Girls. That's probably not a surprise to anyone who was following closely through the '90s, but some of these songs I discovered well after the fact, so I've just personally come to the realization that males should never be allowed to sing punk-rock again; women add beauty, sadness, reverie, and lots else that might not have worked so well for Slaughter & the Dogs, but that now seems like the only way to do it. "I Believe in Nothing" also feels elegiac, something it shares with "Get Away" and other compilation-closers along the way like "Teen Age Riot" and Dinosaur Jr. and "Smells Like Teen Spirit." I'll get into the election below, but in a year that was resoundingly about Yes, I found the Vivian Girls' No especially poignant.

(#1, year-end ballot, 2008)

"Red, White and MILF," Figghole

I'm tempted to quote the lyrics in their entirety; it's not unusual at all for me to come around to ordinary words because the accompanying music draws me in, but with Figghole playing the kind of generic metal-rap that normally makes me wince, I may well be voting for lyrics here. (Except, except...somewhere in that mysterious alchemical process whereby songs are written, the words are so good that suddenly the generic metal-rap seems exciting again.) From the very first line—"She came to us from the hills of Wasilla/The babes are hot, but the winters are a killer"—the election's great Monster from the Id is transformed into a comic-book myth, Paul Bunyan in heels, shooting wolves from helicopters and drinking Miller beer. The YouTube clip has the Ted Nugent singer traipsing around town surrounded Robert-Palmer style by a trio of Palins; piling on one lurid image after another (enough so that you have to sign in now to view it), it plumbs Palin's softcore appeal as ingeniously as Tina Fey did. On my favorite line of the year, they get all meta: "She might not know about foreign stuff/She might not know about knowin' stuff." Swear to god, until this song, I didn't even know what a MILF was.

(#6, year-end ballot, 2008)

"I Gotta Feeling," Black-Eyed Peas

Did this have a lengthier run at #1 than "Boom Boom Pow"? Not sure—but I'm predicting that it'll be making people happy long after its predecessor's expert flash is relegated to the sidelines (after first taking a moment to salute its great line about being so 2000-and-eight; I spent a couple of weeks last spring laying that on everybody I spoke to). It's amazing how far these people have come in such a short time: not more than a couple of years ago, they were more or less a monstrosity. "I Gotta Feeling" exists somewhere inside a November election-eve euphoria that never ended, a moment a world apart from Joe Lieberman, Orly Taitz, Glenn Beck, Sgt. Crowley, Matt Taibbi, Joe Wilson, and the, um, exigencies of governing that have made the past year such a prosaic slog. (I say that as an interested Canadian who believes the President's doing just fine; Iowa, however, 2009 has not been.) As melodic and graceful as it is propulsively anthemic, "I Gotta Feeling" brings to mind "Holiday" and "Roam" and (of course) the Vengaboys, and I'll even throw in "1979" in terms of the video. Seeing BEP doing it on one of the award shows after descending from above on giant rocketships was easily my musical high point of the year. Again, these weren't just any rocketships—they were super-huge giant ones.

(#1, year-end ballot, 2009)

"Check It Out," Nicki Minaj & will.i.am

This is the second year in a row where will.i.am has topped my list; I must now seriously consider the possibility that he's a genius on the order of Chuck Berry or Bill James. (Three years ago I thought he was the Antichrist, or at least one of many Antichrists. My thinking has evolved on this matter.) The story has moved along since "I Got a Feeling," a spectacularly buoyant, endlessly playable, but nonetheless conventionally structured dance-pop primer. Half of "Check It Out" is that, the other half is compelling, speaking-in-tongues Missy Elliot weirdness. Which brings me to Nicki Minaj. I look at her and I'm Kevin Bacon in *Diner*, resigned to the fact that there's stuff going on in the world that I don't know about. For better or worse, I grew up sneaking into my (pretty sure closeted) uncle's room to look at his *Playboy*s from the '60s and '70s. Now that I'm about to turn 50, there is, sadly, still a part of my conception of female sexuality that goes back to the women in those magazines. Sorry—we are what we are. (George Costanza from the infamous cleavage episode: "What, am I trying to win an award here?") So, to get to the point: just when I finally manage to get my head around Beyonce in the "Telephone" video as the last stop in comic-book voluptuousness, the very end of history, the image people throw Nicki Minaj at me. This is not good. This is not right. This is not fair.

(#1, year-end ballot, 2010)

"It's Not Meant to Be," Tame Impala

Swirly, trippy, majestic. It might more accurately be my #1 of the year, but "Check It Out" is out there, it has some meaning in the world, and my inclination with what basically amounts to a coin toss is to vote for the hit. Someone may see my list and think "Oh, I know that, that's great," whereas Tame Impala are a band I stumbled over on a blog. That's not even like buying some Homestead or SST record in 1986 and trying to get people interested—it's closer to a mirage, wrapped in a reverie, inside an abstraction. Which is a good description of what "It's Not Meant to Be" sounds like. Which is nice.

(#2, year-end ballot, 2010)

"Gone Missing," Wussy

The *Wussy* LP is so good, it's hard to know which song to pick; I got out a Ouija board, dart board, and magic 8-ball, and this is the one. There's no way I should like Wussy as much as I do. There's a basic heaviness to a lot of their songs (definitely present on "Gone Missing") that's normally not my kind of thing, and Chuck Cleaver's voice has the kind of Gordon Gano/Robert Smith quaver that I usually recoil from. (As always, my points of reference are impressively up to date.) Maybe Lisa Walker being there to temper all of that puts them over for me, but it's not like she's a shrinking violet either—actually, it may be her more than anything that gives them a really sinister undertow. Great lines, too, which I never notice till the third or fourth time through: my two favorite on Wussy are "reflecting on the never-ending question why we've been born" and "I finally got your letter, and your punctuation hit me like a truck." Punctuation is something I think about a lot. I use dashes and semi-colons way too often, and there's always the never-ending question of where to place all the commas. And O.P.P. (other people's punctuation), geez. That does indeed hit me like a truck sometimes.

(#4, year-end ballot, 2010)

"Telephone," Lady Gaga & Beyonce

A song about a young girl in her 20s who's too busy to text her friend or talk on the cell phone; based on informal observations walking around the city, this immediately moves it into the realm of science fiction. The video's outrageous. Doesn't matter to me where it steals from, or how much—I'm sure a list of its antecedents would take up several pages. (Here's looking at you, Tura Satana.) I give Beyonce all the credit in the world for agreeing to participate. Lady Gaga: "No one's going to even notice me—you'll be the star of the show, promise." A friend told me that he thinks Beyonce's an intrusion, but to me she's just amazing. I was mulling over what I wanted to say about "Telephone" on the way home one day, and "Saturday Night's Alright for Fighting" came over the radio. Thinking about how elaborately over-the-top the "Telephone" video is, and thinking about Elton in Ken Russell's *Tommy* film, I'm going to propose that one of the better things god ever did was keep a videocam out of Elton's hands until he got old and boring. Here's looking at you, god—well played.

(#10, year-end ballot, 2010)

"Never Will Be Mine," Rye Rye & Robyn

More proof of the Rob Sheffield Rule, which says you can't write a bad song about waiting by the phone; this is a great one. Robyn is as eloquent and as magisterial (in the good sense—I think there's a good sense) as she was on "With Every Heartbeat," wrapping her voice around resignation and transforming it into a balm, while Rye Rye's childlike jibber-jabber is pure Judy Holliday. I'd be quite content living without a phone. I pay six or seven hundred dollars a year for the privilege of being rude to telemarketers, charitable foundations, and political canvassers. A couple of times a month I call out for pizza.

(#5, year-end ballot, 2011)

"Take Care," Drake & Rihanna

I like the Miguel and Frank Ocean songs I've heard, but I don't think they have the pitch perfect calm found here. I had to teach dance to my grade 6s this year, which basically amounts to a couple of classes spent twisting and frugging and hitchhiking, then they get into small groups and come up with their own dances. Four of my girls chose "Take Care" for their music, so thanks to them for making sure I didn't miss this. I don't have any more interest in Rihanna's ongoing dramas than I did when I voted for "Cheers (Drink to That)" last year, no more than I once did in Madonna's, or Mary J. Blige's, or Eminem's, or whomever's. (Don't mean to sound callous—I realize Rihanna's were triggered by something qualitatively different.) But they're there, on "Cheers" and again on "Take Care," where her opening line (about knowing when people have been hurt by the way they carry themselves)[6] seems made to order for Hugh Barker and Yuval Taylor's *Faking It*, which I finally got around to reading. Maybe that line was written specially for her, and maybe that's the first thing most listeners will remember about this song, if they remember anything at all. But without the expert contribution of the Canadian childhood TV star she's paired with (whose background seems eminently middle-class to me, although his Wikipedia entry tries hard to blur that), and especially without the studio hands who provide all the atmospherics, it'd just be words on a page that I probably wouldn't even notice.

(#2, year-end ballot, 2012)

"Pizza King," Wussy

Not a good year for pizza kings. One wanted to be president (not really, just play along), but he had a past, and sometimes he'd forget his lines. A couple almost had their businesses run into the ground by a rogue Supreme Court justice and the selfishness of sick people. Another made it to the World Series, but ran into funny-looking round man and got swept in four games. No idea who Wussy are singing about, but well timed anyway.

(#4, year-end ballot, 2012)

"Avant Gardener," Courtney Barnett

Australian—same part of the world as Lourdes, give or take a time zone or three. I thought "Royals" was striking the first few times; skip forward a few weeks after hearing it constantly as my grade 7 art classes listened to the radio, and I'd had enough of "Royals" for several lifetimes. Would that be true of "Avant Gardener" if it had been the fluke hit instead? I don't think so—or rather, I think it's a song that would eventually emerge on the other side and sound fabulous again. That happened to me with "Loser" once. When I finally had a chance to write about it in my old fanzine, soon after it had fallen off the charts, I was so tired of it I just gave it a rating and left the gushing to everyone else. Today, it again sounds like the greatest thing in the world.

---

6 A famous Bobby Bland lyric I missed until someone pointed it out to me on the ILM message board.

"Avant Gardener" does in fact meld Beck, one of his spacier slide-guitar songs, with Liz Phair. Instead of fragmentary gibberish about loveseats and chimpanzees, I'm guessing Barnett is an actual asthmatic singing drolly of her actual daily ordeals. (I don't know—tried to confirm this and couldn't.) She neologizes as imaginatively as Clipse: "I'm breathing but I'm wheezing/Feel like I'm emphysemin'." I've never seen an episode of *Breaking Bad*, but "I guess the neighbours must think we run a meth lab/We should amend that" makes me want to catch up. As everything winds down, there are a few seconds of noodling around that sound like they're lifted from Three Dog Night's "Mama Told Me (Not to Come)," which was also about someone who had trouble catching his breath.

(#5, year-end ballot, 2013)

"Knowing We'll Be Here," Daniel Avery

Occupies some space between bliss and grace, like "Inspector Norse" from last year, minus the crazy drug fiend in Todd Terje's video. Words like "bliss" and "grace" are the limits of my ability to write about a song like this—sometimes I'll throw in "serene," too, and that's about it. I was checking one publication's list of Top 50 Dance Songs online, and along with every video clip there was a capsule write-up, seemingly all of them by the same writer. As I idly read a few while playing the clips, I found myself more and more impressed by the writer's ease and assuredness in micro-differentiating between songs and sub-sub-genres that would blur together for almost anyone, me included. Not that the songs all sounded the same, they didn't, but the language this writer was able to summon went above and beyond the call of duty. I couldn't do it.

I'm also impressed, and amazed, by the way "Knowing We'll Be Here" and "Inspector Norse" are able to reach me. I'm as far away from their intended audience as possible. My only connection to the clubs where they were meant to be heard is when I drive across Richmond Street, through Toronto's club district, after a late film at the Lightbox. Drunken sparkly people half my age spill onto the street—I'm worried one of them will pound the side of my car as I come to a stop at an intersection, which might cause me to want to intentionally run that person over, and that'd be bad. I navigate my way through, drive the rest of the way home, listen to "Knowing We'll Be Here," and construct my own club in my head.

(#1, year-end ballot, 2013)

"Work Bitch," Britney Spears

A lot of songs on here appeal to—embody—my sense of beauty, so I'm glad to include this one bit of insanely funny shamelessness. Britney Spears has been pretty much the most useless pop star on the planet for me the past 15 years—I think the only song of hers I didn't mind was her first single, but enough about my bilious private life. Somewhere along the way, rock critics started to like her. I remember "Toxic" did very well in year-end polls. Couldn't stand it; just checked, still can't. I could have listed her twice this year, though—also like "Scream and Shout" a lot. The first time I heard "Scream and Shout," via video, I thought that if any song ever had a chance to redefine gruesome, this was the one; before long, it added to my sense that will.i.am possesses a peculiar kind of pop-music genius.

"Work Bitch" makes me think back to TLC's "Waterfalls," where they counselled moderation and patience right around the time they were setting things on fire and declaring bankruptcy. Here, the lecture is on initiative and perseverance—if you want stuff, really important stuff like parties in France, you need to stay focused, hold your head high, call the governor, make the bubble up...well, she starts speaking in tongues a bit, but the message is clear. And if it isn't, there's always the helpful "You better work, bitch/Now get to work, bitch!" to clear things up. Good show: if I could hold up one person for my students whose every public action exemplifies the very meaning of work ethic, Britney Spears would be my first choice. (Cheap shot—I imagine she works 40 times harder than I do, albeit with a little bit of messiness attached.)

The music here is amazingly propulsive. I think it's "Superstition," more or less, trashed up and amped up and sped up beyond lawsuits. It slows down and coalesces in all the right places. She throws in a fake English accent on the word "hot." Why, I don't know. She says "bitch" at least as well as Angel Haze, and better than Young Thug. She'll probably make the Rock and Roll Hall of Fame one day—everyone except England Dan and John Ford Coley does now—and because of this song, I'll be okay with that.

(#7, year-end ballot, 2013)

Malapropisms

I'm casting a bonus vote for my Dad, who recently asked if I was "still writing for the Village People." It was his greatest malapropism since my parents were apartment-hunting a few years ago and he mentioned a place as being "$850, including utensils." I was enjoying the moment too much to really answer him, so yes, Dad, I am, now and again, but I try to save all my best stuff for the Silver Convention.

(year-end ballot, 2001)

constantly aware of all the changes that occur

More stories—all the ones that don't have anything to do with high school or my hometown. (Not true. You'll find both of them in here, too.) These ones concern friends, co-workers, libraries, baseball, donut stores, giggling fits, teaching, and various other matters. Sometimes they're tangents spinning off from a piece of music or a film, sometimes not. I'm glad I had, when they were written, the option of pursuing those tangents whenever I felt like it—not just in the fanzines I wrote for, where such freedom was a given (freedom's just another word for writing-for-free, as the song lyric goes), but in other venues too, like *Nerve* and *Graffiti* and even the *Voice*, both paid and unpaid. I tend to teach the same way, too. Lots of tangents and stories, with a little bit of bluffing here and there.

I probably haven't written as much about my years as a grade-school teacher as I could have, or should have; the nine or ten months a year I spend in the classroom have been far and away the dominant fact of my life for the past 15 years. Writing about what goes on in the classroom is tricky—you have to do so with a certain degree of discretion (real names are obviously verboten; the piece that follows about a long-term placement I once had in a grade 2 class is the one time in this book where I changed names wholesale), and, as with power-pop, I've had it in the back of my mind that I would one day attempt something lengthy on the subject. I'm not sure that'll happen; I'm five years away from retirement and pretty worn out at this point.

Also: the two or three baseball-related inclusions have had all mention of on-base percentage, runs created per 27 outs, and Pythagorean Wins removed. A reluctant concession to the world most people live in.

Five Favorite Years for Pop Music

1) 1972
2) 1982
3) 1979
4) 1994
5) 1986

I'm approaching this as a list of years where my connection to music was at its deepest, regardless of whether or not I was connecting with music released in that year. Usually I was, but in 1979 and 1986 I was playing catch-up to a degree. I like Michaelangelo's description of 1969 a lot, and he almost makes me want to make room for that (I'd add *Volunteers* to his list of I-want-to-spoil-the-party downers), but it was past the statute of limitations when I first heard some of the stuff he mentions. I'm leaving out 1965 and 1966, home of more music that I love than any of the years above except #1, for the same reason—my dim four-year-old memories of 1965 pretty much begin and end with "Downtown" in the back seat of the family car. So, chronologically: 1) As I've related to many people already, the origin of the universe, the be-all and end-all, my own private Rosebud. I remember an old "Real Life" column where Greil Marcus called 1972 "the least scary year ever" for pop music. Maybe, but at age 11 it was awash in mystery for me, and that initial sense of discovery has never abated. The high-water mark of singer-songwriters as hitmakers: "Doctor My Eyes," "Without You" and "Coconut," "Anticipation" (which I've always preferred to "You're So Vain," same year), "Mother and Child Reunion," all the *Harvest* singles, "Sweet Seasons," weird epics like "American Pie" and "Taxi" and "The First Time Ever I Saw Your Face." Exquisite neoclassical soul: "Let's Stay Together" *and* "I'm Still in Love with You" (like getting "Eight Days a Week" and "Ticket to Ride" in the same year), "Betcha By Golly, Wow," "I'll Be Around," "Oh Girl." Bleaker Nixon hangovers from War ("The World Is a Ghetto"), the Staple Singers ("I'll Take You There"), Curtis Mayfield ("Freddie's Dead"), and Stevie Wonder ("Superstition"). Brilliance scattered all over the Top 40: "I Saw the Light," "You Wear It Well," "Rocket Man," "I Can See Clearly Now," "Tumbling Dice," "Black Dog," "Everything I Own," "Rock and Roll Lullaby," Badfinger's "Day After Day." The five Lisbon girls: Pauline Boone, Yolanda Sluik, Anita Woychesko, Lee Johnston, Susan Dey. And, of course, "Hurting Each Other," the last great Carpenters single. 3) Early in the year, my high-school Neil Young obsession reached critical mass with *Rust Never Sleeps*, which he'd previewed a few months before at Maple Leaf Gardens; in the summer, just before starting university, my new friend Peter introduced me to *The Ramones* and *The Clash*. I loved the first and didn't much care for the second. In the fall, after a few months of going to punk shows, I shared the mike for a few seconds of "White Riot" with Joe Strummer. 2) *Album Generic, Back from Samoa, The Fire of Love, Wild Gift* and *Under the Big Black Sun, Damaged, The Days of Wine and Roses*, Fear's *The Record*—if it came from California, we loved it (except for the Minutemen, who were just confusing). I didn't hear Hüsker Dü, the Replacements, or R.E.M. until the following year, and thanks to them and some others, '83 and '84 were just as momentous for me. But '82 looks more exciting from here. There was still such a thing as Top 40, I think; I hardly noticed until 5) I started working at a downtown record store, where, much to my Rip Van Winkle-like disorientation, the manager made it clear that the great majority of customers didn't want to hear *Psychocandy* at 11:00 in the morning. So we played *True Blue* and *Please* and "Rumors" instead, and a part of the musical landscape I'd more or less ignored for a long time—the biggest part—came into full view once again. It wasn't quite Emerald City: there was also Europe's "The Final Countdown" to contend with. 4) I wanted to include one year from *Radio On*'s lifetime, when I was keeping up with the radio and videos like I kept up with Slash and SST in the early '80s. Scanning my year-ends, '94 looks like a good choice: "Fantastic Voyage," "Miss World," "Cut Your Hair," "Gin and Juice," "At Your Best (You Are Love)," "Self Esteem," "Do You Wanna Get Funky," "Worker Man," and "Pay No Mind" all made my Top 10, a representative mix of the big hits and underground heroes I've bounced back and forth between the past 30 years, except that in 1994 they were sometimes one and the same.

(rockcritics.com, 2002)

Quality Time with Balaam & the Angel

My first submission to *Nerve* was a page-long review of the Ramones' "Bonzo Goes to Bitburg" in either July or August of '85. *Nerve* had been around for maybe a year at that point, but I'd only really taken notice of it the last couple of issues. In particular, it was a long R.E.M. piece by Howard that made me think it might be a good place for me to try sending something. I'd done a little music writing through university: a review of *Damaged* for a journalism friend at Ryerson; reviews of Hüsker Dü, the Butthole Surfers, and the Gun Club for *The Varsity* my last year at the University of Toronto; and a letter published in *The Newspaper*, UT's other student newspaper, in which I was very distraught that the Psychedelic Furs and Joe "King" Carrasco had been left off a pre-emptive best-of-the-'80s list compiled by their writers. (One of them, Sam Guha, who I came to know through the campus radio station a few years later, would die very young of a heart attack; I imagine all the guilt he carried around over the Joe Carrasco slight played a role.) Life in general had gone steadily downhill in the intervening year-plus since graduation, and however awkwardly, I think I was able to get some of that feeling into the "Bonzo" review. I sent a copy to *Nerve*, and also one to the *Voice*. I didn't hear back from New York—it's my understanding that they reluctantly passed following a series of high-level editorial meetings—but within a couple of weeks, I got a call from Dave at *Nerve* telling me that it was too late for anything to be included in the issue they were just finishing, but I should drop around and try to set something up for the issue after that.

I went in to a nearly empty Ryerson either that weekend or the next and met Dave. I don't remember if Nancy was there or not, I don't remember what we talked about, and I don't remember if I came away with a specific assignment then and there or whether I had to follow up later. I do remember being tremendously excited as I headed downtown that day. My first two reviews ran in the September issue: X's *Ain't Love Grand* and an album by the Proletariat "featuring Lydia Lunch," a rather optimistic sales come-on that I pounced on for laughs. I was a regular contributor for the rest of *Nerve*'s two-year-plus run, album reviews only for the first few issues and eventually live reviews, interviews, and other stuff too. Yes, live reviews—if you know me at all well, that's pretty funny.

More than just getting me started as a music writer, *Nerve* had a huge effect on me socially. Basically, it was the first time in my life I made a number of new friends beyond the handful I'd been close to since middle school. I started working at a downtown record store around the same time, widening my social circle some more—it seemed like I knew a lot of people all of a sudden. Fifteen years later, the circle has contracted back to those same middle-school friends and the handful of *Nerve* people who remain, which is what you'd expect. But as meaningless as almost all of that activity ultimately was, I'm glad I experienced it—everyone should get to play Edie Sedgwick at least once in his life.

Those first two reviews, especially the X, got kind of mangled in the editing process, and if there's one thing I'll be arrogant enough to take some credit for at *Nerve*—I'm sure other contributors have a similar story—it was in getting Dave and Nancy to pay more attention to typos, and to be less quick to change copy without talking to the writer first. As I remember it, Dave was partly amused by how agitated I was over the X review—I probably did blow everything out of proportion. But as time went on, you could much more reliably expect that what you'd read in each issue was pretty much what you'd written. Too much so in my case.

My writing more or less passed through three phases at *Nerve*. I was earnest and fussy at the beginning, occasionally (as with the Proletariat review) getting some humour across, but still half-dedicated to that stilted kind of writing you fall into at university. As clunky as those early reviews were, though, they strike me as better than what came next: the self-important know-it-all, alternately glib (when imitating Bangs) and pretentious (when imitating Marcus), sometimes both at once. (No reflection on Bangs or Marcus, just an acknowledgment of how destructive their influence can be when misappropriated.) Unfortunately, phase two accounted for much of my stay at *Nerve*, making a lot of the writing I was so enamored of at the time hard for me to look at today. Somewhere along the way, I settled down and wrote some stuff that still reads well to me: a largely autobiographical look at obsessive record buyers, pieces on the Angry Samoans and the Gun Club, interviews with Roger Ashby (a DJ with CHUM) and Paul White (a former Capitol A&R guy I ended up working with at the aforementioned record store; he played a surprisingly large role in breaking the Beatles in Canada). I'm also inordinately proud of a Mel Torme space-filler I wrote towards the end, inspired by the discovery that an old album of his shared the title *Right Now!* with a recent Pussy Galore release. Pigfucker esoterica very much of its moment.

The timing of my involvement with *Nerve* was perfect in terms of the chance it gave me to interview some people who figured prominently in my imagination at the time, and to do so while the idea of interviewing somebody was still new and exciting: Bob Mould and Grant Hart, Joey and Dee Dee Ramone, Paul Westerberg, Curt Kirkwood, Marcus and Chuck Eddy, Schoolly-D, the Beastie Boys (possibly their first Canadian interview, a few months before *Licensed to Ill*, and gross enough that I wrote it up under a pseudonym), Richard Berry, and, for *Graffiti* (another Toronto publication that many *Nerve* people also wrote for), Johnny Thunders and the Pet Shop Boys. And again, whatever I might feel about the whole interview process today, everyone should get to play Barbara Walters at least once in his life—it's very satisfying that I got to talk to those people, especially in view of the fact that some have passed on. In keeping with the no-free-lunch rule, the trade-off for such access was quality time spent with the Thrashing Doves, Balaam & the Angel, the Raunch Hands, Matt Bianco, and various other mid-'80s luminaries. As you might expect, there wasn't a lot left to ask the Thrashing Doves that the whole world didn't already know.

I'll second a couple of Tim's observations: monthly *Nerve* parties ("meetings") at Dave and Nancy's were great, and Dave was a little bizarre. His two standard greetings: "Let's wail, babe," after something Huey Lewis once said to me, and "Phil D, totally out of control," after something Dale Martindale (don't ask) once said to him. He sometimes spoke in code, all of which carried a specific meaning and all of which I've forgotten except for "Did you tell her your life story?" Sometime in the mid-'90s, long after *Nerve*'s exit, Dave ran into Scott on Yonge St. "Scott Woods—hey." Scott had been living in Vancouver for four or five years, and they probably hadn't spoken in seven or eight. That won't make any sense unless you know Dave. The magnitude of his deadpan at such moments is very hard to convey.

Nancy, Dave's girlfriend and Nerve's co-publisher, was synonymous with two things above all else. First, there was her spacey interviewing style, the "If you were a major food group, which one would you be?" school of interrogation that's weird enough when practiced on regular famous people, doubly so when Zodiac Mindwarp is at the receiving end. (He was a self-identified meat or meat alternative, if memory serves.) Also, half or more of us had major crushes on Nancy at one time or another. That's an old story to the participants not worth dwelling on, but it was definitely a large part of *Nerve*'s dynamic.

I have a weird kind of relationship today with the music of that time, the music of the mid-'80s, both what *Nerve* covered and what it didn't. When I began, I was perfectly in sync with *Nerve*: Hüsker Dü, the Replacements, R.E.M., the obviously misguided certainty that whatever was hugely popular was almost always worthless (albeit a certainty that was sometimes the source of a compelling kind of us-against-them special pleading). Under Dave's influence, I added the Jesus & Mary Chain to my list of heroes. And then, sometime in 1986, my interest in Top 40 was reawakened by the record-store job. (I started to hang around with Scott at this point, and he also influenced me in that direction.) Dave was always good about letting writers pursue whatever they were interested in at any given moment, so soon I was reviewing Lisa Lisa, Alexander O'Neal, Madonna, and Bananarama for *Nerve*. Today I hardly ever listen to or think about any of that stuff—not the Amerindie end of it, and not the pop hits that followed. I connect more with my favorite '90s music, the songs that went into *Radio On*, and more still with my favorite '70s music. It's not that I think what I listened to during *Nerve* days is bad or overrated or anything like that. It's all just kind of walled-up for me for the time being, the Blow Monkeys included. I'm sure it'll sound great again at some point.

Overall, I have nothing but good feelings about *Nerve* 15 years later—not necessarily about the writing I did, but rather the heady sensation of being right in the middle of a fledgling publication that felt like the most important thing in the world at the time. That has a lot to do with the fact that *Nerve* was basically the first publication I wrote for—I doubt that it retains the same significance for Tim or Howard, both of whom had already been writing for a while when *Nerve* came along. When I read Robert Draper's history of Rolling Stone a few years back, I found myself really caught up in the early chapters, which were charged with the same kind of excitement I experienced at *Nerve* (and, in very different circumstances, that I experienced again when *Radio On* started to feel like something special). There have been numerous occasions since during my time as a music writer that I've been extremely happy about one thing or another, but I can honestly say that it never got any better than scooting around Toronto in the back of a van with Dave and Nancy, delivering that month's *Nerve* to record stores and clubs around the city.

(rockcritics.com, 2003)

With which character on The Simpsons *do you indentify most closely? Why?*

I think I have a little of six or seven characters in me. There's some Milhouse left over from grade-school—loyal friend, awed by the fact that Bart's standing over there "doin' stuff"—some Martin Prince, too. Whenever I hear that some local publication I despise has folded, I always let out a very satisfied Nelson-style raspberry. I share Apu's sentimentality and Homer's nostalgia, and I can also be as calculating as Mr. Burns. I don't see much of myself in Bart, though someone who knows me might disagree (in high school, yes). Most of all I hope I'm Lisa; everyone should aspire to be Lisa.

(*KITSCHener*, 1997)

Come Back to the Five & Dime, Jeffrey Lee, Jeffrey Lee

Beginning with a letter dated 4/23/82—"I went to the record store the day after talked to you and they had neither the Ornette Coleman album nor the Gun Club album"—the ongoing correspondence between my first-year roommate and me entered a new era: The Gun Club Letters. For the next three years, nary a letter went by without at least passing reference to the latest activities of L.A.'s fattest, I mean finest. Tom was in Toronto recently, so I waited until he wasn't paying attention and asked if I could excerpt some of his letters in an upcoming record review. He didn't say no. For starters, there was a constant attempt to unravel the psyche of the Club's charismatic leader, Jeffrey Lee Pierce: (1/83) "My brother Joe bought a copy of *Boston Rock* while he was home, an end of the year issue that included a group of quotes—one by Jeffrey Lee Pierce which I will paraphrase. He said the high school he went to was a mixture of every ethnic type in L.A. They all call each other names but eventually they make babies together—that's what's important. I think he must have said it better. Maybe not. If nothing else it shows what a poor racist he is." There were photographs of Pierce culled from various sources and passed along: (undated) "It's a terrible thing to say about one's idol, but I think that Pierce looks like a trapped pig about to be slaughtered. I made a copy on each of the three settings for shade. Maybe you can put them together for some artistic effect of your own choosing." There were nudges on the shoulder about letting down the Gun Club Team: (7/83) "I can't believe you haven't bought the 7-inch "Death Party" (new take-home size). It would make a great single if "Come Back, Jim" were on the other side, but because of the different artwork, it still seems to me an indispensable part of my collection." There were cryptic Club references that would make no sense whatsoever to an outsider: (11/83) "Incidentally, the old Plugz fan mail address was on Highland Ave. I wonder if Tito has a glass eye." There was a letter from Peter Holsapple, member of the dB's and then part of the Gun Club's management crew: (2/84) "Dear Tom, thanks for your letter. At the present time, the Gun Club is not on tour. Jeffrey is out in California, writing songs and (once again) reorganizing the band. Are you aware that there is a new Gun Club album called *The Birth, the Death and the Ghost*, recorded in and around Los Angeles? The personnel on the album is JLP, Kid Congo, Terry Graham and Rob (credited as "Bob") Ritter. Sorry about the delay in answering your letter. Keep in touch." There was follow-up action: (4/84) "I wrote to Peter Holsapple again, just to keep in touch. I asked him for Jeffrey Lee's address, believe it or not." There was lots more, too, every letter a grab-bag of Gun Club fun, facts and trivia. Near the end, there was mostly just a big guffaw: (12/83) "I was just looking at the *NME* with Pierce on the cover, and I got an idea for a new TV series. It's called *The Gun Boat*: past and present members of the Gun Club find romance and adventure aboard a reconditioned WWII destroyer. Jeffrey Lee Pierce is your captain." The joys of shared obsession.

(*Nerve*, 1988)

Marking

I'm marking a set of stories right now—truthfully, my least favorite thing one has to do as a grade 6 teacher. Anyway, just encountered a great title: *The Island of Treasure*. Better than *The Wake of Finnegan*, not as good as *The Complaint of Portnoy* or *The Dick of Moby*.

(ILX, 2011)

Have you ever stalked anyone? Why, and what happened?

No, but I have done some flaky things over the years that demonstrate stalking-like tendencies. When I worked in a property management office in the mid-'80s, I would always keep a lookout from my desk for this exotic-looking blonde who worked in one of the government offices upstairs. If I saw her coming out of the elevator and going to the coffee stand around the corner, I'd often wait two or three minutes and then leave the office to ride back up with her. Never said anything and came right back down after. I've had full-time obsessions with three donut-store girls, a supermarket cashier, and an optometrist's clerk at various times in my life. Donut stores are good, because you can go back every day without raising undue suspicion. A supermarket isn't bad either, though it's more of a weekly thing, unless you have the patience to do your grocery shopping two or three items at a time. The optometry industry is tough—once you have your glasses, there's not a lot you can do. I did sign up for a course in Mandarin Chinese (eventually cancelled) just so I could drop in and tell her, but I don't think she was much impressed. I've always believed I was the reason she left her job soon after.

(*KITSCHener*, 1998)

Joe Carter

Believe it or not, I actually consider myself a fan of Joe Carter's. He's one of the best interviews in the game, and on the field he's intense and emotional when he needs to be, playful and talkative the rest of the time—he's just generally a lot of fun to watch. I think his defense is a little underrated: I've seen him make a number of nice catches and strong throws since he's been with Toronto, and I hardly ever recall him looking bad (having witnessed George Bell and Candy Maldonado, bad is something I recognize). As a hitter Carter's mercurial: terrible slumps, and then two or three stretches each year where he hits six homers in a week and no one can get him out. (This season he binged for a month-and-a-half, with something like 50 RBI after 40 games.) He hit the home run that will probably always be my number-one baseball memory, right up there with Aaron's 715th, Fisk in Game 6, and Reggie's third in a row in '77. When I'm 93 years old and can't even remember how to fold paper in half, much less what Joe hit in late-inning pressure situations, I'll still remember his famous home run—in the long run, it will be all that matters. Did I mention he has a gorgeous wife? He does, and the runs created formula doesn't give him any credit for that. But there is nothing inherently remarkable about Carter's RBI totals, and—the key—given good health, I think there are 30 other guys in baseball who would knock in just as many or more under similar circumstances. The Jays would not have won a World Series without Alomar, and they wouldn't have won one without Winfield and Molitor. I doubt very much whether they would have won without Henke and Ward. I don't know whether they would have won without Joe Carter: I think his bat's a lot more replaceable than people imagine, but then you get into the other things that he brings to a team, and that's where I'm not so sure of the answer.

(Here's something really amazing: I went and looked up Carter's player profile in the 1985 Zander Hollander guide—i.e., back when nobody knew who he was—to see if I could find a prophetic quote to fill this space at the bottom of the page, and it turns out that either Zander Hollander printed the wrong picture, or else Joe was formerly a white man who bore a vague resemblance to Jason Alexander. If this is true, he certainly never mentions it in interviews.)

(*Radio On*, 1994)

Guess Who

Part of the fun of doing this for me is trying to piece together the story of what I liked at different times in my life, and when exactly I liked it. The Guess Who figure prominently in that story. They were my second favorite-group; not my second-favorite after someone else, but the second time I was consciously aware of having a favorite musical act. The first, as I've mentioned many times before, was Ray Stevens; my grade-school friend Martin had a copy of *Ray Stevens' Greatest Hits*, and we used to love "Gitarzan," "Ahab the Arab," and "Bridget the Midget." A couple of years after that wore itself out, I talked my dad into taking me to see the Guess Who at Toronto's old Exhibition Stadium (original home of the Blue Jays, now a parking lot). That would have been either '73 or '74; *Rockin'* would have been the only full-length LP I was familiar with at that point, although I knew all their hits well from the radio. I'd go back every August for the next two or three years with my cousin Glen, each time their encore-version of "American Woman" getting longer and more elaborate. I owned a bunch of their albums at one point—*American Woman, Wheatfield Soul, Artificial Paradise, Live at the Paramount, #10, Road Food*, possibly one or two more—but most of them either went to Randy or, the ones that were bought before I started collecting in earnest, were discarded because of wear and tear. There was also an 8-track of *The Best of the Guess Who* I used to play endlessly. The mere fact that I've listed a non-hit in the mixworthy group tells you all you need to know about how much of a fan I was—I mean, I actually used to get wrapped up in Burton Cummings' emotional well-being, something he was never shy about documenting on those mid-'70s albums no one remembers anymore. ("Those Show Biz Shoes" from *Artificial Paradise* was a good example of Burton as Sylvia Plath.) It all seemed very adult, very FM, very rock, very meaningful. I didn't realize till later that most of what made the Guess Who so good was the exact opposite of how I then perceived them—they were AM, they were pop, and they were often quite loopy ("Rain Dance," "Glamour Boy," "Albert Flasher," etc.). But that's OK. They really were pretty great, and looking back, they made for the perfect segue from Ray Stevens to all my later high-school obsessions.

(record inventory, 2005-06)

"Stop," Spice Girls

The Spice Girls' hold on my grade 3 class last year was at times like the *Simpsons* episode where the yo-yo troupe comes to Springfield, and every question from the kids for the next two weeks has to do with yo-yos. Ms. Hoover, exasperated: "Is this about yo-yos, Ralph?" Me: "Is this about Scary Spice, Natalie?" Class sharing time for the final two months became the Home Shopping Network for Fly-by-Night Spice Girls Merchandise, and for the school talent show auditions I had one group of girls lip-synching to "Spice Up Your Life," another to "Too Much," and a third to "Stop." We sent the former on to the big show, along with my own class favorite, Richard Brown lip-synching to "It's Not Unusual." (So as not to confuse anyone, we rechristened Richard as "Welsh Spice.") The mania was widespread: a friend who teaches grade 2 at another school wondered how you were supposed to promote good citizenship when you were busy breaking up fights over who'd get to be Sporty Spice at recess. Peer pressure built up on all sides: In a draw for our class hockey pool, Rickey chose the Spice Girls rub-on tattoos over the deck of cards and the key chain, not because he really wanted them—Rickey's much more of a card-playing type—but because it was inconceivable last year that you'd take anything else. (Also, in Rickey's case, so he could prevent the rest of the class from getting them.) In the end, all I could do was try to keep up. When I was looking to fill time the last week of school, I had an art activity where the kids named and sketched themselves as the new replacement for Ginger Spice. It took up two periods and kept them happy. Hopefully we can put the Spice Girls behind us in September and strike out for new territory, maybe measure the circumference of Green Day or something. (6.5)

(*Radio On*, 1998)

What personality type on the Myers-Briggs test do you think would be most suited to a career as "dictator" or "cult leader"? Why?"

I don't have an answer to the question at hand, but I do have a Myers-Briggs story. Last year, in order to get paid for the second week of an extended March break, I had to attend a series of half-day teaching workshops. As far as I could tell, they really didn't have much of anything to do with teaching, they were just what any elementary teacher would recognize as busy work. (Miss Hoover: "Before we pass out our Valentines, class, we're going to construct some special Valentine's Day mailboxes made out of cardboard." Lisa Simpson: "But isn't that just pointless busy work?" Miss Hoover: "Bingo—now get cracking.") The worst of them had to do with *The Seven Habits of Highly Effective People*—pure nonsense, reminded me of some kind of cult. More interesting was the Myers-Briggs workshop (I'm always interested in analyzing myself), which was preceded by a similar but simplified version called "True Colors." This latter involved answering a series of questions about yourself, after which you were designated as one of four personality types represented by a particular color (as opposed to

Myers-Briggs's more elaborate grid of 16 different types). I forget what the colors were or what each one represented, but let's say I was a Blue—the cautious, methodical type, doesn't react well to surprises. Once you had your color, you got into a group with the other 10-15 people having the same color. Each group was then supposed to write an acrostic poem describing its color and present the poem to the workshop. Fine—pointless busy work, but no worse than cardboard mailboxes. Being the cautious, methodical group, we all agreed that we'd go for the simplest presentation possible: one person would stand up and read the poem on behalf of the whole group. So we wrote the poem and waited for our turn. As the two groups ahead of us presented—whole-group sing-alongs both—you could see the panic begin to spread among the Blues. We're going to look really bad if just one person stands up and reads; we'd better do what the other groups are doing. So about 30 seconds before it was our turn, the rest of the group decided that we'd all go up together and sing our poem. Presumably the melody would just come to us spontaneously when we got up there. I couldn't believe they were serious. I pointed out that we'd already decided how we were going to do it, that it was too late to change—besides which, to what end? But my objections didn't have any effect, we were going to sing and that was that. I reacted the same way I often do when I feel overwhelmed by events; as the group stood up and moved to the front, I mumbled something like "This is stupid" and ducked out of the room. I came back four or five minutes later, by which time they were finished and seated again. I didn't ask anyone how it went because I really didn't care. I felt infantile about what I'd done, but I also wanted to point out to everyone in the group that, for better or worse, I was the only one who remained true to character. I wanted to tell them that they were just a bunch of fake Blues— misplaced Reds and closet Greens, not fit to share the Blue experience with me, the real thing.

(*KITSCHener*, 1997)

"Soixante-Sept," Hylozoists (2009)

I was out for my sister's birthday tonight with a few of her friends. When I mentioned to my sister that I thought our waitress, somewhere in her early 20s, was cute—did you know that restaurants sometimes hire cute waitresses?—my sister pointed out that she was such-and-such's daughter. Are you serious? In the mid-'70s, when I was 14 or 15, my family and I went to New Orleans with such-and-such and her family for a Lions Club convention, and she and I went to some kind of social event one night that had been organized for the teenagers who were stuck there doing nothing. As you might guess, she was really good-looking too. I don't think we said six words all night. So here I am, 35 years later, eyeing her daughter.

There's a Pierre Berton book called *The Last Good Year*, all about 1967. He didn't have that quite right—as per Scott's "Gasoline Alley" comment above, 1972 was the last good year (there've been three or four pretty good ones since)—but it's a great title anyway. If you're Canadian and old enough to remember 1967, you're familiar with the people and events he writes about: the Centennial, the Leafs winning the Cup, the ascent of Pierre Trudeau, and most of all Jean Drapeau and *Expo '67*. My family and I didn't make it to Montreal for Expo, but we did see the *Man and His World* exhibit a year later. Unlike the States, where they seemed to be experiencing a collective nervous breakdown in '67 and '68, in Canada it was seen as a moment of great optimism—that's how I remember it, and Berton's book reinforced this for me. You can hear it in the Hylozoists song, too, right down to the opening invocation from Drapeau. There's not a lot of art I can look to that evokes strong feelings in me for my country, but "Soixante-Sept," a song I discovered about a year ago, joins *Goin' Down the Road* and maybe "Helpless" right at the top of the list.

(#19, Facebook Top 100, 2010-11)

Renée Crist

Soon after I got going with e-mail the winter before last, I tracked down Rob's address on a University of Virginia page. I sent him a short letter to see if it was indeed him, Renée intercepted (shared account), and for the next year-plus she quite unexpectedly became my closest e-mail friend. We wrote two or three times a week, mostly about baseball, mostly trying to one-up each other in silly wordplay and jokes and trying to make each other laugh. Baseball's really good for that if you're attuned to its endless absurdity. Renée was, and it became a completely pleasurable and important correspondence for me.

That wasn't all we wrote about, of course. Renée's letters really helped me through a terrible flu I had the spring before last (having gone through something similar herself, she had a calm and clear idea of what course it would run; I'd never been so sick before, so I was a little panicky at the time), we went back and forth on Dole a lot (I like him, Renée couldn't stand him, and we both had a great time making fun of him), and she provided sound and funny counsel on another matter I've been jabbering away about for a couple of years (as did Martina Eddy before her; I make friends with the husbands, but I stay for the wives). But mostly it was baseball and more baseball. I think I did some of my best baseball writing ever in those letters, a reflection of how much I enjoyed and looked forward to writing to her.

I wish I had Renée's letters with me; I would love to be able to go through them and pick out a bunch of stuff to reprint here. That's the worst thing about my Free-Net-plus-outdated-modem set-up, not being able to print and save e-mail. Things she liked to write about included Clemens and Sele and Nomar from the Red Sox (her favorite team), Maddux and Lopez and Chipper Jones from the Braves (second favorite), some of the local Charlottesville Blues players who'd done promo spots for her radio show (she sent me a great Blues T-shirt that I wear all the time), Alex Gonzalez and Shawn Green after seeing a game at the Skydome last summer (periodically inquiring whether Green still had the good-luck beard he was maintaining at the time), Pettitte and Jeter, the evil Orioles (just about the only team Renée disliked), and that great Denny's commercial with Gwynn and Sosa. She liked the Rockies, too. In one of the last letters I wrote her, I dutifully pointed out that Galarraga and Bichette and Castilla weren't nearly as good as they seemed to be, that their impressive numbers were mostly a park illusion. That's me; with Renée, I think she just thought it was a funny team of cast-offs playing in a freakish park, and for that you had to love them.

I didn't write to Renée the last few days because I knew she was on the mend from a fall she'd taken at a wedding. But I almost did anyway. I was really anxious to tell her about something in an old *Sporting News Register* I'd just picked up at a garage sale: in the general information section of Yogi Berra's profile (coaching for the Yankees at the time, when the *Register* still included coaches), he listed his hobby as "sports." Renée must have had Yogi in the back of her mind somewhere when she wrote her Quad City DJ's review last issue.

(*Radio On*, 1997)

interrupting my train of thought

George Thorogood

Okay, enough fooling around. This one's actually true: I spent part of a summer working in Georgetown's Greenwood Cemetery alongside Godfrey Thorogood, a cousin of George's. Really, could there be a more surreal connection to third-tier rock and roll fame? Godfrey was studying to be a minister at the time, so of course he was preoccupied with matters of right and wrong, humility, forbearance, etc., etc.—except when he got into a snit because he felt I was getting a disproportionate amount of time riding around on the John Deere (as opposed to trimming around headstones with a hand-mower). I'm being unfair—after I, uh, vigorously explained to him why things were happening the way they were (a long explanation, the general thrust of which I still remember but won't get into here—trust me, he had nothing to complain about), he gave the matter some thought and did the one thing that always makes me really uncomfortable: he apologized. I thrive on arguments; if you want to shut me up, say something gracious. Anyway, looking at the link above, I'm not exactly sure what "Disciplemaking" is, but I'm confident that whatever it entails, a strictly enforced equal-time rule on all vehicular machinery is part of the package.

(record inventory, 2005-06)

2004 Top 10

#3: *Être et Avoir*: I didn't think this was a great film, but anyone who teaches elementary school will be absorbed by it the whole way. It's most effective getting at the ordinary everydayness of the job (maybe a given if you keep the camera in any grade-school classroom long enough), and the kids are an interesting mix. In the young guy who gets kept in at recess to finish his work, the film even has a milder version of *Spellbound*'s Harry Altman. What bothered me, though, was the way the director practically hangs a halo on Georges Lopez, the teacher. He's shown to be a man of infinite patience and grace, never handling any situation with anything less than textbook decorum, never letting slip an ill-chosen word. Big surprise: it ain't like that. They left out all the parts where you snap invective at some kid much more sharply than you really should; the times when you're up there making it up off the top of your head, meanwhile stepping outside yourself and hearing how preposterous you sound while doing so; or where three unrelated problems jump up out of nowhere and create chaos in eight seconds flat, and instead of patiently trying to sort out what's what, you take a deep breath and let loose—"SIT DOWN!" I was also aware throughout of some of the everydayness that was absent: curriculum, the ludicrous whims of educational reform, the scrounging around for resources that never ends. It's there in a way: on the last day of school (and therefore the last day of Lopez's career), you can catch Lopez give a little shrug of resignation just after everyone files out, and that rings very, very true.

(rockcritics.com, 2003)

What is (are) the most useless item(s) of trivia that clutter up your brain and keep you from remembering more important things?

Baseball stats. There was a logjam up there in the late '70s; most of them I've forgotten, but if I stop and think hard for a minute, a few linger. Wayne Simpson was 14-3 in 1970. Fred Lynn hit .333 with 39 home runs in 1979. Donn Clendenon knocked in 97 runs in 1970. Joe Torre hit .363 in 1971. Luis Tiant's E.R.A. was 1.91 in 1972. Orlando Cepeda hit 34 home runs in 1970, Bob Bailey hit 28, Danny Walton hit 18. (The first baseball book I ever bought was Zander Hollander's guide to the 1970 season, so that year figures prominently.) Sam Rice had 2,987 career hits. Jackie Robinson hit .342 in his MVP year. Alex Johnson won the batting title by less than a thousandth of a point in 1970 with a .329 mark. I think I have every Cy Young winner and every MVP back to about 1960 filed away, and I'll sometimes go over them working backwards when trying to fall asleep at night.

(*KITSCHener*, 1998)

Fraser & DeBolt

Fraser & DeBolt, an early-'70s Canadian duo, used to be managed by the most unusual person I've ever worked with: Willie Weckesser of Woolco-Woolworth. I proofread advertising flyers there for a year or so after I left the record store, and Willie was my supervisor. It's difficult to know where to begin in trying to describe what was so unusual about him, but here's a quick story. Willie liked all the push pins on the bulletin board used by the proofreaders to be arranged neatly—rows, columns, evenly spaced. There was this guy John who worked with us for a few weeks (it was obvious he wasn't going to be around for long), and one day, to mess with Willie's head, he scattered the push pins all over the bulletin board before leaving work. Willie didn't say a word about it the next morning, but all the pins had been returned to their usual rows and columns. Ever seen the dish-towel scene from *Sleeping with the Enemy*? It was kinda like that.

(record inventory, 2005-06)

Draw a social map of your high school or some job or other place, and, like, you know, how people talked, and stuff, and categories like "hoods" and "preppies" and "dirtbags"; or write about your life, or something.

Because I'm putting in about 60 hours a week at my job right now—I inherited a grade 2 class from a teacher who moved into a VP position elsewhere—I find that it's almost pointless for me to try writing about anything that isn't work-related. I attempted a year-end movie summary for Scott Woods's internet publication a couple of months ago and didn't get anywhere. My job has shut down my mind to the outside world.

I can't really draw a social map of my school's teaching staff. I can see its outline, but I'm still a newcomer and an outsider. The few times where a teacher has said something negative to me about another teacher's methods (or where I've overheard such complaints), an "I don't need to name names" has been attached. I know of one instance where a teacher drew a second name for the "Secret Friend" gift exchange because she thought the first name would have created problems. There's murmuring here and there about the Vice-Principal. These are exceptions, though. Certain people hang around with each other, and that's where all the good stuff must get voiced. Outside of one's group, everything's quite civil and innocuous.

Instead of social maps, here's a rundown of my students. I'm going with "write about your life, or something" off the *WMS* topic list.

Selamawit — Brightest student in the class. She poses a problem for me because she's so far ahead of the others in math (e.g., multiplication, which we've recently started, is technically not even part of the grade 2 program—only "pre-multiplication readiness"—and Selamawit knows her tables up to 12). So low, middle, and high activities aren't enough when I plan math, I usually have to create something extra for Selamawit. Her writing skills are solid, but not outstanding in the way that her math is; her thinking is sophisticated, so she's the number-one target audience for my brilliant dry wit.

Karanjit — One of my five ESL students (I had a sixth who moved to a different school last month), in India for the first few weeks after I took over. Nice boy, takes forever and a day to get his work done, stares at me sometimes like I'm some strange being from another universe.

constantly aware of all the changes that occur

Jeetinder — Hardest worker in the class, third or fourth brightest. I get the impression from his parents, and from the fact that his homework book is initialled by dad every night, that there's a lot of pressure from home to succeed. Jeetinder races through his work, he's jittery all the time, he interrupts constantly, and he craves approval (which wears me down after a while; many times I've basically waved him away). If you were to watch him closely for a day, you'd come away convinced that he's going to have a nervous breakdown before he's 11.

Happy — The anti-Jeetinder, probably the most easy-going student I have. Writes more freely than anyone in the class. Always smiling; the name's too perfect.

Wendy — Slower than Karanjit—takes forever and a day to not get her work done. She's easy to lose track of, too; 15 minutes after the work has been assigned, I'll remember to check Wendy (I've moved her out of the group twice) and she'll still be printing the date. It's not because the work's too hard for her. What is she doing over there? Is she surreptitiously building a bomb inside her desk? I keep meaning to check that.

Nthatisi— I was warned by the outgoing teacher, by the VP, and by mom that I might get lots of attitude and resistance from Nthatisi, who supposedly wasn't very happy about the change. There's been a little of that, but basically (reason #53 why I'm not good at this) she has me wrapped around her finger. She's precocious, theatrical, stubbornly independent, and she cracks me up, so I let her get away with lots that I shouldn't. Wednesday: working in groups, the kids are supposed to use various materials to build some kind of shoe accessory. Thursday: explaining why her group hasn't done anything yet, Nthatisi tells me that "We had an idea yesterday, Mr. Dellio, but as the days go by we forget."

Supreet — Slower than Karanjit, slower than Wendy—slower than time standing still. Verbally she's bright and alert, she just has an aversion to pencils and paper. Another master psychologist—not in Nthatisi's league, but running a strong second.

Navpreet — Almost puts in as many hours as I do—the schoolday proper is from 8:30 to 3:00, but Navpreet's there in the after-school program from 8:00 until after 5:00. Very bright, always complaining about the "workload," trudges down the hall at the end of the day with her books and her coat and her backpack like an overloaded bellhop.

Tanvir — Fifteen of my students are Indian; I recently saw *Pather Panchali* for the first time, and the young, angelic-looking Apu reminded me most of Tanvir. A couple of weeks ago, the kids were painting ceramic shoes they'd made on a field trip to the museum. Each pair of partners was given some gold and silver paint, and they were allowed to pick two more colours between them. Tanvir's partner chose red. "Tanvir, what other colour would you like for your group?" "Red." "Is that a good choice? Your partner already chose red." (Earnestly and angelically) "But I like red."

Rahul — My very own Ralph Wiggum. Blurts out answers that, if he's not merely repeating what's just been said, often have only the most tenuous connection to the question at hand, sometimes not even that. "What's the same about the square and the rectangle?" Rahul: "Is it clouds?" He blurts them out nonstop—he remembers to put up his hand so infrequently, it's pretty much automatic that I praise him when he does. It's funny to sit here at the computer writing about Rahul, but day-by-day he's very exasperating. Partly it's an ESL problem; the ESL teacher says there's something else going on there.

Sahanna — She's only been with me for a week. All I know for sure so far is that if you sometimes like to sing that Bohannon song where he chants his own name, you can use Sahanna's name instead.

Fariya — The prototypical sweet little 8-year-old girl. Came back from six weeks in India with some story about the lights going out and a boy dressed like Michael Jackson. I didn't really get the gist of it myself, but the class had a big laugh.

Sangeeta — My favorite along with Nthatisi and Fariya. Even more earnest than Tanvir—helps everyone, speaks carefully and with the utmost gravity, will say that someone is "judging" her rather than teasing her. Actually listens to everything I say. I look around, see fidgeting and whispering and tuning out, then I come to Sangeeta and she's focused as intently as can be. May be hanging on every word, may just be judging me.

Manraj — Big wrestling fan, keeps me posted on the exploits of someone named Shawn Michaels. Shy, always works hard, never misbehaves; I

constantly aware of all the changes that occur

feel bad for him (and Sangeeta, and a few others) because he has to spend so much time listening to me drone on and on as I try to get through to the rest. Feeling his way with my jokes; looks at me warily for a few seconds, averts his eyes as the joke clicks in, then breaks out in a big grin.

Jason — For the first month, accounted for a good 25% of my stress; he's starting to settle down a bit, so I'd put him somewhere between 10-15% now. Gets picked on, cries, strikes back, can't look after anything—he lost three pencils in the space of an hour one morning; we just found out he's been wearing a size-1 matched with a size-3 boot the last couple of weeks—and, no surprise, has pronounced language difficulties to go along with all the behavioural and emotional problems. (Not an ESL student; he's from Newfoundland.) When the class lines up to move elsewhere, as often as not he remains at his desk until I ask him to join the line. Needs three or four reminders to get started on his work, otherwise he'll just sit there. Hits himself on the head when angry or frustrated.

Amrinder — He's been with us for about a month. Good student, master of hangdog irony, up-and-coming class clown.

Sukhneet — ESL, just starting to get over her fear of writing—she's writing a lot of extra journal entries, almost every one the same sentence about playing at her cousin's house. Follows me around when I'm out for yard duty (which amounts to walking 10 yards in one direction and then walking back), interrogates me, seems to think it impossible that I'm 35 years old—not necessarily that I'm younger or older, there's just something about the number 35 that throws her.

Sameer — I'm supposed to get to know every student in the class, but after three months I essentially know nothing about Sameer. He completes his work quickly and without difficulty, keeps his thoughts to himself, and has a knack for instigating without drawing attention to himself. So I let him go his own way. This is not right, it's just one less thing for me to think about.

Andy — Was just tested for giftedness along with Selamawit (they scored in the "6th and 7th stanines"; true giftedness is supposed to reside in the 8th and 9th). Supremely bored—gets his work done with the minimum effort possible, then wastes time with Patrick and Amrinder. He needs a different teacher.

Patrick — Reigning class clown. I didn't think mentioning Uranus would leave me vulnerable in a grade 2 class; I was wrong, planetary discussions must be carefully screened. I'm after Patrick a lot, which is too bad because when he's not bouncing off walls, he's diligent and conscientious with his work. He takes me in stride, and always comes back the next day ready to bounce around some more.

Priya — Was away in India when I started, still there three months later. I've seen her picture on the wall.

I can't remember at what point grade 2 starts to blur together in a kid's mind with all the other grades (by grade 6?), but until that happens, I would guess that one or two of mine will look back on this half-year as one of their best school experiences; twice as many will remember it as one of their worst; and almost all of them will remember it as a really odd time, somehow different from all the other years. They may or may not connect this feeling to the fact that the teacher was never really sure of what he was doing, if they haven't made the connection already.

(*Why Music Sucks*, 1997)

Tom T. Hall

A character who was almost a match for Willie Weckesser: Jack Mahoney, the pro at the golf course where I worked my last couple of summers in high school. He used to sing Tom T. Hall's "Old Dogs - Children and Watermelon Wine" over and over again while puttering away in his workshop, except he'd never get any farther than the title lyric. Soon after I quit, he fled town with a member's wife and relocated in Florida, where I bet he's still re-gripping and de-gripping the same three-wood he always seemed to be working on 25 years ago.

(record inventory, 2005-06)

Diodes/Dion & the Belmonts

This is the least interesting group of records I've posted in a while, so just a couple of quick personal associations. 1) I took a couple of film courses at the University of Toronto with a Diode, John Hamilton. I don't recall him ever sitting in class looking especially tired; he seemed very well rested. 2) Also dating back to that time, I used about 10 seconds

constantly aware of all the changes that occur

from Dion & the Belmonts' "I Wonder Why" in *Wild Christ*mas, one of two super-8 films I made my final year. From the same film: some voiceover by Alan Freed lifted from the album *Alan Freed's Memory Lane*, Darlene Love's "Christmas (Baby Please Come Home)," Ritchie Valens' "La Bamba," Little Richard's "The Girl Can't Help It," and the Angry Samoans' "Steak Knife." It was a festive splatter film. Six years later, Scorsese had the nerve to steal the whole Darlene Love concept for *Goodfellas*. I don't know, maybe it's me, I'm a little fucked up maybe, but let me understand this, Marty: I'm here to provide soundtrack ideas for you? I amuse you, I give you ideas?

(record inventory, 2005-06)

Hasil Adkins

Tomorrow I'll try to explain who Hunter S. Thompson was to my grade 7 class. Outside of whatever value his writing had or didn't have (I loved *Fear and Loathing* when I read it in university, and never had any desire to pick up anything else by him, all of which looked like more of the same stretched a hundred different ways), you have to be really careful with something like that. I want to convey what was really funny about *Fear and Loathing*, and why Thompson felt he had to go to Las Vegas and take a whole bunch of drugs in order to say something about his country, while at the same time making it clear that they must never ever try to do something that stupid themselves, and that Las Vegas itself is an evil town filled with people like Paul Anka and Joe Pesci. I had the same problem when I tried to explain Hasil Adkins to them earlier this year (I was playing *Songs the Cramps Taught Us* during an art class). "Well, he was this guy who wrote a lot of songs about...well, they were about cutting people's heads off. Please understand that these were just songs, and that in reality Hasil Adkins was just like any other normal person. Maybe not normal like you and me, but normal enough that he never cut anyone's head off for real. Not that I'm aware of, anyway. I'm getting sidetracked—look, just don't ever cut anyone's head off, OK? It's the wrong thing to do."

(record inventory, 2005-06)

interrupting my train of thought

"Sending My Love," Zhane

The way that Zhane pronounce their name makes me think of Sade, which in turn reminds me of an argument I once had with an old university friend, Tom. He was smarter than I was about most everything, and even though he had a big influence on me, there was a certain amount of resentment on my part that he was so casual about all the stuff that he knew and I didn't—I could never dismiss him as pretentious or pedantic, and that would work on my own insecurity. How I'd sometimes handle this would be to go out of my way to be an obstinate buffoon when we'd argue about something, be the guy you just couldn't talk sense to. When Sade came along in 1985, I said to Tom that it was dumb, perhaps even completely wrong, how she pronounced her name. He pointed out to me that just because our alphabet works a certain way, that doesn't have anything to do with how someone else's alphabet might work. Because this struck me as perfectly sensible and obvious beyond words, I wouldn't relent—it was dumb anyway, and she should learn how to pronounce her name properly. Sometimes I think my obstinacy was accidentally on the right track in these arguments, like the time that Tom was caught up in a book on subliminal advertising and he insisted I'd be able to see naked women in the ice-cube patterns of a Coke ad if I only looked. I couldn't see them, until finally he became exasperated to the point where he said I was like a "poster boy for Freud" (I remember the phrase clearly). The truth was that I couldn't see them—but I also wanted to ruin his interest in something I didn't know anything about. (6.0)

(*Radio On*, 1994)

Brent Sclisizzi

I'm going to take a couple of days off from the album inventory to pay insufficient tribute to Brent Sclisizzi, a good friend who passed away last week at the age of 42. Like anyone who knew Brent but didn't know anything of his long-term health problems, I'm stunned that this could have happened.

I met Brent 20+ years ago at university, where we were both enrolled in the University of Toronto's film studies programme. I think we maybe took two or three courses together, although the only one I specifically remember is the production course we took with Gino Matteo at St. Mike's. Brent served as cameraman on the two student films I made. One was shot inside the McGibbon Hotel, famous in my hometown of Georgetown because somebody was supposedly once murdered there, perfect for a would-be splatter film entitled *Wild Christmas*. For travelling shots, I pushed Brent around in a wheelchair. I'm not sure if he made any films himself for that course—if so, I never saw them.

We lost touch after graduation, but a few years later I ran into him at a rep screening somewhere around town, and within another few years we began getting together fairly regularly for films—once every month or two for the next decade, usually at the Cinematheque.

Movies were the foundation of our friendship, but being almost exactly the same age, we also had a lot of the same stupid reference points from the '70s in common. When I looked through one of Brent's photo albums the other day, it was like looking at photos from my own life, right down to the old black-and-white novelty shot taken inside the Fantasy Island jail. His grade-school class photos may as well have been my own. Call it whatever you want—life experiences, psychic landscape—but looking through that album, it really hit home with me that we came from the same place.

Brent's taste in films always fascinated and puzzled me. This is a simplification, but his enthusiasms basically carried him in three different directions. He loved a lot of foreign directors I either didn't care for (Fellini, Bunuel) or knew nothing about (he always named Raul Ruiz as his favorite director). There was also Saturday-matinee Brent—literally; he regularly went to the Cinematheque's Saturday afternoon screenings—who loved the Marx Brothers and film noir and *Casino Royale* (his favorite movie). Finally, the one tangent I could never figure out, he'd faithfully rush out and see the junkiest first-run fare imaginable. *Dude, Where's My Car?* is the first film I think of along those lines; seems we had a number of conversations where he tried to explain to me why I needed to see *Dude, Where's My Car?*

My original idea was to incorporate commemoration of Brent right into the album inventory, but I've either already bypassed all his favorites—Jethro Tull, Genesis, Philip Glass—or don't own any of the more obscure ambient and 20th-century music he was passionate about. We had everything and nothing in common when it came to music. Last Christmas, I sat with Brent and his girlfriend Tara and excitedly played Danger Mouse's mash-up of Jay-Z's "99 Problems" and the Beatles' "Helter Skelter" for them. With a smile, as always, Brent suggested I might be too old to be listening to such things. It was so funny and good-natured the way he did so, it never even occurred to me to bring up *Dude, Where's My Car?*

Brent worked for the CBC, where I attended an in-house memorial this afternoon. He obviously had had a huge effect on the people he worked with. The thing that kept coming up again and again from the different speakers was a view of Brent I share whole-heartedly: how even-tempered he was. In the twenty-plus years I've known him, I never saw so much as a flash of anger or sourness about anything. His calm was almost eerie, and I think one of the things that always amused him about me was all the whining and complaining I do. The most inspiring thing I heard this afternoon, though, was hearing one of his co-workers eulogize how Brent always took a week or two off in September to volunteer with the Toronto Film Festival. Well...it's true that he always booked off work during the Festival, and it's also true that he voluntarily saw as many films as humanly possible during that time, but I think he'd maybe been putting one over on his employers for years. Good show, Brent.

(homepage, 2005)

"Kotton Krown," Sonic Youth

I'm never going to be comfortable in social settings involving large groups of people (me plus three others; seven or eight is fine if it's people I know well). I can fake my way through in a way that I merely look bored or "quiet and thoughtful," but what's really going through my mind is something close to what Michael Corleone hears just before he kills Sollozzo and McCluskey—a dull, dead, shapeless roar. Something of that is still there when I finally get away, but the feeling of being trapped lifts, and an incredible sense of relief and wide open space takes over. What I hear and feel then is in "Kotton Krown." (9.0)

(*Radio On*, 1997)

Gabriel Giffords

I was telling my grade 6 class about the 9-year-old girl yesterday, and they seemed to fully grasp the weight of what happened. I don't often connect to these awful events on a personal level, but in the case of the girl, because I teach kids around the same age, this time I have. From everything that I've read about her, I recognize her very well, and invariably have a handful of kids just like her in my class every year (almost always girls): the student that lives to please her parents and her teachers. They fuss over everything. You assign something that you know is just intended to tie you over until you get something ready for tomorrow, and within five minutes they've asked three questions because they want to get it exactly right and make you happy. Unbelievably sad.

(ILX, 2011)

Retro

One last thought having to do with the radio show I mentioned earlier. College radio hasn't changed a bit in 15 years. I used to get grief then for mixing in Janet Jackson or Vanessa Williams—not a great deal, I did an overnight and was pretty much left alone, but the guy who did the show in front of me, for one, would have been happy to see me run over by a transport. I'm a lot more circumspect now about sneaking in something hugely popular (a change that's paralleled my own listening habits, so it's been an easy adjustment), but sure enough, when I played Nelly's "Hot in Herre" a couple of weeks ago, the metal girl before me called me on it; she wasn't overly confrontational or anything, but she did want me to justify why I was playing commercial hip-hop. "Because it's a great song?" wasn't good enough for her, so I pointed out that I'd heard New Kids on the Block played on the Saturday afternoon dance show a couple of months ago (true), and that the station's hip-hop shows played the likes of 50 Cent all the time (I made that one up). Playing New Kids on the Block is acceptable, it turns out: "But that's retro." Oh. I can't think of word, or a concept, that creeps me out more than "retro." I'm guessing that virtually anyone who writes about music feels the same. Whatever I love at any given moment always exists in the here and now, whether it came out last week, 10 years ago, or in 1963. "Outta Control"'s main competitors for my favorite song of the year were the Spikedrivers' "Often I Wonder," the Cellos' "Rang Dang Ding Dong (I Am the Japanese Sandman)," Hot Tuna's "Sea Child," Yo La Tengo's "Satellite," and a dozen other going, gone, or long-gone things that felt every bit as wondrous as 50 Cent's record. (That his gave up nothing to any of them is why he's #1.) Really, it's a completely meaningless distinction to me.

(year-end ballot, 2005)

Three Willies

I haven't written about baseball on this site for ages. I don't have the energy at the moment to sort through my evolving feelings about the game over the past few years, but I'm less of a fan right now than at any time since starting university 30 years ago, when I (rather pretentiously) ignored everything from the We-Are-Family Pirates of '79 through to my discovery of Bill James and the concurrent ascension of the Jays in '83.

I sat down yesterday, though, and watched the original NBC broadcast of the '71 All-Star Game, given to me by a friend who's been transferring his VHS library onto DVD; he obtained it from a TSN rebroadcast dating back to '94, when they were running famous old games during the strike. The '71 All-Star Game was only the second one I would have watched as a kid, on the heels of the '70 game in which Pete Rose more or less shortened Ray Fosse's career by a decade. The game is still remembered for Reggie Jackson's monstrous home run off a light tower in Tiger Stadium's right-field corner; it was also the sole American League victory during a 19-1 NL run spanning three decades.

Before the broadcast got underway, TSN's Paul Romanuk mentioned that the game would feature 18 future Hall of Famers. I stopped the tape, grabbed a pen, and, almost without pause, jotted down 18 names: Mays, Aaron, Clemente, Kaline, Billy Williams, Yaz, Lou Brock, Reggie, Frank Robinson, Bench, McCovey, Killebrew, Stargell, Brooks Robinson, Seaver, Palmer, Hunter, and Gibson. I started in the outfield and worked my way in, doubling back once because I missed Frank Robinson, a telling indicator of how much he played in the shadow of Mays and Aaron.

By my count, Romanuk ended up being off by one—15 of my guys were there, three weren't, and I missed four, bringing the total to 19. Billy Williams, Catfish, and Gibson were absent, while Aparicio, Carew, Marichal, and Jenkins all got into the game. I shouldn't have missed Carew or Jenkins; I mistakenly thought Marichal had pretty much had it by '70 (he went on to finish 18-11 in '71, with the Giants taking the NL West), and Aparacio never even crossed my mind (he in fact had no real business being there, based on his in-season performance; he went into the game hitting .206, and finished the year with an offensive line that was dismal across the board). Seeing as Seaver warmed up but didn't get into the game, I assume Romanuk's number was lifted from the actual box score.

A few random notes:

1) Some comic relief right off the top: Sparky Anderson has Mays leading off and Aaron batting second. You'll sometimes hear about teams having power at the top of the lineup, maybe a couple of middle infielders with 15-20 home runs apiece. On this particular night, the NL had 1200+ home runs setting the table.

constantly aware of all the changes that occur

2) If you want to mark a moment in time in a particular sport, look past the Hall of Famers and take note of the second-tier stars. Willie Mays might mean 1954 and The Catch to one person, 1965 and the Roseboro incident to another, and 1973 and the sad ending to a third. But if you roll out names like Don Buford, Lee May, Glenn Beckert, Bobby Murcer, Cookie Rojas, and Rick Wise, you can only be talking about the early '70s.

3) If you blink, you'll miss Reggie's home run. He hits it six or seven pitches into the count: contact, cut to the camera attempting, unsuccessfully, to follow the flight of the ball while Curt Gowdy goes nuts (unless I've got worse eyesight than I even think I do, the camera is panning across empty space, the ball far above; you only see it on its way down, after it bounces off the light tower), and, as Reggie trots the bases, a shot of the light tower. Takes about four or five seconds. No replay, because there isn't really anything to show.

4) Has there been a great black starting pitcher since Dwight Gooden? African-American black, not Hispanic—Sabathia was born in California, but I'm not sure if his ancestry is Hispanic or not. The '71 game pitted Vida Blue (in the midst of one of the greatest seasons ever for a starting pitcher) against Dock Ellis, with Don Wilson coming on in relief.

5) Speaking of which, it was hilarious to hear Gowdy and Kubek make reference to Ellis's no-hitter from the year before, as puzzled as anyone that he walked eight and a hit a batter en route. We now know that Ellis was tripping on acid during that game.

6) Also from an alternate universe: Blue was coming off two starts in which he'd pitched 9 and 11 innings, having left the latter game with the score 0-0.

7) Most entertaining pitcher was Mike Cuellar. In the top of the 6th, he strikes out Willie Stargell on...some kind of double-reverse backup Eephus pitch; Stargell is still busy unknotting himself.

8) The players are much more businesslike. Think about all the theatrics in recent All-Star games: Johnson and Kruk, Johnson and Walker, Bonds and Tori Hunter, etc. With Brooks Robinson playing third, Bench tries to drop one down in the 7th. He misses, before singling past Robinson on the next pitch. Remember that this is only a few months removed from Robinson's acrobatics in the '70s Series, where one of his primary victims was Bench. There is no visible reaction from either player after the missed bunt, and none following the subsequent single. Rerun the same sequence with the same backstory today, and I think you'd see mugging galore from Robinson and Bench. Different game—better or worse, I'm not sure (I thought Kruk was pretty great patting down his heart against Johnson).

9) Clemente is every bit as unorthodox a hitter as legend has it: as plain as day on the replay, he hits his eighth-inning home run completely off his front foot.

10) Player I most wanted to see who was there but didn't get into the game: Sudden Sam McDowell.

My friend also gave me tapes of Games 6 and 7 from the '71 Series. I was rooting for the Orioles, so it would be the first time baseball really made me sad.

(homepage, 2009)

"Complete Control," Clash (1977)

In a comment I posted last night to the "Regrets" entry, I talked about various influences that have guided my listening the past few years. I failed to mention one of the biggest: how much my job affects me. I regularly make reference to teaching in my writing, but I don't often acknowledge the degree to which it shapes my experience as a listener these days.

One way in which this influence plays out should be obvious: now and again, I'll latch on to (or at least come to enjoy) a song that the kids all love and that probably would have gone right past me otherwise. A few years ago, I voted for one of those "Crazy Frog" records on my year-end because my students were going crazy to it at our Christmas party. It sounded like a work of genius that day; I don't remember a thing about the song anymore, which was also probably the case within 48 hours of the party. Soulja Boy, "Poker Face," "Adam's Song," Chingy—there've been a number of these songs and artists over the years, although fewer of them recently.

The more interesting and harder to explain influence is in how I hear my own favorite music when I play it for students. This is something that I do all the time: entry music over the P.A. each morning, as a supplement to "Today in History" readings (e.g., a Dylan song on Dylan's birthday), as weird intros for lessons (Eno's "The True Wheel" when we start ratio), a bunch of music videos we look at in connection to media literacy, etc. Although I've never specifically played "Complete Control" for one of my classes, I do remember when it started to reach me in a way that it had never done before. This would have been when I was revisiting a lot of stuff from '77 and '78 in advance of the punk-rock assembly I mentioned a while back. It wasn't exactly a case of my all of a sudden being able to hear the song through the ears of a 12-year-old, which just can't happen no matter how much you may try to wish that into being. It was more like I was trying to get a sense of "What might this sound like to a 12-year-old?" And, "If I play this at the assembly as the kids file into the gym, what will that feel like for me?" (I ended up using other music for some reason.)

I've never been a big Clash fan—"Police on My Back," "Should I Stay or Should I Go?" a couple of other songs; *London Calling* leaves me cold, and *Sandinista!* I got through once—but with those questions hanging in the background (and, no getting around it, the residual shock of Joe Strummer's improbably early exit), "Complete Control" began to sound like the most moving thing I'd ever heard, and five years later it still does. I've got two nominations this time vying for one of the five greatest moments on any record ever: "That means you!" of course, but also those beautifully soft chords during the break, just before the ensuing cacophony. The whole last minute is epic. Making sixty seconds feel epic is not an easy thing to pull off.

I'm sure that sounds like a very convoluted explanation of why it took me forever to hear a record that many people had long since decided was one of the greatest ever made. But that's more or less how it happened.

(#14, Facebook Top 100, 2010-11)

CHUM (Roger Ashby interview)

The emotional pull a Top 40 radio station can have on you when you're growing up is one of life's great wonders—trying to reconstruct it through memory, of recapture it years later, is not that easy. That's why Alan Freed remains as shrouded in myth as Johnny Ace, Frankie Lymon, or anyone else you can name: Freed represents something as mysterious as the music he played.

Like countless people from the Southern Ontario area, I spent my years as a crumbcrusher listening to CHUM (AM, that is, though at the time the distinction was unnecessary). CHUM wasn't the only listening alternative in 1973—if you were a social outcast you could listen to the new kid CFTR, and if you were really exotic there was CKOC out of Hamilton, where they actually did chart 40 songs (CHUM stuck with 30), and there was always some bizarro item like Sweeny Todd's "Roxy Roller" up at the top. But CHUM ruled the universe: best logo, catchiest station I.D. ("C-H-U-M, 1050 Toronto!"—hum it if you're with me), the great "Jungle" Jay Nelson and "Big" Scott Carpenter, the CHUM midway at the Ex, answering the phone "I listen to CHUM" to win $1,000, the Top 300 of all-time (again, CKOC went for the jugular with the Top 500), solid-gold weekends, on-air requests (I made it on once asking for "Mississippi Queen")—all of it totally ridiculous, of course, but it shaped the way I feel about pop music far more than any single album or song I've ever listened to.

(*Nerve*, 1988)

Clubhouse Blues

The accompanying look at the Texas Rangers is the story I was seeking, but for me a much larger one unfolded: what it's like to interview major league ballplayers for the first time. It wasn't easy; it wasn't particularly enjoyable.

There were two primary problems: there was me, and there were the players. First off, cliché though it may be, I was in total awe of everything. The day began around 11:30 a.m., with Avrum (our photographer) and me killing some time around the cage while the Jays took BP. An omen of things to come—I was fully aware that I was walking on turf for the first time, how odd it felt. From there on in, I would constantly be distracted from what I was supposed to be doing by the consciousness of me doing it. Camus goes to the ballpark, so to speak.

It was difficult to drag myself away from the cage: the chatter, the closeness of the players, and their individual rituals—Jesse Barfield instructing himself to "move him over," "hit and run," and so forth before each pitch—were overwhelming.

Once inside the Rangers' clubhouse, a kind of miniature Disneyland, things really fell apart. Avrum would patiently suggest that I approach some players, because soon they wouldn't be available; "Yeah, I think I'll go talk to Parrish," I would reply, and then stand there motionless for another minute. An inescapable question was clouding my mind: why would anyone here possibly want to talk to me?

Interviews themselves are not new to me; the past year I've spoken to recording artists whose records sell from next-to-nil (Schoolly-D) to a reasonable amount (Joey Ramone) to a boatload (Huey Lewis). I was never uncomfortable, though, because the interview was always to their advantage—they were trying to sell records. Now, we're supposed to believe that players are responsible for selling the game at all times, but while watching them get ready, many sitting there lost in thought, that didn't seem relevant. Inside the clubhouse, I absolutely felt like an intruder.

Once I began speaking with players, I was quickly reminded why many of my views about the game have been irrevocably shaped by *Ball Four*. More on that when (and if) I fulfill my ambition to interview Jim

Bouton. For now, suffice to say that baseballese just strikes me as so much drone. It goes back to something Martin wrote about Earl Weaver last issue: "It's as if he can't believe anybody but a numbskull reporter, desperate for copy, would faithfully copy down absolutely anything the great man says, profound or banal makes not matter." You can judge for yourself whether the quoted Rangers actually convey any information—to me, their thoughts were completely rote. Darrell Porter in particular betrayed a machine-like impersonality; obliging enough to answer, but without the slightest trace of emotion the second we finished.

A learning experience, but more than ever I understand Bill James' decision to view the game entirely from an outsider's perspective.

(*Innings*, 1986)

Have you ever bought a book solely because you thought it would look impressive on the shelves?

As someone who buys 10 books for every one that I actually read, that's a very good question. Any book I buy, I really do feel that it's something I might want to open up one day; at the same time, not being the fastest or most dedicated reader in the world, I'm sure I already have more books than I could realistically expect to finish in my lifetime, yet I continue to buy more books. So if I'm buying books that deep-down I know will never be read, maybe I am buying some of them for decorative purposes. I do know I'm on the intellectually insecure side—I'm 100% sure of my opinions and aesthetic judgement, but, tangled up with not getting into graduate school 12 years ago, I'm a little intimidated by highly-degreed people (unless they say things like "the inevitability of an Africanist cyberspace," in which case my insecurity takes the form of ridicule)—and that's exactly the kind of person who'd be most likely to embellish his bookshelf. But in actual fact, I consciously bury the most esoteric/incomprehensible of my books, moving them to the bottom or to the back where they won't be seen. There's not a lot of them, but they're there. If, after moving things around to make room for something new, a Norman O. Brown or Roland Barthes ends up staring out at me, I move it somewhere less conspicuous. It makes me feel silly, and anyone who sees it is going to get the wrong idea about me. Worse, I might be asked if I've read it; worse yet, like with the Roland Barthes, maybe I have read it and I might be asked what I thought about it. (Don't ask me where this parade of people traipsing through my bedroom comes from. Work with me here.) The mere fact that I'm so self-conscious about all this stuff—that I think about it all—shows that I do have definite problems in this area.

(*KITSCHener*, 1997)

But You Promised

Another teacher and I had some grade 6s decorating the gym on Friday afternoon for an upcoming concert. One of the guys helping—well, he's a motormouth who never shuts up, and I asked him to help rather than send him to gym class, where there was a substitute teacher in for the day. Anyway, the other teacher overheard the following exchange after we had cleaned up and the kids were headed out to their busses:

Motormouth guy: "That was fuckin' crazy!"
His female friend: "You said you were off the cussing."

Yes, completely crazy—they were putting pieces of masking tape on student art.

(ILX, 2011)

What is the most inappropriate place/situation that you've ever had an uncontrollable giggling fit? How did you try to cover it up?

The best, most inappropriate giggling fit I've ever had is a story I've probably already told to a half-dozen people. It dates back to the fall of 1984. Tom Mayock, a university friend who'd dropped out after first year and was living with his family in Illinois, had moved back to Toronto for a few months so he could write. (As you know, there are bylaws in Illinois against writing.) We were sharing the first floor of a house on Bathurst St. and going to a lot of movies. One afternoon we went to the AGO to see two Michael Snow films, *New York Eye & Ear Control* and *Back and Forth*. Normally I have little interest in weird non-narrative film, but I'd seen *New York Eye & Ear Control* in a class a couple of years earlier, and I retained a vivid memory of how the soundtrack was played off against some dramatic head shots of famous musicians; also, Michael Snow was going to be there, so it seemed like something worth attending. The films finished and Snow stood up at the front of the theatre to take questions. Having just sat through a movie that consisted of nothing but a camera on a tripod moving back and forth for an hour or three, naturally questions were a little slow in materializing; on top of that, Snow was every bit as warm and gregarious as you'd expect the maker of such a film to be. As I remember it, the first question was taken care of with a one- or two-word answer of bottomless indifference, after which there was a half-minute of embarrassed shifting around in seats and very conspicuous silence (the AGO theatre being a rather somber chamber at the best of times). It was at this point that either Tom or I leaned over to the other and whispered, "Ask him what he thought of *Ghostbusters*." I remember the line like it was yesterday, but for some strange reason I can't say with any certainty who said it; it's the kind of thing that could have come from either of us. That's how it started, and for the next five minutes, as Snow continued to field questions sporadically, Tom and I tried as best we could to make ourselves disappear. For me this involved covering my face with my hands, pretending to reach down for something on the floor, burying my head in my jacket, taking deep breaths...that part of the story's a blur. I probably looked like I was having a seizure. Eventually I managed to calm myself, perhap owing to nervous exhaustion. I still wonder what he thought of *Ghostbusters II*, which would not appear for another five years.

(*KITSCHener*, 1997)

Lisa Lisa & Cult Jam

I spent approximately two years in the mid-'80s doing interviews for *Nerve* and another local publication. People I spoke to during the first half of that run: Joey Ramone, Bob Mould, Richard Berry, Johnny Thunders, Paul Westerberg, Greil Marcus. Towards the end: Lisa Lisa, LaToya Jackson, Apollonia. I can't quite put it into words, but something happened between Point A and Point B.

(record inventory, 2005-06)

Write about weird things you did as a child, or weird things you did as an adult, or weird things that you've failed to do but should do. Or something.

If I ever decide to become a Trappist monk, I'll have had some valuable training recently in the vow-of-silence part. Today was the kind of day that I seem to have once or twice every couple of weeks now—what I've

interrupting my train of thought

come to categorize as days where I speak fewer than a hundred words. I started to become conscious of such days a few months ago, and while they're a little alarming and depressing, at this point I'm still more fascinated than alarmed or depressed by them. I never consciously set out to have such a day, I'll just catch myself looking back at the end of one and realize that I have.

They're more frequent during the summer, maybe twice a week on average. When school's in and I'm getting steady calls for supply teaching, there might only be the occasional Saturday where it happens. But when work's slow, like it is right now the first week back after a teachers strike, I'm liable to get one at any time. Today was one for sure.

Thinking the day through tonight, at first I thought I'd only spoken to two people. Going over it a little closer, I realize it was actually seven:

1) Just before leaving the house at 9:00, I got a call for a Mr. Whiner. I've had calls for this person before, though I'm pretty sure it wouldn't be spelled that way, it must be Mr. Weiner. I'm trying to write kind of a downbeat mood piece here, so I hate to have to start off with news of a Mr. Weiner. "Hello" and "You've got the wrong number" was all I said.

2) The usual pleasantries at the donut shop where I get my coffee and cinnamon ring—"Good morning," "Thanks" (coffee), "Thanks" (cinnamon ring), and "Thank you" (change). It's a little different at a second donut shop I sometimes patronize, where I actually have to say what it is I want. But I've been going to the other place more often as of late, so it's only a matter of time before I have it down to six words there, too.

3) Next I headed up to Richview Library, the main branch in the Etobicoke system. Richview's about a 15-minute drive north from where I live, but it opens up two hours earlier than the two libraries right in my neighborhood. (They see me way too much at the local branches anyway, especially during the summer, so I always feel like the librarians are watching me and trying to figure out what my story is. The psychological maneuvering that goes on between me and some of the librarians at New Toronto and Long Branch is an article unto itself; it's good whenever we can get some additional time away from each other.) I got to Richview just as it was opening, and headed to the upstairs information desk to sign up for one of the internet terminals. There was a woman waiting ahead of me but no librarian. I answered a couple of questions she had—was this where you signed up for the computers, what did you have to do to print? Twenty words, maybe.

4) The librarian appeared shortly thereafter. Signing up required little more than giving my name—five or ten words.

constantly aware of all the changes that occur

5) Once online, I tried to check a free e-mail account I keep. The computer I was at wouldn't give me access—it wasn't "accepting cookies"—so I went downstairs and signed up for an internet station down there. (You're only allowed one 30-minute internet session per day, therefore I had to relocate to avoid detection.) Five more words, still no cookie acceptance.

6) I went for lunch at a nearby mall around 12:30, which involved 10-15 words to the Pizza Pizza guy.

7) Five more words buying a chocolate bar at the pharmacy next door.

And that was it for the day—I didn't speak to another person from 1:00 p.m. on. After lunch I went back to the library and read for a couple of hours. At some point a bunch of little kids and a few parents invaded the reading area where I was sitting, a twice-daily recreational thing they have at Richview. I might have exchanged silly small talk with one of the kids if I'd been in a lineup at the supermarket, but a) I haven't worked all week and therefore haven't shaved, so I look a little disreputable at the moment; b) there's something vaguely drifter-like about anyone my age at the library in the middle of a workday anyway; and c) I was reading a book about the Stonewall Riots of 1969. Not that there's anything wrong with that, but all-in-all it seemed like a bad combination.

I moved elsewhere and killed another hour—checked e-mail on one of the regular Free-Net computers, read a little more, did whatever it is I do in there; I spend so much time in libraries I'm more or less sleepwalking—and then headed home. I ate in, and there were no phone calls through the evening. I tried my parents a couple of times around 7:00, but they weren't home. It was just a couple weeks ago that I spoke to my parents about not calling me so often. Have you seen the *Seinfeld* where Jerry's mom calls to ask where she can get some ice for Morty? That's what was happening with me for a while, a call every other day about nothing. It finally became too much when my mom called for something like the third day in a row one night, and five minutes after getting off the line my dad called wanting to know if I knew where to get the address for *Wheel of Fortune*. "Enough" I pleaded at Thanksgiving dinner the following weekend.

Adding everything up, I count between 50 and 70 words. The floating commune that lives next door has seemingly been out all night—I swear it's the first time that that's happened in two months; the silence has been unnerving—so I haven't done any yelling through the walls. I did talk back to the TV a couple of times. It's second nature for me to curse out other drivers, and I probably did a little of that earlier in the day without realizing it. (If you were to reduce my most commonly voiced epithet to an acronym, it would have two out of three letters in common with "Most Favored Nation.") Even with all of that, I'm still safely under a hundred words.

I guess this belongs in the Weird Things I Do as an Adult section—not necessarily for almost getting through a day without talking, which is weird but possibly not all that uncommon if you live alone and have a day off, but for being preoccupied enough with the matter to be counting words. If such days become any more frequent than they are now, I'm sure that one day I really will have the makings of a colorful weird-things-I-do-as-an-adult list. I don't think they're going to become any less frequent. I've spent my thirties playing Schoolly-D with the names on my phone list: one by one I knock them out.

(*Why Music Sucks*, 1998)

Poll: What's the Worst Part of Getting Old?

This'll sound—what's that word again?—tautological, but the worst part of getting old (50 in October) is realizing I won't be young again. I can't see *Taxi Driver* for the first time again, I can't hear *After the Gold Rush* for the first time again, etc., etc. Ninety-seven percent of the music, films, and baseball players I'll ever care about are behind me. (I figure I've got more latitude with books, so that's good.) And I tend to run that stuff into the ground, with nothing to replace it.

(ILX, 2011)

"Blues Run the Game," Jackson C. Frank (1965)

> *Maybe tomorrow, honey, someplace down the line*
> *I'll wake up older*
> *So much older, mama*
> *I'll wake up older*
> *And I'll just stop all my tryin'*

Wow—as Snoop Dog would say, I think about those lines like every single day. They're not encouraging. They don't make me eager to skip forward 10 or 20 years. Jackson C. Frank wrote them when he was 22. His Wikipedia entry is harrowing:

"In 1984, Frank took a trip to New York City in a desperate bid to locate Paul Simon, but he ended up sleeping on the sidewalk. His mother, who had been in hospital for open heart surgery, found him gone with no forwarding address when she arrived home. He was living on the street and was frequently admitted and discharged from various institutions. He was treated for paranoid schizophrenia, a diagnosis that was probably correct, though he had always claimed that he actually had depression caused by the trauma he had experienced as a child."

Well, I don't expect things will ever get so dire for me—no great traumas from childhood to haunt me, no desperate bids to locate Paul Simon. I do worry about the "just stop all my tryin'" part, though. Like a lot of people I bet, much of my life seems to be structured around a never-ending series of projects. (When I first e-mailed Scott with the countdown idea, the subject line read "new project!") Generally, I'm very good on following through once I start one of these—to abandon something is to admit failure, and if too much of your own sense of self is tied into these projects (not married, no kids, guilty as charged), that's a road you don't want to go down. So right now it's the countdown, which we're almost finished. Before that, I had a couple of radio interviews to take care of. We had a *Nerve* anniversary show a few months ago—that was a project. A couple of major ones happened on my homepage (my Hall of Fame projects, along with this one): writing almost every day on the 2008 election, from the Iowa caucus through to Nov. 4, and a record-by-record inventory I did of my album collection seven or eight years ago. *Radio On* was a decade-long project that kept me busy and alive through the '90s. In between, lots and lots of smaller ones. Keeping the mp3s in my media library properly tagged and with the correct cover art is a never-ending project. (Until it ends, that is—until mp3s and media libraries are ancient history five years from now.)

As focused as I am on carrying things through to completion—which really amounts to not starting something unless I'm sure it's manageable—sometimes I stumble. I was all excited last summer about hooking up with a local rep theatre and presenting a series of pop-music films (*Rushmore, Boogie Nights*, etc.); that got off to a promising start, then died. I've got an old grade-school friend who works in film, and a few months ago I tried to convince him that we had to make a documentary about Denny McLain. He didn't say no, so I went off to start researching Denny McLain...and lost interest 50 pages into one of his memoirs. They don't all work out.

"Projects," of course, is basically a metaphor for "tryin'"—a way to feel productive, something to look forward to at the end of the day, a means of staying engaged with the world. I've already contacted somebody about one that will start up once this finishes. For as long as there are projects, I'm basically happy. But when they run out, or when you can't be bothered to initiate them anymore, that's scary. That's where "Blues Run the Game" begins.

(Just to be clear, Jackson C. Frank's words are about 30% of why "Blues Run the Game" is my seventh-favorite song ever. The rest has to do with the guitar playing and what happens in the space between those words.

(#7, Facebook Top 100, 2010-11)

people always live and die in 4/4 time

Anyone who knows me will be amused by the *L'Avventura* and Bunuel talk in the intro to the movie section. My film-going life has been dominated by two overlapping obsessions, neither of which involves subtitles, austere Swedish landscapes, or Delphine Seyrig puttering around a kitchen. (I like the latter two just fine; always hated having to read subtitles, though.) The first, all over this book and pretty much everything I've ever written about movies, are American films from the '70s, a window of excellence that was just drawing to a close as I started university. (Towards the beginning of my second year, I saw *Raging Bull*; toward the end, *Heaven's Gate*. Another simplification, but a tidy dividing line.) The other is how pop music is used in films. I'm unduly disappointed when it's misused, and I start to cut slack for any film that gets me to take notice of even a single song. I say overlapping because it was probably seeing *American Graffiti* soon after it came out that started me down both paths, and there was a screening of *Mean Streets* at Toronto's old Cinema Lumiere that figured in heavily too. Someone once chastised me on the ILX message board that directors aren't DJs. But sometimes they are, I'd argue—and when some of them get out of the DJ booth, like Wes Anderson, they become a whole lot less interesting to me.

The two longish pieces on the subject of pop music in movies that frame this section were written within a few months of each other. The *Voice* piece, "Freeze Frame" (I remember I wanted to call it "Everyone's Gone to the Movies" instead), came first, and then, somewhat mysteriously, I did it all over again for *Cinemascope*—I think the motivating factor may have been the appearance in the interim of *The Virgin Suicides*. Anyway, while a lot of the same names and films turn up in both, I think they're sufficiently different to justify including both. The first one's basically an overview of the terrain, the second—be forewarned—has a thesis in mind. I know that, because you can regularly spot me jumping through hoops as I try to keep the thesis on life support.

Just for fun, I'll start with the second and finish with the first.

Strange Magic: The Pop-Music Soundtrack from American Graffiti to Sofia Coppola

On the second-last day of school this year, I showed my grade six class *American Graffiti*. Pop music and film already exert some influence on most of my 29 kids, though clearly not as much as television, the Internet, or Digimons. My hope was that this would be the first time they'd experience pop music used expressively in a film, as opposed to merely decoratively or cross-promotionally (i.e., the Nine Inch Nails/Red Hot Chili Peppers/Busta Rhymes kind of soundtrack with which they're familiar), and that a few might be as permanently affected as I was at their age when I sat through *American Graffiti* twice one summer afternoon in 1974. If such an awakening did take place, those affected were pretty quiet about it; some fidgeted, most looked bored, and the only time they got into the spirit of things was when Paul LeMat barreled into the parking lot to save Charles Martin Smith from a beating. For those 30 seconds, my guess was that they were responding to what seemed a little like a Jackie Chan film.

American Graffiti appeared more or less simultaneously with *Mean Streets* in 1973, and even though the style and sensibility of their directors are worlds removed from each other, the two films are closer than you might think in the way their characters relate to pop music. The music in *American Graffiti* and *Mean Streets* primarily belongs to George Lucas and Martin Scorsese; characters make occasional reference to what they're hearing—David Proval's insistence on "only oldies tonight" in *Mean Streets*, LeMat's dismissive preference for Buddy Holly over the Beach Boys in *American Graffiti*—but for all intents and purposes, the soundtracks express the tastes, personalities, and autobiographies of Lucas and Scorsese much more than that of their characters.

In *Mean Streets*, this seems especially obvious. When De Niro makes his flashy entrance into a bar accompanied by "Jumpin' Jack Flash," the effect is virtuosic, but it's highly likely that Johnny Boy has only the dimmest awareness of who the Rolling Stones are. Even Charlie (Harvey Keitel), through whose ambivalent eyes we're seeing Johnny Boy, is more a product of the soundtrack's Italian standards than he is of *Beggars Banquet*. And the one time that Johnny Boy responds directly to what we're hearing—when he does his little spastic dance outside the getaway car to the Miracles' "Mickey's Monkey"—you're again aware that he's not someone who'd ever actually own a Smokey Robinson record, much less think, talk, or develop any kind of an opinion whatsoever about Smokey Robinson. The Miracles, the Rolling Stones, and to a lesser degree the doo-wop and girl-

people always live and die in 4/4 time

group music that takes up the bulk of *Mean Streets*' soundtrack, are there because Scorsese wants them to be there. The decision of whether to use "Jumpin' Jack Flash" or "Street Fighting Man," for instance, is one of infinite meaning and nuance for Scorsese, the difference between the "everyday inferno" (Pauline Kael's words) he's after and the easy period-identification that would be enough for a lesser director. For his characters, though, such distinctions are nonexistent: it's all just amorphous background din.

American Graffiti, where the music would seem to be of paramount importance to Lucas' cross-section of seven California teenagers, is somewhat trickier. Every kid listens to Wolfman Jack's radio show incessantly, they go to their school homecoming and dance to "At the Hop" and "The Stroll," and their dress, mannerisms, and talk reflect the teenage worlds vividly mapped out in songs by Chuck Berry, Eddie Cochran, and Dion DiMucci. For all of that, however, pop music often doesn't have any more of an emotional pull on Lucas' nascent surfers and hippies than it does on Scorsese's low-rent hoods—less, actually. Do Richard Dreyfuss' Curt and Ronnie Howard's Steve seem like pop obsessives, the kind of characters who'd mark the events of their lives by specific songs heard in specific situations, who'd look to pop music for a deeper understanding of themselves, who'd maybe even romantically (and foolishly) weigh a life decision against a line from a favorite song? To me, no, they're too level-headed, and so is Cindy Williams' Laurie. (LeMat, Smith, and Candy Clark, maybe; Mackenzie Phillips, definitely.) The music drives the narrative forward—the Monotones' "Book of Love" when Phillips flees LeMat's car, Booker T.'s "Green Onions" as an omen of disaster—and it routinely mirrors what characters are feeling, but again, it's first and foremost a directorial device. You're hearing what's inside George Lucas' head, not what's in Curt's or Steve's.

I've singled out *American Graffiti* and *Mean Streets* because together they set a framework within which most of the worthwhile pop-driven films of the past 25 years can be located: a director visualizes a particular scene or sequence through the filter of some favorite piece of music, and the music in turn is used to shape and choreograph the scene in a way that is meant to resonate deeply. Generally, the song has only the most incidental or casual connections to the characters on hand, and sometimes not even that. This holds true for Creedence Clearwater Revival's "Fortunate Son" in Jonathan Demme's *Melvin and Howard* (Paul LeMat's Melvin Dummar is the very definition of who John Fogerty was trying to find a voice for, but, for that very reason, Dummar himself wouldn't know the first thing about

CCR)[7]; the Byrds and the Turtles in Jonathan Kaplan's excellent *Heart Like a Wheel* (housewife-with-kids Shirley Muldowney's sole connection to music is the country & western her dad used to sing for her; the Byrds and the Turtles come out of Kaplan's life); and *Goodfellas* (the slow-motion shot of De Niro underneath Cream's "Sunshine of Your Love" gets to the core of Jimmy Conway's spiritual rot like nothing else in the film, even though Jimmy himself couldn't possibly be any more removed from the world inhabited by Cream). The same dynamic is evident in the more recent mastery of *Boogie Nights* (where Paul Thomas Anderson's porn-happy ensemble essentially has the same relationship to disco that *American Graffiti*'s teenagers have to rock 'n' roll: music's a plaything, an ever-present ambience that fills the space around them and gives them something to dance to, but it's far from the central fact of anybody's life) and *Rushmore* (Jason Schwartzman's Max Fischer is like one of Pete Townshend's misfit heroes come to life, but Max's own tastes are better represented by the cheesy seduction tape he plays for Ms. Cross than the Who, Kinks, and Creation songs Wes Anderson chose for *Rushmore*).

In each case, there's a disconnect between the film's characters and its soundtrack, a pattern that reaches its logical conclusion, at once comical and hypnotic, in Lars von Trier's *Breaking the Waves*. Here, the narrative is literally stopped at various points for a series of static landscape shots underneath a progression of 1970s art-glam songs (David Bowie, Jethro Tull, Roxy Music). I suppose someone could develop a reasonable case for how these songs are intricately linked to the psyches of von Trier's characters, but to me their inclusion is much more easily explained: they're the director's favorite songs, and he was going to get them into his film no matter what. If von Trier had instead been directing *The First Wives Club*, I'm willing to bet that the same soundtrack would have been part of the package.

There are exceptions in these films and others—stray moments when a character reveals a deeper attachment to whatever music's playing in the background, when ownership of the soundtrack passes from director to character. Towards the end of *Boogie Nights*, in the celebrated firecracker/"Sister Christian" sequence, there's a close-up of Mark Wahlberg's Dirk Diggler as his attention shifts from the surrounding mayhem to the lyrics of Rick Springfield's "Jessie's Girl" from one of Rahad Jackson's "awesome mix tapes." Dirk loses himself in the song, gets caught up in the way Springfield tells the story of Dirk's own feelings for Julianne Moore's Amber Waves, and the trace of a smile starts to cross his face. It's a profound

---

7 No idea why I wrote that; of course Dummar would have been familiar with CCR—everyone was, not least of which a guy who had dreams of writing a hit song.

pop-music moment, the best cinematic translation I've ever encountered of an old Steely Dan lyric: "All night long, we sang that stupid song/And every word we sang I knew was true." Anderson went on to give his characters an even greater emotional stake in *Magnolia*'s soundtrack during the great "Wise Up" montage.

Three recent films have appeared that may or may not signal a new kind of pop-music movie, one in which the soundtrack is less in service of a director's personality and is more intimately connected with the thoughts, actions, and aspirations of the film's characters—in short, where characters either talk directly about the music we hear, ruminating on its place in their lives or using it as a sounding board for their theories about the world, or, in one extraordinary instance, consciously choosing soundtrack music that is going to speak for them. *The Virgin Suicides*, *High Fidelity*, and *American Psycho* are very different films in terms of tone and genre, yet their soundtracks all feel like clear departures from the Scorsese/Lucas-influenced style of the past quarter-century.

Mary Harron's *American Psycho* is the weakest of the three, a heavy-handed art-splatter film whose one idea, that the materialistic excesses of the Reagan era produced monsters in our midst (with Reagan himself, predictably enough, dangled out there as the biggest monster of them all), was handled with more wit and economy in TV's *Family Ties*. That aside, Harron sticks close to the digressions and detours of Bret Easton Ellis's novel, preserving for us the bizarre juxtaposition of Christian Bale's Patrick Bateman expounding earnestly on the significance of Huey Lewis, Robert Palmer, and Phil Collins just before putting his victims out of their misery in more ways than one. Speaking as someone who worked at a record store during the summer of 1986, Ellis's intuitive grasp of the music which came to define that precise moment in pop history is flawless. Lewis, Palmer, and Collins, along with maybe Lionel Richie and Billy Ocean, are locked into place as surely as Bateman himself—weird, immaculate, anonymous spaces that still linger. Mary Harron's musical voice can be found in *I Shot Andy Warhol* and old issues of *Punk* magazine; *American Psycho*'s soundtrack is meticulously and presciently programmed by Bateman, as precise a pop critic as he is serial killer.

Bateman's Top-40 monologues are an opportune time to bring up Quentin Tarantino, whose most famous musical set piece, the Stealer's Wheel scene from *Reservoir Dogs*, would fit comfortably into *American Psycho*. Tarantino is something of a bridge between the Scorsese/Lucas tradition and the recent blip of character-driven soundtracks. Unlike Scorsese's hoods, Tarantino's characters reveal an intellectual, if not always emotional, attachment to pop music: observe the Madonna roundtable and Chris Penn's close analysis of "The Night the Lights Went Out in Georgia" in *Reservoir Dogs*, or Sam Jackson trading thoughts on the Delfonics with Robert Forster in *Jackie Brown*. In the first two cases, it's hard to hear the talk that accompanies the music as coming from anyone other than Tarantino himself. When Mr. Brown and Mr. Blue start dissecting "Like a Virgin," it's like a great in-joke on the gulf between Jimmy Conway and Cream in *Goodfellas*—the words are Tarantino's, not Mr. Brown's, and they carry about as much spiritual weight as Homer Simpson wistfully pining for the bygone days of Supertramp. But in *Jackie Brown*, you really do hear the Delfonics through the ears of Forster and Pam Grier, signalling a move from Tarantino to his characters as the controlling sensibility.

There's probably more talk about pop music in *High Fidelity* than in any narrative film ever made, much of it lifted verbatim from Nick Hornby's novel. Too much talk, sometimes—after a thrillingly resonant opening, "You're Gonna Miss Me" blaring over a close-up of a spinning 45, the music drops out and John Cusack needlessly starts explaining what the Thirteenth Floor Elevators' monument to spite and self-pity has already made perfectly clear. Far from channeling its characters and its music onto two separate tracks—with the narrative looking after the former and the director in charge of the latter—*High Fidelity* immerses Cusack and his record-store buddies in the daily rituals, idiosyncrasies, and private enthusiasms that grow out of a full-fledged pop obsession. Sometimes the surfeit of detail works fine: You could see *High Fidelity* six times and still have fun scanning the frame for familiar album covers, and the one time when the record store's busy and we hop from fragment to fragment of overheard conversation—Stiff Little Fingers, *Blonde on Blonde*, *Psychocandy*, the Beta Band—director Stephen Frears lowers the volume on Cusack a bit and lets the film find its own rhythm. In the end, however, the movie has all the surface noise of Hornby's novel without the underlying melancholy.

Sofia Coppola's *The Virgin Suicides* is pitched far away from *High Fidelity*'s esoteric clutter, but its austerity and restraint are deceptive: no matter how encyclopedic Cusack's pop-music I.Q. is in *High Fidelity*, or how much his record collection dwarfs the solitary milk crate owned by Kirsten Dunst's Lux in *The Virgin Suicides*, it's Coppola's film that comes closer to capturing from the inside the experience of what it's like to give part of your life over to pop music—closer, maybe, than any film ever has. In *Dazed and Confused*, an earlier version of growing up in the '70s, Richard

people always live and die in 4/4 time

Linklater's teenagers seemed barely cognizant of the Foghat and Edgar Winter that played non-stop on the radio as they drove around town. Linklater had the songs down cold, but I only rarely sensed that any of them meant anything to the kids—whatever feeling of kinship I took away were for Linklater, who clearly shares some biography with me, not for his characters. The *Virgin Suicides* uses about one-seventh the amount of music heard in *Dazed and Confused*, but every second registers. Sometimes, like with the incredible introduction of Trip Fontane to Heart's "Magic Man," Coppola sticks close to Scorsese: pick the right song, play it loud and let it play, and let the music do the rest. Even there, though, "Magic Man" pointedly speaks for all the girls hanging off their lockers and swooning as Trip walks down the hall, so when "Crazy on You" accompanies Lux's and Trip's seismic first kiss soon after, it's as if Heart has been officially designated as a talisman to the kids, something that closes off their world to outsiders. From there it's a short step to the homecoming dance, where Electric Light Orchestra's "Strange Magic," 10cc's "I'm Not in Love," and Styx's "Come Sail Away" speak a secret language of longing and desire understood immediately by anyone who went to high school at the time. Which would not, significantly, include Sofia Coppola—I haven't read the source novel for *The Virgin Suicides*, from which I take it some of the songs are lifted intact, but in any case the music is wholly an extension of the characters, not Coppola (who was five years old at the time).

All of this serves as prelude to the fallout from the dance. First, Mrs. Lisbon's record-burning edict, the first time in the movie one of the daughters is forced to articulate the role that pop music plays in her life. It's important that Mrs. Lisbon's ultimate punishment should target Lux's record collection: as Lux clings to her milk crate to the point of being dragged down the stairs behind it, the same music that has already been established as a binding force among the film's teenagers is now moved into the realm of the purely personal, the realm of the pop obsessive. The sight of a record (any record) going up in flames might not resonate like the sled in *Citizen Kane*, but to anybody who collects vinyl it's a disturbing image nonetheless. (For a whole gallery of traumatized record collectors, see Alan Zweig's recent documentary *Vinyl*.)

Finally, there's what I've come to think of as the playing-records-over-the-phone sequence. I'd place it alongside the Copa entrance in *Goodfellas* (to the Crystals' "Then He Kissed Me"), the pool party in *Boogie Nights* (Eric Burdon's "Spill the Wine"), and Max's extracurricular resume in *Rushmore* (the Creation's "Making Time") as the scene against which all pop cinema should be measured. For no apparent reason other than the simple truth that there's nothing one can say that hasn't been said with perfect eloquence somewhere in a pop song, the Lisbon girls and their worshipful chorus of boy admirers renew contact by playing records to each other over the phone. The songs are carefully chosen and a story emerges. The boys lead with Todd Rundgren's "Hello It's Me," a smile and a new beginning; the girls respond with Gilbert O'Sullivan's "Alone Again, Naturally," which talks of suicide. The boys come back with the Bee Gees' "Run to Me," an intimation of safety and acceptance; the girls promptly cut them off with Carole King's "So Far Away," leaving only distance and resignation. I might have extended the scene to find room for Badfinger's "Day After Day" and Harry Nilsson's "Without You," but otherwise, perfection. Coppola takes one of the most basic instincts of pop fandom, the desire to share your obsessions with the world—"Hey, you've got to hear this"—and retells the film in miniature.

Coppola, who like most directors her age has been influenced to one degree or another by music videos, suggests a new kind of synthesis for pop cinema: a combination of Scorsese's dazzle, Lucas' command of period, a complex and carefully developed affinity between character and soundtrack, and something more elusive—an intuitive feel for the kind of atmospherics needed to sustain the best music videos across minutes of wordless narrative. Music and image are melded in *The Virgin Suicides* in a manner that gives resonance not just to the dynamic high points (where Scorsese and Lucas operate), but also to the quieter, Air-scored passages that give the movie an enigmatic dreaminess befitting the five Lisbon sisters. The scene where the boys read from Cecilia's diary, triggering a fantasy of Lux frolicking in sun-drenched fields underneath Air's "Ce matin là," is video-influenced in the best sense, the sensual elevation of mood and gesture above all else. Coppola's husband, Spike Jonze, is probably the most celebrated video director of the past decade, and her brother Roman directed Green Day's "Walking Contradiction," on the short-list of my favorite videos ever. Clearly Coppola has benefited from some helpful familial ties in terms of drawing on the conventions of video, and she uses them exceedingly well. In doing so, she opens up new possibilities for the pop-music soundtrack.

(*Cinemascope*, 2000)

people always live and die in 4/4 time

Heart Like a Wheel

Jonathan Kaplan's biography of drag-racer Shirley Muldowney ranks high on my list of favorite '80s films; Pauline Kael more or less shrugged it off as a safe and self-consciously genteel B-movie, but to me it has the kind of grace and quiet truth that are usually associated with such art-house directors as Truffaut and Ozu. It also has a couple of unexpected pop-music moments that send me away every time I watch the movie. "Happy Together" turns up after an emotional moment of reconciliation between Shirley (Bonnie Bedelia) and her mechanic husband Jack (Leo Rossi)—Shirley has returned from an unsuccessful sojourn to Michigan to find a sponsor who'll build her a car, a trip she undertook against Jack's wishes, and now Jack has promised to build the car himself. They embrace, fade to a title card announcing "Raceway Park, 1966," the Turtles song starts up, and the camera begins a slow, majestic tracking shot that starts high and glides down to take in first Connie Kalitta (Beau Bridges), an established star signing autographs as he moves through a wave of female admirers, and then Shirley, who as Kalitta passes out of view (the two haven't met yet) is revealed standing against a post, nervously looking around as she waits for her first-ever attempt to qualify for an NHRA race. It's an intricate, beautifully choreographed shot: the euphoria of "Happy Together"'s chorus and the arrangement of Shirley and Connie within the frame tell you everything you need to know about the way these two people will eventually come to dominate each other's lives. The Byrds shot is even better. It's a couple of years later, Shirley's not making any headway on the circuit, and both she and Jack have just brushed off some unsolicited advice from Connie when he stops by their pit one day. Shirley and Connie make an unspoken connection, though, and as "Turn, Turn, Turn" fills the soundtrack, there's a slow-motion, double-reverse tracking shot as they part. (I think that's what you'd call it; Scorsese uses the same technique sometimes, like in *Taxi Driver* whenever Travis eyes someone walking away from him.) They look each other over carefully, and Connie gives the strangest little smile just before he disappears from view.

(*Popped*, 1996)

interrupting my train of thought

So Sad About Max

I'm disappointed that *Rushmore* didn't get a better reception. It did get a fair amount of attention, so that might seem like a strange thing to say, but to me it's the kind of film that should have galvanized movie audiences the way that *The Godfather*, *Nashville*, and *Taxi Driver* did 25 years ago. "Should have galvanized movie audiences"—that's my bad Pauline Kael imitation, and it's probably from having read so much Kael that I still root for my favorite films to make hundreds of millions of dollars and become big topics of conversation everywhere you turn. I don't feel the same way about my favorite music, where I'm more or less indifferent to whether it makes #1 on *Billboard* or has an audience of me and five others. (With me the range is more like #1 in *Billboard* to #93 in *Billboard*—me and 500,000 others.) With films, though, I turn evangelical, as I have recently with *Rushmore*.

It's a film that brings together a number of things that at one time or another made a lasting impression on me: *The Graduate* (*The Graduate* specifically, but *The Heartbreak Kid*, *The Sterile Cuckoo*, *Nobody Waved Goodbye*, *You're a Big Boy Now*, and—I'm guessing, I haven't seen it—*Harold and Maude* are there too), *The Catcher in the Rye* (*Rushmore* is as much of a film version as you could ever hope for), and the handful of early Who songs I'm most in awe of ("Substitute," "I'm a Boy," "Circles," "Don't Look Away," "Pictures of Lily," "See My Way," "I Can't Reach You"). Especially "I Can't Reach You"—when Pete Townshend sings "You're so alive and I'm nearly dead," he could be *Rushmore*'s Herman Blume standing at a distance and looking at Max Fischer, or Max looking at Rosemary Appleby, or Margaret Yang looking at Max, or Herman looking at Rosemary, or maybe even Rosemary looking at Max. In the end, as it should be, it's Max looking at Margaret. "You fly your plane right over my head/You're so alive and I'm nearly dead"—when Max opens his eyes and sees Margaret for what amounts to the first time, one of his three or four great moments of acceptance in the movie, she actually is flying her plane right over his head. I don't know if Wes Anderson had "I Can't Reach You" in mind when he envisioned the scene on the tarmac, but *Rushmore* is so steeped in the spirit and the fact of those early Who songs—"My name is Max and I'm a head case" would have worked as the film's opening line—he might have.

Rushmore's connection to *The Graduate* and *The Catcher in the Rye* is no less overt, but Anderson plays around with them and, in many ways, makes them better. Besides its basic premise, *Rushmore* lifts specific images and effects from *The Graduate*: Herman disappearing into himself as he floats to the bottom of the family pool, Max lying in wait for Herman inside the car, Rosemary's "Goodbye, Max" perfectly echoing Mrs. Robinson's "Goodbye, Benjamin," the close parallel between the "I Am Waiting" and "April Come She Will" sequences. But outside of Max's shared weakness for half-baked ideas (where he goes Benjamin Braddock ten better), he couldn't be more unlike Ben. I can understand why some people have no patience for Ben's doddering around in *The Graduate*, where Hoffman seems to be working out his *Rain Man* character 20 years before the fact; for me, it's all of a piece with everything I love about the film, but if I were seeing *The Graduate* for the first time today, I doubt I'd find Ben so endearing. Some of Ben's mannerisms linger on in Bill Murray's sad and rumpled Herman Blume, who is more a version of Ben 30 years later than Jason Schwartzman's Max is of Ben five years earlier—Ben gone on to the world of steel instead of plastics, but still hiding behind trees and still unable to put together a sentence when he stands before Rosemary in front of her house. Max, on the other hand, never dodders. He's on overdrive all the time, brilliant and emphatic and spinning off into 30 different directions at once. He's Holden Caulfield, not Benjamin Braddock—a creative whirlwind, a force.

But Max isn't really Holden, either. I last read *The Catcher in the Rye* over 10 years ago, and it's not a pleasant memory. The book's unrelenting sourness was hard to take; it is what it is, but the way that Salinger was so quick to close off every last chance for Holden to find his place in the world—for every Phoebe, there'd be a wall with "fuck you" scrawled over it—felt suffocating. *Rushmore* doesn't punish Max the way that Holden's punished in *The Catcher in the Rye*. Max shares Holden's misfit/outsider status, and he thrives on the same kind of healthy loathing for the Magnuses of Rushmore Academy, but Max is able to come out the other side of his breakdown in a way that I don't remember Holden doing. Taking Herman in to meet his father, understanding how mean he's been to Margaret, orchestrating Herman and Rosemary's reconciliation—these are profound moments, and they give *Rushmore* a sympathetic lift that's absent from *The Catcher in the Rye*. That's not something you need from Salinger's book when you're 15, but 20 years later, it's a difference that means a lot.

For me to love a film as much as I do *Rushmore*, there's a good chance that pop music's going to figure prominently. There's music all through *Rushmore*, a mid-'60s mix of second-tier hits and semi-obscure album tracks from Britain, and as is true of all the best pop directors—Rule Number One—Wes Anderson puts the music front and center, sometimes for minutes at a time. Along with a spare-sounding Kinks song I'd never heard before (just right for the image of Herman tossing golf balls into the pool) and Cat Stevens' original "Here Comes My Baby" (also a discovery: it's always been a Tremeloes song to me), *Rushmore* has three musical detours that are epics unto themselves. There's the Who, of course, a couple of minutes from "A Quick One While He's Away." It's used as counterpoint—"You are forgiven" over and over again at the very moment when Max and Blume are ready to kill each other—but it's also an inspired match for the look on Max's face as he emerges, slow-motion, from the hotel elevator after funnelling honeybees into Herman's room: an expression of adolescent hate as fixed and as blank as the one worn by Pete Townshend on the *My Generation* LP cover. It's the look you hear in "I Can See for Miles," but that would have been too easy a choice. "A Quick One" functions as a more abstract backdrop to the same feelings.

After Max concedes Rosemary to Herman, he turns away—from them, from Margaret, from school, from himself. He's George Minafer towards the end of *The Magnificent Ambersons*: he's gotten his comeuppance, ten times over. What follows, as the Rolling Stones' "I Am Waiting" plays (I've never owned *Aftermath*, so that was new to me too), is as affecting a snapshot of self-pity as I've ever seen in a film. I've always thought self-pity the most underrated of emotions—you don't want it to overtake your life, but every so often, it's not a bad thing. As much as anger or revenge or anything else, it's an emotion that cleanses. Anderson apotheosizes self-pity for the duration of "I Am Waiting": Max closing the drapes on Margaret is an image of tremendous purity.

Best of all, just as *Rushmore*'s getting underway (so don't show up late, which I hope you wouldn't consider anyway), is the montage of Max's extra-curricular activities set to the Creation's "Making Time." Again, new to me; I'm not even sure if I'd ever come across the group's name before. You can find singular depictions of hate and self-pity in other movies, but I don't know that there's ever been anything like the "Making Time" sequence. The choreography is stunning—each tableau more intricate than the last, everything culminating in the shot of Max leading the "Bombardment Society." I can't give a name to whatever it is that this sequence gets at. It gets to the core of something.

My favorite student in my own class the past two years has been Marshall Buck Tremblay (I had him as a 3 last year and asked to have him back in the 3/4 split I'm doing now). Marshall doesn't know he's my favorite student, because two or three times a day I'm yelling at him. He's exasperating. He reads about three grade levels ahead of the rest of the kids, and he's intensely interested whenever I'm talking about Richard Nixon or

Aretha Franklin or *Citizen Kane*. Last year, as part of a newspaper unit, I had the class trying to write editorials on whether the younger grades should be allowed to attend school dances; yes, wrote Marshall, because all kids need to "feel the flow of freedom." Meanwhile, his marks are average or worse because he just doesn't care, and he's not much past the kindergarten level when it comes to the social graces—he's still eating snow and rifling around garbage cans for fun. I told his mom that she needed to see *Rushmore*, that it was about a kid who was Marshall in five years. (Quickly adding that I meant that only in a good way, that I wasn't saying that Marshall would be pulling down 40s and 50s in high school—the truth is, that's in part exactly what I meant.)

I hope Marshall sees *Rushmore* one day; I know he'll see himself up there, and if he catches it at the right moment, I'm sure it will affect him like *The Graduate* and *The Catcher in the Rye* affected me. And if I were 15 myself right now, I'm guessing that *Rushmore* would have the capacity to permanently shape how I viewed the world, or at least how I viewed myself. I'm not, so that's already been taken care of by other films, books, and records. But *Rushmore* touches something inside me that comes from the same place.

(homepage, 1999)

"Winter Lady," Leonard Cohen/"Sing Me Back Home," Merle Haggard

Early-'70s film music: "Winter Lady" is one of the Cohen songs in *McCabe & Mrs. Miller*, a version of "Sing Me Back Home" appears in *Goin' Down the Road* (a Canadian film famous here and little-known elsewhere; you may have seen the *SCTV* parody, where Joe Flaherty and John Candy cheerfully set out for Toronto in hopes of landing two of its unlimited "doctorin' and lawycrin' jobs"). I can't remember where exactly "Winter Lady" turns up in *McCabe*, but it instantly evokes for me all of that movie's elliptical, snowbound beauty. The *Goin' Down the Road* scene takes place in Toronto's Regent Park, as a street musician sings the Haggard song for a small group of nostalgic Maritimers. When a couple of local winos serendipitously wander into camera range (cinéma vérité then in its heyday), lead characters Joey and Petey break away to share a bottle with them. It's quite an amazing scene, not false or heavy-handed at all. (The winos are so far gone they're oblivious to the camera.) In part because of *Goin' Down the*

Road, I went through a time in the early '80s where my friends and I would seek out the worst bars in the city we could find, most of them in the Dundas and Parliament area around Regent Park. I'm not especially proud of such behaviour looking back on it today; it's called slumming, and it's kind of pathetic. Anyway, in one of those bars I encountered Paul Bradley, the actor who had played Joey some ten years earlier. The experience was sad, inspiring, and a little bit unreal, like having a movie that's running through your mind suddenly materialize in front of you. The line separating Bradley from Joey was nonexistent. When I told him how much *Goin' Down the Road* meant to me, not the first time he'd heard this I'm sure, he said that he'd just been at Don Shebib's house the night before (the film's director), working on a script that had been in development for a number of years and which was now ready to be produced. I'm not saying what he was telling me wasn't true, but I do know that it was Joey who was sitting there talking to me: drunk, wistful, hanging his hopes on something that was never going to happen. (Maybe I'm wrong. If the film did go forward—I still remember the title he gave me—it did so in complete obscurity. I'm almost certain it was never made.) Running into him under those circumstances, I had to wonder if Bradley maybe had more in common with the Regent Park winos than with Doug McGrath, the actor who played Petey and who later went on to a number of smaller roles in some prominent films. It's something I think about every time I look at the film now.

(*Tapeworm*, 1996)

The Perks of Being a Wallflower

I'm somewhere between the *** and **** ratings for *Perks of Being a Wallflower* above. Haven't read the book, and couldn't figure out when it was set—the mix-tapes probably put the early 2000s as an end-date, but if there were any other clues that narrowed that down, I missed them. The music interested me: Tone-Lōc, the Smiths, an excellent "Come On Eileen" sequence, and all those mix-tapes—I wonder what Rob Sheffield thinks of this. I missed "Teen Age Riot" altogether—must have been when I was glaring at bright-cellphone-woman in the next aisle—but liked hearing "Pretend We're Dead." Something that stretches credulity: high school students who know the Shaggs and Nick Drake but have never heard "Heroes." Something else: the lead guy is supposed to be in grade 9? Because he looks just as old as his wallflower friends, and doesn't act like a 14-year-old, you accept that, but if you start thinking about the plausibility of him getting involved with high school seniors, well, it was too big a leap for me. I've got other nitpicky complaints, but some of it worked fine. Taking the Smiths off the turntable at a party and putting on Tone-Lōc reminded me of *Quadrophenia*. The gay character struck me as 1,000 times less of a caricature than the equivalent in *Scott Pilgrim*. Didn't foresee where everything was headed.

(ILX, 2012)

35 mm Jukebox: The 20 Best Uses of Pop Music in a Martin Scorsese Film

1. "Then He Kissed Me," the Crystals, in *Goodfellas*: Henry leads Karen into the Copacabana through a backdoor network of corridors and kitchens, passing out twenties and greeting well-wishers the whole way. It's all one shot, lasting for the duration of the song and beyond; I'm sure it'll one day be as famous as *Touch of Evil*'s opening shot, being just as elaborate but much more emotional. You experience everything through Karen's eyes—you find yourself as awestruck and as caught up in the passing swirl as she is—as Scorsese manages to visualize the storybook idyll of "Then He Kissed Me" from the inside, from the same place where Spector invented it. This is probably my favorite three minutes of film ever.

2. "Sunshine of Your Love," Cream, in *Goodfellas*: Jimmy standing at the bar, taking refuge from the flaky wig salesman Morrie, who's been pestering Jimmy for his share of the Lufthansa robbery. As played by Chuck Low, Morrie's patter is sprinkled with things like "unconscionable" and "cultivating"; he's my favorite character in the movie, an erudite lowlife. (Low also has a great bit in *The King of Comedy* as the guy in the restaurant who mimics Rupert.) De Niro's not doing anything except standing there thinking, but Scorsese shoots him in slow-motion anyway; combined with the song and De Niro's screwy expression—Jimmy's paranoia is starting to flip him out—it's a tremendously sinister moment.

3. "Be My Baby," the Ronettes, in *Mean Streets*: The synchronization of Hal Blaine's drums to the jump-cut of Charlie laying his head back on the pillow is undoubtedly what first attracted more people to Scorsese than

anything else. It's an astounding shot the first time you see it, and has great resonance for as many times as you watch the film again.

4. "Life Is But a Dream," the Harptones, in *Goodfellas*: Henry and Karen's wedding reception, which I like to think of as the Peter, Paul & Marie scene. The mood is one of romantic exaltation similar to the Copa sequence above, culminating with Henry and Karen circulating the dance floor as Willie Winfield hits and holds the song's final notes.

5. "El Watusi," Ray Barretto, in *Who's That Knocking at My Door*: A long, audacious anticipation of *Mean Streets* and everything else that Scorsese would ever do. Leaving behind the movie-at-hand for four minutes, Harvey Keitel and his mook friends toss around a gun and play pretend bang-bang in a slow-motion mixture of dissolves and tracking shots. There's a glimpse of Scorsese seated at a table as the sequence starts, and it all ends with the sound of gunfire and a startling cut on the soundtrack to Jr. Walker's "Shotgun." It must have been something to have been sitting there in a theatre in 1969 and been floored by this.

6. "Jumpin' Jack Flash," the Rolling Stones, in *Mean Streets*: Johnny Boy's slow-motion entrance into Tony's bar, Heather Weintraub on one arm and Sarah Klein on the other, what God sends through the door instead of the forgiveness Charlie asks for. This is the shot that best captures what Pauline Kael meant when she described *Mean Streets* as "hallucinatory," "operatic," and "dizzyingly sensual."

7. "Layla," Derek & the Dominoes, in *Goodfellas*: The fallout from Lufthansa, with dead bodies turning up in parked cars, garbage compactors, meat freezers, and elsewhere. The deaths themselves are far from tragic—bumblers like Johnny Roastbeef with his pink Coupe de Ville, or Carbone, the guy who thought that Joe Pesci really did want that coffee to go—but they feel that way thanks to the lyrical sweep of the music and Scorsese's artfully tracking camera. It's a sequence of genuine grandeur.

8. "Love Is Strange," Mickey & Sylvia, in *Casino*: Sam encounters Ginger for the first time: poker chips float overhead, time slows down, the music takes over. Scorsese has shot this same moment many times before—Travis's first glimpse of Betsy in *Taxi Driver*, Jake eyeing Vickie by the pool in *Raging Bull*—but he's so good at it that he makes it purer

each time out. There was a trailer for *Casino* with "Gimme Shelter" and "Can't You Hear Me Knocking" that was alive and epic in a way that the movie only rarely is; "Love Is Strange" is the one time it rises to the level of *Goodfellas*.

9. "Big Noise from Winnetka," Bob Crosby & the Bobcats, in *Raging Bull*: A few seconds of no particular consequence, but for me one of Scorsese's most striking shots. Jake has just followed Vickie out of a church-sponsored summer dance, and as he stands on the outside step amidst a throng of activity, he watches her pull away in a car with Salvy's crew—as always, in a state of disembodied slow-motion, punctuated by the strange whistling of the Crosby song overtop.

10. "Atlantis," Donovan, in *Goodfellas*: The scene where Tommy beats the living hell out of Billy Batts, the first indication that he's not just volatile but psychotic. (Pesci gives the same actor, Frank Vincent, a severe beating in *Raging Bull*; when Vincent finally lets loose on Pesci in *Casino*, it's like a little in-joke.) It's not surprising that Scorsese is able to make such evocative use of doo-wop in his films—doo-wop is an underused and largely unknown genre, and its dreaminess is perfectly suited to movies. I am surprised when he creates unforgettable moments out of overplayed classic-rock standbys, as he does here and with #s 2, 6, and 7, songs I thought I was immune to by now.

11. "Late For the Sky," Jackson Browne, in *Taxi Driver*: Scorsese's singer-songwriter film: Travis gives Betsy a copy of Kris Kristofferson's *Silver Tongued Devil* LP, the Jackson Browne song plays on *American Bandstand* (or maybe just in Travis's head, or in Scorsese's) when Travis absentmindedly kicks over his TV set, and the whole movie would seem to be based on Harry Chapin's "Taxi," especially in the coda they share.

12. "Come Rain or Come Shine," Ray Charles, in *The King of Comedy*: As an image, this freeze-frame underneath the opening credits describes the film succinctly: Masha's hands in full grab, Rupert on the outside looking in, a garish blue camera flash for illumination, Jerry out of view. The lyrics of "Come Rain or Come Shine" also preview the story, as Masha will vividly demonstrate to Jerry later on. What's anomalous is the song's warmth, which has no connection to the sick corrosiveness of what follows.

13. "We Belong Together," Robert & Johnny, in *After Hours*: *After Hours* sits somewhere in the middle for Scorsese, but whenever I think back on it, certain moments like this one—a slow tracking shot in on Terri Garr, the ultimate accident-waiting-to-happen in a night filled with them—come back with great clarity.

14. "Beyond the Sea," Bobby Darin, in *Goodfellas*: Henry's description of wiseguys serving time recalls nothing so much as the scene in *The Godfather* where Clemenza instructs Michael on how to make spaghetti sauce—prison as an overeater's paradise, where the preparation of food is a precise ritual and dinner doesn't commence until there's red and white on the table.

15. "Tell Me," the Rolling Stones, in *Mean Streets*: Charlie's crowd-pleasing antics with Diane, the stripper whose overpowering allure gives him one more thing to hide from. "Be My Baby," "Tell Me," and "Jumpin' Jack Flash" ring out one after another within the first 10 minutes of *Mean Streets*—it takes a while to clear your head and get your bearings again.

16. "Lonely Nights," the Hearts, in *Raging Bull*: A beautifully framed shot of Jake, balancing full champagne glasses on top of one another, after-hours entertainment for a dwindling array of admirers and ambulance chasers. Doo-wop is used as woozy, early-morning drunk music here, a mixture of reverie and self-pity.

17. "Speedo," the Cadillacs, in *Goodfellas*: Our introduction to Jimmy Conway: a neighbourhood legend at 30 for his style, his passions, and his fluid wad of hundred-dollar bills, he's as close to a perfect match for the Cadillacs' Mr. Earl as you could hope for. Young Henry is dazzled; "It was a glorious time," he recalls in narration.

18. "Mickey's Monkey," the Miracles, in *Mean Streets*: Johnny Boy is constantly short-circuiting in *Mean Streets*, doing the one thing he shouldn't be doing at any given moment, and this is his most inspired bit of foolishness: as he and Charlie flee from Michael, he takes time out for a little frug around their getaway car. Charlie is immobilized by these outbursts; they come from somewhere he doesn't understand.

19. "Werewolves of London," Warren Zevon, in The Color of Money: There's obviously a lot of Johnny Boy in Tom Cruise's Vincent, nowhere

more evident than in his choreographed bravura here. And just like Charlie above, Paul Newman is left to look on uncomprehendingly—Vincent's ecstasy is outside his experience, or was at least lost to him somewhere back in The Hustler.

20. "Pay to Cum," Bad Brains, in *After Hours*: Mohawk Night at Club Berlin, a spectacle far more terrifying than it is funny—especially Scorsese's cameo, where he can be seen operating the lights from above in a kind of robotic, Nazi trance.

The biggest factor in compiling such a list is whether you prefer *Goodfellas* or *Mean Streets*, which taken together are going to dominate almost any configuration. I have eight songs from *Goodfellas*, four from *Mean Streets*; someone else might reverse the numbers. I think I could have even squeezed all 20 songs from *Goodfellas*, as there are many things I left off (Cleftones, Shangri-Las, Chantels, Drifters, the whole collage of the helicopter sequence) which I like just as much as what's there, but I tried to spread the list around a bit. *Goodfellas* is the best film of the decade by a wide margin, and for me it edges out *Raging Bull* as Scorsese's greatest achievement to date.

A quick account of some omissions...*Alice Doesn't Live Here Anymore* has Mott the Hoople's "All the Way From Memphis," and Neil Young's "Time Fades Away" is in *American Boy*—great songs both—but I don't have a strong recollection of either, so I guess they didn't make much of an impression on me at the time. There's lots to choose from in "Life Lessons" from *New York Stories* and (obviously) *The Last Waltz*, but I'm not a big fan of either, and *The Last Waltz* is something different anyway. *Cape Fear* has "Patience" and "Been Caught Stealing," and maybe if I didn't hate the film so much, I'd remember them a lot better than I do. *Italianamerican*, *The Last Temptation of Christ*, and *The Age of Innocence* don't qualify—there might be a few seconds of Snoop Doggy Dogg in *The Age of Innocence* but I'm not quite sure—and I still haven't seen *Boxcar Bertha* or *New York, New York*. Also, this is a pop-music list; I've left off *Raging Bull*'s "Cavalleria Rusticana" section and Bernard Herrmann's score for *Taxi Driver*, both of which would otherwise be up near the top.

(*Popped/Real Groove*, 1995/96)

Kenneth Anger, *Inauguration of the Pleasure Dome* (1954) and *Rabbit's Moon* (1972): Two more Kenneth Anger films—they showed all nine at the AGO this year. *Pleasure Dome*, which could be called *All My Rowdy Libertine and Satanist Friends Are Coming Over Tonight*, is hilarious; Anger added an Electric Light Orchestra soundtrack sometime in the '70s, so you get to watch all these unsavory lunatics prance around and conduct their arcane little rituals to the strains of "Boy Blue" and "Can't Get It Out of My Head." *Rabbit's Moon* is flaky too, but it also gets as close as anything I've ever seen to the far-reaching desire and eerie stillness of my favorite doo-wop music. Inside a bluish-silvery forest, a clown tries to woo his love by lassoing the moon, like Jimmy Stewart promised Donna Reed in *It's a Wonderful Life*; the Dells, the Capris, the Flamingos, and Mary Wells play overtop, interspersed with strange bits of indeterminate drumming and electronic filler. It all made me wish that I had some grounding in mime and ballet and other things I know nothing about.

(#2 video, year-end ballot, 1997)

The Virgin Suicides (Sofia Coppola, 1999)

Later tonight, I'll attend grad night for the grade 8s at my school. Sheer coincidence—I slotted *The Virgin Suicides* for #22 about three weeks ago—but this is Prom Film #3 on my list. I said there'd be five, but I scrapped *American Graffiti* somewhere along the way. The fourth will involve not a full-out prom, but something that serves the same function.

I took the time to re-watch *The Virgin Suicides* over the weekend, and I'll admit that I've had some second thoughts. It's such a mood piece, and this time I don't think I was in exactly the right one. I also just finished squirming through 140 minutes of *The Tree of Life*, which must be one of the biggest hunks of Kael bait I've ever seen—it's not the most opportune moment for me to be listing something elliptical and self-consciously poetic and so-not-Ridgemont-High. I considered reverting back to a film I'd dropped earlier on, *Rushmore*, which appeared almost simultaneously to *The Virgin Suicides* and also affected me quite a bit. But I'll stay with Coppola's film, because a) it had already held up over the course of six or seven previous viewings, and b) even this time, I found the beauty of certain passages as stunning as ever. And as improbable—I still do not know from what life experiences Coppola was able to conjure up a world that more or less matches my own romanticized version of the mid-'70s. She was four years old at the time.

Well, if you believe one of the boys narrating *The Virgin Suicides* (which essentially means if you believe Coppola), it's because she's a female—she intuitively understands everything about me, while I'm forever trying and failing to make sense of her, from the time I'm in grade school until, presumably, the day I die. I can go with that; I don't necessarily believe it's true, but when I connect with a film on some level that runs deeper than the rational/intellectual, I'm usually okay with whatever it wants me to believe. The adult Trip Fontaine (seemingly in rehab) thinking back on Lux Libson across the decades: "She was the still point of the turning world, man." I think that's as valid a moment as Mr. Bernstein recalling the young woman on the ferry in *Citizen Kane*.

I haven't read Jeffrey Eugenides' novel; I've come across people who prefer the book, and others who prefer the film. It's not difficult to imagine what the book can get at it in more detail than the film—though all the voiceover narration does try to give some semblance of interior lives—but the film can give you Todd Rundgren, Carole King, Heart, and others in a way that a book simply can't. The clip I've linked to is inner-circle hall of fame when it comes to pop music in movies. What I really took notice of this time around was the scene where Rundgren's "A Dream Goes on Forever" plays, the party where the boys get the Down Syndrome kid to do funny, entertaining things. They mean well. Cecelia quietly leaves the room and kills herself. It's such an excruciating scene to watch, you don't necessarily question the logic of what she does.

Something else I thought of for the very first time (I don't know why it took me so long to remember this): in the mid-'70s, we had a family of Libson sisters move into the corner house on my own street. The Martinique sisters, or something like that. They were French-Canadian, there were four of them, and their age range lined up almost exactly with that of the Libsons. I don't think I ever thought of them as the still point of the turning world (that was Nancy Phillips), but I do know my friend John and I spent a lot of time cycling past their house one summer.

(#22, Facebook Top 50, 2011)

"Heart and Soul," Cleftones

A famous single I include in connection to Wolfman Jack's recent death: it's the song that plays in *American Graffiti* as Richard Dreyfuss takes a last look over his shoulder and discovers he's just been talking to the real Wolfman Jack. Whatever mystique that Wolfman Jack took away from that moment was obviously lost over the next 20 years of bad TV shows and infomercials, but every time I watch *American Graffiti* I'm amazed at how moving his one scene is, how subtle a performance he gives as himself pretending to be someone other than himself. The way he explains why he's content to toil away in obscurity at the station, his friendly pleas for Dreyfuss to take one of the melting popsicles, the advice he dispenses, there's not a trace of falseness in any of it. I could never reconcile the quiet perfection of that scene with all the garish celebrity stuff that came later.

(*Tapeworm*, 1995)

Fast Times at Ridgemont High (Amy Heckerling, 1982)

This isn't really my 31st favorite film of all time. It's more like #71—top 100 for sure. But I'm going to slot it here for three reasons:
1) As Steven hinted about his own list, mine is just about to become very canon-predictable. It'll be a different canon than Steven's, but there aren't going to be many surprises the rest of the way. So whatever my real #31 pick is, I can guarantee that *Fast Times* is more fun to watch, and more fun to write about.
2) On the music countdown, I would occasionally let YouTube availability decide a close call. Well, not only was I able to find one of my favorite *Fast Times* scenes on there—with a throwaway line ("No, I don't have any Blue Oyster Cult…") that's been inexplicably lodged in the back of my mind for 30 years—the clip was posted, if the comments are to be believed, by the guy who played the kid looking for the BOC tickets.
3) I've tried to honour the serendipitous accident throughout these countdowns. And on Q-107 yesterday morning, *Fast Times* was the answer to one of their "Stump the Chump" questions: what early-'80s film popularized the word "dude"? Sounds a little iffy to me, but add it all up, and there you go—#31.

Fast Times is sort of like *Saturday Night Fever*, in that it's famous for various reasons that obscure how serious and how brutal it is at times. If you think of *Fast Times*, the first thing that pops into your head is Sean Penn's Spicoli, possibly one of the three or four greatest comic inventions ever, and then you probably remember the cast in general: it belongs to a group of films (*American Graffiti, Animal House, Diner*) where an ensemble is filled with people who later went on to various levels of fame. (Although for me, the best performance after Penn is given by Brian Backer as Mark Ratner, and he basically vanished.) Actually, let me backtrack: the first thing you might remember is Phoebe Cates, who in a single scene manages to justify the existence of the Cars.

But watching it last night, I was again reminded of how incredibly up-front it is about teenage sex—to a degree that I'd sometimes think, "Could you get away with that today?" It's just so casual about things like Jennifer Jason Leigh's 16-year-old Stacy losing her virginity to the creepy 26-year-old stereo salesman, or the scene in the cafeteria where Cates conducts her tutorial on oral sex. Even the jokier stuff can take you aback: when Judge Reinhold recites his pre-emptive breakup soliloquy, he's staring into a mirror with "big hairy pussy" scrawled all over it.

There's all that, and then there are moments of subtlety that would be at home in a Truffaut film. Big-brother Brad waiting around for Stacy after her abortion; the way Stacy says "You're so nice" to Ratner at the hospital; the truce between Ratner and Damone at the prom (after their beautifully handled locker-room confrontation). These are the moments that elevate *Fast Times* to something beyond what it would be without them, which would still be a very funny and smart film.

The soundtrack is somewhat famous too; not being an '80s guy, most of the time it's just background for me. I like a few things. Jackson Browne makes for an odd icon of teenage libido, but the song of his that plays during Stacy's two big sex scenes is pretty good. There's a new-wavey thing called "I Don't Know," inspired by Spicoli, that I like—I checked the credits and it's Jimmy Buffett! Penn's rendition of "Wooly Bully" at the prom is righteously gnarly; how did this guy ever end up hectoring us about what a fine actor Jude Law is? And there's one truly great musical moment, what I'd probably always assumed was a Fleetwood Mac song till I checked the credits last night: Stevie Nicks' "Sleeping Angel" as Damone scrambles around to pay for Stacy's abortion.

My greatest regret in life as an elementary teacher: I will never once get the opportunity to say, "What are you people—*on dope*?"

(#31, Facebook Top 50, 2011)

Wild Palms

"Love Child," Supremes

It's midway into the second night, and thus far pop music has only lurked around the edges of *Wild Palms*: snatches of the Zombies and Lou Christie, people trading offhanded quotes from the Beatles and Bob Dylan, two middle-aged housewives dancing to Don Gardner & Dee Dee Ford's "I Need Your Loving" while their husbands huddle in the foreground and plot corporate strategy. "Love Child"'s appearance is the first indication that something more adventurous might start to take shape. After Harry discovers the Wild Palms symbol on his hand—he screams out to Grace as the Wyckoff children, in sinister *Village Of the Damned*/Diane Arbus formation, watch silently—there's a cut to Senator Kreutzer lounging around poolside, absorbed in a holographic image of three Japanese women lip-synching the Supremes song. The women are stunning, done up vintage Supremes-style in sequined gowns and luxuriant bouffants, and they're shot like go-go dancers in an old *Laugh-In* party scene, all sectional body shots and subliminal jigsaw editing. The Supremes have never looked or sounded more erotic; they make great holograms, which (a good joke whether intentional or not) is kind of what the Supremes were anyway. That "Love Child" was actually an autobiographical tale of poverty and deprivation—a girl-group protest song—only makes the displacement all the more powerful.

"House of the Rising Sun," Animals

The rescue of Chickie Levitt, and also the rescue of "House of the Rising Sun": no matter how many thousands of times you've heard it—the song was all but dead for me before *Wild Palms*—all the urgency and foreboding that you first heard as a kid is here restored full force. As far as Chickie goes, I'd be lying if I said I fully understood why it's so important for the Friends to get him away from the Fathers and down to the beach so he can die; by this point, the story has more or less been lost to me and I'm just enjoying the all-around weirdness. The Fathers think Chickie has the Go-chip, it's really in Japan with Ushio, unless Ushio has secretly implanted it in Harry's hand, in which case why was Harry dreaming about rhinos all along?...Well, I'm sure it can all be logically mapped out on paper. In any event, the song combines with a whirlwind barrage of falling bodies (I love the shot of Stitch getting machine-gunned down as the rescue van starts to pull away) and Mimezine-induced cathedrals to make it seem as if the fate of the entire world hinges on getting Chickie to the beach. It's like an apocalyptic, guerrilla-style reprise of *Midnight Cowboy*'s last few minutes.

"No Expectations," Rolling Stones

The exquisite slide playing that makes "No Expectations" one of the prettiest of Rolling Stones songs here serves as perfect accompaniment to Interrogation-by-Mimezine (following Death-by-Mimezine and Orgasm-by-Mimezine earlier in the film). The result is an inspired bit of druggy screen surrealism, as pleasurable in its way as the brainwashing scenes in *The Manchurian Candidate* or Mia Farrow's impregnation in *Rosemary's Baby*, encompassing both Wild Palms' funniest line ("Something's *weird*...", Harry's shrewd appraisal of the situation as his recently-dead wife cheerfully describes to him her annoying little flesh wound) and its single scariest image (Harry's long-dead father headbutting him in the pool). Harry emerges from it all as a simpering basket case—they took him to the station, they put him on the train, he's got no inclination to pass through there again.

(Popped, 1996)

Boogie Nights

Big surprise. There's so much here, and it's used so well and so surprisingly—"Driver's Seat" and "Sister Christian" were completely new to me—that whatever misgivings I have about the film itself just fall away. (Briefly: William Macy is wasted, the scenes with Wahlberg's mother are needlessly hysterical, and there's something a little mechanical about the rise-and-fall plotting, as if now everything must fall apart just because we're at that point in the film where everything's supposed to fall apart. Cf. *Casino*.) The music, direction, and performances create a world, and the world draws you in. Terrific: Apollo 100's lost-cause "Joy," "Brand New Key," "Mama Told Me (Not to Come)" of course, "Machine Gun," "Magnet and Steel," "Ain't No Stoppin' Us Now," "Jungle Fever," and (another salvage job; it's bland on record) Roberta Flack's "Compared to What," all of it topped by the poolside nirvana played out against "Spill the Wine." It's been widely pointed out that the pool-party sequence borrows/plagiarizes from *I Am Cuba*, which I remember Cameron Bailey commending for its "delirious Marxism." Much of *I Am Cuba* is tedious, hollow speechifying; the delirium of Eric Burdon & War is so much more delirious. (One other complaint: I wish Paul Thomas Anderson had gone for "Do Ya" over the end credits instead of "Livin' Thing." You shouldn't sacrifice a lesser song for the sake of a joke—and "Do Ya" would have worked as a punch line too.)

(#1 video, year-end ballot, 1997)

Freeze-Frame

Gavin Smith: Pop music is used in films, at least at one level, to cue the audience to what era it is.
Martin Scorsese: Oh, no, no, forget that, no.
—*Film Comment* interview, 1990

In any given year, 80 percent of my musical epiphanies take place in the car, one percent happen in front of the stereo, clubs and concerts account for zero percent, and the rest I get from the movies. When it comes to melding pop music to image, 20 years of Madonna, the Beastie Boys, or anybody else on MTV hasn't produced anything quite so startling as sequences found in recent films by the Andersons Paul (*Boogie Nights*) and Wes (*Rushmore*). These musical detours are elaborate enough and sufficiently self-contained that you could yank any one of them right out and you'd have a contender for Greatest Music Video Ever Made, and the same can be said of ready-made videos scattered across the work of Martin Scorsese, Quentin Tarantino, and other pop-crazy directors.

Scorsese, of course, represents the single most inescapable reference point for any director today who tries to choreograph movie narrative to a pop-music backdrop. Almost every Scorsese film has a signature musical moment or two (high on my own list would be Jackson Browne's "Late for the Sky" in *Taxi Driver*, Ray Barretto's "El Watusi" in *Who's That Knocking at My Door?*, plus at least a dozen inspired matches found in *Mean Streets* and *Goodfellas*), but by the time of 1995's *Casino* he was straining to outdo himself. This year's *Bringing Out the Dead* again finds Scorsese in a holding pattern. The Clash's "Janie Jones" and the Cellos' "Rang Tang Ding Dong (I Am the Japanese Sandman)" leap out thrillingly for a few seconds before being cut short, while Big Brother's "Combination of the Two" is regrettably buried in the background. Scorsese betrays the two most fundamental rules he's been teaching disciples for years: Let it play, and play it loud.

Quentin Tarantino and Paul Thomas Anderson learned better than anyone, emerging in the '90s as the first really serious competition Scorsese's ever had as cinema's number-one cut-creator. Tarantino, you know about—deservedly or not, *Pulp Fiction*'s (1994) bang-bang mix of Dick Dale, Chuck Berry, and Dusty Springfield generated more widespread awareness and adulation of a rock and roll soundtrack than anything since 1973's *American Graffiti*. As much as I like how Tarantino used all of the above, he also committed the major sin of wasting Al Green's "Let's Stay Together" in the same film. I much prefer not only *Reservoir Dogs*' (1992) seismic K-Tel jolts (George Baker Selection, Blue Swede, Stealer's Wheel) but also the serene world-weariness that marks the Delfonics, Bobby Womack, and Johnny Cash in 1998's *Jackie Brown*.

Maybe Tarantino suddenly felt old after he saw Paul Thomas Anderson's *Boogie Nights* (1997), which felt like one of those "Oh yeah?—top this" dares that McGwire and Griffey throw at each other during All-Star Home Run Derbys. Anderson's sympathetic ensemble piece matched the freewheeling sweep of *Goodfellas* to the esoteric junkiness of *Reservoir Dogs* and advanced the art of the rock and roll soundtrack a little further still: the pool party sequence to Eric Burdon and War's "Spill the Wine," a deviant's living-room Fourth of July festivities to Night Ranger's "Sister Christian," the vacant rot in Burt Reynolds's face posed against the Chakachas' "Jungle Fever" and Melanie's "Brand New Key." Toward the end, a profound pop-music moment—with chaos breaking loose all around, Wahlberg finds himself caught up in Rick Springfield's "Jessie's Girl" and a smile of deep recognition begins to cross his face.

Wes Anderson's (no relation) *Rushmore*, a last-minute '98 release I've seen six times this year, may be even better. Certainly it's something new—*Boogie Nights*, *Reservoir Dogs*, and *Goodfellas* belong to the time-honored tradition of low-life mooks that goes back to *The Wild One* and *Blackboard Jungle*, but *Rushmore* is more like *Being Pete Townshend*, a prep-school fantasy that comes from somewhere inside the same head that imagined the misfit heroes of "I'm a Boy," "Pictures of Lily," and *Quadrophenia*. The Who actually do turn up in *Rushmore*, a generously uninterrupted two minutes of "A Quick One While He's Away" as Jason Schwartzman, Anderson's own misfit hero, squares off against his equally maladapted mentor (Bill Murray) in a spectacularly vindictive display of one-upmanship. Elsewhere, semi-obscurities from the Rolling Stones ("I Am Waiting") and the Kinks ("Nothin' in the World Can Stop Me Worryin' 'Bout That Girl") definitively capture adolescent self-pity and middle-age spite, while buoyant contributions from Cat Stevens, the Faces, and John Lennon mirror the more irrepressible side of Schwartzman's Max Fischer. The movie opens with the Creation's "Making Time" over an indescribable résumé of Max's extracurricular pursuits, including such high-profile campus favorites as fencing, beekeeping, model aviation, and bombardment. If I had to choose, the "Making Time" sequence in *Rushmore* would be the one: my nomination for Greatest Music Video Ever Made.

No other film in 1999 came anywhere close to *Rushmore* as a pop-music event, but a few things caught my attention. I spent the first half-hour of *Lock, Stock, and Two Smoking Barrels* fidgeting through the by-now-familiar drill of déjà Tarantino, but then the Castaways' "Liar, Liar" appeared out of nowhere and the same old clichés seemed vital again. *American Beauty* is at its wildest when Kevin Spacey punches up the Guess Who's "American Woman" on the car radio, with a too-few seconds of Free's "All Right Now" further underscoring Spacey's liberating descent into the kingdom of who-gives-a-fuck. *The Limey* opens with the Who's "The Seeker," which it serendipitously shares with *American Beauty*, and ends with a poignant old clip of Terence Stamp strumming Donovan, secret hero of '90s film scores (cf. *Goodfellas*, *To Die For*, *Election*). And though I don't often take much notice of newer soundtrack music, the combination of Nicole Kidman eyeing herself in the mirror and Chris Isaak's "Baby Did a Bad Bad Thing" was the one time *Eyes Wide Shut* lived up to the promise of its amazing trailer.

On the downside, David O. Russell's *Three Kings* starts off like it's going to salvage those strange few months in pop history between Milli Vanilli and Nirvana (Snap, Public Enemy's "Can't Do Nuttin' For Ya Man," Rare Earth standing in for M.C. Hammer), but the music soon dries up completely in the Kuwaiti desert; Russell does manage to sneak in "In God's Country," the only U2 song I've ever really loved, over the end credits. *Boys Don't Cry* has the Isley Brothers, Timmy Thomas, and Lynyrd Skynyrd, but to little effect; when the Cure-originated title track finally appears and turns out to be a cover, you feel cheated. Spike Lee's *Summer of Sam* stands alongside *Bringing Out the Dead* as the year's major letdown. Lee's done some terrific things in the past with "Livin' for the City" and "Erotic City," but he stumbles badly with the Who's "Won't Get Fooled Again" and "Baba O'Riley," resulting in a couple of big showcase montages even more overwrought than the rest of the film. I barely remember a thing from *Outside Providence* or *200 Cigarettes*, both of which belong to the *Flamingo Kid* school of soundtracks: "Hey, the Drifters—it must be 1960."

Thanks to the Andersons, the rest hardly matter. *Rushmore* and *Boogie Nights* have meant more to me the past couple of years than my favorite new music during that time, and I'm betting that both will become sacred texts to a new generation of rock and roll filmmakers. Being someone who once had aspirations of making the Great Pop Movie myself (until all that technical stuff about knowing how to write scripts and operate cameras got in the way), watching them's also a bit of a bittersweet experience. When someone really gets it right, which in the 35 years since *A Hard Day's Night* and Kenneth Anger's *Scorpio Rising* has happened surprisingly infrequently, there's always a part of me that wishes it'd been me instead.

(*Village Voice*, 1999)

in and around the lake

One of my secretly important little gestures known only to me was alphabetizing the songlist for each issue of *Radio On* by song title rather than artist. So it was "Counting Blue Cars," Dishwalla, rather than Dishwalla, "Counting Blue Cars." Seems like the obvious thing to do in retrospect—we were rating and writing about songs, trying to figure out why blue cars were being counted and how we felt about that, not artists—but in terms of how rock criticism works, doing so was almost counter-intuitive. To this day, Pazz & Jop's year-end singles list places artist first, song title second. If you're thinking *"Who could possibly care?"* right about now, sympathy. And for all I know, Pazz & Jop's formatting may amount to nothing more than clerical convenience.

But trying to hear music apart from whoever happens to be making it—or at least to minimize the biases and preconceptions and general noise that get in the way of hearing and responding to something for what it actually is—is an ongoing challenge I've been preoccupied with for as long as I've been writing about music, especially in the pages of *Radio On*, where you were confronted by all manner of surprises-waiting-to-happen if you were open to them. Or, as Greil Marcus once put it, "On Top 40 (I don't care what it's called now), Pia Zadora could make the best record of 1987, and we'd all (those of us honest enough to admit it) be scurrying to figure out what that meant. It wouldn't mean anything, other than that the radio is still a good, weird machine." (As always, please substitute modern-day equivalents for my antiquated reference points: Dishwalla = Imagine Dragons, Pia Zadora = Robin Thicke.)

So The-Song-Not-the-Singer is, as much as humanly possible, a guiding principle. Which doesn't mean I don't have my favorite artists—of course I do, like anyone does. (It's always a good idea to introduce something with a convoluted attempt to explain the exact opposite.) Here then is my own personal pantheon, along with, in a convention of the record inventory called "mixworthy," accompanying lists of the songs that put them there. I've left the lists as originally posted (there was a 10-song maximum in place), with a few exceptions: those for Madonna and the Pet Shop Boys have been expanded (adding some key CD-era songs), and—call CNN—a Yo La Tengo mixworthy list has been created special for this book.

Apologies to the Byrds and Sly & the Family Stone—they belong here too, just couldn't find anything I've written about them that I liked enough. Wussy, you're on your way.

----

interrupting my train of thought

Beatles

"Eight Days a Week" and "Every Little Thing," *Beatles for Sale*; "I Need You," "Ticket to Ride," and "Tell Me What You See," *Help!*; "I've Just Seen a Face" and "Norwegian Wood," *Rubber Soul*; "She Said She Said," *Revolver*; "Long, Long, Long," *The Beatles*; "Rain," *Hey Jude*

Three years ago, I organized a school-wide Beatles assembly where I teach. I was so completely immersed in everything to do with the Beatles for the weeks leading up to the assembly—music and quizzes on the morning announcements, a display case, posters, rehearsing four students to re-enact the Sullivan performance—that I've been a little Beatled-out ever since. (The assembly was amazing: being in a gym filled with 400 kids clapping along to the "Ticket to Ride" sequence from *Help!*, roaring with laughter, was as good as teaching ever gets.) But that doesn't mean I'm tired of my favorite Beatles music in the way that I can get tired of the Beach Boys or the Rolling Stones. Obviously there are specific songs I'd be content to never hear again—"Day Tripper," "Come Together," and "Drive My Car" would head the list—but I think I can honestly say I never get tired of *the Beatles*; there's never a time where I won't hear something like "Ticket to Ride" or "Eight Days a Week" and just be floored by its brilliance. I have a theory that in the whole history of the universe—the whole thing, from ground zero till today—the Beatles have brought more happiness into the world than any other four people who ever lived. Religion? No chance. Christ, Allah, the Buddah, whatever—however much happiness and comfort you want to attribute to any religious figure, real or imagined, there's a lot of misery and guilt and destructive zealotry on the other side of the ledger. With the Beatles, there's no downside—there's just thousands upon thousands upon millions of people who have also heard a certain song at a certain moment and had everything else just fall away as complete and utter happiness takes over.

(record inventory, 2005-06)

Shiva Shiva, Y'All

I didn't find out about George Harrison's death until the morning after, just as I set out on my drive into work. Stories a few weeks earlier had said he was gravely ill, but the news still came as a surprise. I turned the car around and hurried back to tape something to play for my grade six class.

Quick decision: what?

Not surprisingly, all you heard on the radio that morning was "Something" and "My Sweet Lord," with rock stations veering as far afield as "While My Guitar Gently Weeps." I like them all, but I knew they weren't what I wanted the class to hear. I considered the ecstatic chime of "What Is Life" instead, or maybe "I Need You," one of my two or three favorite Beatles songs. *The White Album*'s luminous "Long, Long, Long" was also a possibility.

I chose "Norwegian Wood." After trying to convey to the students something of the significance of George's death—that while he wasn't a colossus like John or Paul, he had been a living Beatle nonetheless, a precious resource in increasingly short supply—I told them that the song they were going to hear wasn't one of George's, but his contribution to it was integral, and I thought it stood as his greatest two minutes as a Beatle.

Students have always responded favorably to whatever Beatles music I've played in the past, but I wasn't sure how they'd react to the sheer strangeness of "Norwegian Wood." Their response was one of the most gratifying things I've experienced as a teacher. They listened attentively, following along with the lyrics I'd written on the board, and when the song finished—no sentimental exaggeration at all—two or three of them spontaneously began to clap. They stopped just as quickly as they started, undoubtedly feeling a little goofy, but the point had been made. I think, and hope, that those two or three students were thinking they'd never heard anything so quiet, so still, so perfect before.

(*Village Voice*, 2002)

John Coltrane

"My Favorite Things," *My Favorite Things*; "Chasin' the Trane," *Coltrane "Live" at the Village Vanguard*; "Out of This World," *Coltrane*; "Afro-Blue" and "Alabama," *Coltrane Live at Birdland*; "Part 1 – Acknowledgement," *A Love Supreme*

It was my first-year roommate at university, Tom Mayock, who first played John Coltrane for me. It was a compilation, I think. Trying to piece together the exact sequence of events that led to me ending up with 19 albums is difficult, but I know that the turning point was when he sent me a copy of *A Love Supreme* after my second year. (I think I'd already acquired *My Favorite Things* on my own by that point; Tom dropped out in spectacular fashion after failing all but one of his first-year courses, which, I probably don't need to add, was not a measure of anything except the fact that he never wanted to be there in the first place—one of the smartest guys I've ever met.) The really bizarre thing—this part of the story mystifies me—is that I had to pick up the album (there were two, actually—one of the live records the other, I think) from Paul McGrath, a guy who covered pop music for *The Globe and Mail* years ago. You'll see a quote from Paul on that famous full-page ad for the Ramones' first LP, the one that mixed ecstatic raves with horrified aneurysms; Paul's quote was one of the most horrified. I think he was a friend of Tom's brother, and that's as much as I can figure out—why was I picking up these albums from him?! Anyway, I have an amazingly vivid memory of listening to *A Love Supreme* for the first time—it's kind of corny, but absolutely true. When I put it on, I'd been up for some 30 hours finishing an essay, my last one of the year—a weird badge of honour among university students, something I used to be able to do easily, whereas now I have difficulty staying awake through a two-hour movie. A great calm always settles over you when the school year finishes—I still experience it today as a teacher—so as I listened along to "Part 1 - Acknowledgement," half hypnotized by its tranciness and half drifting in and out of sleep, it felt like I was in the middle of some meaningful brush with serenity. And then, towards the end, the chanting: "a love supreme, a love supreme..." I clearly remember wondering if I was hallucinating when the chanting started up; a voice was the last thing I expected to hear, and there was a flat, druid-like quality to it that seemed to belong to the world of hallucinations. (If it had been 1991 instead of 1983, I'd have been checking under the bed for Bob from *Twin Peaks*.) It remains one of the great musical moments of my life, right up there with similarly life-altering encounters with "Cowgirl in the Sand," *Taxi Driver*, and *The Catcher in the Rye*. Over time, "My Favorite Things" has become the song I play most often, and I'm fairly sure I've listened to that more than any other piece of music I own. I think it's one of those works of art that contains the world—it's *Ulysses*, it's *Citizen Kane*, it's "Guernica," it's one of the great achievements of human history. (Please don't ask me if I've read *Ulysses*—work with me here.) And I'll stop there, because I have to keep a few superlatives in reserve for *Black Vinyl Shoes*.

(record inventory, 2005-06)

in and around the lake

"My Favorite Things," John Coltrane (1961)

I wrote a fairly detailed account of how I came to John Coltrane when I inventoried my album collection a few years ago. The short version: *My Favorite Things* was the first jazz album I ever owned. I also have the song itself on a couple of CDs—an expanded Rhino reissue of the original LP, which appends both halves of the 45 issue of "My Favorite Things" (yes, it was released as a single, with an A-side running 2:45; I find that kind of amusing), and also the Ken Burns Coltrane collection. I don't own the *Sound of Music* soundtrack, and haven't seen the film in 40+ years.

One thing that's clear to me is that the circumstance of having "My Favorite Things" as my introduction to jazz ensured that there would always be a limit to how much of a fan I would ever be of the form. Everything I've ever heard subsequently gets measured against "My Favorite Things," and everything falls short. Everything: Monk, Charlie Parker, Billie Holiday, Charles Mingus, Duke Ellington, Sonny Rollins, etc., etc., etc. Grachan Moncur's "When" comes close—because, guess what, it reminds me of Coltrane—Oliver Nelson's "Stolen Moments" comes close, and so do a couple of Miles Davis tracks, "Flamenco Sketches" and (with Coltrane playing alongside) "Milestones." (And, within Coltrane's own body of work, "A Love Supreme.") But everything else, even though I can (and do) enjoy it and understand its importance, ultimately it's something I appreciate more than respond to emotionally. I started at the top of Mount Everest, then began to survey the land below. Again, that's me; for someone else, maybe Louis Armstrong's Mount Everest.

I started reading Ben Ratliff's *Coltrane: The Story of a Sound* a few months ago, and the bookmark hasn't moved from page 29 since a week after I began. It's a meticulously technical book, undoubtedly very insightful if that's the prism though which you respond to Coltrane. For me, music's an abstraction. Some people like for that abstraction to be explained, to learn how it was put together, and some people are very good at explaining it. I have, over time, learned to respect the idea that knowing a lot about the inner workings of music is very useful, and worth imparting to others if you're able to do so. Sounds weird that anyone might believe otherwise, but otherwise is somewhere close to where I used to be—a belief that the more you knew about the technical side of a piece of music, the more you'd find yourself distracted from zeroing in on what was really important about it. I don't believe that anymore. But on a personal level, I still have an impressionistic understanding of music, and I don't see that ever changing. I'm able to figure out that what I most love about "My Favorite Things" has more to do with

McCoy Tyner's long middle section than with Coltrane himself. Tyner's part of the song is where I lose myself; Coltrane is the frame. That's about as technical as I'm capable of getting when trying to describe what I hear in a jazz or classical piece of music. Well, also that Tyner's playing always makes me think of "Linus and Lucy" from *A Charlie Brown Christmas*.

I also respect the idea that sometimes what's most important about a piece of music is beyond articulation. That's a convenient way for me to sneak out of here without ever saying what it is I hear in "My Favorite Things," but I do believe the truth of that. It would take a great deal of time and a great deal of effort to find exactly the right words, but in the end, I don't think you could do it. I couldn't, anyway.

(#2, Facebook Top 100, 2010-11)

Creedence Clearwater Revival

"Bad Moon Rising," *Green River*; "Fortunate Son," *Willy and the Poor Boys*; "Ramble Tamble," "Up Around the Band," and "Who'll Stop the Rain," *Cosmo's Factory*

Seeing the Cramps, Crazy Cavan, the Crawdaddys, and Creedence in the same batch is instructive as to the paths available to anyone whose worship of the past becomes a guiding principle: you're either a novelty act from the outset (Crazy Cavan and the Crawdaddys); an inspired imitation for an album or two, until your lack of a second idea reduces you to a novelty act (Cramps); or you reinvent what you love and reflect your times in complicated ways that are still difficult to get a handle on 35 years later—that would be Creedence Clearwater Revival. I think that among people in my general demographic—rather than give an age bracket, I'll just say anyone who remembers hearing "Up Around the Bend" while it was still on the charts—there's more goodwill towards Creedence than virtually anyone from the era. Maybe anyone, period—you'll see the Beatles get knocked around now and again, but I don't know that I've ever come across a truly negative word said or written about Creedence Clearwater Revival. They were brilliant, they owned Top 40, and they came and went in the blink of an eye.

(record inventory, 2005-06)

"Ramble Tamble," Creedence Clearwater Revival (1970)

New Year's Day—you need something to wake you up, I can tell. "Ramble Tamble"'s one of the greatest album-openers ever (1970 was a spectacular year for album-openers), with two minutes of what I believe is called, in Creedence-speak, "choogling"—yes, choogling—giving way to a wash of majestic and atypically (for CCR) meditative drone. Unlike "Bad Moon Rising" or "Fortunate Son" or "Up Around the Bend," it's the rare masterpiece of theirs that hasn't been played to death on classic-rock radio. I used to own an 8-track of *Cosmo's Factory*—I bet "Ramble Tamble" had program one all to itself. A user comment from YouTube: "38 years ago when I was on a ship in Viet Nam I used to BLAST this song on the mess decks while I was scrubbing pots in the galley." I can't beat that.

(#65, Facebook Top 100, 2010-11)

Bob Dylan

"She Belongs to Me," *Bringing It All Back Home*; "Like a Rolling Stone," "Just Like Tom Thumb's Blues," and "Desolation Row," *Highway 61 Revisited*; "Rainy Day Women #12 & 35," Blonde on Blonde; "I'll Keep It with Mine," *Great White Wonder II*; "Can You Please Crawl Out Your Window?" *A Rare Batch of Little White Wonder - Volume 3*; "Positively 4th Street," *Bob Dylan's Greatest Hits*; "You Ain't Goin' Nowhere," *Bob Dylan's Greatest Hits Vol. II*; "Tangled Up in Blue," *Blood on the Tracks*

Owning *Royal Albert Hall* (ninth-generation copy? I bought it in '79 or '80 from the Record Peddler, which always racked a few dozen bootlegs before they vacated the Queen St. address) and the two *White Wonder* albums doesn't seem like as big a deal as it used to be, before CBS released all that stuff legitimately. My version of "I'll Keep It With Mine," which to me is Dylan's most stunningly beautiful ballad ever, is missing the insane banter with Tom Wilson that prefaces the sanctioned CBS version: "This one's called, uh, 'Bank Account Blues'!"...I just finished *Memoirs* this past weekend, having gotten about two-thirds of the way through many months ago before putting it aside. It's such a weird book—whatever version of Dylan you carry around in your head, there are enough anomalous juxtapositions and almost surrealistically mundane bits of description scattered throughout to stop anyone short:

interrupting my train of thought

"Whether he really said it or not, it didn't matter. It's what I thought I heard him say that mattered, and I never forgot it. It was all the recognition and encouragement I would need for years to come. Sometimes that's all it takes, the kind of recognition that comes when you're doing the thing for the thing's sake and you're on to something—it's just that nobody recognizes it yet. Gorgeous George. A mighty spirit."

From anyone else, a passage you wouldn't even notice. From the guy who imagined a world where Ezra Pound and T.S. Eliot trade barbs while Cinderella does Bette Davis impressions and down-on-their-luck monks recite the alphabet, kind of disorienting—in a good way, I think...Even if albums were still the format of choice, I bet my Dylan collection would stop mid-'70s nonetheless. I'm just not that interested in his acclaimed work of the past 10+ years. I haven't heard nearly enough of it to make a convincing case as to why I feel that way, but I do. (I listened to *Love and Theft* in its entirety and got very little out of it. I have a feeling I'd like *Time Out of Mind* better.) The short version: he's not a very good singer anymore, and by "good," obviously I don't mean in a technical sense. The irony is, I'm sometimes acutely aware of situations where an artist continues to do great work beyond a point where people have decided that he or she isn't vital enough to warrant close attention anymore. The Pet Shop Boys immediately come to mind. With Dylan, though, those mid-'60s albums that had such a profound effect on me in high school were enough. Even if the story has indeed broadened and deepened these past few years, the first telling was rich enough for me that nothing more ever needed to be said.

(record inventory, 2005-06)

Logorrhea (Top 10 of the 2000s)

#7: *No Direction Home: Bob Dylan* (Martin Scorsese, 2005): A friend of mine has assured me that this is Dylan's film, not Scorsese's—starting with the fact that all of Dylan's interviews were conducted with an interviewer of his choice, probably even wholly scripted by him (cf. Nate Hentoff in 1966, if legend is to be believed). Maybe; I honestly don't know, and I'm not sure it makes a difference. There's just so much stuff to lose yourself in here, and out of the morass, the chaotic sweep of events, a story does come into focus, one that has something to do with the way Dylan spends much of the film trying to disengage himself from those events, constantly reminding the interviewer that all of that—politics, folk music, glamour, "the sixties"—was their thing, not his. Nothing new, I guess, he's been feinting and dodging forever; *I'm Not There* might have been a good title too. There's a multiplicity of other stories that come into focus, too, criss-crossing all over each other, and they're harder to sort out. In one of my favorite conceits in the film, the Beatles get acknowledged exactly twice: once verbally (something along the lines of "Would you ask the Beatles that?!" at one of those toxic press conferences), the other time as a listing in *Billboard* (in a close-up of the chart where "Like a Rolling Stone" hits #2, you can see the Beatles sitting at #1 with "Help"). "Oh yeah, those guys..." That very noticeable omission is a pretty good story in and of itself.

(homepage, 2010)

Al Green

"Let's Stay Together," *Let's Stay Together*; "I'm Still in Love with You," *I'm Still in Love with You*; "Have You Been Making Out O.K." and "You Ought to Be With Me," *Call Me*; "Sha La La (Makes Me Happy)," *Al Green Explores Your Mind*; "Tired of Being Alone," *Greatest Hits*

Al Green Explores Your Mind might be my favorite album title ever—definitively psychedelic, but also suggestive of *They Saved Hitler's Brain* or some other grade-Z horror film. The cover's just a shot of Al smiling; they could easily have come up with something a lot more twisted...I'm glad I never had to make any effort to discover Al Green. I likely would have taken to him no matter what, but who knows, if I were a few years younger, he might have been someone where I'd read too much about him beforehand for his records ever to live up to expectations. I think that's something that plays a part in understanding my indifference to James Brown and Otis Redding; it has much more to do with matters of style (and sure enough, as Al Green veers closer to Otis Redding on something like "I Can't Get Next to You," I stop liking him), but the fact that I'd read so much deification of *Live at the Apollo* and *Otis Blue* before I ever owned either album almost guaranteed some measure of letdown. With Al Green, all of that is a non-issue; he was there, on the radio, right alongside the Carpenters, Bread, Badfinger, and all my other favorite music when I first started obsessing over Top 40 radio in 1972, so he's thoroughly embedded in the mystery and romance of that moment for me. If equating Al Green with the Carpenters seems nonsensica to you, all I can say is that a) you weren't 11 years old in 1972, and b) you need to see *The Virgin Suicides* a.s.a.p.

(record inventory, 2005-06)

Hüsker Dü

"Everything Falls Apart," *Everything Falls Apart*; "Real World" and "It's Not Funny Anymore," *Metal Circus*; "Something I Learned Today," *Zen Arcade*; "Books About UFOs," *New Day Rising*; "Flip Your Wig," "Makes No Sense at All," and "Divide and Conquer," *Flip Your Wig*

I don't feel the need to relisten to any Hüsker Dü; I've listed the same eight songs I would have listed 20 years ago, with the other two spots reserved for "Eight Miles High" and "Love Is All Around," both 45-only. The only other music that ever dominated my life to the extent that Hüsker Dü's did from *Metal Circus* through to their break-up was Neil Young's my last three years of high school. (I've recently downloaded pretty much the entirety of Stereolab's output, but the non-Stereolab part of my life proceeds exactly as before. It's not quite the same thing.) The timing was perfect. *Metal Circus* came out as I was heading into my final year of university—I didn't hear the two earlier, lesser releases till later—and everything about the record and the group just clicked with me. It was loud and abrasive, like most of what I listened to at the time, but there was also a majestic wash of songcraft and melody carrying the din along, and that spoke to the 12-year-old pop fan in me who'd never really forgotten "Hello It's Me" and "Baby Blue," even if I hadn't given them any thought for years. It's a little harder to reconstruct how the words hit me—meaning there was a lot about myself then I don't necessarily want to think about now—but they got those exactly right too. After a step back with *Zen Arcade* (the record generally singled out as their greatest; I've always been in the minority there), they went farther with *New Day Rising*, farther still with *Flip Your Wig*, then finished with two albums that, even though I don't have room to list anything from either, were both very good. I was right with them the whole way, and when they packed it in at the precise moment when my own tastes were starting to change drastically, the timing was again perfect. How imperfect the timing was for Hüsker Dü is something you could think about for a long time and not get anywhere. They affected me much more than Nirvana did, but the fact remains that Hüsker Dü didn't reach even 1% of the people "Smells Like Teen Spirit" did, and there's no reason to think they would have under any circumstances. They likely wouldn't even be famous if *Metal Circus* had come out eight years later than it did—I'm pretty sure they didn't have a video as monumental as the one for "Smells Like Teen Spirit" anywhere inside them, the launch point for everything that transpired with Nirvana, and absent that, *Metal Circus* might have come and gone quietly in 1991, with not even enough critical interest to secure a follow-up. So maybe the timing was perfect for them, too—not on a personal level (you read some very strange stories about Grant Hart), and not financially, either, but in creating the context in which they thrived: Michael Jackson and Madonna and Bruce Springsteen doing important things over there, but for anyone who didn't need to hear about that, there was Hüsker Dü doing important things over here, and doing them so amazingly well that over here felt like a world much, much bigger than it ever actually was.

(record inventory, 2005-06)

"Divide and Conquer," Hüsker Dü (1985)

For most of my life, I've told people I'm not political. Mostly that's been true, and it mostly still is. But: if you've been voting for one side, without exception, for 30 years, and if you more and more find certain tendencies of the other side to be increasingly obnoxious, obviously you're something of a political person. I suppose I'm also becoming political in the worst way: I'll shrug off the faults of politicians I support—yes, I'm talking about Obama here—being of the mind that pushing back too vociferously, or deciding that you'll voice your disappointment by not voting at all, creates the conditions whereby the other side takes over, and then, good luck, you're welcome to whatever you get. Which, understandably, is going to exasperate anyone who's more political than I am. Which I why I still say I'm not political.

I was much less given to such mundane resignation ("realpolitik" I think it's called, even though I try to avoid such terms) in my 20s; I reliably voted liberal, but basically hated the whole charade, putting me perfectly in sync with the inchoate disgust found on a number of Hüsker Dü songs. I've had them, not surprisingly if you know me, on every one of my previous Top 100s, but I tended to tilt towards the Grant Hart pop side of the band— "It's Not Funny Anymore" on one of them, and "Books About UFO's" on the CKLN list. (I can't remember, but I may have gone with "Eight Miles High" on the third.) And that's still the side that I'm partial to. But on "Real World," "Something I Learned Today," "Newest Industry," "Eight Miles

High," and "Divide and Conquer," they communicated everything I felt at the time about pretty much every politician out there (excepting Trudeau). Which was what? I don't know—inchoate disgust is difficult to formulate into words. The closest I can come is "I'll sit around and smoke cigarettes/ And babble 'What the fuck?'" from "Newest Industry." Except for the cigarette smoking, that was me in my 20s. I also like that they had the good manners to spell out "What the fuck," before everybody was in such a hurry. "Divide and Conquer" is a whirlwind bridge between the pop side and the inchoateness (I had to check, but yes, it's a word). It's like "Complete Control," in that it finds Bob Mould exceedingly agitated about things like zip codes, shopping malls, and, in what must be a shout-out to Wire, lines of longitude and latitude…I'm kidding; it's about globalization, and urban sprawl, and loss of privacy, and money-changes-everything, and lots of serious stuff. But it's Hüsker Dü, not the Disciples of Hiphoprisy or Rage Against the Machine (or whoever their 2011 equivalent is), so all of his babbling is housed inside a hypnotic cascade of ringing guitar and an unexpected grace-note of la-la-la's towards the end. I continue to be awestruck by how great Hüsker Dü were on songs like "Divide and Conquer."

(#11, Facebook Top 100, 2010-11)

Five Favorite Covers

1) "I Say a Little Prayer," Aretha Franklin (1968)
2) "Love Is All Around," Hüsker Dü (1985)
3) "I'll Keep It with Mine," Nico (1967)
4) "Only Love Can Break Your Heart," St. Etienne (1992)
5) "Where the Streets Have No Name/Can't Take My Eyes Off You," Pet Shop Boys (1991)

1) I doubt that Aretha Franklin set out to cover Dionne Warwick (whose version made the charts a few months earlier) as much as she just wanted to get something written by the then-very-marketable Burt Bacharach onto one of her albums. Given the choice between a show-offy soul version and a sweet pop version of the same song (the difference between Otis Redding and Al Green, roughly speaking), the pop version will sound better to me almost every time. This is the exception, and it's not even close. I can barely even remember Dionne Warwick's "Say a Little Prayer" anymore. 2) I'd compare this to "Rainy Day Women #12 & 35": a joyous romp, a work of supreme confidence, appearing at the end of a masterful run. Out-

side of a perfectly placed "doo-doo-doo" at the end, I never thought there was even a trace of jokiness about it, just a bunch of guys my age (and from Minnesota, besides) swooning nostalgically for that slow-motion image of Mary Richards tossing her hat into the air. You could probably just as easily hear nothing but jokiness, and that'd be fine too. 3) Speaking of Bob Dylan, I've been listening to certain songs from the '65-66 period a lot recently: "She Belongs to Me," "Just Like Tom Thumb's Blues," "Desolation Row." I have five songs from *Love and Theft* on tape; they must be the wrong five, because I'm at a complete loss to understand how anyone who loves the former can consider the latter to be in the same stratosphere. I was used to Nico's "I'll Keep It with Mine" by the time I got the original on a bootleg; comparing the two, hers is sufficiently different and just as beautiful. 4) A rebuke to the eternally pointless *Trans*, where Neil Young had the idea that using machines meant he had to make his music sound inhuman. 5) I like this a lot, but just on the merits, I'd rather hear the Turtles' "You Showed Me," SWV's "Right Here (Human Nature)" (which may not really count as a cover), Sinead O'Connor's "Nothing Compares 2 U," Ace of Base's "Cruel Summer" (eligible under the sufficiently-different-unless-it's-virtually-identical rule), and probably a few dozen other things I missed. I couldn't think of any way to round up candidates beyond just scanning my record shelves, and with at least a thousand covers buried in there, I know I must have missed something. Anyway, I love the story behind the Pet Shop Boys record. Neil Tennant used to ridicule U2 every chance he got around the time of *The Joshua Tree*—for good reason, as it must have dismayed him to see the singles from that album finish higher in critics' polls than "What Have I Done to Deserve This?" Tennant was really funny about it, too, but in a way he came across as a different version of the same purist Bono is: one wanted you to believe that the Pet Shop Boys could never make a record as good as B.B. King, the other was unable to concede that U2 might have it in them to write a pop song as good as Rick Astley. To Tennant's credit, he did admit as much with "Where the Streets Have No Name." I don't think Bono would ever be able to make the same imaginative leap with a cover of "West End Girls" or "Being Boring."

(rockcritics.com, 2002)

Jefferson Airplane

"Let Me In," "Come Up the Years," and "Run Around," *Jefferson Airplane Takes Off*; "Today," *Surrealistic Pillow*; "Won't You Try/Saturday Afternoon," *After Bathing at Baxter's*; "We Can Be Together," *Volunteers*; "It's No Secret," *Bless Its Pointed Little Head*; "Runnin' 'Round This World" and "Mexico," *Early Flight*

Yes, the Jefferson Airplane match up with almost anybody for me. It's their sound that I love—the folk-rock drone, the harmonies, the fact that at their strangest, they usually managed to come up with melodies that lifted even their most pretentious songs back to life. (No argument here—they definitely knew how to get pretentious.) *The Worst of Jefferson Airplane* was also one of the first half-dozen albums in my collection, and that proved to be an excellent gateway into the regular-issue LPs I went on to buy a few years later. A quick ranking of the first five: 1. *Jefferson Airplane Takes Off*; 2. *After Bathing at Baxter's*; 3. *Surrealistic Pillow/Volunteers/Crown of Creation*. The first two are mostly great from start to finish, the other three have strengths and weaknesses in almost equal measure. Not sure why, but I passed on *Bark* and *Long John Silver* a number of times. I wish now I hadn't—I bet there's at least a song or two on each worth saving. Jefferson Starship wasn't bad; Starship was easy to confuse with Survivor, Sheriff, and Michael Sembello; happily, they seem to have called it a day before Ship ever materialized.

(record inventory, 2005-06)

"Genesis," Jorma Kaukonen (1974)

Or maybe it's "Jorma Kaukonen" by Genesis, how should I know? (old Chuck Eddy joke)…The first of three Airplane-related songs on my list, and also the first of three found in Noel Baumbach films. In this instance I knew the song before seeing the film, but just barely—I found it on my own maybe a year before it turned up in *Margot at the Wedding*. Nothing especially noteworthy about how it's used; the principals are sitting around Jennifer Jason Leigh's living room talking, and "Genesis" plays on a turntable or CD player in the background. I don't know how Kaukonen's *Quah* LP escaped my attention for so long, meaning I didn't even know of its existence—there's an entry for it in the first *Rolling Stone Record Guide*, right after important work by Kansas and Gabe Kaplan (nothing in Christgau's

'70s book, though). I've been trying to find an exact release date, as I'm curious about its proximity to Nixon's resignation. The last tracks were laid down in May of '74, so it likely appeared very close on the heels of August 9. One more gateway into a moment in time like no other.

(#51, Facebook Top 100, 2010-11)

"Sea Child," Hot Tuna (1972)

"This is what God sounds like," writes whoever posted this onto YouTube. A bit melodramatic, but I'll more or less second. I could list it much higher, but I've got one more Jorma Kaukonen band coming up—who could it possibly be?—and I want to spread them out a bit. I'm pretty sure he's the only guy who's on my list three times. (Jack Casady produced the Kaukonen song I listed earlier, so you could maybe count him too.) Hot Tuna's such an awful name for a band, I never went near them for 30 years; I believe I mentally filed them away with Meat Loaf, Sleepy LaBeef, and other artists named after popular meats. I don't remember exactly how I came to their LP *Burgers* (named after a popular meat), but now that I know they're mostly a blues band, I haven't made an effort to investigate them any further. "Sea Child" just leaps out of the fray, though, a total anomaly. In terms of the rest of the album, that is—anyone at all in love with Kaukonen's other band is going to connect with it instantly. I really need Sun Grope Guy back here to physically give shape to the intricate rhythmic beauty of "Sea Child." And words—it has words: "Through your hair, across my eyes/The twilight shafts in soft surprise/Reminds me once again how nice/It is to be with you." Hippies just wrote silly cosmic stuff, right? I don't know if those lines are good enough for actual poetry (never something I took to when I was expected to study it), but add Kaukonen and Casady overtop doing their swirly kaleidoscope thing, and they most definitely are. It's a moot point anyway. As a piece of music, "Sea Child" goes places poetry can't.

(#27, Facebook Top 100, 2010-11)

"Thunk," Jefferson Airplane (1971)

I feel like Sollozzo in the first *Godfather* right now: "I'm gonna speak Italian to Steven."

If I were posting on the message board, I'd already have six people yelling "Challops!" at me. (Provocation for provocation's sake; I didn't know what it meant either.) Beyond drawing a blank from anyone who only knows the Jefferson Airplane through "White Rabbit" and "Somebody to Love"—which, thank-you radio, probably accounts for 95% of the pop audience who knows them at all by this point—I doubt "Thunk" would be very well-received by the other 5%. It might even be a song (I'm just guessing here) that's reviled by a lot of Airplane fans. It has very little to do with most of the things I love them for—no Kaukonen/Casady rave-ups, no soaring Grace or ethereal Marty, no Fillmore swirl. It's a near-a capella abstraction that, although it clocks in at three minutes, feels more like a fragment than an actual song. It's weird beyond words.

I saw the Phil Ochs documentary last night, and it was very specific about a transitional moment that interests me a lot: what became of the anti-war movement as it started to wear down around '71 and '72. The film's version of events jibed with what I've read and seen elsewhere—that you either became violently radicalized to a degree that was beyond the pale, like the Weather Underground, or you basically turned away. Which might have meant retreating to a commune, or making a joke of your past (like Ochs), or going the Jerry Rubin route, or any number of things. That's a simplification, I'm sure, but one that's not without validity.

I hear that transitional moment on "Thunk." It's basically about a guy who's sitting around trying to figure something out—superficially, it's a love song, and that's probably all it was meant to be—but gets stuck on the realization that thinking and thinking "ain't do me no good." That's where the song starts, and that's where it ends. Along the way, there's a brief passage that sounds like a hymn: "only a dream" repeated three times. They sound lost and defeated, and I find it all tremendously moving. The Airplane stuck it out for another album or two, I imagine a sad relic by 1973 ("decline and dissolution" is how Wikipedia puts it), at which point they found their own means of turning away.

I've loved the Jefferson Airplane since buying their *Worst Of* compilation early in high school. I'm not completely sure why they've had such a strong hold on me for so long. I bought *Heavy Cream*, *Weird Scenes Inside the Goldmine*, and Hendrix's *Smash Hits* at almost exactly the same time, and, for the duration of high school, more or less played them all to death. With the Doors and Hendrix, whatever appeal they had for me ended immediately upon entering university; my interest in Cream, as indicated by the earlier pick, ebbs and flows. But there's never been a time when I didn't love the Jefferson Airplane. I wish they were viewed with the same kind of reverence as the Beatles or Bob Dylan.

(#16, Facebook Top 100, 2010-11)

Led Zeppelin

"Good Times Bad Times" and "Your Time Is Gonna Come," *Led Zeppelin*; "Whole Lotta Love," *Led Zeppelin II*; "That's the Way" and "Brony-y-aur Stomp," *Led Zeppelin* III; "Black Dog," "Misty Mountain Hop," and "Four Sticks," *Led Zeppelin IV*; "Over the Hills and Far Away," *Houses of the Holy*; "Black Country Woman," *Physical Graffiti*

My favorite thing ever written about Led Zeppelin is Billy Altman's reference to "the indescribably chaotic 'Black Dog'" in *The Rolling Stone Record Guide*. That one short phrase has been lodged in the back of my mind for 25 years; besides getting "Black Dog" exactly right—what a monumentally bizarre song; I can't imagine anyone actually sitting down to write "Black Dog"—it captures something fundamental about Led Zeppelin in general, their indescribability as much as how chaotic they could be. The true mark of genius to me is when you hear or look at or read something and wonder, "Where did that come from?" I think that all the time when I listen to Led Zeppelin. They were so far off on their own tangent at times, and had such an extraordinarily intuitive understanding of what they were doing at a time when the big concern seemed to be how much they were stealing from the blues—a complaint that now seems insanely funny—that to this day I see no credible points of comparison with what came before them, what was around while they were making records, or what followed in their wake. The Beatles sort of go with the Rolling Stones, the Velvet Underground kind of belong with the Stooges and the Dolls, but who can sensibly be compared to Led Zeppelin? Black Sabbath? Deep Purple? Thor? There's an unbridgeable gap in complexity, in surprise, in playfulness, and in all-around inventiveness right down the line. Meanwhile, their chaotic side was marked by a purity and a spontaneity that seems even more impressive to me than, say, the chaos of *Funhouse*, as great a record as that is. The Stooges obviously made it their mission to record the most chaotic album anyone had ever heard, and many would say they succeeded. I doubt that Led Zeppelin ever had anything similar in mind with "Whole Lotta Love," "Black Dog," or "Misty Mountain Hop"—I think they just wanted to make the loudest and liveliest noise they were capable of—but chaotic those songs are, with enough going on in any one of them for five songs. And then there's the improbable delicacy of their slow stuff ("That's the Way"), their gift, when they felt like using it, for pop music ("Over the Hills and Far Away"), and their inexplicable ability to pull off something like "Fool in the Rain." (The timing of *In Through the Out Door* prevented it from ever becoming a part of my life—I didn't buy it until years later—but they definitely signed off with a flourish.) I'll stop there, because I'm just going around in circles. They've regrettably been replaced by Pink Floyd as the house behemoth on Q-107, but Led Zeppelin's place on the shortlist of greatest-ever otherwise seems to become less and less a point of contention with each passing year. *Sui generis* to the max, give or take a borrowed blues chord or two for anyone still keeping track.

(record inventory, 2005-06)

Madonna

"Holiday," *Madonna*; "Shoo-Bee-Doo," *Like a Virgin*; "Get Into the Groove," 12-inch B-side; "Open Your Heart," *True Blue*; "This Used to Be My Playground," *Something to Remember*; "Bad Girl," *Erotica*; "Ray of Light," *Ray of Light*; "Beautiful Stranger," *Austin Powers: The Spy Who Shagged Me (O.S.T.)*; "Don't Tell Me," *Music*; "Miles Away," *Hard Candy*

I mentioned earlier that we wrote a lot about Michael Jackson in *Radio On*; take that and triple it, and that's how much there was on Madonna. By the time I reviewed *Music* a few years later, I think I'd said everything I'd ever conceivably want to say about Madonna. I'll use her instead as an example of something I've noticed while making my way through this, something that applied equally to Janet Jackson when I wrote about her, and that will later apply to the Pet Shop Boys and R.E.M.: that it feels odd writing about people who have large, or at least important, parts of their careers on both sides of the vinyl/CD divide. Most of the artists I'm writing about here are (posthumous compilations excluded) strictly vinyl. There are a lot of others who, even though they've continued to record into the CD era, are (to me, anyway) vinyl artists in spirit if not fact. Rod Stewart would be an obvious example, but I'd also include Neil Young, Dylan, and Lou Reed in that group; the only stuff of theirs I care about predates CDs. The flipside of that would be my favorite music of the past 15 years made by people who (without getting overly nitpicky about it) belong strictly to the CD era. That group is much smaller: Imperial Teen, Stereolab, Yo La Tengo, and a couple of others, none of whom I'll be writing about in this context.

in and around the lake

(Yes, I know, Yo La Tengo dates back to the mid-'80s—one of their early albums will be listed here. But all their best music comes later, well after CDs had dislodged vinyl.) And then there are the in-between people like Madonna and R.E.M. I have albums by them—famous ones like *True Blue* and *Murmur*, LPs that seem very much part of a vinyl continuum stretching back through *Rumours* and *Sgt. Pepper* and *The "Chirping" Crickets*—but they also put out music I love that may not even exist on vinyl: "Ray of Light," "Beautiful Stranger," *Automatic for the People*. (I bet there were a few hundred copies pressed of the latter.) There's vinyl-Madonna and there's CD-Madonna, and the continuity between one and the other feels a little strange to me. Does that make sense?

(record inventory, 2005-06)

"This Used to Be My Playground," Madonna

Is it fair to say that how much you get out of this—not just as a Madonna record to compare to other Madonna records, but as something to hold on to from the inside—depends largely on how much time you spend in the past? Some people spend lots of time there, some very little; it's no secret that those who think about the past very little generally move forward in life, and those who think about it a lot and are able to turn that into something eventually move forward in life, and those who think about it a lot and keep getting tangled up tend not to make out so well. Being the kind of person who wastes sorry amounts of time going over stuff that happened three, five, ten years ago, it's nice to hear a song that says that's OK, that reminds you there's nothing wrong or unusual about that. Satchel Paige had the right idea, but it just doesn't work, I've tried many times. (8.0)

(*Radio On*, 1992)

"Human Nature," Madonna

"Oops! I didn't know I couldn't talk about sex"—good point, it's discouraging how you're not allowed to talk about sex these days. You can be like Jodeci or Adina Howard and talk about freaks and freaking, or be like Primus and talk about big brown beavers, and you definitely don't see enough sex on TV or at the movies anymore, especially if it's something with Michael Douglas or Demi Moore or Sharon Stone. Why doesn't Sharon Stone get over her shyness and make a movie about sex? There's clearly an attractive woman hiding under all those frumpy clothes she insists on wearing...I'm overstating the point, but that's the kind of befuddlement brought on by such an inane line. I know what the counter-argument is: much of what's acceptable today is at least partly so because of Madonna (true), and whereas Madonna really does delve knowingly into the subject of sex and push taboos, all that other stuff that thrives off the climate she helped create is merely superficial and cheap (the subtleties of this second argument are lost on me). "Human Nature" isn't bad on the radio, lots of odd voices weaving in and out, and there are some images in the generally ridiculous video (e.g., spanking the dog; arranging for a monkey in the middle of a video shoot is probably tougher than you think) which catch my eye. But much like "Scream," the persuasiveness of "Human Nature" hinges on a premise which you either accept or don't accept, and if you don't, the record comes across as more than a little self-serving. (5.0)

(*Radio On*, 1995)

"Beautiful Stranger," Madonna (1999)

There was one of those spectacularly awkward reaction shots of Madonna on this year's MTV Awards, right after "Beautiful Stranger" lost Best Female Video to "Doo Wop (That Thing)." As I remember it, her very visible disgust had something on the order of "You fickle, unappreciative bastards" written all over it. Seeing as that's more or less what I was thinking myself (no knock on "Doo Wop," which is great), I may be overstating. I think "Beautiful Stranger" is probably Madonna's greatest single. It has the misfortune of sounding too much like "Ray of Light," and also the stigma of soundtrack-expediency attached to it, so it seemed to slip past a lot of people, both in print and on the charts. It goes even farther than "Ray of Light," though—better melody, better vocal, better light show. It's about the trippiest, most propulsive above-ground dance music since the first two minutes of Led Zeppelin's "How Many More Times"; I hereby christen this exclusive genre Misty Mountain Step-Hop. Getting back to the award show, Madonna got a lifetime's worth of attention around the time of "Justify My Love" and "Erotica" for some very dubious music. Now that her every last thought isn't news anymore, great work unrewarded seems to have her perplexed and impatient. She wears it well.

(#1, year-end ballot, 1999)

in and around the lake

Act of Contrition

Back when Madonna was deep into her silly season—starting as early as "Like a Prayer"'s bombast but really spinning out of control during the months of *Truth or Dare*, "Erotica," and (as we grade-school teachers call them) the picture book—it seemed to be an article of faith, certainly among pop writers who were now paying closer attention to her than ever before, that she was this endlessly fascinating person whose every last public utterance merited some kind of analysis. You weren't supposed to be just a fan of her music anymore, and if that's as far as your allegiance (and attention span) extended, you were missing the bigger picture. Madonna was first and foremost about "transgression"—of taboos and assumptions surrounding sex, gender, race, religion, celebrity, the whole litany. She was debated on *Nightline*; the Pet Shop Boys, who put their name on more cerebral records, never even made it onto *Sunday Morning with Charles Kuralt*.

That was one version of Madonna, that she was slyly and perceptively rewriting the whole culture, but for me she was instead the ultimate slave to what one writer dubbed the John Waite Rule. In brief, the John Waite Rule says that John Waite and Bruce Springsteen hit upon a great record in exactly the same way: by trying this, that, and the other thing until every now and again, purely as a matter of luck, they hit pay dirt. You can argue about specific cases, but for the great bulk of stuff out there, the rule is unassailable. And if anybody has made a career out of trying this, that, and the other thing—with this and that looking pretty foolish, while the other thing produces terrific results—it's Madonna.

Flash back to her infamous Letterman appearance, an emblematic souvenir of the Madonna Spectacle Industry. It's difficult to pinpoint chronology, but if memory serves, her obscene needling of Letterman came during a lull of some kind: in the months leading up to *Bedtime Stories*, or after the first single had run its course and faded—a point where nothing much was happening. As Madonna let loose and I sat there squirming, the embarrassment was double, not only for what seemed like her most desperate attempt yet to kick-start the publicity cycle, but also for the lurking suspicion that it would work, that there'd be a whole army of acolytes who'd interpret her Andrew Dice Clay impression as a brilliant affront to the Midwestern sensibilities of Letterman, his touristy audience, and that sweet old couple in the front row the camera kept cutting to for reaction shots. Instead, Letterman seemed to mark the end of Madonna's Camille Paglia period—or maybe it was "Human Nature," where Madonna petulantly complained that she didn't know she wasn't supposed to talk about sex, a little hollow at the precise moment when Adina Howard sat in the top 10 with the most outrageous fuck song imaginable. Sex talk on the radio had been commonplace for years; it was all those bald hermaphrodites and sadomasochistic Chihuahuas in the videos that left some of us mystified.

Ancient history by now, but for anyone who believes "Crazy for You" will long outlive "Justify My Love," a quick look back serves to underscore how gratifying Madonna's re-emergence into normalcy has been post-*Evita* (one good song: Antonio Banderas cooing, "I know your name's Evita/'Cause your perfume's smelling sweeta/Since when I saw you down on the floor"). "Ray of Light," "Beautiful Stranger," and the new *Music* are the work of someone worth rooting for again: a little older, a little humbled, happy just to enjoy the party and let others wear the lampshades, a bit of an underdog even. Motherhood, yes, but it would have happened anyway. When there's no one left to scandalize, you move on.

Music breaks down neatly into three discrete sections, on which I'll hang the very technical names the dance part, the good part, and the dirge part. The good part, so named because it's really good, accounts for half of *Music*'s 10 songs, conveniently nestled into tracks four through eight inclusive, so you can play that section over and over again without interruption. (A moot point, perhaps, as CDs can allegedly be programmed according to your specifications anyway. Sounds complicated.) And seeing as some of the good part can be danced to and some of the dance part's good, just about any listening configuration should play well.

Nonetheless, "Impressive Instant," with its munchkin voices, elastic bassline, and impressive flashes of alliteration ("wingy-wingy-wingy"'s especially euphonious), would have been a better opener than the title song, which has already dashed inexplicably to number one. Anything purporting to celebrate music's powers of transcendence should be epic and transcendent itself, something along the lines of the O'Jays' "I Love Music," or that one about getting into the groove. "Music" instead gives you Daft Punk knob-twiddling and a thump-thump Teutonic beat, neither of which is going to transport anyone anywhere. "Impressive Instant" also shares some useful inside information should you ever run into Madonna at a club: she likes to samba and rhumba, so don't bother trying to win her over with an invite to do the Jackie Gleason.

After some more generic stalling, you're plunged into "I Deserve It"'s two strummed chords like you've accidentally wandered into some faraway singer-songwriter album from 1971. The transition is dramatic, hinting that *Music*'s finally ready to mess around some. Both "I Deserve It" and its companion piece, "Nobody's Perfect" (a/k/a "Farewell, Bubba," a ready-made mea culpa for Bill's memoirs), are excellent variations on a genre Madonna does better than anyone: the Memory Song, à la "Live to Tell," "Oh Father," "This Used to Be My Playground," "I'll Remember," and other scattered ruminations on people and places she carries around in her head. On the assumption that "Nobody's Perfect" lifts its title from *Some Like It Hot*'s famous closing line, I've gone ahead and conceptualized the video: Madonna (who was at her best on *SNL* singing "Happy Birthday" to Phil Hartman's Clinton) as Marilyn, Kevin Spacey and Vince Vaughn in drag, meticulous shot-for-shot re-creation from Spike Jonze.

It was disappointing last year to see "Beautiful Stranger" lose year-end polls to a pleasant bit of nothing like "No Scrubs." I count it as Madonna's masterpiece, her own "Erotic City," with a hypnotic abandon that a friend correctly identified as rooted more in Creedence Clearwater than "Ray of Light"'s electronica. "Amazing" is another tale of obsessive-compulsive behavior with an equally unlikely texture—strip away the vocal and you're left with one of the faster numbers on Joy Division's *Unknown Pleasures*. What amazes her, incidentally, is what a boy can do to a girl, a powerful hold that will forever remain a mystery to the boy because he'll never really know "What It Feels Like for a Girl." Which happens to be the name of my favorite song of all, the perfect answer record to *The Virgin Suicides* (where boys indeed stand on the side of the street looking uncomprehendingly on girls), thanks in no small part to the gossamer-like synthesizer percolating in the background (Air bubbles?).

No point in dwelling on the dirgey stuff, except to observe that Madonna's more fun going loco than going Nico. If you plan on taking in *Music* piecemeal via the radio over the next few months, hang around—better and weirder things are on the way. Meanwhile, should Madonna do anything really dubious in the next while to draw some attention to herself, please disregard parts of this review.

(*Village Voice*, 2000)

"Miles Away," Madonna (2008)

Controversies involving the Rock and Roll Hall of Fame are very much of the tree-falling-in-the-forest variety, so for anyone who missed it, the Mother of All Rogue Diva's induction last March generated some not unexpected derision. Leonard Cohen, who also went in, generated none. I have the same question today that I did at the time: *in what universe is Leonard Cohen more rock 'n' roll than Madonna?* I love a few early Cohen songs, but I honestly do not understand the mindset that sees him as belonging but Madonna as an interloper. Elsewhere, she underscored how peripheral she's become by backing the wrong candidate for the Democratic nomination, and when she eventually came over to Obama, she jumped in with embarrassing overkill: her concert montage linking McCain to Hitler thankfully didn't get a lot of attention, but I'm sure I wasn't alone among Obama supporters in thinking "please make her disappear for a few months." And then, of course, the divorce, the genesis of which she openly addresses on "Miles Away." Not one of Madonna's great memory songs—the miles are actual physical distance, not metaphorical—but it feels like one anyway. The lilt in her voice when she sings "so far away" is worth any number of HOF inductions.

(#8, year-end ballot, 2008)

New York Dolls

"Personality Crisis," "Looking for a Kiss," "Trash," and "Subway Train," *New York Dolls*; "Who Are the Mystery Girls?" and "Human Being," *In Too Much, Too Soon*

      Chronic substance abuse, abject co-dependency, the farthest reaches of human deviancy— but enough about New Edition, I'd rather talk about the New York Dolls. (Hands up if you saw that one coming a mile away.) I was definitely aware of them in 1973, and have a dim memory of seeing the first album on sale at the record store that used to be in Brampton's Shopper's World, but because they got no AM airplay, they were just a curiosity from some world that didn't make much sense to me at 12. (Much like a couple of other strange encounters I carry with me from the same time: some band on local cable flailing around wildly while singing about staining the carpet, and Rainer Schwartz, a DJ on Toronto's CHUM-FM through the '70s, playing "Golden Years" on a show he must have hosted on TVO.) Finding their first album as an import during my great punk-rock plunge in 1979 or (more likely) 1980 had as much impact on me as anything between Neil Young and Hüsker Dü. I can't say for sure what it was that prompted me to buy it—possibly Christgau, though more likely it was the Sex Pistols' "New York," or maybe I saw it cited in some interview I read at the time. Except for "Private World" (which in context works fine), I loved the album from start to finish almost immediately, and the fact that it was something I discovered on my own, ahead of my friend Peter who got me going on punk in the first place, gave it an extra layer of secret-society appeal. *In Too*

Much, Too Soon wasn't as overwhelming as a whole, but the covers were funny, "Mystery Girls" was funnier still, and "Human Being" was the greatest sign-off ever. Unlike some other people who define that time for me like the Cramps or Joy Division, the Dolls sound more or less as good today as they did then. Pop historians that they were (which I think means some combination of Johansen, Thunders, and Sylvain, although maybe the other two shaped the group's aesthetic more than I realize), both albums are marked by a perfect mix of girl-group savvy, heavy-metal whomp, and Bo Diddley swagger, so much so that the context in which they first captured my imagination—their privileged place in the punk-rock chain of-being—hardly matters anymore. The Dolls filtered their genius for pop music through a very different sensibility than Led Zeppelin's, but both bands had an uncanny ability to stay nimble at a time and within genres where many turned leaden. My friend Tim was lucky enough to see them live circa 1972 at Toronto's Victory Burlesque Theatre, with a very glammy Rush opening—wow. The bootleg listed above features possibly the most tasteless album covers in my collection: a bleached-out shot of Johansen in pillbox hat, sitting beside JFK in the assassination limo. I'm ashamed to say I love knowing that it's there.

(record inventory, 2005-06)

2005 Top 10

#3: *New York Doll*: I liked this just slightly less than the Ramones documentary from last year, but it was really good in ways I didn't expect; I'm going to place it behind two films I was less predisposed to like, but this could just as easily occupy the #1 spot. I'll again bring up Michael Moore in connection to director Greg Whiteley's treatment of Arthur Kane's Mormon co-workers. They all come across as sane and articulate, and even with the two older ladies who generate some laughs, one of them has a beautifully dignified moment when Arthur dies. I think they would have been caricatured in the hands of Moore; not necessarily cruelly, but I think he would have handled them condescendingly, and would have treated their religion as a joke. (It's true that Whiteley's a Mormon himself, but, based in part on a Q&A he did after the screening I saw, I think his balance is more a matter of temperament.) The scene that will stay with me the longest from *New York Doll* is when David Johansen arrives for the first time during the Dolls' practice sessions for their London reunion show. First of all, it's hard to find words that adequately convey the depths of Johansen's cragginess—I even had to consult the dictionary to check "cragginess." And the way he saunters into the room as the band plays "Out in the Street" and slowly starts to join in—still the star of the show, the guy who knows that all eyes are on him (especially Arthur's, having waited a couple of decades for this moment) but kind of half-pretends to be just one of the guys—is brilliant; possibly staged to one degree or another, but brilliant anyway.

(rockcritics.com, 2005)

"Dance Like a Monkey," New York Dolls (2006)

I heard this for the first time when they did it on Letterman, and it passed the debacle test instantaneously and with ease (which, if you're an optimist, amounts to "Please don't let this be embarrassing"; if you're a pessimist, it's more like, "How embarrassing is this going to be?"). There's a little too much "Lust for Life" about it, but it's also got some of the old "Frankenstein" in there, especially in the emblematic din after the line about inheriting the wind. I've got a friend who produces an arts show for a local television station, and a few months ago, Johansen and Sylvain were in his building doing an interview. He tracked down Sylvain and got him to autograph his old copies of the first two LPs, mentioning that he was there for the group's show at Toronto's Victory Burlesque Theatre in 1973, with Rush opening. Johansen arrived soon after, and Sylvain reminded him of the long-ago show. Johansen's response: "Geddy Lee...he's a *funny guy!*" I like the story as much as the song.

(#6, year-end ballot, 2006)

Pet Shop Boys

"West End Girls," *Please*; "What Have I Done to Deserve This?" *Actually*; "Left to My Own Devices" and "It's Alright," *Introspective*; "Being Boring," *Behaviour*; "I Wouldn't Normally Do This Kind of Thing," *Very*; "The Samurai in Autumn," *Release*; "Flamboyant," *PopArt*

(record inventory, 2005-06)

"The Samurai in Autumn," Pet Shop Boys

Not the single (I like "Home and Dry," too), but really, when the last time you heard it like this? 1990, I guess—*Behaviour*'s very autumnal too, and that side of the Pet Shop Boys has been there since the beginning. I also like two or three songs on the Beck album, and almost put "All in Your Mind" on my list. This will happen to you too, Eminem: one day your "moment" will have passed (the quotations because the true value of such alleged moments is highly overrated), and you'll emerge on the other side with a wistful and pretty set of songs that serves to assure your remaining audience that everything's OK, you're still around and still making music.

(#8, year-end ballot, 2002)

The Status of the Gay Question

      Getting this interview transcribed—or, even better, digitized and posted—was something Scott and I first discussed a few years ago, but there wasn't any real context for doing so at the time. I wasn't even sure I could still find the cassette where it resided—I knew I had two or three boxes of cassettes stored away downstairs, a mad scramble of mix-tapes and esoterica and some of the interviews I'd done in the '80s, but I hadn't looked through them for quite a while. Deterioration had also crossed my mind.

      Happy to say that I found the tape (along with some other interviews I'm glad I still have: Joey and Dee Dee Ramone, Johnny Thunders, John Candy...Huey Lewis—I won't get sidetracked explaining that one), and now, with all these podcasts Scott's been posting, we've got something approaching a rationale for putting it out there, and enough technology to avoid the transcribing I was always too lazy to do anyway.

      The interview dates back to the fall of 1988, just after *Introspective* came out. (Possibly just before, I'm not sure—maybe I had been listening to a promo, but I don't think so, else the copy I have now would be that very same promo, which it isn't.) For me, it was the exact zenith of the Pet Shop Boys' Imperial Phase, coming off of *Actually* and "What Have I Done to Deserve This?" with an instantaneously striking, self-assured album that looked like it was going to sell even more, chart even higher, and be reviewed even better. The interview was done for a magazine out of Toronto named *Graffiti*, where, after reviewing records and contributing various pieces (some co-written with Scott) for the past couple of years, I'd just been brought on as an associate editor. So it was also the zenith of my own Imperial Phase, even though mine was secret and lasted only three months. *Graffiti* went bankrupt right before the interview made it to print, which is why it's been languishing in a shoebox ever since.

interrupting my train of thought

What I remember…There was me, Neil Tennant, Chris Lowe, and a record-company woman. It took place at a prominent Toronto hotel (no idea which one), I think up in a swanky room but I'm not sure, and it was one of those junkets where I was slotted in the middle of a whole bunch of other interviews. I vaguely recall wanting to make them realize that I was different than everybody else, that I actually cared about the record and wasn't just there for a byline and a cheque (cf. Matt Bianco, Men Without Hats, Balaam & the Angel, and some of my other illustrious work from that era). So I made sure we spent the first five minutes talking about Simon Frith. I felt confident that the people from *Rock Express* and MuchMusic would not be talking about Simon Frith. Something I'd forgotten: that the record-company woman seemed to want to steer the conversation away from Neil and Chris making fun of U2. They weren't on the same label, and I don't think there was a great deal of overlap in their audience at that point (probably more true three years earlier), so I'm not sure why that bothered her.

It's of course an odd experience to travel back twenty-five years and listen to yourself at 27. The one condition I set forth for Scott in following through with this was that there could only be an acceptable level of cringe-worthy moments on my part. After listening to almost the whole thing, I'm 73% sure that that level is indeed acceptable. I'm a little too look-at-me in proclaiming my antipathy towards political music. (Basically true, but I did have "Bonzo Goes to Bitburg" on my year-end in '85.) I suggest at one point that I'm older and presumably more sagacious than the Pazz & Jop voters who by-passed *Actually*; again, I'm 27. And as for the best moment of all, well, that's how you get titles for published interviews. Basically, and surprisingly, I sounded pretty much the same then as I do today.

Excuse all the mysterious ambient crashes and thumps. My best guess is that, just to keep things lively, I threw something across the table at Chris Lowe every 30 seconds or so.

(rockcritics.com, 2014)

Ramones

"Loudmouth" and "Today Your Love, Tomorrow the World," *Ramones*; "Oh Oh I Love Her So," "Carbona Not Glue," and "Now I Wanna Be a Good Boy," *Leave Home*; "Sheena Is a Punk Rocker," *Rocket to Russia*; "It's Not My Place," *Pleasant Dreams*; "Bonzo Goes to Bitburg," 12-inch single *in and around the lake*

I spent about two minutes flipping through the Ramones LPs and deciding which songs I'd most want to save; I'd have to set aside at least a night to accurately see where I stand right now—I haven't listened to any of the albums for years—so I'm not at all confident of the mixworthy list. "Bonzo" (used beautifully in *School of Rock*), "Sheena" (never a favorite until I included it on a "'70s Mastermix" for a school assembly three years ago), and "Oh Oh I Love Her So" I'm fairly sure of, the rest no. I had "Pet Sematary" on a year-end once, so maybe that would go on too; I hardly know anything at all from their last two or three albums. My period of greatest interest in the Ramones coincided exactly with my start at *Nerve*, so I ended up writing about them on five separate occasions within the space of about 18 months: a review of "Bonzo" that was the first thing I ever submitted to *Nerve* (not published); an LP-by-LP career overview for *Rock Box*, a hardcore hip-hop fanzine put out by Scott Woods; a review of *Animal Boy* for *Nerve*; an interview with Joey and Dee Dee, also for *Nerve*; and a review of *Halfway to Sanity* earmarked for the *Voice* that was either lost in transit (something called "fax machines") or is still undergoing a thorough edit 18 years later. I'd all but shifted into full-out deification of the Ramones around that time—not their newer music, but something less tangible, something they seemed to represent—I think because they were a nostalgic step back from a lot of the noisier and weirder (and often useless) stuff I was then listening to, back to my introduction to punk a few years earlier. I don't know; they seemed very heroic and forgotten in 1986. Anyway, after all of that I'd worn them out, and it was only last year's documentary, Joey's "Maria Bartiromo," and of course all the deaths that closed out their story abruptly which brought them back into focus for me after 15 years of not caring what they were up to. And that's that. For as long as I'm teaching, I'll try to play them for my students once a year on the anniversary of Joey's death, likely something from album #1, and try to explain why their sitting there giggling and looking befuddled is no different than the giggling and befuddlement that greeted the Ramones in 1976—as well, that is, as someone who was listening to the Alan Parsons Project in 1976 is able to explain.

(record inventory, 2005-06)

R.E.M.

"Carnival of Sorts (Box Cars)," *Chronic Town*; "Radio Free Europe," *Murmur*; "(Don't Go Back to) Rockville," *Reckoning*; "Driver 8" and "Life and How to Live It," *Fables of the Reconstruction*; "It's the End of the World as We Know It (And I Feel Fine)," *Document*

Six songs, three with parentheses—Yes, I Was a Total R.E.M. Sap (And I Guess I Still Am, to a Degree). I actually thought I'd be listing more than six, but looking over the albums one by one, even half of what's above would be enough: "Rockville" and "Life and How to Live It" are old favorites that I haven't taken the time to re-listen to, and "It's the End of the World" is borderline spent. Six is a much more accurate reflection of how obsessively I listened to those first five records, though, and the extra songs also stand in for a couple I'd take post-vinyl: "New Orleans Instrumental No. 1" and "The Great Beyond" for sure, maybe one more. I never expect to like anything by R.E.M. anymore, and probably haven't going as far back as *Document*, so I'm surprised by how often I do; even something as marginal as *Reveal*, which I found cheap a while back, has a couple of songs I like a lot. It wouldn't be fair to call them the ultimate one-idea band, because a) they mess around enough that there's a certain amount of variety and change through the years, and b) anyone who hates them might want to know what exactly that one idea is, and I'd be stuck for an answer. ("Uh, parentheses?") For me they've always had more of a one-mood/one-amorphous-feeling appeal: what I liked about "The Great Beyond" was the same thing I liked about all those unintelligible fragments on *Murmur*. If you have no use for slavish devotion to surface beauty, then you have no use for R.E.M.; that's about the beginning, middle, and the end of what they have to offer. I still find it puzzling that "Losing My Religion," which to my ears has very little of that beauty—and no parentheses—is the song that opened up a much larger audience for them, and also brought around at least one critic, Greil Marcus, who had despised them up to that point. But I'm glad it allowed them to spend some time at the top of *Billboard* for at least a while.

(record inventory, 2005-06)

"Flamboyant," Pet Shop Boys/"Bad Day," R.E.M./"Maria Bartiromo," Joey Ramone

I was not expecting to be voting for any of these. I didn't have more than a passing interest in the Joey Ramone album when it came out last year, and when it comes to the Pet Shop Boys and R.E.M., I'm Michael Corleone at this point: every time I think I'm out, they pull me back in. "Flamboyant" and "Bad Day" haul out tried-and-true straw men as targets—a shallow nightlifer for the Pet Shop Boys, a Republican president for R.E.M. ("Bad Day"'s typically oblique, but I assume the creepy auctioneer is Bush)—while Joey goes out on a brilliant joke-that's-not-really-a-joke: I know he wasn't rich-rich, but after 25 years of steady if unspectacular earnings as a Ramone, I'm guessing he *was* in a position to be keeping tabs on Yahoo and Amazon stock. (That's how he would have stumbled over Maria Bartiromo in the first place, right?) The object of his affection should be floating on air for the rest of her life: the idea of a dying punk rock icon recording a love letter to a glamorous courtier of Wall Street is worthy of a fairy tale. (I think I always wanted to write the same song myself: to Ona Fletcher, to Gail Smith, to Thalia Assuras...) In the end, though, the subject matter of all three of these songs is almost incidental. What they're really about, and what makes them so removed from everything else that dominates popular music right now, is how each represents a very singular evocation of capital-B Beauty for the three artists in question. I don't have the words to adequately describe how they convey this beauty, but I can point to the specific moments where I hear it, and they're all embedded in the "grain of the voice" and all that ephemeral stuff: the rise and fall in Neil Tennant's voice on "you're so flamboyant," Joey when he sings "those eyes make everything OK," and the background swooning underneath "please don't take a picture" in "Bad Day" (Mike Mills always sings those parts, I think). So even though there's a part of me that realizes "Flamboyant" is a very minor song that the Pet Shop Boys have probably done a dozen times already—I feel like I'm Andrew Sarris in the mid-'60s, grasping onto ghosts in *Seven Women* or *El Dorado*—I also know they're refining and deepening that song in ways that, even at their most withering, achieve a kind of majesty and serenity that continues to speak to me: "It all takes courage, you know, when just crossing the street/Well, it's almost heroic."

(#2/7/8, year-end ballot, 2003)

Replacements

"Johnny's Gonna Die," *Sorry Ma, Forgot to Take Out the Trash*; "Kids Don't Follow" and "Go," *Stink*; "Color Me Impressed" and "Within Your Reach," *Hootenanny*; "I Will Dare" and "Answering Machine," *Let It Be*; "Left of the Dial," *Tim*; "Alex Chilton," *Pleased to Meet Me*

As surprised as I was that I didn't feel the need to list more R.E.M. songs, I'm even more surprised to have so many by the Replacements. It's not that I play their albums any more frequently than R.E.M.'s —I really don't listen to either of them anymore, though I know I'll be much more inclined to go with the Replacements on the radio. (I threw in "Color Me

Impressed" two shows ago and it sounded great. Playing R.E.M. on a college station in 2005 would just somehow feel unseemly.) Again, the list is essentially what I would have posted 18 years ago—first Al Gore and I would have invented the internet, then I would have posted—with no second-guessing and no re-listening. There's such an immense likeability factor attached to those first few Replacements records, and such a indelible gift for melody coursing through even the songs that are meant to be foreboding ("Johnny's Gonna Die," "Go")—that to me they're a band that doesn't drag around any of the baggage synonymous with the Amerindie mid-'80s: noise as schtick, artiness, self-righteousness, etc., etc. There was hardcore, there was pigfuck, there was obscurantism, and there was the Replacements. That they probably hung around a couple of albums too long doesn't diminish their stature in my eyes, nor does whatever Paul Westerberg is up to today (the two CDs I have of his both have their moments).

(record inventory, 2005-06)

"Alex Chilton," Replacements (1987)

I know I had the Replacements on at least two of the other lists ("I Will Dare" and "Answering Machine"), possibly all three. I didn't expect they'd make this one, but a couple of things happened. 1) I started watching *Feeling Minnesota* last week, and, before bailing, there was the scene where Cameron Diaz and Keanu Reeves sang along to "I Will Dare" in the car. It felt like this was a really famous scene that I should have known about; I didn't. 2) I found a remaindered copy of the Replacements compilation put out a few years ago by Rhino, so cheap that I superfluously bought it for the car (I already had 17 of the 20 songs). The compilation happens to be perfectly in sync with my own version of the Replacements, so I've been playing it all week.

"Alex Chilton" also takes care of something else: some recompense for the fact that (apologies to Rob and Renée) I've always thought Big Star a little overrated. They had two songs I'd be happy to list here—"September Gurls" or "Thirteen," not what you'd call surprising—and a third, "The India Song," that I like a lot. Past that, they start to lose me. "Alex Chilton" resonates with me in a way that most of their own music doesn't, and obviously Chilton's death a few months ago adds extra poignancy to a song that was already the ultimate fan letter. (Move it ahead of "Maria Bartiromo" and "Janis" in that department.)

in and around the lake

Westerberg's fandom is expressed much more obliquely than Joey Ramone's or Joe McDonald's, but there's something else going on here anyway. I'm pretty sure Westerberg is writing about himself as much as he is Chilton, not that he'd ever admit as much. For almost all of the people who've been following this countdown, the Replacements are as much a fact of life as the Beatles or Rolling Stones. It's easy to forget that for most of the music-listening world, they're not—not then, not now. I'm guessing that most of my teacher friends here—Anita, Jen, Karen, Tina—have never heard a Replacements song. And I'm sure that by 1987, Westerberg had thoroughly internalized the mantle of prophet without honour, resigned himself to the fact that (like all the Michael Azerrad bands) he just wasn't going to cross over into any kind of radio play or commercial success. So he's probably feeling a little sorry for himself here, imagining children by the millions waiting for "Color Me Impressed" and "Unsatisfied" and "Within Your Reach," but knowing that they'll never hear those songs. Except he recasts them as Alex Chilton, because fan letters are a lot more appealing than self-pity.

"If he died in Memphis, that'd be cool"—I'd forgotten all about that line. Did he? I don't know. But it's a nice thought, not mean or ironic or glib at all. Just nice.

(#34, Facebook Top 100, 2010-11)

Smokey Robinson/Miracles

"Mickey's Monkey," "You've Really Got a Hold on Me," and "Way Over There," *Greatest Hits from the Beginning*; "Ooo Baby Baby" and "A Fork in the Road," *Going to a Go-Go*; "The Tears of a Clown," *One Dozen Roses*; "Why Do Happy Memories Hurt So Bad," *One Heartbeat*

I definitely gave Smokey Robinson a privileged place in the pantheon for a time. I guess it would have been the middle and later part of the '80s when I was putting the six songs listed above on one mix-tape after another—it's harder to pin down when exactly you were most interested in someone on the basis of music recorded years earlier, as opposed to people you were immersed in during their peak years. *One Heartbeat* dates to my time with *Nerve* and CIUT; I'm not sure if I reviewed it, but I played "Why Do Happy Memories Hurt So Bad" all the time on the radio, a much richer song than either "Being with You" or "Cruisin'." You've got to have *Going to a Go-Go* for "A Fork in the Road," a B-side that lives up to its mystique; close call with (the overlooked) "Way Over There" and "Ooo Baby Baby," but it's probably Robinson's greatest song. I don't have any Vanity LPs, therefore sidestepping the difficult issue of where to file the interview promo. (Smokey has a great bit about the importance of sad songs on *The Motown Story*, an early box that's otherwise rendered useless—for taping purposes, anyway—by all the intrusive interview clips.) I was actually surprised and somewhat disappointed to learn about Robinson's former drug problems. I say "actually" because the combination of pop stars and drug problems usually registers all the surprise of a George Steinbrenner hissy fit—you can set your watch by such phenomena. But Smokey always seemed like such an oasis of sanity and wisdom. Dylan's famous quote about Robinson being America's greatest living poet (I may have read somewhere that the quote is apocryphal, but I remember coming across the exact interview where he said it) is the second most inspiring thing Dylan ever said about another musician, after his breathless recollection of what it felt like when the Beatles took over the Colorado airwaves in 1964.

(record inventory, 2005-06)

Todd Rundgren

"We Gotta Get You a Woman," *Runt*; "I Saw the Light," "Couldn't I Just Tell You," "Cold Morning Light," and "Hello It's Me," *Something/Anything*

And if not Cheap Trick or Steely Dan as the answer to "Explain the '70s to me," then maybe *Something/Anything*. There can't be more than a handful of studio-albums proper in my collection where I've listed, or will list, four songs; I've got four from *Something/Anything*, and almost added "It Wouldn't Have Made Any Difference" for a fifth. The strange thing is, I don't consider it among my favorite LPs—it's a double, and beyond those five songs, there's nothing else on there I care the least about. I've had it since '77 or so, by which time the original gatefold was gone; it was side one I always played through high school, not paying too much attention to either "I Saw the Light" or "Hello It's Me," radio hits I knew from five years earlier. I'm not sure exactly when or why, but sometime in the mid-'90s I rediscovered "Hello It's Me" and "I Saw the Light," and it was one of those overwhelming epiphanies where something clicks and you're transported back to some time and place—and all the feelings associated with that time and place, even if you couldn't quite give them a name—that still occupies a much larger place in your being than you would have guessed. (All of this probably happened in close proximity to a fanzine piece I wrote about my high school years in Georgetown.) Ever since, I've thought of both songs as being as important to me in an autobiographical sense as almost anything else I can think of—*Everybody Knows This Is Nowhere* cuts even deeper, and that might be it.

(record inventory, 2005-06)

"We Gotta Get You a Woman," Runt (1970)

I'm being annoyingly technical here—this is Todd Rundgren, of course, but (something I didn't know until 30 seconds ago) it's from an album that, on release, was credited to the band Runt. I didn't realize it came out so early, either; I was thinking '71, maybe even early '72.

I have a harder time pinning down the appeal of Todd Rundgren than probably anybody else from my (roughly speaking) favorite couple of years ever. I suspect the *Creem* and *Rolling Stone* critics who tried to write about him at the time had exactly the same problem. It hasn't gotten any easier 40 years later. He was a singer-songwriter who was worlds away from the whole Carole-James-Joni way of doing things. He was sort of glam, but not really. (You've got to take a look at the "Hello It's Me" link I've added below, though. People who look like that do not deserve to make music like this.) I've often read that there are affinities between Philly Soul and his most famous songs. I guess so…I don't really hear that myself. He gets away with stuff that could only be gotten away with in 1972; like on "Hello It's Me," he promises just to pop over every now and again to have sex with the object of his desire, no obligations whatsoever, and he frames this as something of a thoughtful, sensitive gesture. He was, as they say, *sui generis*. As I've written before, there are four or five songs of his (all but this one from *Something/Anything*) that are like godhead to me.

Rather than "Hello It's Me" or "I Saw the Light" (#6 on my CKLN list), I'm going to go instead with something that, the two times a year it turns up on Q-107, is as good as car radio ever gets (something the linked YouTube gets at nicely). If you've never heard it, stay with it till the very end; it's got a punch line as ingeniously droll as Grin's "I Lost a Number."

Don't know about Leroy, but thinking about Bebe Buell—and let me add, rather enviously, that people who look like Todd should not be ending up with Bebe Buell—his busybody friend made out okay.

(#37, Facebook Top 100, 2010-11)

Rolling Stones

"It's All Over Now," *12 x 5*; "The Last Time," "19th Nervous Breakdown," and "Get Off of My Cloud," *Big Hits (High Tide and Green Grass)*; "Back Street Girl," *Between the Buttons*; "Out of Time," *Flowers*; "Street Fighting Man" and "Prodigal Son," *Beggars Banquet*; "You Got the Silver," *Let It Bleed*; "Sway," *Sticky Fingers*

Well, what do you know—I used up all 10 spots before even getting to *Exile*. Rather than knock off a song or two—I wouldn't want to be without anything above—I'll just say that *Exile* is their greatest album and can stand as a phantom 11th pick unto itself. One huge omission from the two or three early LPs not listed, all of which I've managed to download in the past few months: "I Am Waiting" from *Aftermath*, a great album that's maybe not quite as great as its reputation ("Goin' Home" drags, and there are a couple of minor throwaways). Only two post-*Exile* LPs—I had *Goat's Head Soup* a long time ago, before I started collecting in earnest—and as long as you're OK with that, I am too. (There's a parallel universe out there where people advocate that the likes of *Emotional Rescue* and *Tattoo You* aren't just formulaically good records, they're in fact more vital than *Exile*. This argument has not extended to *Voodoo Lounge* or "She's the Boss" thus far, but you can never be sure where such roads lead.) The Rolling Stones have systematically squandered more goodwill than anyone in pop music history save for Michael Jackson, and it's difficult to take a step back and write about them as if that's not a factor. I don't think I knew much at all about the Stones prior to their 1972 stop in Toronto (I must have been familiar with at least a few of their '60s hits from the radio, but I don't think I had any sense of their place alongside the Beatles in the overall scheme of things), the tremendous fanfare over which I still remember. Urjo Karedo wrote a splashy overview of the band's career up to that point for the *Toronto Star*, there was a big radio special I recall listening to, and I quickly became aware that this was something that mattered a lot. I bought *Hot Rocks* shortly after and played it to death for the next couple of years; my favorites included most of the warhorses I'm now completely sick of ("Satisfaction,"

"Brown Sugar," "Sympathy for the Devil"). I survived the mid-'70s still loving all the '60s hits, and then towards the end of high school my fandom peaked as I discovered all the amazing album cuts on *Beggars Banquet* and *Let It Bleed*. That's about all I can do at this point: piece together my own history as a fan, which is that of someone who was too young to have had my world turned upside down by the first half-dozen albums—I've never really had any feel for their early blues covers—but just old enough to have jumped on board at the tail-end of the Mick Taylor period. That it took me about a minute to list 10 unassailably mixworthy songs without drawing from what I count as their greatest album says far more than whatever ambivalence, exasperation, or just plain boredom I might feel about the whole saga at this late date.

(record inventory, 2005-06)

Shoes

"Boys Don't Lie," "Not Me," "Capital Gain," and "Nowhere So Fast," *Black Vinyl Shoes*; "Tomorrow Night," "Too Late," and "Now and Then," *Present Tense*; "Yes or No," *Tongue Twister*; "Curiosity," Boomerang; "Running Wild," *Silhouette*

(record inventory, 2005-06)

Rejected *33-1/3* Book Proposal for *Black Vinyl Shoes*

Are you sure you want this to be a book that sells? There's a lot of pressure and a lot of time commitments that go along with a best-selling book—have you given any thought to that?

I'm not sure if there's a readership out there for a book on the Shoes or not. They've got a highly specialized fan base: two well-known rock critics out of New York, various relatives in and around Zion, Illinois, and me. It would be almost generous to say they existed at the margins of pop history, although when I was looking through old *Billboards* a few months ago to see if any of their albums charted—I was trying to prove to a friend that they were more famous (relatively speaking) than Suicide—I discovered that *Present Tense*, their second LP, made it as high as #50 in 1979. I don't know what that meant in terms of actual album sales, but I've come across more than a few copies of *Present Tense* in thrift shops over the years, confirming that there were indeed people who purchased Shoes records. The fact that those records now reside in thrift shops probably doesn't strengthen the argument for a book 25 years later.

In any case, I do believe that if you did it right, a book on *Black Vinyl Shoes*, the Shoes' debut that preceded *Present Tense* by a couple of years, could tell a story every bit as compelling as the stories Peter Guralnick uncovered in *Lost Highway* and *Feel Like Going Home*, books that similarly found their subject matter at the margins of musical history. Guralnick wrote about blues and country artists, many of them largely forgotten when the books first appeared, but I think it was likely *Lost Highway*, especially the chapter on Charlie Rich, where I first got the idea for a book on the Shoes. I bought *Lost Highway* and *Black Vinyl Shoes* roughly around the same time in the early '80s, and by 1986, I was writing to Minor Threat's Ian MacKaye to see what he thought about a possible book on the Shoes, the Chantels, and his own group. I had only the vaguest sense at the time of what linked these obviously disparate artists in my mind, and I was lucky MacKaye was gracious enough not to dismiss me as a crackpot. He said he was intrigued, wished me luck, and that was the end of that—the part about actually writing the book never came to pass.

I now understand the link better. The Shoes, like the Chantels and Minor Threat, made music that was so singular in its purity, so rich a distillation of the space it occupied, that you realize immediately you're inside a world far more expansive and detailed than whatever genre the music formally aligns itself with—'70s power-pop, '50s girl-group, '80s hardcore—a world that was instead shaped, imagined, dreamt inside the head of a pop visionary. With Minor Threat, the visionary was MacKaye; with the Chantels, some combination of 15-year-old singer Arlene Smith and producer George Goldner; with the Shoes, I'm guessing it was the Murphy brothers, John and Jeff, but that's one of the things I'd want to find out in the course of writing the book. Whoever it was, I use the word visionary cautiously but with total conviction: I honestly believe that the music contained on *Black Vinyl Shoes* (and on parts of each of the Shoes' other LPs; every one they made had at least two or three songs as good as *Black Vinyl Shoes*' best) is marked by the same kind of obsessiveness and complexity as the creations of Brian Wilson and Phil Spector, two other artists I'd feel comfortable referring to as visionaries.

So I'd want to get inside that space and explore it, and I'd also want to veer off into the following:

- The Shoes' relation to "new wave"; how is that Blondie, the Cars, and the Police sold millions of records, while the Shoes only caught a glimpse of the mountaintop and then quickly faded into oblivion? There must have been some kind of push from their record company (Elektra) if they managed to land an album in the Top 100, but there must also have been some fundamental failing in the band that prevented them from ever breaking through to a bigger audience.

- The history of "power pop," an amorphous genre that regularly gets compiled onto CDs (not always especially well), but, to the best of my knowledge, has never been accorded a full-length book. Actually, I'm not even convinced the Shoes are best described as power-pop, although *Black Vinyl Shoes* is usually one of the first records mentioned whenever someone starts listing essential power-pop LPs. To me, they're more like gossamer-pop, pop music of such ethereality and intricacy that it barely seems to exist at all (from Christgau's "Consumer Guide" review of *Black Vinyl Shoes*: "Recorded by elves on a TEAC four-track in a living room in Zion, Illinois…"), an elusiveness that paradoxically draws you in deeper. I'd try to situate the Shoes within a whole tradition of like-minded music: the Beatles' "I Need You," the Who's "I Can't Reach You," the Searchers' "Don't Throw Your Love Away," the Merry-Go-Round's "On Your Way Out," the Flamin' Groovies' "Shake Some Action," all the way through to the Posies' "Any Other Way" and Yo La Tengo's "Moby Octopad." As part of my proposal, I've sent you a CD that will make clearer what I'm talking about—it should reach your office by the middle of next week.

- The Shoes vs. Big Star. Somebody put out a book on Big Star last year, and over time they've been deified by critics as the '70s' great lost pop band. I like them fine—"September Gurls" is one of power-pop's greatest creations—but on the whole, the Shoes were much, much better. There's a temptation to say that the Shoes did intuitively what Big Star went about doing very self-consciously, but I think a great deal of design and deliberation and artistic aspiration did go into the Shoes' music, so that would be too easy. They had a more reliable command of chime and melancholy and the infinite space between, though, and there's a beauty that courses through *Black Vinyl Shoes* that I rarely hear on Big Star's LPs.

- A story of prophets without honour. This is where *Lost Highway* comes in—much as Guralnick caught Charlie Rich still pursuing some semblance of a career years after his one brief flirtation with success, three-quarters of the group that made *Black Vinyl Shoes* was still at it in the early '90s, putting out new material on their own record label and reconfiguring older albums for CD release. Why? For whom? Pop music had passed them by a few dozen times in the intervening years, but they hadn't changed a bit. I'd like to interview band members as part of the project, which I'm guessing would be as complicated as getting hold of a Zion telephone book and looking up the name Murphy.

- Finally, I'd want to start listening closely to the lyrics on *Black Vinyl Shoes* and get an idea what the songs are actually about. It's an album with so much surface pleasure, so much in which to lose yourself on a non-verbal level, that after spending 25 years with it, I'd be hard-pressed to quote specific lyrics. Girls are mentioned a lot, and they seem to be a perennial source of disappointment.

(2005)

Steely Dan

"Reelin' in the Years," *Can't Buy a Thrill*; "King of the World," *Countdown to Ecstasy*; "Rikki Don't Lose That Number" and "Pretzel Logic," *Pretzel Logic*; "Doctor Wu," *Katy Lied*; "Sign in Stranger," *The Royal Scam*

By all logic, I should feel the same kind of antipathy towards Steely Dan that I do for the Gang of Four, Todd Haynes and Todd Solondz, Antonioni, *2001: A Space Odyssey*, and lots of other music and films where I always get the impression that not only am I supposed to be thinking instead of feeling—ideally, I like art that inspires me to do both—but that feeling would be bad form. (Obviously, my own perspective on the aforementioned—I realize that anyone who loves *L'Avventura* gets lots of feeling out of it.) Not that Steely Dan were necessarily arty through the '70s, but they did, willfully or otherwise, radiate aloofness, austerity, and a brooding kind of mind-over-heart severity—one of the first things that comes to mind when I think about them are those withering images of Donald Fagen on the covers of *Katy Lied*, *Pretzel Logic*, and *Can't Buy a Thrill*, where he seems to be looking right through you and saying, "You might like this, but it won't be easy and it won't be fun."

in and around the lake

That's all background scenery, though—in actual fact, there's this weird kind of joy that fairly leaps out of songs like "Pretzel Logic" and "Reelin' in the Years," and, just as I wrote about Led Zeppelin earlier, I can't think of any other music that's comparable. Trying to assign special calendar significance to certain events ("The '60s ended with Altamont") is a corny thing to do, so naturally I do it whenever I think I've hit upon something. Two theories in that direction: the '60s began—or least what we think of as "the '60s" were anticipated by—the close-up of Janet Leigh's eye in *Psycho* (I've seen that one floated elsewhere, too), and the '70s didn't really leave the '60s behind musically until the opening 30 seconds of "Rikki Don't Lose That Number." I know I'm talking about a song that came out in 1974, and that Led Zeppelin and Bowie and lots else that was definitively '70s preceded "Rikki," but there's something absolutely jarring and *sui generis* about that opening, while the rest of the song is built upon cryptic fragments and strange time-shifts that have no business working so brilliantly in a sing-along pop hit that made it to #4 on *Billboard*. I recently made a three-CD '70s compilation for a departing custodian at my school, with some Nixon excerpts mixed in throughout. "Rikki" entered the Top 100 on 5/11/74, three months before Nixon's resignation. I had everything arranged more or less chronologically on the CD, so, punctuated by a clip from Nixon's resignation address, I heard "Rikki" in a way I never had before (at the risk of obviousness, Rikki = Richard):

> We hear you're leavin', that's OK
> I thought our little wild time had just begun
> I guess you kind of scared yourself, you turn and run
> But if you have a change of heart...

Yeah, I know, it's really all about a guy named Ricky and his stash, but the juxtaposition was striking ("Knockin' on Heaven's Door" from the same compilation was similarly transformed, even if it appeared a year earlier: "Ma, take this badge off of me/I can't use it anymore..."). Anyway, *Pretzel Logic* was another one of my most played albums in high school—one where I can really hear the evidence today, with pops and crackles all over the place—and after barely thinking about Steely Dan at all through the '80s, the past few years my favorite songs of theirs have rejoined music by Neil Young, Todd Rundgren, Rod Stewart, Cheap Trick, and, yes, David Bowie at the top of my '70s list. Those days are gone forever, over a long time ago. (Sorry, couldn't resist.)

(record inventory, 2005-06)

interrupting my train of thought

Rod Stewart

"Handbags & Gladrags," *The Rod Stewart Album*; "Gasoline Alley," *Gasoline Alley*; "Every Picture Tells a Story" and "Mandolin Wind," *Every Picture Tells a Story*; "You Wear It Well," *Never a Dull Moment*

Only six Rod Stewart picks, but it's no exaggeration to say that collectively they might not just be my favorite music ever made, but also my favorite art of any kind. The only real regret I've ever had about the '70s book I wrote with Scott Woods is that it was so single-minded in its pursuit of jokes, I sometimes feel like it was a bad-faith betrayal of a lot of music that carried me through school, helped shape who I am, and still means a great deal to me today. Not to be melodramatic—the feeling only applies to some of what we covered in there, and I don't carry around a lot of guilt over our refusal to thoughtfully engage the collected works of Gentle Giant and Paper Lace. But with Neil Young, with Al Green, with the first four Rod Stewart LPs, I can see where someone could come away from the book wondering if we even like this music at all, a trade-off we boxed ourselves into when we decided from the outset that we'd try for a funny book through and through, and that we'd leave the other book the decade deserved to someone else. I'm not totally sure why those early Rod Stewart songs effect me today to the degree that they do—again, as with Steely Dan, there were many years in there where I never gave them a moment's thought, and at the time, when "Maggie May" and "You Wear It Well" were on the radio, I liked them a lot, but there was other music I gravitated more towards. Today, when I often wonder why I don't show the requisite emotion when it comes to real-life events—those that fill the news, and those that are closer to my own life—I can think of at least three occasions when an unexpected Rod Stewart song off the radio had me kind of welling up. (The punch line is that one of them was that most sensitive of all '70s love-lyrics, the Faces' "Stay with Me.") "You Wear It Well" especially gets to me; if *Every Picture Tells a Story* is Stewart's high-water mark during that run, the album where it all comes together and everything seems effortlessly within his grasp, then "You Wear It Well" is the warm afterglow of someone taking a moment to luxuriate in his mastery before it slips away. Lyrically, it's word-perfect, with the extraordinary lines about Madame Onassis and feeling like a millionaire even more evocative now because they were sung at a time when Stewart's still dreaming about that world and not yet part of it. (There are also lines that mention Minnesota and the homesick blues—not sure who he had in the back of his mind there.) I honestly believe it's superior to "Maggie May," which, I should add, I regret leaving off the mixworthy list—just a little tired of it right now.

(record inventory, 2005-06)

"Gasoline Alley," Rod Stewart (1970)

"You Wear It Well" topped my CKLN list; I could have listed it #1 again (especially having since discovered this phenomenal live clip that I'll link to below), but there's a group of core Rod Stewart songs that are so central to my life, I want to get one of the other ones on the list this time. All the usual suspects: "Mandolin Wind," "Handbags and Gladrags," "Every Picture Tells a Story," and—back in the inner circle, after writing that I was tired of it when I did the record inventory—"Maggie May." You can throw in "Stay with Me" and "That's All You Need" by the Faces, too—I was originally going to lead this list with "That's All You Need," but Ian Anderson came to me in a dream the night before we began and guided me towards "Witches Promise." That's eight contenders, including the song I've settled on, and my preference for any one of them over any other is microscopic and forever changing. People will often point out that, contrary to conventional wisdom, Rod Stewart didn't fall off the edge of the earth soon after *Never a Dull Moment*—that he continued to release good music, and that the arc of his career is much more fluid than he gets credit for. Count me on the side of conventional wisdom. "Tonight's the Night" is fine for what it is, but what it is ain't "Gasoline Alley."

Basically you've got Stewart's version of "Penny Lane" or "Helpless" here. I've been trying to think of other songs that belong with those three—call it the *Wild Strawberries* genre, where somebody revisits specific locales associated with childhood or adolescence—but for some reason I'm coming up blank; there must be dozens, maybe hundreds (not to mention a book or two). Neil provided a useful checklist for such songs: dreams, comfort, memory, despair. "Gasoline Alley"'s got them all, plus it has a mandolin. The violin and mandolin playing on the best of those early Rod Stewart songs is their greatest contribution to the history of music and the history of the world. It's the doorway that opens up onto all those great words that tumble forth from the singer and makes them resonate.

(#20, Facebook Top 100, 2010-11)

Velvet Underground

"Sunday Morning" and "Heroin," *The Velvet Underground & Nico*; "White Light/White Heat" and "Here She Comes Now," *White Light/White Heat*; "What Goes On," "Jesus," and "After Hours," *The Velvet Underground*; "Sweet Jane" and "Rock & Roll," *Loaded*; "I Can't Stand It," *VU*

I've had the 10-song rule in place the whole way—or at least since the Beatles necessitated putting it there—and I'll continue to honour it, but the Velvet Underground make for a tougher call than anyone I've dealt with thus far. (It may be an even bigger problem when I get to Neil Young.) I've bypassed seven songs—"I'm Waiting for the Man," "Femme Fatale," "All Tomorrow's Parties," "I Heard Her Call My Name," "Some Kinda Love," "Oh! Sweet Nuthin'," and "I'm Sticking with You"—that I love approximately 1% less than what I've listed. If the Velvet Underground had been a baseball player, they'd have been a sabermetrician's dream. Their rate stats—percentage of great albums (4/4 in the studio, giving them a pass on *Squeeze*); percentage of great songs (running around 50% for me, maybe even higher for most people)—are undoubtedly the best ever for anyone who put out at least four LPs. Their peak value was so high, it translates into a healthy career value just on the basis of four years. Their peak value *was* their career value—there was no downtime in there. I'm not sure how many runs they created per 27 outs, but they probably score well there, too. I'd been aware of the Velvet Underground going back to middle school, an awareness that most likely began with Lillian Roxon's memorable entry for them in *The Rock Encyclopedia*: "There is no word for their sound but sometimes it seems as if a presence has taken it over, perhaps even His Satanic Majesty himself. You can easily imagine someone performing black masses with the Velvet Underground's albums." If that seems like kind of a narrow reading, it's worth noting that only the first two albums had appeared at that point; in any case, the bit about black masses sure made an impression on me. So I harbored some curiosity about the Velvet Underground right from the time I started buying records, but the problem was—it's easy to forget things like this living in the era of instant access to almost any music ever recorded, first because of all the catalogue excavation that accompanied the transition to CDs, and now again thanks to file sharing—there was a block of around 15 years where every one of their LPs was out of print domestically. That's my strongest association with the Velvet Underground outside of the music itself, and it's what I want to write about here; how much of

in and around the lake

an adventure it ended up becoming trying to assemble this small core of four studio albums. Long before I did buy anything, I'm almost positive I once stood inside Sam the Record Man looking at a copy of *White Light/White Heat*—this would have been 1974 or 1975, maybe—and that missed opportunity only added to my later desire to get my hands on their albums. I eventually began with the first LP and *Loaded*, both of which I bought either right at the end of high school or sometime during the following summer. I can't remember which one I got first, but they're both oddball imports that are probably almost as hard to track down today as original copies; my Nico album is a German import on Polydor, unpeeled banana on the front and no band pictures on the back, while *Loaded* is also a German pressing belonging to a strange series called "Original Rock Classics"—I say strange because the six other titles pictured across the bottom of the back cover include Vanilla Fudge's *Renaissance*, Iron Butterfly's *Heavy*, and the Electric Prunes' *Mass in F Minor*. Which of the four seems out of place? Also on the back cover is a captioned photo of the band in which Lou Reed is nowhere to be seen, even though he's identified as one of the four people—that confused me for years. Okay—two down, two to go. My next big project was to get *White Light/White Heat*, that vague memory of the copy in Sam's still in my head, and that turned out to be a nightmare. Occasionally a copy would turn up at the Vinyl Museum, but always selling for a minimum of $20, and I just wasn't someone to pay that much for an album, no matter how much I wanted it—I had learned by then that something would always turn up eventually at a reasonable price if you had a little patience. (I'm assuming no copy surfaced at Vortex during this time, because they would have priced anything at maybe $12 and I would have bought it. The original Vortex was the best record store the city ever had.) My friend Norm, the one who worked in the basement of the Vinyl Museum, managed to get me a French import for almost nothing at one point, and, for as long as I had it, that was probably my most treasured record. And to prove it, it met an untimely death in the trunk of my friend Dave's car when it was left overnight and came out looking like a piece of bad sculpture. Why was it in there in the first place? I don't know—we did some flaky things back then. To fill the void, I bought a two-record import collection when I was visiting an American friend—this is now '82 or so—which included almost the entirety of *White Light/White Heat*. It wasn't the same as having the actual album, though, so I went on to trade that one to Norm, who'd somewhat improbably started collecting everything he could from the band, including an original 45 of "White Light/White Heat." (Norm's temperament seemed light years away from the Velvet

Underground.) Within a couple of years, I found another unusual pressing of *White Light/White Heat*; I'm having trouble remembering what it looked like, but it was an early-'70s reissue on MGM, with a different cover than the standard all-black. That's the one I kept until Polygram finally started reissuing the original albums in the mid-'80s, I think in advance of *VU*'s release, at which point I bought a new copy and gave the other one to the aforementioned Viveca Gretton—another one of my sad, heroic gestures lost to history. At some point during all this *White Light/White Heat* juggling, I found a very cheaply priced British copy of album #3 in the small used bin Records on Wheels kept. Not sure where or when I found *1969 Velvet Underground Live*, but I think the impetus for buying it was that it turned up very high in the Gambaccini book; similarly, I bought the *Golden Archive Series* collection, even though I already had every song on it, because it was Ellen Willis' pick in *Stranded*. I think I've seen a copy or two of *Squeeze* over the years, but it's never held any real interest for me, ditto the *Max's Kansas City* LP. The one thing I would still like to get is the companion volume to *VU*. To get back to the idea of instant access, every time something is gained in life, something is lost. Obviously it's great that anyone who wants to investigate the Velvet Underground can do so easily today—it's sad how record companies held back so much music for so long until a new technology gave them a proprietary reason to suddenly rediscover it. There's a part of me, however, that misses all the work that went into tracking down certain albums. I'm not sure how much of that is the record-collector snob in me and how much is the music writer snob—about half and half, probably—but when you finally got what you were after, there was a tremendous sense of gratification that made you value the music even more.

(record inventory, 2005-06)

Who

"The Kids Are Alright," *My Generation*; "I Can See for Miles" and "I Can't Reach You," *The Who Sell Out*; "Bargain," *Who's Next*; "I Can't Explain," "Happy Jack," "Pictures of Lily," "Substitute," and "I'm a Boy," *Meaty Beaty Big and Bouncy*; "Circles," *Two's Missing*

I took a couple of days off from this to think about the Who, but then I remembered I'm on summer vacation, during which time thinking too hard is against the rules, so I instead did a Homer Simpson and just filled my mind with images of space aliens and dancing cows. So I guess I'll just have to wing it. Twice in my life the Who were up near the very top of the list: from the end of high school through to the beginning of university, first for (of course) *Who's Next* and then later because of the simultaneous appearance of *The Kids Are Alright* and *Quadrophenia* in theatres, and then again in the mid-'80s, when I reviewed *Two's Missing* for *Nerve* and spent some time re-listening to all the singles collected on *Meaty Beaty Big and Bouncy* (also a high school favorite). It was during that second period of intense interest that I felt sure that, on "Substitute " and "I Can't Reach You" and "Pictures of Lily," the Who had hit upon a version of pop music that may have been even closer to God than what the Beatles had crafted a year or two earlier. There's a mix of fragility and calm and intricacy on "I Can't Reach You" (not a famous song—if you don't know it, it leads side two of *The Who Sell Out*) that, as I've said about other stuff on here, makes me wonder "Where did that come from?" I say without hesitation that Pete Townshend was a genius from 1965 through 1967, and he created a body of work during that short span of time that you could spend a lifetime trying to take apart and adequately articulate its complexity. That's the good news; on the other side of the ledger, though, there's more baggage than even the Rolling Stones carry around in trying to perpetually hear that body of work fresh. First and foremost is the improbable reluctance of Townshend and Daltrey to put the "Closed" sign up once and for all—for a long time, nothing all that out of the ordinary, but bizarre after Entwistle's death. They suffer from overplay on one radio format as much as anyone out there, covering all phases of their career from the sublime ("My Generation") to the ridiculous ("Who Are You"). (On a related note, one song I should detest by now but don't is "Baba O'Riley"; most times it comes on the radio it still resonates with me, and if there were sufficient room above, I would be comfortable listing it.) The *Tommy/Who's Next/Quadrophenia* second phase of their career is a problem in general: there's greatness there that just does not hold up as well as the first phase, and—for me, anyway, and notwithstanding what I just finished saying about "Baba O'Riley"—I have a hard time getting past the image of a bare-chested Daltrey to want to give those albums the attention they deserve anymore. (Not a problem with the Rolling Stones, as I consider their parallel phase—from *Beggars Banquet* to *Exile*—as their best.) And then there was all that ugly business with Townshend a couple of years ago, and that inevitably interferes: one thing I always got from those early songs was a certain kind of purity (even when about cross-dressing or masturbation!), and that's been compromised, though not vitiated altogether—great art's too durable for that, right? All of these obstacles matter, and to remain a fan, you almost have to take that '65-67 period and quarantine it as something that exists apart from everything else you know about the Who. I guess that's what I've been able to do, because a fan I remain. One last note: if I had *A Quick One* on vinyl, I'd be listing "Don't Look Away" and "See My Way." To make room, I'd drop two of "Happy Jack," "I'm a Boy," and "Bargain".

(record inventory, 2005-06)

The Who's *Two's Missing* and Peter Townshend's *Another Scoop*

Working at his peak, the young Peter Townshend possessed an intuitive feel for how far the pop song form could be advanced that operated on some higher plane—how much detail it could support without losing its buoyancy, how its surface frivolity could couch the most serious matters (or, if need be, the most frivolous), how its essential grace and fragility and power to intoxicate could be pushed to a point just short of disappearing into thin air. The Beatles of "I Need You" and "Every Little Thing" could do that too, but for a brief moment Townshend refined the process a little further. I bet he looks back at that moment now and hasn't a clue where those early songs came from. How good could he be? "Happy Jack" and "The Kids Are Alright" you're familiar with, but the more obscure "I Can't Reach You," which kicked off the "serious" side of *Sell Out*, remains Townshend's most eloquent approximation of pop song perfection. In keeping with his supposition that the simple things you see are all complicated, "I Can't Reach You" works on about eight different levels. Like "Substitute," it's a fan's imitation of the point/counterpoint structures that Smoky Robinson (whom Townshend writes of reverentially in the liners to *Another Scoop*) handled with such astounding ease during his heyday. It relates someone's story: a guy standing off somewhere and gazing at a girl he feels unworthy of. It's as ethereal as a Christmas carol, say "Hark, the Herald Angels Sing." It's about masturbation, Townshend's signature. It's unspeakably sad—"You're so alive and I'm nearly dead." And, in retrospect, it serves as Townshend's farewell to pop song perfection, his tacit acknowledgement that he'll never be able to say everything he wants to in a two-and-a-half minute format.

(*Nerve*, 1987)

in and around the lake

Wire

"Mannequin," *Pink Flag*; "Sand in My Joints" and "Too Late," *Chairs Missing*; "Map Ref. 41°N 93°W," *154*; "Come Back in Two Halves," *A Bell Is a Cup*

(record inventory, 2005-06)

"Too Late," Wire (1978)

"Is it too late to change my mind?"—apropos for one more last-minute bump. ("Is it too late to change-a my mind?" to be precise. Inside the Top 10, little things mean a lot.) Just the song, though, not the artist. I knew right from the start that Wire would be in my Top 10, just as they were on the CKLN list. They've actually dropped a spot—last time I had "Mannequin" at #7.

The past couple of months, ever since I saw Olivier Assayas's *Carlos*, I've had it in my mind that "Dot Dash" was going to be my Wire pick. A somewhat embarrassing admission: I'd never heard "Dot Dash" until Assayas's film. I've had Wire's first three LPs for a long, long time, but "Dot Dash" was a stray single that never made it to LP until many years later on a *Pink Flag* reissue. It's an amazing song—in the context of the film, as unforgettable as "El Watusi" in *Who's That Knocking at My Door?*—and I'll provide a link below. In the end, though, I didn't want to have a Top 10 song that I'd only known for such a short while. I probably haven't yet listened to it 15 times.

I could go with "Mannequin" again—la-la-la's as improbably Monkees-worthy as those found on "Divide and Conquer"—but "Too Late"'s another one that my band had been considering, so it's been on my mind lately. We ended up passing: it's the same basic bar-chord as everything else I'm able to play moved up and down the fretboard, but they move it around extra-fast, they move it to at least six different locations, and, as all of that sorts itself out, you're supposed to simultaneously match some words and some drumbeats to all the different locations. That's just way too much happening in one song—never even mind what sounds to be an organ or some such instrument overtop. As rudimentary and as primitive as it all sounds, there's actually some musicianly stuff going on here.

I haven't heard Wire's new album yet, but I've established a new Bill James-like metric in honour of them: "Wire Peak Value," meaning how well your four best songs (not three, and not five—four) match up against anybody else. The greatest WPV of all time belongs to Wire. (8.391, if you're interested—I don't have time to explain.) On "Too Late," "Mannequin," "Dot Dash," and "Map Ref. 41°N 93°W," they were the greatest ever—better than the Beatles, Dylan, anybody.

(#8, Facebook Top 100, 2010-11)

Yo La Tengo

"Detouring America with Horns" and "Satellite," *May I Sing with Me*; "Sudden Organ" and "I Heard You Looking," *Painful*; "Blue Line Swinger," *Electr-O-Pura*; "Moby Octopad," *I Can Hear the Heart Beating as One*; "From Black to Blue," *And Then Nothing Turned Itself Inside Out*; "How Some Jellyfish Are Born," *The Sounds of the Sounds of Science*; "The Race Is On Again," *I Am Not Afraid of You and I Will Beat Your Ass*; "I'll Be Around," *Fade*

New Wave Hot Dogs

New Wave Hot Dogs is an album I can definitely envision a long-term attachment to, if only for the half of it that's gentle and sweet and lyrical; even better than the Reed song is "Lewis," plus four or five others that work a similar style. Unfortunately, the half that tries to live up to the name of leader Ira Kaplan's defunct rockmag, *New York Rocker*, gets in the way. The edgy, almost Human Switchboard-type songs just aren't very convincing. I firmly believe that anyone with a gift for melody, as Yo La Tengo obviously possess in a big way, should milk it for all it's worth—total wimpdom, just like, the Shoes.

(*Nerve*, 1987)

"Moby Octopad," Yo La Tengo

An iridescent wisp of a song, like "Tattoo" or "I Can't Reach You" from *The Who Sell Out* (it may even sample "Armenia City in the Sky"), and there are traces of the Who in the title, too; Scott says it has something to do with a brand of keyboard Pete Townshend used to use, while it makes me think of those mopeds driven around by the kids in *Quadrophenia*. According to a Yo La Tengo page I checked, parts of Burt Bacharach's "Bird Bath" are "embodied" by "Moby Octopad"—I've never heard of that song, I don't know if "embodied" is supposed to be a euphemism for "sampled," and in any case the result doesn't sound very Bacharachish. I never thought I'd be checking a Yo La Tengo page in this lifetime. Ten years ago I reviewed *New Wave Hot Dogs* (a hard title to forget), and I haven't once thought of Yo La Tengo since. I'm somewhat shocked to hear something so exquisite from an old wave group I'd never bothered to pay attention to (I would have missed this, too, if I hadn't stumbled over the great "Sugar Cube" video one day). For me, "Moby Octopad" comes very close to the breaking point of how much beauty a song can sustain without shutting you out, without turning into something you admire but don't feel, an empty pretty picture like the movie *Days of Heaven*. Close, but it goes places: a rolling start, a bit of a changeup in each of the first three verses, a sudden stop and a half-minute's worth of dissonance (without losing the shape of the song—it threw me the first time, but now I think it's perfectly placed), then a reprise, more beautiful still because you weren't sure if the dissonance had brought the really good stuff to a premature end. I don't know what any of it's about. Yes I do, it's about a Moby Octopad; I'm getting together with Mark Morrison to write the sequel, "Return of the Moby Octopad." (9.0; from the same album, "Sugar Cube," "Return to Hot Chicken," and "Damage" are also excellent, and there are a number of other good songs. If you could extract the best 11 or 12 and shuffle them up the right way, I think you'd have an old-fashioned 40-minute pop album for the ages.)

(*Radio On*, 1997)

"How Some Jellyfish Are Born," Yo La Tengo (2002)

One last perverse choice, but I don't know that anybody in the group is as attentive to Yo La Tengo as Steve is to the Jefferson Airplane, so this one may pass by unnoticed. But it's from an album that Christgau again brushes aside with the dreaded bomb icon, and he's a big YLT fan. That damn Christgau, undermining my list every chance he gets.

Yo La Tengo is my favorite band since Hüsker Dü. The Pet Shop Boys occupied that spot for a time, then my interest in them started to wane; skip forward a few years to where getting hold of a band's entire catalogue became a much faster and cheaper proposition, and one Yo La Tengo album after another, a picture started to emerge of a band that was building a sizable body of work slavishly devoted to the two or three things I love most: melody, beauty, and drone. Almost comically so—an *Onion* piece from 2002 provided me with the phrase "The Great Sebadoh Fire of '93," which is the name of the folder where I keep all my Yo La Tengo-type music. Scott gave me credit for "Back & Forth" the other day, so I'll return the favour and credit him with taping *I Can Hear the Heart Beating as One* for me soon after it came out; that was what started it all. (Jeff Pike made me a tape soon after, and that played a part too.)

Now it's me who does the proselytizing. I've got a CD-700 that I've made for a number of people, and it's comprised of some of the same songs that most fans would put on there—"Moby Octopad," "Sudden Organ," "Blue Line Swinger"—mixed in with an array of personal favorites ("From Black to Blue," "Satellite," "The Race Is on Again," etc.). I could have gone with many of them for this list. I don't include "How Some Jellyfish Are Born," however; there are already a few long songs on there, and with so much to fit in, "Jellyfish" stands too much apart from what Yo La Tengo does to make sense. Again, perverse: ostensibly my favorite song by my favorite band, and I leave it off my hand-picked best-of that's supposed to convert friends into loving them as much as I do.

I couldn't begin to estimate how often I've played "How Some Jellyfish Are Born" the past few years, though—I can recall a few stretches of time where I played nothing but in the car for days on end. It serves the same function as songs I've already listed by Arvo Pärt, Grachan Moncur, and Kim Hiorthøy, with a couple of more still to come. Melody, beauty, drone, and enough empty space in which to turn off your mind, relax, and float downstream. So really, it doesn't stand apart from what Yo La Tengo does at all.

At the risk of sending us off on a tangent, I actually believe this: someday, they'll be inducted into the Rock and Roll Hall of Fame. It won't happen for a long time, but eventually their Bert Blyleven-like case will win out.

(#13, Facebook Top 100, 2010-11)

"I'll Be Around," Yo La Tengo

My favorite video this year was, predictably, the one that Vania Heymann put together for "Like a Rolling Stone." Next—I see very few videos these days—would be Yo La Tengo's for "I'll Be Around." I can't imagine where it would ever get played, so I'm sure it exists nowhere except on YouTube. Close to 200,000 views, though, some of them not by me.

in and around the lake

It's set in a forest clearing, then in a kitchen. Text is all over the screen—what looks to be a short story but on closer inspection is a mishmash of Yo La Tengo lyrics past and present, excerpts from said mishmash, and a recipe for Spicy Tortilla Soup. Once inside the kitchen, the band putters around and makes their soup, they sit down to dinner, then a couple of cops come and take James McNew away. Ira and Georgia look perplexed. I'm not sure...maybe the joke is trying to introduce some adventure and intrigue into three of the most domesticated lives imaginable. (A title card early on says "Based on Actual Events," which is then amended to "Inspired by Actual Events"—there may be some poetic license.) Or maybe McNew is about to leave the band, and this is their way of breaking the news. It's quite cryptic.

Fade has everything you might love or despise about Yo La Tengo. After two or three songs I don't care for (including "Om," the one song that seemed to get some attention), I think it's a perfect album. "I'll Be Around" continues a tradition (shared by Neil Young) of stealing titles from famous songs; the Spinners' "I'll Be Around" is one of my favorite songs from my favorite year ever, and I think I like Yo La Tengo's "I'll Be Around" even more. Their whispery ambience has never felt closer, or, at the same time, just as out of reach. Always just out of reach.

(#3, year-end ballot, 2013)

a friend i've never seen

The only possible way to end. Neil closed out the record inventory (more or less), he closed the Facebook countdown, he closed my high school years in Georgetown when I saw him preview *Rust Never Sleeps* at Maple Leaf Gardens in 1978, and he's closing this book. All roads lead to Neil. Except for the country roads that take you home. They lead to West Virginia.

"The Loner," *Neil Young*; "Cinnamon Girl" and "Cowgirl in the Sand," *Everybody Knows This Is Nowhere*; "Only Love Can Break Your Heart," and "Till the Morning Comes," *After the Gold Rush*; "Ambulance Blues," *On the Beach*; "Albuquerque" and "Tired Eyes," *Tonight's the Night*; "Barstool Blues," *Zuma*; "Sugar Mountain," *Decade*

You can see how silly it is for me to narrow down my favorite Neil Young songs to 10—if you move "Sugar Mountain" to where it belongs chronologically at the front of the list, I've used up six spots by album number three, and even there, I had to ignore at least three or four other songs from those first three LPs that I love more or less as much as anything I've listed. There are so many alternates that just narrowly miss, I won't bother naming them as I did with the Velvet Underground. There's one thing that is accurate, though—even if I expanded the list to 20 songs, it would still pretty much end at *Zuma*; maybe "Powderfinger" would make it, maybe "Like a Hurricane," too (automatic many years ago, until I wore it out), but in terms of how I feel about Neil Young right now, the music he made up until 1975 just dwarfs everything he's done since. (A couple more qualifications. I was able to cheat earlier by including work he's done as part of CSNY and the Stills-Young Band; "Ocean Girl," which came out in 1976, would make any list of 20, and would even contend for my 10 favorite. And from his resurgence in the early '90s, I'd definitely include "Over and Over.") Anyway, enough bookkeeping. My first two Neil albums were the first two anybody should start with, *After the Gold Rush* and *Everybody Knows This Is Nowhere*. For two records that would become so incomparably important to me, I'm very hazy on the details of when and why I bought them. I may have picked up both at exactly the same time, I'm not sure—if not, within weeks of each other, I'm positive. They were probably bought in '76, but it may have been as early as '75; I remember being in Florida when *American*

interrupting my train of thought

Stars 'n Bars was on the new-release rack in 1977, at which point I was already a fan, so it had to be '75 or '76. I mentioned before how much some of what I listened to in high school was influenced by the senior basketball team, something that was true of Neil Young more than anybody, but again, how that influence translated into my choosing to start with *Gold Rush* and *Everybody Knows* is a little unclear; the most vivid memory I have of the seniors' Neil fixation is them singing "Roll Another Number" on the bus, but I wouldn't buy *Tonight's the Night* until later. Whatever the exact timeline—and I should mention that an 8-track of *Harvest* preceded all of this by a few years, and that the singles from that album were very much a part of my immersion into Top 40 radio in 1972—finding my way to those two early LPs, and then to *Tonight's the Night* and *Zuma* and *Time Fades Away* soon after, remains one of the defining events of my life, doing more to shape me as a listener, and as a person, than any other music I've ever encountered. There's a great quote from Lou Barlow that I've made reference to before, about how "Being 17 and in a hardcore band is just about the pinnacle of human experience," but I'd have to say that being 15, fumbling around aimlessly in a small Ontario town in the mid-'70s, and having "Cowgirl in the Sand" get inside your head is even better. I still have a piece of paper tucked away in a yearbook going back to June of 1979 and my last few weeks of high school (see facing page).

More than anything I can say, this one surviving document of my Neil Young obsession from that time—there's just that and the albums themselves—gives a glimpse into how much, as I prepared to clear out of Georgetown for Toronto and university (never, I mistakenly thought, to look back), I had begun to view my life through the prism of some fuzzy, Vilmos Zsigmond-photographed movie populated by the characters and fragmentary images that floated through *Everybody Knows* and *Zuma* and *Gold Rush*. I suppose the meaning of it all is fairly self-explanatory, an all-encompassing farewell to our classmates that my friend Steve and I intended to post around school during the final week. I'd like to think we did just that, but something's telling me we backed down. You can see who the good guys and the bad guys were—actually, outside of us, there were no good guys, it was just good girls and bad girls and bad guys. Three things come to mind as I look back at our handiwork 25 years later. One, you can't beat a typewriter for character; two, I didn't know the difference between a full and a semi-colon; and three, I was well on my way to becoming the pretentious fuck I turned into at university. The film was conceived as something real, a vague outline I'd carry around in my head all through U of T, with the grand plan being

a friend i've never seen

```
attention, last week only;

ambulance fever: or, the story of the last five years as seen through a
    businessman's eyes

* starring;

i fell in love with the actress; she was playin' a part that i could
    understand...

karen gregson / the ocean girl / in a jungleland by the sea and the sand
    can i meet you there
jane mcintyre / the cinnamon girl / you see us together chasing the
    moonlight
sandra smith / the girl just down the aisle / once i thought i saw you
    in a crowded hazy bar dancing on the light from star to star
jennifer thompson / the country girl / i am lonely but you can free me
    all in the way that you smile

...well all that glitters isn't gold; i know you've heard that story
    told...

alice armstrong / isabella / you're only real with your makeup on
nancy phillips / the cowgirl in the sand / when so many love you is it
    the same
janice snow / the stupid girl / you really got a lot to learn

...and stars sit at bars and decide what they're drinking...

james hansen / danger bird / he rides the wind back to his home although
    his wings have turned to stone
robert hatcher / mr. soul / i was raised by the praise of a fan who said
    i upset her
william rivers / the cripple creek ferry / doesn't mean that much to me
    to mean that much to you
derek todd / the emperor of wyoming / ain't it funny how you feel when
    you're findin' out it's real
terrence waldrum / cortez / what a killer

...while the lonely mingle with circumstance.

leopold bloom / the old man / back in canada i spent my days riding
    subways through a haze i was handcuffed i was born and raised
stephen dedulas / the loner / so all you critics sit alone you're no
    better than me for what you've shown with your stomach pumps and
    your hook-and-ladder dreams we could get together for some scenes

original soundtrack written and performed by the broken arrows...
                                    available on borrowed tunes® records

produced by: david briggs
directed by: elliot roberts
```

that I'd go on to York's graduate program in film and that *Ambulance Fever* would be my very own *Mean Streets*. It all kind of fell by the wayside when I never got into York, not being someone who had the initiative and certitude of self to pursue anything on my own, absent some kind of structure to lead me along. I'd been progressively losing interest in Neil Young by that point too; *Trans* was the first album of his I'd ever flatly disliked (an understatement; I was appalled), *Everybody's Rockin'* and *Old Ways* barely registered, and *Landing on Water*, which I reviewed for *Nerve*, was so bad I authoritatively stated Neil would never again make music that affected people in any meaningful way. I've since realized that that's always a stupid thing to say of any singer whose primary resource, his voice, hasn't lost a thing over the years, and sure enough, *Freedom* and a return to something approximating his greatest work was close at hand. The other thing I remember about that review was that I barely even hinted at how important Neil Young had been to me just a few years earlier; there was something very self-satisfied about the way I dismantled this really awful LP, and even though I was 100% right, not providing some necessary context for my dismissal was an odd omission. I actually think there was a subconscious link in my mind between Neil, my anger and disappointment over York's rejection, and the realization that I wasn't going to be a filmmaker after all, and that *Ambulance Fever* would remain a piece of paper hidden away in a yearbook. So I'm glad I finally get to make some use of it here. I would eventually come full circle and again experience the full force of those early Neil Young LPs, not because of *Freedom* or *Ragged Glory*, but triggered by a fanzine piece I wrote in the mid-'90s in which I revisited high school less from a musical standpoint than how it affected me socially. (Let me mention in passing that I liked *Freedom* when it came out, and I had "Hangin' on a Limb" on a year-end CIUT list; *Ragged Glory* appeared at a moment when I was paying less attention to music than at any time since I first started listening to the radio, so it was only a year or two ago that I finally bought that one on CD.) I continue to be aware of Neil's newer releases, occasionally hearing something that sounds pretty good ("Razor Love"), occasionally thinking he's hit a new low (the 9/11 song), but I haven't bought anything on release since *Old Ways*. The early albums are still important to me, and always will be. I'm not sure if even the upcoming box set can find its way into that fortress; I know there'll be lots of stuff on there that falls into place chronologically in terms of Neil's biography, but not mine.

(record inventory, 2005-06)

Neil Young Journeys

Saw *Journeys* tonight. (Same friend I saw the '78 Maple Leaf Gardens show with—instead of getting high beforehand, we went to Starbucks.) I liked all the old stuff, especially what he does with "After the Gold Rush." Half the show is *Le Noise* material, which I was hearing for the first time since La Nuit Blanche a couple of summers ago. Can't say I liked much of that..."Sign of Love"'s pretty good; "Hitchhiker" seemed less impressive;

"Love and War" made me cringe. I really liked Neil in the car, drolly talking about taking nickel dares as a kid and stuff like that—early on, you get the idea this will make up half the film, but in the end it's much less. What's really missing: a tour through Toronto. Demme does something weird with the camera during "Down by the River" and "Hitchhiker" that's really funny, but accidentally so, I think: *Dr. Tongue's 3D House of Neil*.

(ILX, 2012)

Purple Words on a Grey Background[8]

In the winter and spring of 1972, right around the time I commandeered a transistor radio lying around our house and began listening religiously to Toronto's 1050-CHUM, there was a six-month window when Neil Young was something of a radio star. "Heart of Gold" made it to #1 in March, followed soon after by "Old Man," a more modest hit. "The Needle and the Damage Done" also got some AM airplay (in Toronto, at least), and when "Heart of Gold" fell out of the #1 spot, it was supplanted by America's "A Horse with No Name." I have a very dim memory of America insisting at the time that "A Horse with No Name"'s similarity to Neil (ditto their "Sandman") was purely accidental; just like the Osmonds and "Yo-Yo," America's sound was their very being, impervious to outside influences. Meanwhile, less covert cover versions of Neil had been on the radio within the past couple of years: Buddy Miles (1970) and Joey Gregorash (1971) both charted with "Down by the River," Matthew's Southern Comfort (1971) included "Tell Me Why" on the same album as "Woodstock," and somebody named Tommy Graham (no recollection of him at all; he sounds like he should have been in Deep Purple) made it onto CHUM's Top 30 with "After the Gold Rush" in 1972. Neil's liner note on *Decade* about not liking the middle of the road very much following the massive success of *Harvest* wasn't altogether an exaggeration; if he wasn't exactly Elton John, you didn't have to search very far to hear him, someone who sounded like him, or someone singing one of his songs in 1972.

And that was pretty much it for Neil Young and AM radio. Neil himself had another half-dozen very minor hits over the next decade (none making it higher than #61), and two more cover versions charted: Linda Ronstadt's "Love Is a Rose" (1975, a B-side) and Nicolette Larson's "Lotta Love" (1979). No more Top 100 singles of any size for Neil after that, and

---

8   A few excerpts from a much longer survey; a web address for the full piece can be found in the appendix.

no more hit cover versions. But cover versions did continue to appear—lots of them. Lots and lots and lots of them.

With the help of various online resources, I began a few months ago to track down as many of them as I could. I had an eye towards writing about whatever I eventually assembled, but I also wanted to put together a box set for a friend. Obviously, you need to have access to a good file-sharer to even think about such a project; as the old K-Tel commercials used to warn, going out and buying the necessary CDs individually would set you back a couple thousand dollars (besides which, some of what follows exists only in the ether, never having been actually released). As it stands today—I'm more or less finished, but every now and again I turn up something new—I've collected 277 individual songs (including versions drawn from four multi-artist tributes), plus another four full-length single-artist tributes, almost 22 hours' worth of music in all.

Simultaneous to all of this, I've also been collecting cover versions of the Beatles and the Velvet Underground. I'm going to hazard a guess that Neil is the third most-covered artist in the history of pop music. The Beatles, as you might imagine, are in another stratosphere altogether—I've got 115 hours of Beatles covers on the computer, and I know there are at least another 115 hours still out there, possibly even twice that. I've got about 12 hours of Velvets covers, so let's say they're good for fourth- or fifth-place; I sense they've been covered more often than the Rolling Stones or Chuck Berry or anyone else you could name, but I might be wrong. I would assume Dylan sits second behind the Beatles.

The Neil box for my friend ended up comprising 10 CD-700s, a winnowing down that gave me the latitude to leave out all of the bad stuff and most of the merely ordinary. For the purposes of this piece, though, I'll run through the entire haul, arranged alphabetically by song. On the eve of these long-rumored anthologies of unreleased archival material finally seeing the light of day, here's another tangential piece of the Neil Young puzzle.

"Ambulance Blues" (*On the Beach*, 1974)

R.E.M. w/Neil Young (Holiday Single, 1999)

I'm going to cheat and call this a cover, seeing as it was issued as R.E.M.'s 1999 Christmas single for fan-club members. Neil handles vocals, Peter Buck plays banjo, Michael Stipe is not involved; it's a live recording, from where I'm not sure. Neil begins with a disclaimer that he's going to work from a cue sheet, amusing to me because after listening to the original approximately three zillion times through high school, it's the longest song I know where I have every last word down cold. The one significant change from the original—Neil follows his cue sheet closely, and the mood and the pacing are just right (a few extra seconds actually push it over nine minutes)—occurs in the Patty Hearst verse:

> *I saw today, in the entertainment section*
> *There's room at the top for private detection*
> *To mom and dad, this just doesn't matter*
> *But he still screwed around, and now he won't even look at her*

The first three lines are familiar, the last comes out of nowhere and is startling—as casually as can be, Neil takes the greatest of Nixon songs (with all dissenting votes for Jefferson Airplane's "Mexico" and the Undisputed Truth's "Smiling Faces Sometimes" acknowledged) and sets it down squarely in the Clinton/Lewinsky moment. Divine inspiration or a disclaimer to the disclaimer? I'd like to get hold of that cue sheet.

"Cinnamon Girl" (*Everybody Knows This Is Nowhere*, **1969**)

Andy Curran (Borrowed Tunes: A Tribute to Neil Young, 1994)
Big in Iowa (This Note's for You Too: A Tribute to Neil Young, 1999)
Brett Anderson & Terence Trent D'Arby (undated)
Dream Syndicate (Out of the Grey, 1986)
Killdozer (Intellectuals Are the Shoeshine Boys of the Ruling Elite, 1984)
Loop (The Bridge: A Tribute to Neil Young, 1989)
Los Lobos (undated)
Malc Brookes (Be the Rain, 2006)
Mark Lanegan (undated)
Matthew Sweet & Susanna Hoffs (Under the Covers Vol. 1, 2006)
Motorhead (All the Aces: The Best of Motorhead, 1978)
Radiohead (Live@Music Planet2Nite, Paris, 2001)
Replicants (Replicants, 1995)
Smashing Pumpkins (Live@WZRD, Chicago, 1989)
Type O Negative (Symphony for the Devil, 1999)

"We need to cover something a little less obvious…Hey, I know—let's do 'Cinnamon Girl!'" Fifteen covers—almost twice as many as "Cortez the Killer"'s nine and "Heart of Gold"'s eight, the runners-up—make "Cinnamon Girl" Neil's "Yesterday." Happily, it's not a song that's going to end up on a Ray Conniff album—that's something "Heart of Gold" will have to contend with through the years. (My references are out of date…substitute "Nickleback" for "Ray Conniff.") I recently counted down my 100 favorite songs on a college radio show I do out of Toronto, and I had "Cinnamon Girl" at #2, behind Rod Stewart's "You Wear It Well." The original figures so prominently in my imagination—the mood of which is perfectly conveyed by *Everybody Knows This Is Nowhere*'s cover shot, something I'm not sure I could explain, other than to say it's a Canadians-in-flannel thing—that any kind of an overly faithful run-through is going to go right past me, like the Brett Anderson/Terence Trent D'Arby and Los Lobos versions.

You have to mess around with the song to even have a chance, and most of these people do. The metal and noise bands (Killdozer, Motorhead, Loop, Type O Negative, Replicants), not surprisingly, slow it down and accentuate its essential heaviness; Killdozer's typically over-the-top yowling is so engagingly inane that they come off best, while Type O Negative forget there's still a song there and ruin it. Thom Yorke and Billy Corgan are both in full whine, which actually works well in this context—I like their versions fine. Susanna Hoffs brings a female voice to a definitively male song, and that's worth something (truthfully, you can barely hear her until the very end—Sweet dominates). Best bet? I don't know anything about Mark Lanegan except the little bit that I've read online, but he does a terrific Richie Havens-like version for an Italian radio station, complete with some breathless Italian patter from the host at the end. And there's his secret—he's alone and confused and far away from home. Ma, send him money now, he's gonna make it somehow, he needs another chance.

"Country Girl" (*Déjà Vu*, 1970)

Steve Taton (Be the Rain, 2006)
Mike Durham (Be the Rain, 2006)

The original, from *Déjà Vu*, rarely gets mentioned in anything written about Neil Young, having long since been subsumed into the shadow of "Helpless" and the tracks that classic-rock stations cling to ("Woodstock,"

"Teach Your Children," "Our House"). I count it as one of his greatest songs—four minutes of opaque, orchestral doom-and-gloom, culminating in that ecstatic moment when everything breaks in half and the sun comes cascading through: "Country girl, I think you're pretty…" Enough drama for Phil Spector, and when you compare it to the two aforementioned Graham Nash warhorses, well, you know that Neil and his bandmates weren't really on the same page. Steve Taton tries to go it alone, and, as much as I applaud his calling attention to a neglected masterpiece, a substantively different song emerges: some of the moodiness remains, but the high drama's absent. Mike Durham proceeds from something I'd forgotten, that "Country Girl" is technically comprised of three movements, each with its own subtitle ("Whiskey Boot Hill"/"Down, Down, Down"/"Country Girl (I Think You're Pretty)," and he lifts out the middle section as a standalone. Strange, to say the least—everything's build-up, stopping just short of the moment you live for in the original—but he actually gets much closer to what I love about the song.

"Cowgirl in the Sand" (*Everybody Knows This Is Nowhere*, 1969)

Benalto (undated)
Byrds (Byrds, 1973)
Indigo Girls (undated)
Iron and Wine (Live@Bowery Ballroom, NYC, 2004)

Unlike "Cortez," nobody takes on "Cowgirl in the Sand" full-out—all of these versions run between three and four minutes, and three of them are acoustic, a major overhaul of Neil's 10-minute, guitar-mad epic. (A brief salute to the one electric version, Benalto's frat-house yelping; it's quite likely the single worst thing in this survey, and standing out from 250 other covers in any way is worth something, I suppose.) In one of those parallel universes I spoke of earlier, Iron and Wine (and Calexico) do a great "All Tomorrow's Parties," and they do almost as well with "Cowgirl"; they're masters of the spooky dirge. The prize here, though, goes to the Byrds, a live version taken from the not very well regarded reunion LP they put out in 1973. I've never heard the whole album, just the two Neil covers (cf. "[See the Sky] About to Rain" below), but to me you've got the real Byrds, all five of them together, intersecting with an emerging colossus who shares both their strangeness and their brilliance. It's Einstein and Freud, walking together on the beach, and I'm very grateful to learn that such a meeting took place.

"Down By the River" (*Everybody Knows This Is Nowhere*, 1969)

Buddy Miles (Them Changes, 1970)
Low & Dirty Three (In the Fishtank, 2001)
Meters (Kickback, 1975)
Undisputed Truth (Cosmic Truth, 1975)
Wild T. & the Spirit (Borrowed Tunes: A Tribute to Neil Young, 1994)

I haven't done any research above and beyond the songs I write about here, but chances are that Buddy Miles did the first-ever Neil Young cover, so all credit to him. My completely uninformed sense of Miles before hearing "Down by the River" (I've never heard anything else by him) pretty much amounted to two scare phrases: "jazz-rock fusion" and "drum solo." So I don't think anyone else in this survey surprised me as much as he did—I love what he does with the song, re-imagining it in a way that brings to mind the Chambers Brothers singing about how their soul's been psyche-DEL-i-cized. Weirdly enough, it's his version, rather than Neil's original, which then becomes the blueprint for the Meters and Undisputed Truth, with all three of them incorporating a recurring "sha-la-la, the weather" refrain that comes out of left field and makes you wonder how Neil missed it. The two rock covers have opposite problems: Wild T is exceedingly shrill, Low & Dirty Three so low-key they're barely there (it's almost funny—in a nine-minute version, they don't finish tuning up until the six-minute mark). I led off my friend's box set with Buddy Miles, just so I could sneak in Chris Farley beforehand: "You're gonna end up eating a steady diet of government cheese, and livin' in a *van down by the river.*"

"Heart of Gold" (*Harvest*, 1972)

Black Label Society (Alcohol Fueled Brewtality Live + 5, 2001)
Boney M (Nightflight to Venus, 1978)
Johnny Cash (Unearthed II: Trouble in Mind, 2003)

a friend i've never seen

Lawrence Gowan (Borrowed Tunes: A Tribute to Neil Young, 2006)
Richard Lloyd (This Note's for You Too: A Tribute to Neil Young, 1999)
Stereophonics (Have a Nice Day, 2001)
Steve Dahl (Be the Rain, 2006)
Tori Amos (Strange Little Girls, 2001)

Inevitable that this would generate the second most covers on this list; it was Neil's only #1 single ever, and, 35 years later, it easily remains his most famous song. ("Hey Hey, My My [Into the Black]" and "Rockin' in the Free World" get more airplay on Toronto's biggest classic-rock station, but even there, "Heart of Gold" still pops up a lot.) I wonder how many of the covering artists above share the same kind of nostalgia for the song that I retain. I realize it's not anywhere near to being one of Neil's greatest songs, and all the overplay has drained it of whatever emotions it once stirred, but it was my introduction to Neil Young in 1972, on the air when I claimed that transistor radio, and *Harvest* soon after became the first album of his that I ever owned (on 8-track, no less), so there's still something there for me that's impossible to destroy. I know that Johnny Cash didn't come to the song that way, and I'll take a wild guess that Boney M didn't, either, but the other six, maybe. Black Label Society (gothic metal) and Tori Amos (skronky noise) get credit for reinventing the song, but truthfully, they both sound kind of silly. Cash, Gowan, Lloyd, the Stereophonics, and Steve Dahl—whom I assume is not the Steve Dahl who burned disco records at Comiskey Park in 1979; if it is, I hope he doesn't mind being listed alongside Boney M—are varying shades of faithful to the original.

Boney M split the difference: they can't help reinventing the song to a certain extent, just because of who they are, but they also include some excellent harmonica playing (a young Rob Pilatus from Milli Vanilli, perhaps) that reminds me more of Neil than anything else on this list. I used to have a claque of Boney M acolytes who wrote for *Radio On*, a Top-40 fanzine I put out through the '90s. I think they were a claque; they might have been a cadre, or even something really sinister, like a cell. A few of the issues featured a *Radio On* canon of the greatest artists ever, drawn from contributors' lists of their 100 favorite songs, and, humorless drudge that I am, I would make sure to rig the rules so Boney M didn't end up nestled in amongst the Beatles, the Rolling Stones, and Madonna at the top. Well, mea culpa, sort of: I like Boney M's "Heart of Gold" better than anybody's.

"Ohio" (7-inch, 1970)

Coal Porters (This Note's for You Too: A Tribute to Neil Young, 1999)
Dandy Warhols (Come On Feel the Dandy Warhols, 2000)
Toxic Reasons (Dedication 1979-1988, 1988)
Ween (Freedom, 2001)
Isley Brothers (Givin' It Back, 1971)

My favorite overtly political song ever ("overtly" meaning the ones that actually name names). A big part of what's kept it so vital for me is that I play it for my middle-school students every May 4. I give them the backstory, post the lyrics on chart paper, and pass around the famous photo from Kent State; of the 40 or 50 songs I play for them during the course of the year, I'd say they're as attentive to "Ohio" as anything. (I always follow up by asking them what they think the line "we're finally on our own" means.) The Isleys' version runs almost nine minutes, dissolving into Jimi Hendrix's "Machine Gun" towards the end; no surprise that it wanders, but, appearing in 1971 as it did, it's almost as much in the moment as the original, and that counts for a lot—like so many songs and films of that era, Nixon's there lurking, and not just in the words.

I like the Dandy Warhols' spooky slow-motion version even better. I was only eight when the killings happened, so my sense of Kent State is only second-hand (or third-hand, being Canadian), but I'm sure that along with the anger and outrage—which is where Neil focuses his energy—there was a feeling of falling endlessly through empty space, like a collective bad dream that just kept getting worse with each successive post-Dallas event. And that's where the Dandy Warhols focus their energy (or lack thereof, to be more precise). One final note: Toxic Reasons contribute the fourth or fifth useless punk cover thus far. Maybe I've forgotten something that comes up later in this survey, but, although your instincts might tell you otherwise, Neil Young + punk is not a good idea.

"Only Love Can Break Your Heart" (*After the Gold Rush*, **1970**)

Corrs (VH1 Presents the Corrs Live in Dublin, 2002)
Elkie Brooks (Shooting Star, 1978)
Everlast (Big Daddy O.S.T., 1999)
Juliana Hatfield (Gold Stars 1992-2002, 2002)

a friend i've never seen

Psychic TV (The Bridge: A Tribute to Neil Young, 1989)
Saint Etienne (Foxbase Alpha, 1991)
Waltons (Borrowed Tunes: A Tribute to Neil Young, 1994)

I wouldn't say the original is the most famous song on *After the Gold Rush* ("Southern Man," probably), and it doesn't get much airplay on the classic-rock station here, but it has the ability to summon forth something extra in those who cover it; at least three of these are exceptional, and only the Waltons are less than really good. (Yes, it's one of my own favorite Neil songs, and it's always tricky to separate my feelings about the originals from the covers. There are a number of originals I rank just as high, though, and their covers just don't have the same impact as some of these.) Everlast (rough-edged folk, with a Hawaiian twist), the Corrs (orchestrated folk), and Elkie Brooks (mid-tempo disco) all approach the song differently, and it proves eminently pliable. (I retain a funny memory of a former girlfriend, British, dancing to an Elkie Brooks album in her living room.)

I mentioned back in the introduction that Linda Ronstadt and Nicolette Larson were the only two people to chart with a Neil cover after 1972; if the memory of Saint Etienne's version made you think I must have miscounted, it actually only barely made it onto the UK Top 100. Radio's loss—I put it in my Top 10 that year, and it's only gotten more hypnotic with time. Juliana Hatfield's rendition is all swoon—beautiful singing, quavering instrumentation to mirror the song's fragility, and a minor alteration to the melodic progression that adds an extra little lilt. And that leaves the bug-eyed, transgendered Satanist with the lengthiest and best version of all, the strangest thing about which is how very unstrange it is. There's a lifetime of disappointment and missed opportunities in the counsel kept by "Only Love Can Break Your Heart," and while the lifetime that Psychic TV's Genesis P-Orridge brings to the song is undoubtedly a lot more unusual than where Neil was coming from, all that matters in the end is the way he invests every last bit of it into the delicate fall of "Yes, only love can break your heart" each time he hits the chorus. Perfection.

Rusted Moon: ***The String Quartet Tribute to Neil Young*** **(2002)**

Strings are dramatic. You could take the collected works of Mr. Mister, Billy Vera, and My Chemical Romance, and if you set it all to strings, there'd be drama. There's something about the violent swoop of violins that brings out the best in almost anything, and Neil's work lends itself to the full treatment beautifully. The songs I most love, "After the Gold Rush" and "Ohio," stand up fine; the big rock statements I'm tired of, "Rockin' in the Free World" and "Southern Man," are charged back to life; and even "Lotta Love," possibly the most lightweight thing Neil ever wrote, seems vital. Quotations from "Pachabel's Canon" are snuck into "Harvest Moon," and while I don't quite get the connection, musically they mesh together seamlessly. (Oh—that must be the connection.)

Best of all is the album's one original composition, "N.Y.T.," a loose paraphrase of "After the Gold Rush"'s melody. The only misstep is "Down by the River"—it starts off promisingly, but there's a clear alteration in the chorus's melody that throws me. Seeing as side two of Neil's debut led off with "String Quartet from Whiskey Boot Hill," it was probably preordained that he'd one day be the subject of a string quartet tribute. I'm kidding... the Beatles' recent orchestral experimentation notwithstanding, do you think anyone in 1969 thought that rock music would eventually be acceptable territory for classical musicians? Also highly recommended: *The String Quartet Tribute to the Velvet Underground & Nico*, a remake of the entire first album. Same label, different musicians, same story—dramatic.

(*Stylus*, 2007)

"Ocean Girl," Stills-Young Band

This is the album that Neil put out between *Zuma* and *American Stars 'n Bars*. Four out of the five songs that are his are just sort of average—including "Long May You Run," the one song from the album that has become well known—but "Ocean Girl" is as good as almost anything he did in the '70s. The Neil Young that affected me most deeply then, and still does, is the one who wrote about the same mythical girl again and again—the ocean girl, the cinnamon girl, the country girl, the girl just down the aisle in "Sugar Mountain"—the girl who walked along forgotten shores and chased moonlight (I don't know how one does that either; it's the thought that counts), the same girl I was going to meet myself someday soon. Those songs and that feeling are bound together for me, and listening to them now, or watching an old favorite movie from the same time in my life, is the best way I have of remembering how I felt back then.

(*Tapeworm*, 1995)

a friend i've never seen

"Downtown," Neil Young

All my live music comes off the TV nowadays, where two of the best things I've seen in recent years were performances by Neil Young. One was his version of "Just Like Tom Thumb's Blues" on the Bob Dylan special: as much as I love the original, Neil somehow managed to make it just a little bit better. (I don't say that lightly, and Neil Young would cringe to hear the comparison made at all, but I've seen it twice and think it's phenomenal what he does.) The other was when he and Pearl Jam did "Like a Hurricane" on the MTV Awards the year before last. As I remember it, Eddie Vedder was stiff and deferential, while Neil looked to be having the time of his life—there was a technical problem at one point that just added to the humour and the madness of Neil bouncing around like a seven-year-old on a tear. There's nothing like that in "Downtown," but it's an appealing bit of nostalgia anyway. I guess mirror balls were standard equipment at the Avalon and the Fillmore, which is strange because to me mirror balls mean disco and disco only; my first choice to name an album *Mirror Ball* would have been the Pet Shop Boys, my second either Gloria Gaynor or Monti Rock III, Pearl Jam would be 2,044th, and Neil would be fifth-to-last (behind Monster Magnet but ahead of Hootie & the Blowfish). I could do without the "Cat Scratch Fever" parts in "Downtown," the rest is fine. (6.0)

(*Radio On*, 1995)

Neil Young's *Archives*

If you're about to shell out for Neil Young's it's-actually-here-for-real *Archives, Vol. 1: 1963-1972*—and forget slapdash affairs like *Apocalypse Now* (five years wait) or *Chinese Democracy* (15 years); the completion of Neil's box falls somewhere between Truman Capote's *Answered Prayers* (21 years) and Brian Wilson's *Smile* (38 years)—here are a few numbers that may give you pause. Based on the nine discs common to all three formats (the DVD/Blu-Ray versions take their first two discs to cover what the CD version covers in one), 89 of 116 songs (more or less—I counted fast) appear on either regular-issue Buffalo Springfield, CSNY, or Neil albums, or on readily available compilations like *Decade* or the Springfield box set. Many are technically new, it's true—alternate takes, unreleased mixes, live versions, etc.—so this may be even more troubling: by my count, 33 of 116 appear exactly as they did on the original studio albums. Indeed, *Everybody*

Knows This Is Nowhere and *After the Gold Rush* are disseminated virtually intact across the middle discs ("The Losing End" from *Nowhere* is all that's missing), while about half of *Harvest* is here in its original form. A number of songs appear three times: not just masterpieces like "Sugar Mountain," "Tell Me Why," and "Cowgirl in the Sand," but even the pleasantly minor "Dance Dance Dance." And, of course, two of *Archive*'s three live discs (*Live at the Fillmore East* and *Live at Massey Hall*) have already been released commercially. To be fair, ample warning was given at the time that they would eventually be part of the upcoming box set—here's hoping that most Neil fans had the patience to hold off.

So superfluity is one problem; for anyone considering the DVD package, there's also the small matter of the visuals. Remember the old Replacements video for "Bastards of Young," the one where the guy plunked himself in front of a TV for a single static shot that lasted the duration of the song? An inspired statement in 1985, one that was also very short and very free. Neil has taken the same idea and run with it for seven of *Archive*'s 10 discs (you get a photo collage of live stills on the *Fillmore East* disc): record players spinning around, reel-to-reel machines, even an 8-track player. Sometimes there'll be a photo of Neil propped against the hardware. As with the Replacements, there's a kind of perverse nobility on display, and, speaking purely as a grade 6 teacher, not feeling compelled to watch allowed me to listen from a different room and keep up with all my marking. If I had just handed over $250 for the experience, though, I suspect the unexpected convenience wouldn't have seemed so swell. I really thought there'd be more in the way of archival footage.

With so much anticipation, and such a prohibitive price tag attached, it's important to state caveats up front. No surprise, though, that there's enough here to justify making the plunge anyway. First of all, almost half of *Archives* is drawn from the years 1969 and 1970; for me, Neil's output during those 24 months (*Everybody Knows*, *Gold Rush*, "Helpless," "Country Girl," and "Ohio") is matched only by what the Beatles and Dylan put out in '65/66. So a lot of what's here is sacred text, and the *Massey Hall* and *Fillmore* discs take you to the very epicentre of that singular moment of genius and mystery and vision. (*Massey Hall* also consists of actual concert footage, although everything's so spectral and murky, I'm not yet convinced it all wasn't concocted in the lab.) The first two *Early Years* discs contain important work that has either only circulated on bootleg or has never appeared anywhere: Link Wrayish instrumentals from '63 with the Squires, a couple of great pre-Springfield folk duets with Connie Smith ("There Goes

My Babe" and "Runaround Babe"), and a beautiful Springfield instrumental called "Slowly Burning." An impressive booklet is included, last year's *Canterbury House* CD/DVD is thrown in, there's a download card that will access mp3s of the entire box, and hidden tracks abound throughout. Some are so well hidden I haven't yet found them, but to make up for it, I'm stumbling over *hidden* hidden tracks that aren't even listed: clips of CSNY doing "Down by the River" on a *Shindig!*-type show in 1969 (hosted by David Steinberg!), Neil running through a "Loner"/"Cinnamon Girl" medley inside a small club in 1970 (segueing to a Madison Square Garden clip, segueing to Neil in Washington Square teaching some guy how to play "Cinnamon Girl"—"just stay modal..."), Neil and Ben Keith in 1972 goofing through "Gator Stomp." There are two versions of "Bad Fog of Loneliness," a *Harvest*-era classic, and some amazing bridges across time are revealed: 1964's "I Wonder" is clearly the blueprint for *Zuma*'s "Don't Cry No Tears," and I was surprised how much I liked 1971's "War Song," a collaboration with Graham Nash, until I realized it was basically "Ocean Girl" (my favorite unknown Neil song) with different words.

Best of all, you get the first DVD appearance of Neil's directorial debut, *Journey Through the Past*, an infamous 1974 vanity project that precedes Dylan's *Renaldo & Clara* by four years. I loved it. It's a mix of awesome live footage ("Rock and Roll Woman" from the Springfield—wow); Carrie Snodgrass looking on lovingly while Neil rolls a joint the size of Manitoba (actually, coming so close on the heels of Snodgrass's affecting performance in *Diary of a Mad Housewife*, I found that clip kind of sad); an absolutely impenetrable *Last Movie/El Topo* storyline in which a bearded guy...well...he walks around a lot, until some hooded horsemen and a matronly old lady arrive at the end; and, at last, the answer to why C, S & Y needed the chirpy Englishman around—absent him, the other three's heads would have exploded from having no one to listen to except each other.

I wish I had room enough to convey how meaningful Neil Young has been to my own life, an attachment that goes back to high school in the mid '70s. Part of it, I think, is a shared obsession with the past: starting as early as "On the Way Home" and "Sugar Mountain," Neil has been looking over his shoulder since almost day one. Much as *Decade* was 30 years ago, *Archives* is the culmination of that side of him (the latest installment, anyway; more boxes are scheduled), and, faults and all, it chronicles an obsession well worth excavating.

(*Eye Weekly*, 2009)

"Driftin' Back," Neil Young & Crazy Horse

I hadn't planned on buying *Psychedelic Pill*—hadn't bought a Neil album close to its release date since *Trans* (not even *Freedom* or *Ragged Glory*, coming as they did after those Geffen monstrosities)—but I was in a used record store before a movie one night, and a couple of minutes of "Driftin' Back" changed my mind. That's as much as I had time to hear; I of course had no idea it went on for 27 minutes, and probably would have been less receptive if I had. Twenty-seven minutes is a lot of room for bad ideas to creep in, reminders that this is now and not then.

I've still only gotten through the rest of the album once ("Walk Like a Giant" goes right past me, except for the whistling, which I hate), but I played "Driftin' Back" on endless loop for about three weeks in the car. I'd put it right up there with "Cowgirl" and "Cortez" and "Over and Over" as Neil's greatest long-player ever. I was a little surprised when the Neil claque on *I Love Music* wasn't as rapturous as I was. The lyrics seemed to be the issue, and indeed, the elliptical Neil of 1970 is long gone; "Driftin' Back"'s litany of complaints is very specific and (to put it mildly) somewhat not in the here-and-now. You don't, for instance, hear a great deal about the Maharishi these days, and those Apple ads with all the iconic faces were several lifetimes ago. I'm not sure what a hip-hop haircut is—Kid 'n Play, maybe, I don't know.

None of which is a problem for me. The words melt into everything else that's going on, and I sing along happily. A song about drifting back ought to be a little random anyway—in the course of a day, my mind drifts back to stuff much sillier than the Maharishi. So I do understand.

(#1, 2012 year-end ballot)

"Only Love Can Break Your Heart," Neil Young (1970)

A true "Mel Brooks is Jewish?" moment for anyone who knows me reasonably well.

I've written a lot about Neil Young over the years. He got a lot of words in the record inventory I linked to yesterday. I wrote a long thing about my high school years for Frank Kogan's *Why Music Sucks* many years ago, and while that was primarily about other matters, Neil Young was all over it. I almost always jump onto Neil threads on the message board—there's a guy named Tyler W. on there whose stuff on Neil is really good. The longest Neil-related thing I've ever written was an overview I assembled a few years ago of all the cover versions that are out there. You'd be amazed at how many there are. I pointed out in the piece that "Only Love Can Break Your Heart" is the most indestructible of Neil's songs for anyone who tries to cover him. I'd collected seven at the time, and all but one was good-to-great (Scott's #60, St. Etienne's version, being one of the great ones). Even today, poking around YouTube, I found another by Jackie DeShannon that I'm baffled I missed the first time.

After the Gold Rush is also the album that I generally name as my favorite ever—sometimes *Everybody Knows This Is Nowhere*, but usually *Gold Rush*. Four of the five songs on side one are contenders for the four greatest melodies ever written. As tired as I am of "Southern Man," I'm glad it's there. A fifth song in the manner of "Tell Me Why," "After the Gold Rush," "Only Love Can Break Your Heart," and "Till the Morning Comes" would be one more than anyone could bear. You'd just disappear into your mind and never be heard from again.

And that's where most of "Only Love"'s genius lies, and what links all of the folk and singer-songwriter picks on my list: their melodies. You'll find that all over my list, of course, but everybody knows that power-pop and mid-'60s radio hits are melody-driven. I'm not sure that's as true of folk and singer-songwriters; you mention folk, and probably a lot of people think of protest and Civil Rights marches, and singer-songwriter might mean the National Lampoon/Lester Bangs version of what a singer-songwriter was all about. And there's validity to that. But Neil Young and Jackson C. Frank and Tim Buckley wrote melodies that said more than their words could ever say.

I don't know if love's the only thing that can break your heart. I'm not sure that I've ever been in love. I may have, and I might be—I don't know. As I explained to a co-worker this afternoon, I think I've been in the vicinity. (Merely to ask the question would be proof enough, for a lot of people, that the answer is no. Again, I don't know—you can convince yourself of anything, if you want to badly enough.) But I think that there are other things that can break your heart too. Fleeting moments of nostalgia can do it. The perfection of certain songs can do it. There's a famous quote from A. Bartlett Giamatti, former commissioner of baseball: "It [baseball] breaks your heart. It is designed to break your heart." I'd subscribe to that, too—happened here in Toronto in 1985, and again in 1987. That felt pretty real. I'm glad, though, that Neil Young didn't decide to write a song called "Only Baseball Can Break Your Heart."

(#1, Facebook Top 100, 2010-11)

appendix

1. record inventory:
   http://phildellio.tripod.com/records.html

2. 2008 election blog:
   http://phildellio.tripod.com/barack.html

3. 2012 election blog (w/scott woods):
   http://dellioandwoods.wordpress.com/

4. facebook top 100 (w/scott woods):
   https://www.facebook.com/groups/127416673986786/

5. facebook top 50 (w/jeff pike & steven rubio):
   https://www.facebook.com/groups/200962099931650/

6. neil young covers:
   http://www.stylusmagazine.com/articles/weekly_article/purple-words-on-a-grey-background-four-decades-of-neil-young-covers.htm

everybody will help you

I saw the Richard Linklater film *Boyhood* a few days ago. I didn't think it quite lived up to advance notice—not very much does anymore—but there's a lot there, and I keep running the film over in my mind. I've also been listening to Wussy's *Attica* in the car, and I can hear some of *Boyhood* in "Halloween": a mood they share, certain lines and moments that seem interchangeable. The two are jumbled up in my mind right now. I wish I could sort out that jumble and get it into these thank-yous.

Self-publishing is a scaled-down exercise—no agent or publicist to thank—but in the couple of years it took to get this project completed, I of course needed help along the way. It was Paul Woods' excellent book on the 1983 Toronto Argos, *Bouncing Back*, that originally led me to Lulu, and once I had everything together and ready for publication, Paul met with me to discuss some logistical matters. Martin Popoff offered some general advice on self-publishing very early in the process. There's a website called *Online OCR* (Optical Character Recognition) that was a godsend just as I was about to begin typing up all the *Nerve* and fanzine pieces in here; faceless website, thank you, you saved me from countless hours of keyboarding. And Vaughn Dragland came in at the 11th hour and rebuilt the manuscript from scratch, fixing all kinds of formatting issues that had been driving me insane. Did you know that a 350-page book becomes a 450-page book once you select the correct paper size? Vaughn did. More on the other people who helped in a minute.

I've spent all my years as a teacher at the same school, Huttonville P.S. The biggest reason I've never felt the need to change is the people I've worked with, past and present. It would be impossible to thank everyone—there's a revolving-door aspect to any school, and over the course of 15 years it can be dizzying—so this list is incomplete: Krista Jarvie, Theresa Iskra, Dianne Mann, Obe Vandertol, Graeme Patterson, Jennifer Evans, Jennifer Rollings, Mike Rawding, Gus Skarlatakis, Susan Currie, Monique Reid, Amanda Hiscock, Satpreet Jagpal, Paul Bennett, Anita Gormley, Doug Chan, Phil Larsen, and Matt Gibson. Special thanks to Sam Sauro and Karen Watts. Sam's departure from Huttonville left a real void in my life; no longer can I make even remotely credible jokes about not being the oldest male on staff. Karen was across the hall from me for many years, during which time she was the art teacher and I was the pretend art teacher. When I asked her to illustrate the cover for this book, I handed her DVDs of *Five Easy Pieces* and Kelly Reichardt's *Wendy and Lucy*: "Here, draw this." What Karen came up with was exactly what I had in mind.

interrupting my train of thought

I made vague mention of influences who didn't make it into the Kael chapter. Chuck Eddy and Frank Kogan were contributors to and supporters of *Radio On* right from the start, and they also edited many pieces found in this book—Chuck at the *Village Voice*, Frank in *Why Music Sucks*. While their musical interests have diverged from mine since those days (diverged even more than then, to be precise), at a moment when I was still trying to find a writing style that felt comfortable to me, both had a key role in moving that along. And I know their own collections—Chuck's *Rock and Roll Always Forgets*, Frank's *Real Punks Don't Wear Back*—had an influence on how I envisioned this one.

Dave MacIntosh was my first editor—it was like getting to start off with Bill Murray as your editor—and he's continued to take an interest in whatever I've been up to in the 30 years since. Dave's contribution to the two Facebook countdowns, not included here, was a book unto itself. Howard Druckman is another friend from *Nerve* days I'm happy to say I still see on occasion. And thanks to Geoff Savage for publishing a couple of books I co-wrote with Scott Woods—doing them made doing this easier.

I've never met Jeff Pike, Steven Rubio, Jack Thompson, or Chris Molanphy, but I've been writing alongside them and sometimes for them for long enough that I feel like I've met them. Jeff and Steven, who I partnered with for the movie countdown, both have blogs that I tried not to think about as I put together this, else I might have stopped and said "They should be doing this, not me."

Everyone likes Rob Sheffield—even Mrs. Rob Sheffield. I was a little nervous about asking Rob to write the foreword. Not Luca Brasi on-the-day-of-your-daughter's-wedding nervous, but, you know, nervous. Rob's been making me laugh ever since I read my favourite made-up lyric of his in an old issue of *Spin*, before I even knew him ("Thoreau is like Ralph Emerson/Ralph Emerson is what I read!"), and his autobiographical Haysi Fantayzee Trilogy of the past few years—*Love Is a Mix Tape*, *Talking to Girls About Duran Duran*, and *Turn Around Bright Eyes*—has been a key inspiration for me.

Tim Powis read about 50% more than what you actually see here, and he helped to choose the pieces that eventually went into the book. Above and beyond that, I like the fact that he's my movie friend, that he saw the New York Dolls in 1972 (what's that, the third or fourth time I've mentioned this?), and that he's right up there with my dad in the malapropism department.

Family and my oldest friends: Pam and Dan Lavallee, Peter Stephens, Norm Ibuki, Steve Keslick, Dave Porter, John Karolidis, Cam Victor, and Fred Ulrich. In my own passive-aggressive way, I know I'm sometimes what's thought of as high-maintenance, so thanks for putting in the time—40+ years for some of you, which ought to be worth a medal or something. I owe all of you a lot.

As you might guess from the 93 times he's mentioned in this book (Scott: "You should include an index"—oh, okay, now I get it), Scott Woods has had a prominent role in just about everything I've written going back to *Nerve* days. Sometimes, like with the record inventory and the 2008 election blog, my entire readership consisted of Scott and a couple of people who'd stumbled in from parts unknown. We co-wrote the two books, we've worked on numerous other projects together, and, along with Tim, Scott had a major hand in shaping this book. His work as an archivist on greilmarcus.net is invaluable, and his own writing constantly makes me reconsider things I thought I'd figured out. Mostly, he's as good a friend as you could ever hope for, and his family—Jackie, Ava, and Elliott—well, the Rolling Stones would have killed to have a family like that. Thanks for everything.

You know what grade-school teachers talk about when we get together outside of school? This would surprise my students: we talk about them. (Actually, in the case of kindergarten students, should you ever run into them in the supermarket or anywhere, they're shocked to find out that you even have a corporeal existence outside of the classroom.) We share stories about the students we're teaching today, and about those we remember from five, ten, twenty years ago. "Amazing kid"—you hear that a lot. And even the students who...*present challenges* (spoken in true report-cardese)... as time recedes, we have nice things to say about almost all of them, too. I don't know if any of the hundreds and hundreds of kids I've taught over the past 15 years (with another five years left to get it right—you never do) will ever see this book. Obviously I wouldn't want any of them reading any of it until many years down the road, and even then, it's a longshot. I guess the question is, would I want them to? Yes, I would. I'd want them to know that that guy who nagged at them about everything, and who often forgot they were still kids, and that kids do stupid stuff, and they like to goof around, and when they don't do their homework it's because homework isn't all that interesting—that he wasn't always that way, and that he did all the same stupid stuff and he actually understood. Most will never know, but this book is for them.

Interrupting My Train of Thought is Phil Dellio's third book. He lives in Toronto, and teaches grade 6 at Huttonville Public School in Brampton. He was watching in 1977 when Reggie hit his third consecutive home run in the World Series—jumped right off the carpet from a sitting position.

I Wanna Be Sedated (w/Scott Woods): Sound and Vision, 1993
Quotable Pop (w/Scott Woods): Sound and Vision, 2001

Made in the USA
Charleston, SC
17 September 2014